Elephant's Edge

The Republicans as a Ruling Party

ANDREW J. TAYLOR

FOREWORD BY NORMAN J. ORNSTEIN

Westport, Connecticut
London

Library of Congress Cataloging-in-Publication Data

Taylor, Andrew J.
    Elephant's edge : the Republicans as a ruling party / Andrew J. Taylor ;
foreword by Norman J. Ornstein.
        p. cm.
    Includes bibliographical references and index.
    ISBN 0–275–98536–9 (alk. paper)
    1. Republican Party (U.S. : 1854–) 2. Political parties—United States.
3. United States—Politics and government—2001–   I.   Ornstein,
Norman J.   II.   Title.
JK2356.T39   2005
324.2734′09′0511—dc22   2005013517

British Library Cataloguing in Publication Data is available.

Library of Congress Catalog Card Number: 2005013517
ISBN: 0–275–98536–9

First published in 2005

Praeger Publishers, 88 Post Road West, Westport, CT 06881
An imprint of Greenwood Publishing Group, Inc.
www.praeger.com

Printed in the United States of America

The paper used in this book complies with the
Permanent Paper Standard issued by the National
Information Standards Organization (Z39.48–1984).

10 9 8 7 6 5 4 3 2 1

Contents

Foreword

To any close observer of American politics—especially to one with a sense of American history—the past decade has been a striking and unusual period. We have had an era of virtual parity between our two major political parties—"the 50/50 nation" has been the frequent moniker given it in the press—that shows no sign of disappearing or evolving into something else. The basic partisan structure in America, including voter identification with parties, has not changed in any fundamental way, through the tumultuous election and aftermath of 2000, the horrors of September 11, the actions in Afghanistan and Iraq, or anything else.

While Republicans after the 2004 election continued to hold all the reins of power in Washington, and added a bit to their narrow margins of power in both houses of Congress, there were other signs that suggested the continuation of parity, including the fact that the aggregate number of state legislators in the entire country—across 99 state legislative chambers—was virtually dead even—the Democrats had 2,704 seats to the Republicans' 2,691.

As Andy Taylor notes in this penetrating and important new book, "For most of American history, one of our political parties has had the consistent and largely unwavering support of the majority of voters." To be sure, there have been other periods in history with close party competition—the era right around the turn of the nineteenth to the twentieth century, the years immediately after World War II—but they seemed clearly to be transitions from an era of party hegemony. This era shows no such signs, either of a move to a realignment, where one party does assume enduring majority status, or to dealignment, where both parties lose support and adherents. If anything, partisanship shows signs of firming up on both sides.

But if there are no signs of an emerging majority party, that does not mean that the parties are equal in their clout or even in their prospects. Start with geography. The Democrats' enduring electoral coalition, the one that gave them dominance of American politics from the 1930s on, was built on a base of a solid Democratic South—a virtually guaranteed bloc of electoral votes and congressional seats that lifted the party to striking distance of majorities and election victories time after time. The Republicans started with their smaller longstanding base in the Northeast and Midwest.

Now the South is the fundamental building block for the Republican Party, in electoral votes, as well as House and Senate seats, leaving Democrats basically with the Northeast, California, and parts of the Midwest. But in a reversal of the previous era of Democratic hegemony, Republicans have their base in parts of the country that continue to grow in population (and thus to add electoral votes and House seats), while Democrats, with a few exceptions, are strong in places that are shrinking relatively in population. At the same time, Republicans are stronger in more sparsely populated regions, while Democrats' strength is in states and areas with concentrated, urban populations—which means, among other things, a GOP edge in the Senate. Which base would you rather have?

Along with that geographic electoral base, Republicans' ascendance to the majority in the House in 1994, and their ability to hold on by their fingernails through 2000, has left the GOP in a position to take advantage of the breakwater provided by successive waves of redistricting. Barely 30 of the 435 House seats are in or close to the toss-up category; upwards of 90 percent of the districts in the House are safe or nearly so for one party or the other. It is not impossible to imagine an election where a party gains or loses fifty House seats. But it would take an extraordinary set of circumstances, akin to an electoral tidal wave, to see a shift of twenty seats, much less fifty.

True, the Republican margins in the U.S. House of Representatives and the Senate are not very robust. But in the House, the ruthless tactics of Speaker Dennis Hastert, Majority Leader Tom DeLay, and Rules Committee Chair David Dreier—using rules and violating norms in ways that Republicans, when in the minority, strenuously decried, and pushing them further every week— have created a kind of party and ideological leverage to move major, controversial policies through the body. In the Senate, the willingness of Republicans to abandon procedures they used when in the minority, like relying on senatorial "blue slips" for individuals to veto judicial nominations, or on filibusters against nominees for the courts, has made the body more like the House, enabling a majority to jam bills through over protests by the minority.

That's not all. Taylor goes on to detail a stream of other reasons for a Republican moment—a time when, despite the party's inability to create an electoral majority, it has maximized its chances of a long run as a ruling party. Republicans have expanded their turf at the state level, including dominating governorships in many of the blue-ribbon "blue" states, like California, New York, and Massachusetts. They have begun to expand the conservative foothold in federal courts and are poised to create an enduring conservative majority in the Supreme Court.

Republicans also have substantive advantages. Post 9/11, the increased priority Americans are placing on security concerns has worked to the benefit of Republicans, who are seen as stronger than Democrats. The same is true of social issues like guns and same-sex marriage. At the same time, Taylor argues, Republicans have narrowed the edge Democrats have had on issues like education and Medicare, and could do the same on Social Security.

Of course, all these assets notwithstanding, Republicans can't count on winning every election. They came within a whisker of losing the presidential contest in 2004. The apparent effort by the Bush administration to shift more Medicaid burdens onto the states, and the discussion within the administration of a tax reform that would take away the federal deductibility of state and local income taxes, could devastate the GOP's hold on power at the state level. The Social Security issue could easily backfire, big-time, on the president and his party. The inability of Bush and his Republicans to deal with budget shortfalls and burgeoning trade deficits could create enough economic upheaval to lead to the tidal wave mentioned above. So could continuing or burgeoning chaos in Iraq or elsewhere in the world. The signs of disarray in Republican ranks in Congress after the 2004 election suggest that the elephant's edge may be less stable than Andy Taylor suggests.

But the fact is that Republicans are consciously and actively trying to use their time in office to leverage their sway for years or decades—even if and when they lose the levers of power—by demolishing mainstay federal programs created and supported by Democrats and shrinking the size, role, and influence of prominent outside groups that are key to the Democratic base. And they are doing so without serious reaction or complaint from a pliant mainstream press that howled in outrage when Democrats used milder versions of their tactics in the 1980s and early 1990s.

Shortly before President Bush's 2005 State of the Union address, here is what two savvy *Washington Post* reporters wrote in a piece titled, "Bush Aims to Forge a GOP Legacy": "A recurring theme of many items on Bush's second-term domestic agenda is that if enacted, they would weaken political and financial pillars that have propped up Democrats for years."

Reporters Tom Edsall and John Harris went on to mention tort reform, which would cut income to trial lawyers; Social Security reform, which could create a generation of individual investors who would be sympathetic to GOP economic policy; and civil service reform aimed at weakening or demolishing federal employee unions. Along with these efforts by the Bush administration, which combine strong (and real) policy preferences with long-term political advantage, one could add the K Street Project, an effort to purge lobbying firms, trade associations, and corporate Washington offices of Democrats and replace them with Republicans suggested by Tom DeLay and his allies—and then turning to the newly minted (and newly affluent) GOP lobbyists for generous campaign donations to expand the Republicans' edge on the money front.

With an impressive command of policy nuance and political trends, a thorough knowledge of the academic literature, and an ability to write clearly and cogently, Andy Taylor has written both an analysis of these trends and a wakeup call to Democrats that their problem is not just related to short-term setbacks or the candidates they choose. They avoid reading, and heeding, this book at their peril.

Norman J. Ornstein
American Enterprise Institute

Preface

"The Republican Party is in a stronger position today than at any time since the Great Depression," observed Bush campaign manager and Republican National Committee Chair designate Ken Mehlman a few days after the 2004 elections.[1] Given that his boss was the first presidential candidate to capture a majority of the popular vote since 1988—Bush also received the support of a record 62 million Americans—it was difficult to argue with him. Indeed, the Republican triumph marked the first time since 1928 that the party had won the presidency and picked up seats in both chambers of Congress simultaneously.

But it was also difficult to claim that 2004 brought about a realignment. In their classic form, realigning elections reveal, quite unequivocally, a dominant party that has the solid support of a new and likely durable majority within the American electorate. The year 2004 exhibited few of the basic characteristics of these historically important contests. It was not, for instance, the expression of political tension that had built up over several years. Quite the opposite, in fact—2004, with the possible exceptions of tax and Social Security policy, was about "staying the course." Party identification, moreover, neither weakened nor strengthened markedly, and both parties experienced rather tranquil nomination contests. The election did not represent the emergence of a new cleavage within the electorate. Indeed, of all of the fundamental qualities of realigning elections described by David Mayhew in his seminal recent book on the subject, 2004 clearly displayed only one: unusually high voter turnout.[2]

Instead, 2004 lucidly revealed the current state of play between the two major political parties. The Democrats and Republicans are, in the context of American political history, evenly matched. George W. Bush has just won two highly competitive presidential elections—the 2000 contest, of course, in the most unusual and controversial circumstances—and GOP majorities in Congress, especially the House, are extremely thin. What is more, neither party can claim the allegiance of a majority of the voting public. About one-third of Americans today consider themselves politically independent.

Yet 2004 also manifested numerous advantages the Republicans have in contemporary American party politics. Cumulatively, these advantages make up what I call the "elephant's edge" and provide for Republican rule—that is, regular GOP control of the elected branches of the federal government, the nation's judiciary, and many state houses. Some of these advantages have been around for a while; most have ripened over the past couple of decades. They include constitutional and statutory rules governing elections and campaign finance, a metamorphosis of important issues in contemporary politics that favors Republican campaigning and governing strategies, shifts in core political values among the public that are consistent with Republican philosophy, and fundamental social and economic changes in American society that are likely to increase the ranks of Republican voters.

This book is essentially a presentation and analysis of this edge. Chapters 2 through 9 describe the Republicans' advantages in detail. In Chapter 2, I show how the Constitution and migration patterns have helped advantage Republicans in presidential and U.S. Senate elections. Chapter 3 furnishes an examination of the contemporary House of Representatives and reveals how Republicans, in rather unideological but ruthless fashion, have taken command of the institution employing the same techniques that allowed the Democrats to control it for most of the second half of the last century. I analyze the remarkable resurgence of the GOP at the state level and how conservatives are utilizing the courts to move policy rightward and mobilize sympathetic parts of the electorate in Chapter 4. In Chapters 5 and 6, I look at developments in foreign and domestic issues to show how

Republicans have used policy for political ends. I show how Republican-crafted American domestic and foreign policies have "trapped" the Democrats. In Chapter 7, I explain how the Republicans have constructed a sophisticated, well financed, and highly disciplined party organization that connects seamlessly to politically effective allied interests—an experience that contrasts greatly with that of the Democrats. I reveal how the Republicans have cleverly exploited the ideas industry and media to make their case for governing in Chapter 8. And in Chapter 9, I examine social and economic changes to show how racial politics, religiosity, and the nature of work and wealth benefit today's Republican Party. I also show how, despite the palpable movement of policy to the right, the public has not reversed its conservative trajectory.

Republican rule should not be confused with Republican realignment. This edge will continue to advantage Republicans in future elections and bring about consistent Republican control of government at all levels—federal, state and local, executive, legislative, and judicial. In and of itself it does not, however, constitute the kind of evolving but nevertheless ineluctable movement toward an enduring Republican majority about which many journalists and strategists have talked. In the concluding chapter I explain the factors that are likely to prohibit the Republicans from fully exploiting their advantages and dominating American politics the way the Democrats did in the thirty years following the New Deal. These factors include internal and intractable tensions within the Republican Party, the parties' sophisticated political information gathering strategies, the innate risk aversion of the campaign industry, and the tendency for the GOP to overreach.

Unfortunately, political science and our understanding of American politics are afflicted by a simple fact: reporters rarely read the work of social scientists but are more broadly informed than academics. As a result, much journalistic writing on American politics is either polemic or takes a litany of anecdotes and reportage that cumulatively make a single simple point. A lot of political science is esoteric and inaccessible. I would like to think that this book helps bridge the divide. Throughout this work I have tried conscientiously to weave academic and applied social science research with the best political journalism.

I have also attempted to make the book of interest to a variety of audiences. Given its provocative argument based upon a broad survey of American party politics, political scientists and members of the public interested in politics will want to read it. So, I hope, will political activists and professionals. I also think academics will find the book a useful supplement to, or replacement for, conventional texts in undergraduate courses in American government and political parties.

Acknowledgments

Many people have influenced my thinking and this book, and they need to be thanked. My editor at Praeger, Hilary Claggett, was quick to recognize the potential of this project. She also worked diligently and patiently with this first-time author all the way through the publishing process. Tom Mann of Brookings, Jack Pitney of Claremont–McKenna College, and Larry Sabato of the University of Virginia kindly read the entire manuscript and provided valuable comments.

I learned a great deal about American government and politics during a year spent in Washington as the American Political Science Association's 1999–2000 William A. Steiger Congressional Fellow. In fact, quite simply, it was a fabulous experience; therefore, just about everyone associated with that year should be thanked. Jeff Biggs, the program's director, is a smart, funny, and generous man who has helped my career tremendously and whose insights on Congress shaped this book directly. My political science colleagues for the year, Rob Boatright and Dan Kaufman, also contributed to my basic pool of knowledge about American politics, as did the people I worked with on the Hill—Representatives Chris Shays of Connecticut, Rules Committee Chair David Drier of California, Budget Committee Chair John Kasich of Ohio, and the staff in Shays' office, especially Peter Carson, Len Wolfson, Kristin Zembrowski, Paul Pimentel, Scott MacKenzie, and Katie

Levinson. Other program participants with whom I had lengthy conversations shaped much of the thinking in this book, too. They include Stan Bach, David Broder, Hank Cox, Chris Deering, Ron Elving, Lou Fisher, Mike Franc, Bill Frenzel, George Hager, Paul Herrnson, Bill Hoagland, Al Hunt, Gary Hymel, Bill Koetzel, Paul Light, Tom Mann, Norm Ornstein, Leon Panetta, Elaine Povich, Cathy Rudder, Jim Saturno, Judy Schnieder, Barbara Sinclair, Matthew Spalding, and Jim Thurber. Norm Ornstein, who donates so much of his time and talent to the Congressional Fellowship Program and the discipline of political science, was kind enough to give some of that to me and write the Foreword.

I also need to thank the dozens of colleagues and friends in North Carolina who have molded this work. They include political-types Erskine Bowles, Joe Bryan, Bill Cobey, Don Carrington, Ran Coble, Brad Crone, Chris Fitzsimon, Dan Gurley, John Hood, Art Pope, David Price, and Eric Reeves. Friends in the media have also assisted me during the numerous conversations we have had—even though they had originally called to ask me a favor. Among the most prominent of these helpful people are Jerry Agar, Jennifer Baron, Mike Blackman, Kerra Bolton, Lynn Bonner, Melissa Buscher, Kelcey Carlson, Rob Christensen, Laurie Clowers, David Crabtree, Tim Crowley, Don Curtis, Steve Daniels, Byron Day, Eric Dyer, Donna Gregory, Anna Griffin, Stephanie Hawco, Adam Hochberg, Mark Johnson, Monty Knight, Mitch Kokai, Amanda Lamb, Cash Michaels, Kevin Miller, Jim Morrill, Shannon Vickery, John Wagner, John Whitesides, and Dallas Woodhouse. Needless to say, local academic colleagues have been superb, too—especially John Aldrich, Bill Boettcher, Mike Cobb, Charlie Coe, Mike Dimock, John Gilbert, Steve Greene, Ferrell Guillory, Michael Hawthorne, Abe Holtzman, Sean Kelly, Walter Lackey, Chuck Prysby, Trace Reid, Carmine Scavo, Roland Stephen, and Jim Stimson. Moreover, I would be remiss if I did not mention other friends in the state who have made an impact, especially those from the old "Grits Gang"—Drew Cline, Matt Curran, Matthew Eisley, Mark Ezzell, Vern Granger, Kelly Hufstettler, Jonathan Jordan, Theresa Kostrzewa, Gilbert Parker, Dwayne Perry, Charlie Perusse, Sean Walsh, Ashley Westbrook, and Frank Williams. And kudos to librarians at North Carolina State's D. H. Hill Library and the University of North Carolina's Davis library for their prompt help in locating materials.

I also need to express my gratitude to the people who have influenced my career the most. David Mayhew's work has become a sort of model for mine. It answers critical questions about American politics in a scholarly fashion but with a panache that makes it accessible to broad audiences. I hope my future projects will emulate his better than this one does. My parents, John and Ronnie Taylor, have thoroughly supported and always taken an interest in my endeavors. So has my brother, Simon. My adviser at Lehigh, Howard Whitcomb, and the graduate director at the University of Connecticut, Garry Clifford, exhorted me through graduate school. For their continual guidance, I should also thank the two department chairs I have served under at North Carolina State, Marvin Soroos and Jim Svara. Finally, three other people deserve special mention. Howard Reiter's encouragement and direction effectively launched my career. And I must thank my wife Jennifer and son Matthew. It is they who give me my edge.

1
American Party Politics Today

In 1969, Kevin P. Phillips wrote a book called *The Emerging Republican Majority*. It caused a splash and was well received in some, most notably conservative, quarters.[1] Phillips believed that the GOP was about to put together a majority from the Rocky Mountain states, rural Midwest, and the "Outer South" (states like Virginia, North Carolina, Texas, and Florida) and by regularly capturing Midwestern states like Illinois, Ohio, and Michigan, as well as the big kahuna, California. The Republicans would also attract consistent support from suburban and conservative Catholic working class or "hard hat" voters in the Northeast. The following year Walter Dean Burnham argued that we were about to witness the rise of a dominant conservative coalition drawing primarily from the middle classes.[2] Such an event would, naturally, benefit the Republicans. But nearly forty years later, the GOP does not have a majority. Ronald Reagan's victories in 1980 and 1984 were dramatic, but they were not breakthroughs. Neither was 1994, despite the fact that Republicans won back the House for the first time in forty years. The year 2004 was important, George W. Bush did, after all, get a majority of the popular vote; but it was hardly paradigm shifting. Like Godot, for whom Estragon and Vladimir wait in Samuel Beckett's play, the solid Republican majority has never come.[3] Indeed, that the GOP even has the solid support of a plurality of Americans is a matter of great contention.

Phillips was technically correct when he started his book with the observation that, "far from being the tenuous and unmeaningful victory suggested by critical observers, the election of Richard M. Nixon as president of the United States in November 1968 bespoke the end of the New Deal Democratic hegemony and the beginning of a new era in American politics."[4] It was just that he was off base with his description of the emerging period. Nixon's victory ushered in not a time of Republican supremacy but what many political scientists say was dealignment. Characterized by split-ticket voting and campaigns centered around candidates rather than parties, dealignment has brought us divided governments—those in which a president of one party must deal with at least one chamber of Congress controlled by the other—over 80 percent of the time since Nixon first won the White House. In other words, at least at the federal level, the Republicans and Democrats have been evenly matched. Unlike the New Deal era bookended by Franklin D. Roosevelt's rout of Herbert Hoover in 1932 and the election that was central to Phillips' analysis—and, indeed, the early twentieth century of Republican Congresses and Presidents McKinley, Theodore Roosevelt, Taft, Harding, Coolidge, and Hoover—no one party dominates contemporary American politics.

The period since the infamous 2000 presidential election reveals starkly the current evenness of the partisan balance. In 2000, the Republican George W. Bush, of course, won a controversial and extremely narrow victory over Democratic Vice-President Al Gore in the Electoral College, 271 to 266. He lost the popular vote, however, by over half a million. At the same time, the country was returning a perfectly split Senate—for only the second time in history—and a wafer-thin, five-seat Republican majority in the House of Representatives. At the state level, the election created eighteen legislatures under Republican control, sixteen governed by the Democrats, and fifteen split by the parties.[5] And, while the National Election Studies (NES) survey found that on election day, November 7, 2000, 49 percent of voters considered themselves "strong," "weak," or "independent" Democrats and 37 percent similar kinds of Republicans, this was a far cry from the 20 percent-plus advantages—at one time it was 31 percent—that the Democrats regularly enjoyed in the 1960s.

The trend continued in the 2002 midterms. On the surface, 2002 looked like a significant victory for the Republicans. The party made historic gains in Congress, largely as a result of energetic campaigning by President Bush in swing states and districts. This was the first time since 1934 that the president's party had gained seats in both the House and Senate during an off-year election. Apart from the four months at the beginning of 2001 before Senator Jim Jeffords of Vermont declared himself an independent, the 108th Congress that began in January 2003 marked the first time since 1954 that the Republicans had won the trifecta of elected federal governmental institutions—they held the presidency, Senate, and House of Representatives all at the same time. But 2002 was no landslide. The country remained heavily split— according to NES, 49 percent considered themselves Democrats, 43 percent, Republicans—and the GOP picked up only two seats in the Senate and six in Congress' lower chamber. What's more, the Democrats enjoyed a net gain of three governors' mansions, taking back Illinois, Michigan, and Pennsylvania and moving to near parity with the GOP at that level. Only the most quixotic of Republicans could agree with the week-after assessment of Bush's political guru, Karl Rove, that "something is going on out there" and that party politics "are moving in a new direction."[6] Most neutrals probably shared Democratic pollster Stanley Greenberg's view that the 2002 elections represented "a minor shift that's explainable by a whole range of things that are kind of one-time phenomena."[7] Democratic National Committee Chair Terry McAuliffe's sentiment that, in the election, "if the Republicans had an edge ... it was tactical rather than ideological" also seemed more accurate than Rove's bold assertion.[8] At that time, even Jeffrey Bell and Frank Cannon, who predicted Bush would be reelected somewhat easily, suggested 2004 would likely be a "lonely landslide"—that is, as in 1972, 1984, and 1996, the presidential election, although one-sided, would not upset the basic terrain of party politics.[9]

By the summer of 2003, however, Republican talk verged on braggadocio. A third Bush tax cut in as many years and the successful prosecution of the war in Iraq had some of them describing a lasting GOP electoral majority. In June, Grover Norquist, president of Americans for Tax Reform, argued that "the Republicans are looking at decades of dominance in the House and Senate, and having the presidency with some regularity."[10] Dan Mattoon, former chief aide at the National Republican Congressional Committee echoed such sentiments the same month in an interview with the *Washington Post*.[11] Simon Rosenberg, founder of the New Democratic Network, assessed the situation for his side this way: "What we're facing is a Republican Party with a minority message on the verge of becoming a majority by practicing a higher order of politics."[12] Commentator Morton Kondracke had detected a swelling of Republican support, especially in swing states.[13] Even some traditionally blue and Democratic states were, according to Bush's 2004 campaign chairman Ken Mehlman, acquiring a Republican reddish hue and "becoming purple."[14]

In the wake of gubernatorial victories in Kentucky and Mississippi and Arnold Schwarzenegger's stunning triumph in the California recall, Republicans and conservatives were further emboldened. Journalist Fred Barnes wrote about a "(finally) emerging Republican majority."[15] The next month, after the week in which the important overhaul of Medicare was passed, columnist David Brooks reported that the Republicans had behaved like a "majority party in full."[16] Analyst Michael Barone was suggesting the Bush presidency paralleled that of William McKinley who constructed "the only lasting Republican majority at all levels of office the nation has seen."[17] And in December 2003 Saddam Hussein was caught in a spider hole just outside Tikrit, Iraq. As a result, President Bush's job approval numbers skyrocketed. Liberal writer Robert Kuttner lamented in the left-leaning *American Prospect* that the GOP strength suggested "the United States could become a nation in which the dominant party rules for a prolonged period, marginalizes a token opposition and is extremely difficult to dislodge because democracy itself is rigged."[18]

Still, as we moved through 2004, any GOP momentum had been fully checked and, arguably, reversed. It became clear that we had reverted to the fundamental principle of partisan parity. English journalists John Micklethwait and Adrian Wooldridge of *The Economist* published a book that tentatively pushed the thesis of Republican hegemony.[19] But the year shaped up to provide a tight presidential election. Continued problems for American governance of Iraq and an anemic and jobless economic recovery meant that Bush's approval ratings continually hovered around and just below the dangerous 50 percent level. In some surveys taken during May and June, only about 46 percent of Americans commended Bush for the job he was doing. The Democrats succeeded in quickly nominating, with minimal bloodshed, Senator John Kerry of Massachusetts to be their presidential candidate. A March 2004 Associated Press-Ipsos poll revealed that 60 percent of Americans believed the country was on the "wrong track." In an ABC News/*Washington Post* poll of the same month, 57 percent of respondents said they wanted their next president to steer the country away from the "course" taken by Bush.

The 2004 campaign was consequently a nip-and-tuck affair. According to numerous polls, Kerry had a slight advantage through much of the summer. Bush edged ahead after a group called Swift Vets and POWs for Truth ran an ad casting doubt on Kerry's purportedly heroic service in Vietnam. The media buy was quite small, but the coverage of the ad, coupled with the Democrats' hesitation in responding to the charges, assisted the president. So did a successful Republican National Convention in which moderates like former New York mayor Rudy Giuliani, Arizona senator John McCain, and California governor Arnold Schwarzenegger starred. A late September Gallup/CNN/*USA Today* poll had Bush up by as many as eleven points.

Calm and in command of the issues, however, Kerry looked presidential in the first debate between the candidates. Bush, on the other hand, seemed stiff and prickly. Like just about all other surveys, a *Time* poll revealed that viewers believed the Massachusetts senator had "won"—in this case 59 percent of respondents declared Kerry the victor. By the time all three debates were done, Bush, who did perceptibly better in the second and third meetings, found himself back in a neck-and-neck race.

Ultimately, of course, the president secured reelection. The margin of victory was wider than 2000, although it could hardly have been narrower. Bush won the votes of 51.1 percent of the electorate, making 2004, with the exception of 2000, the closest race in terms of the two-party popular vote since 1976. Bush also won 286 electoral votes. In this regard, his win, again overlooking the squeaker of 2000, was the closest since 1916. The president began his second term with approval ratings hovering around 50 percent—a figure that was extremely low when compared to former two-term chief executives. Six weeks after inauguration day, a CBS News/*New York Times* poll indicated that 63 percent of Americans felt the president had priorities "different" from theirs when it came to domestic policy. By April 2005, Bush's job approval ratings were solidly below 50 percent in just about every poll.

The Republicans also had a successful time that night in the battle for Congress. They captured five seats retiring Democratic senators had left vulnerable in the South and increased their overall majority by four. In the 109th Congress there were to be fifty-five Republican senators. But the GOP—despite an elaborate Texas gerrymander we will discuss later—won less than half-a-dozen seats in the House and their majority, although now over a decade old and above 230 seats for the first time since 1994, remains very slim by historical standards. Moreover, the party did not add to its twenty-eight governorships and, despite maintaining a narrow twenty-to-nineteen edge over the Democrats in the state legislatures controlled—there were also ten in which the parties shared governance—the GOP suffered a net loss of nearly seventy seats across the country. Liberal analyst Ruy Teixeira seemed to have it right when he said the electorate "tilted, but it didn't tilt very much."[20]

This closeness—contemporary commentators often call the United States the fifty-fifty nation—is revealed by a careful examination of the political map. A perfunctory glance shows much of the map to be Republican red, but this is because the GOP does well in large but rural states. As Phillips predicted, Republicans are in control of the Rocky Mountain and Plains states, a big, rectangular swath of rouge that has as its corners Idaho, North Dakota, Texas, and Arizona. Much of the South, too, is now Republican, but outside these areas, there are important, populous, and reliably Democratic states. The whole Northeast is now blue, and the Republicans, outside of the governorship, are struggling in Nixon's and Reagan's California. The industrialized Midwestern states are key battlegrounds, as are the burgeoning "Outer South" states—especially Florida—that Phillips believed were relatively safe for the GOP.

The demographic makeup of the parties' constituencies reflects the tight competition, too. The Republicans rely heavily on the more affluent, white, male voters, as well as what Stanley Greenberg calls "Country Folk" and "F-You Boys," white, married men under fifty who do not have a college degree.[21] Democrats tap support from racial minorities, union workers, and women. Religious Americans are increasingly Republican, the secular, Democratic. Republican voters are called "retro," Democrats, "metro."[22] In all the theaters of contemporary partisan warfare, the Democrats and Republicans are fighting a fierce battle for superiority that is marked by great energy and intense conflict but ultimately does not push back the enemy very far. It's trench warfare—World War I style. Both sides today have superb intelligence gathering; sophisticated polling techniques have insured this. Both sides also have significant pools of capital and labor and, despite the fact that the public generally considers them to be polarizing toward the liberal and conservative extremes, strategic flexibility. Policy differences are frequently obfuscated and campaigns clouded by advertising campaigns that attack opponents and frame a candidate's position in "apple pie" terms—job creation, educational opportunity, family values, faith, and patriotism.

This book does not seek to answer definitively perhaps the most obvious question posed by the current state of play in American party politics: will one party upset the balance and form a durable majority of identifiers among the electorate? As I shall reveal in the final chapter, I don't think this will happen, at least not in the short and medium terms. Instead, it recognizes that, after nearly a dozen years in control of Congress and at the beginning of a second George W. Bush term, the GOP is a *ruling* party. The book explains a present and future of Republican rule—that is, the GOP as the usual majority in Congress, the accustomed party of the Presidency, a frequent shaper of the courts, and, much of the time, the party affiliation of most elected officials in the states. I will show that there now exist conditions throughout American politics that have established and will sustain this state of affairs. These conditions involve constitutional and statutory rules governing elections and campaign finance, the metamorphosis of important issues in contemporary politics in a way that favors Republican campaigning and governing strategies, shifts in core political values among the public that are consistent with Republican philosophies, and fundamental social and economic changes in American society likely to increase the ranks of Republican voters. They are far less hospitable to Democrats, who find rules loaded against them, face greater difficulties in accumulating critical electoral resources, and discover existing policy, public opinion, and sociological and technological trends constraining their capacity to mobilize voters and to deliver on the demands of their core constituencies. All this, in turn, may lead to an internal discord that could deeply divide the Democratic Party. Together, these phenomena provide the Republicans with a critical edge.

Although not often apparent, Republican advantages are everywhere in American politics. They exist in the elected institutions of the federal government. I will show that the makeup of the Electoral College and Senate load the dice against the Democrats, principally because they allow for the over-representation of smaller, more GOP-friendly states. Moreover, the U.S. House of

Representatives, which was a bastion of Democratic power for forty long years between the mid-1950s and mid-1990s, has come under GOP control as Republicans have discovered ways to protect and promote their incumbents—often by adopting the very tactics that perpetuated the Democratic monopoly.

Republican advantages are a product of current public policy as well. The federal courts continue to hand down rulings that assist considerably in the mobilization of Republican voters. Antagonistic decisions on homosexuality, the role of religion in public life, and the treatment of criminal defendants, for example, have motivated conservative activists to work for Republican causes and provided the basis for effective campaigns designed to question the morality and patriotism of liberal judges and, by inference, most Democrats. At the same time, Republican-appointed judges have been nurturing conservative policies on less evocative and poorly publicized issues such as federalism, property ownership, and business regulation. Foreign policy has traditionally been a GOP strong point, and, as the United States faces the greatest threat to its national security since the Berlin Wall came down, the issue has reemerged as a critical determinant of many votes. With tax rates low and deficits huge, President George W. Bush has also, as Reagan before him, significantly undermined the capacity for Democrats to deliver economic resources and programs to their core constituencies. If Democrats do wish to begin providing the kind of ambitious education, welfare, environment, and health care programs they and their supporters want, they will risk the kind of electoral rebuke experienced in 1994. Then, just a year after President Bill Clinton and the Democratically controlled 103rd Congress had passed a roughly $290 billion increase in taxes and user fees designed to reduce the deficit, the electorate promptly returned GOP majorities to both the House and Senate.

The Republicans have organizational advantages, too. The GOP has greater resources and is better positioned to exploit the ideas industry. Despite the emergence of so-called "527" groups, the McCain-Feingold campaign finance legislation passed in 2002 has accelerated what was an already sizeable advantage the Republicans had in raising certain types of campaign funds. Think tanks like the Heritage Foundation, fueled by wealthy and politically active conservative donors, have challenged traditionally liberal entities like the Brookings Institution at both the federal and state levels. Now Republican policies are fashioned, rigorously tested, and energetically promoted in a way that they could not be prior to the 1980s. These policies, moreover, are received and disseminated by the media that, with new players such as cable television's Fox News channel, are increasingly receptive to them. Democratic positions on trade and social issues cause many from organized labor and other constituent groups to question their relationship with the party, while Republicans have skillfully and seamlessly woven a coalition between the religious right, small government populists, large corporations, and other well-funded and politically sophisticated groups. The Republicans' pool of political talent is growing rapidly, and the party can now field experienced candidates everywhere. It used to be that bright, hardworking young Republicans were groomed for Wall Street and the corporate world; today they are diligently recruited for the public sector as well.

The pattern is the same in contemporary state politics. Democrats no longer control governors' mansions and state capitols with an iron fist. This is the product of stronger GOP organizations at the state and local levels and has meant that Republicans now have considerable influence over critical redistricting processes. Regional and demographic changes in American society have also greatly advantaged the GOP. The party is winning the battle for the hearts and minds of critical swing-voting suburbanites. A large increase in home ownership and the number of people saving for retirement outside of Social Security means that most American voters are more sensitive to company profits and inflation and less so to unemployment. The burgeoning Hispanic community is not necessarily a boon for the Democrats, and the fact that African Americans are increasingly disengaged from the political process certainly helps Republicans.

Interestingly, my analysis takes issue with much of the established thinking about the future of party competition in American politics. In the mid-1990s, just after the GOP had taken control of both chambers of Congress for the first time in forty years, it became fashionable to talk about Republican strength and perhaps, just perhaps, a Republican realignment.[23] After the 1996 presidential election that all changed. In 1997, two very respected liberals, pollster Stanley B. Greenberg and academic Theda Skocpol, co-edited the book *The New Majority: Towards a Popular Progressive Politics*.[24] Arguing that we were about to witness a dramatic left-wing shift in American politics, the book now seems almost quaint, but it is chock-full of theory and evidence explained by prominent scholars. Contributor Paul Starr, for instance, identified several demographic groups—including Hispanics, women, the old, and Gen Xers—that would help the Democrats forge a majority.[25] A year after the book came out, Christopher Caldwell argued that the Republicans were captured by their southern base, a confinement that made them seem too conservative for mainstream American politics.[26]

In 2002, John B. Judis and Ruy Teixeira wrote a book playing directly off of Kevin Phillips' *The Emerging Republican Majority*.[27] Their conceptualization of an "Emerging Democratic Majority" pulls together racial minorities, women, and people employed in the high-tech and service-oriented postindustrial economy into a coalition that can regularly win twenty states and the District of Columbia, placing a Democratic candidate on the brink of the presidency with 267 electoral votes. Although the book suffered from a badly timed launch, just as the Republicans won back control of the Senate in November 2002, it has earned plaudits. Indeed, Teixeira continues to reaffirm his position, despite the Democrats' losses in 2002 and 2004.[28] Democratic pollster Stanley Greenberg has asserted that some slight tactical maneuvering would allow the Democrats to take electoral advantage of demographic and attitudinal developments within the American public.[29] Clinton Labor Secretary Robert Reich, who had for quite some time predicted the "resurgent liberal," wrote a book arguing that not just Democrats but liberals would win what he called the "battle for America."[30] *Washington Post* columnist E. J. Dionne's *They Only Look Dead: Why Progressives Will Dominate the Next Political Era* forwarded a thesis that conditions are ripe for a backlash against the laissez-faire economics of the 1980s and 1990s and a reemergence of the government activism of the late 1800s and early 1900s.[31] According to Dionne, the politics of Teddy Roosevelt will rise again, and, perhaps along with renegade Republicans like Arizona Senator John McCain, the Democrats will be the principal beneficiaries.

What's more, there are Republicans who are sincerely concerned about these arguments. Matthew Dowd, pollster for Bush's 2000 and 2004 campaigns, for example, worries that core constituents of the GOP—namely, white men—are shrinking as a percentage of the American population as the number of minority, especially Hispanic, voters grows. In a similar vein, Republican pollster Bill McInturff argues that "to build a broad coalition that captures a majority of sentiments of this country means a focus on the problems of the new immigrants and Latinos."[32]

Those like Judis and Teixeira, who see the Democrats as most likely to emerge victorious from the current era of parity in American party politics, have a great deal of the data on their side. I have already noted that Democratic identifiers outnumber their Republican counterparts. In the same NES survey of 2000, 19 percent of respondents called themselves "strong Democrats," only 12 percent "strong Republicans." The survey also revealed Americans to have "warmer" feelings about Democrats. The average score for Republicans on a "feeling barometer" on which respondents were asked to give each party a score of zero to 100 was fifty-four—having fallen five points since 1988. For the opposition it was fifty-nine.[33] In an August 2000 Gallup/CNN/*USA Today* poll, one-third of respondents felt the Republicans were too extreme; only one-fourth felt the Democrats were. A June 2001 ABC News/*Washington Post* poll revealed that 57 percent of Americans believed Democrats were most "open to the ideas of people who are political moderates," and only 32 percent felt the Republicans were.

Around the time of their triumph in the 2002 elections, Republicans were beginning to enjoy more favorable ratings with the public. The NES survey that year found that among strong identifiers the Democratic advantage had narrowed to three percentage points. In a November 2002 Gallup/CNN/*USA Today* poll, 54 percent of respondents had a "favorable" view of the GOP; only 48 percent held such a view of the Democrats. Senate Republican leader Trent Lott's remarks at the one-hundredth birthday party of Strom Thurmond, which were widely interpreted as meaning the Mississippian felt the country would have been better off with racial segregation, helped put an end to that. By January 2003, 39 percent of subjects in the same survey had views of the GOP that were "not favorable," whereas 36 percent held such views of the Democrats. A year later, a Gallup/CNN/ *USA Today* poll showed 59 percent to have a "favorable" view of the Democrats, but only 48 percent had such an opinion of the Republicans. Even after Bush was reelected in November 2004, a CBS/*New York Times* poll found that 54 percent had a "favorable" view of the Democrats, but only 49 percent looked on the GOP in the same way.

The origins of the public's reticence to embrace the GOP are not too difficult to discern. Over the past several decades the

Republicans have been frequently and skillfully vilified by the
Democrats and their political allies. We saw this during the
shutdown of the federal government in 1995 and 1996 when
the Clinton administration and congressional Republicans—led
by the ideologically fervent freshman class in the House—could
not come to an agreement on the budget. But the GOP has also
overreached on occasions, making it easier for the opposition to
foster discontent. Prominent examples include George W. Bush's
Iraq war and occupation and the indefatigable pursuit of Bill
Clinton even after it was clear that the public did not want the
president impeached and removed from office for conduct connected to his affair with intern Monica Lewinsky.

To be sure, the Democrats have had their lightening rods: Ted
Kennedy, Tip O'Neill, Walter Mondale, Michael Dukakis, and the
Jimmy Carter of stagflation and the Iranian hostage crisis. This
was especially the case during the 1980s—an indubitably good
decade for the Republicans. In the 1990s and early years of the
new century, however, the line-up of controversial politicians is
overwhelmingly Republican: Dan Quayle, Trent Lott, Tom DeLay,
Jesse Helms, John Ashcroft, Newt Gingrich, and, of course, George
W. Bush. Only Ted Kennedy and Bill—and perhaps Hillary—
Clinton on the Democratic side engender as much negative feeling, but this is largely among ardent Republicans. Indeed, Bill
Clinton's approval ratings closely mirror those of Ronald Reagan,
a man widely believed to be the most beloved president of the
last quarter of the twentieth century. Reagan's mean annual Gallup
job approval ratings were 52 percent, Clinton's 55.[34]

As we moved into 2003, for instance, "Bush hatred" seemed
to take us to a higher level of political opprobrium. The *New
Republic* writer Jonathan Chait claimed to have friends who viewed
George W. Bush's "existence as a constant oppressive force in
their daily psyche."[35] Rather more systematically, pollster Geoff
Garin suggested the loathing of Bush was "as strong as anything
I've experienced in twenty-five years now of polling."[36] Robert
Novak observed that this hatred was greater than that generated
by Nixon, Reagan, or Clinton.[37] Jack Huberman's *The Bush Hater's
Handbook*, published in December 2003, was quite popular, as were
Eric Alterman's and Mark J. Green's *The Book on Bush: How George
W. (Mis)leads America*, David Corn's *The Lies of George W. Bush*,
Maureen Dowd's *Bushworld: Enter at Your Own Risk*, Molly Ivins'
Bushwacked: Life in George W. Bush's America, Bill Press' *Bush Must
Go: The Top Ten Reasons Why George Bush Doesn't Deserve a Second*

Term, and Paul Waldman's *Fraud: The Strategy behind the Bush Lies and Why the Media Didn't Tell You*. Derogatory polemics about the president even went highbrow with Senator Robert Byrd and top-ranking bureaucrats Richard Clarke, Paul O'Neill, Michael Scheuer, and Joseph Wilson attacking Bush's decision making, John Dean's *Worse than Watergate* lambasting the administration's obsessive secrecy, Craig Unger's *House of Bush, House of Saud* suggesting an ominous link between the administration and the Saudi government, and Kevin Phillips launching a devastating attack on the whole Bush family.[38] Even George Will, a reliable supporter of Republican presidents, seriously questioned administration policies in Iraq.

The vitriol could be found all over the Web, as well. Anti-Bush sites included the hostile ReDefeatBush.com, thousandreasons.org ("One Thousand Reasons to Dump George Bush"), onetermpresident.org, bushbodycount.com, nobodydied.com (as in "Nobody Died When Clinton Lied"), and awolbush.com (that casts doubt on Bush's National Guard service in the early 1970s). There were also lighter and more satirical sites like billionairesforbush.com, buckfush.com, and Bush-Orwell '04 (www.gwbush04.com). *Time* magazine devoted a cover story to the polarization of American feelings about Bush in December 2003. Moveon.org, a liberal group initially formed to help President Clinton fight impeachment, took the stinging criticism to the airwaves with aggressive attack ads. Howard Dean, a candidate for the 2004 Democratic presidential nomination, mobilized it, at least for a while, into an energetic and effective political movement. According to exit polls, about 10 million Kerry voters—or just over one in five of those who supported him—did so mainly to get Bush out of the White House.

Still, I will argue that, although the public may seem sometimes to be sympathetic to Democrats in this era of balance, American politics are under Republican rule. In other words, to quote Newt Gingrich in May 2003, "We (the Republicans) are at parity right now, with a slight edge and good prospects."[39] Or, in the words of Republican National Committee chair Ken Mehlman, "It is now fair to say that today the Republican Party is the dominant party in America."[40] In some ways, what I write about is tangentially related to a slow—at least much slower than Phillips and Burnham imagined—shift in the country's center of political gravity. The Nixon and Reagan victories—the second decisive ones in 1972 and 1984 especially—and the GOP's seizing of both chambers of

Congress after the 1994 elections are part of what has been called a "rolling," "secular," or "creeping" Republican realignment.[41] This concept of an evolving, perhaps glacial, but nevertheless ineluctable, movement toward an enduring GOP majority in the electorate, however, is very different to my argument. In this book, I assert that the conditions for consistent and somewhat lasting Republican control of government at all levels—federal, state, and local, executive, legislative, and judicial—are currently in place. Today's politics have embedded within them character- istics that favor and facilitate Republican rule. I do share some of Everett Ladd's assertions in his argument that the postindustrial economy is swelling the ranks of GOP voters. I can agree to some point with Karl Rove that a "new economy based on technology, information and entrepreneurship" is emerging, helping the GOP.[42] Yet this Republican rule does not and will not rest on a discernible and durable Republican majority among the electorate. I do not go as far as Daniel Casse, for example, who has written somewhat confidently about a nascent GOP superiority.[43] I do not quite share Rove's assessment of the 2004 election that "we are seeing part of the rolling realignment," or Michael Barone's that the country is now a Republican-majority nation.[44] And I explicitly reject more sanguine GOP assertions that 2004 repre- sented a sea change within the electorate. Consultants Jeffrey Bell and Frank Cannon, for instance, have labeled the election, "The Bush Realignment."[45] House Majority Leader Tom DeLay claimed the day after the vote that, "The Republican Party is a permanent majority for the future of this country."[46] Even some Democrats admitted that 2004 represented something new. "I think we live in a country that is majority Republican now," was how former Democratic National Committee chair Donald Fowler expressed his party's despair a week after the election.[47]

I do not, however, embrace Ron Brownstein's observation on the eve of the 2004 election that George W. Bush's presidency left the GOP "with a firm hold on about half the country, but with the other half increasingly beyond its reach."[48] Still, there clearly is no stable electoral majority in American politics, and it is unlikely one will emerge in the foreseeable future. The voters will most likely continue to be split three ways—roughly one-third will identify themselves as Republican, one-third as Democrats, one-third as independent. Indeed, I believe Americans will be quite capable of occasionally electing Democratic presi- dents and even evanescent congressional majorities.

There are many reasons why the Republicans will not be able to forge persistent electoral majorities. The pervasive dealignment I discussed above is an important contributor to this state of affairs, but there are others too. In the final chapter, I will examine some of the more critical ones, such as inherent tensions within the Republican coalition, the sophisticated understanding the parties have of public opinion, and the dominance of campaigns by a risk-averse professional political class.

The last chapter, therefore, discusses why Republican rule does not and will not, at least any time soon, rest on a bedrock Republican majority within the electorate. Yet the eight chapters that immediately precede it provide the critical thesis of the book: just about all aspects of contemporary American politics provide the Republicans with a perceptible edge over the Democrats, and it is upon these advantages that Republican rule is built. I start my analysis of these GOP advantages with an examination of the geography of current party politics and the constitutional rules governing the selection of presidents and senators.

2

Uneven Playing Field: The Constitutional and Geographical Origins of the Republican Advantage

On the surface, Karen Olick and Flip McConnaughy have the same jobs. They are both chiefs of staff for U.S. Senators. They must, however, do similar things with dramatically different degrees of intensity. Olick manages what is a large and complex organization for her boss, Democratic California Senator Barbara Boxer. The pace in the Hart Office Building suite that houses it is rapid, the chatter quite loud. Senators from big states have more public requests for meetings, information about legislation, nominations to military academies, assistance in dealing with federal agencies, and help with grant applications. By comparison, McConnaughy oversees a sedate operation. He works for Senator Mike Enzi, a Republican of Wyoming. With fewer constituents, Enzi's phones don't ring as much, and mail sorting is not as onerous for the interns.

Boxer and Enzi reflect a basic principle of contemporary American politics—smaller states tend to favor Republicans in federal elections, and larger ones tend to favor the Democrats. In 2000, for example, Al Gore won six of the ten most populous states, but only four of the ten least populous—as well as the District of Columbia, of course. Excluding D.C., the median size of the states won by John Kerry in 2004 was about 5.3 million, for George W. Bush it was approximately 3.5 million. In the 109th Congress of 2005–2006, Democrats have 51 percent of the House delegation

from the top five states by population, despite occupying only
46 percent of the chamber's total seats. The median state represented by Democrats in the Senate of this Congress is about 4.4
million people; its counterpart for the GOP is about 4 million.

The Constitution turns this simple observation into a critical
Republican advantage in the current competition between the
parties. The document does so because it makes the government
the Founders created not only "national" but "federal" as well.
In a purely national government, James Madison believed that
"supreme and ultimate authority would reside in the majority of
the people of the Union; and this authority would be competent
at all times, like that of a majority of every national society, to
alter or abolish its established government."[1] The national characteristics of the government are found in the House of Representatives where each state has representation based roughly upon
its size. Here, every American is treated the same.

In a government that is fully federal Madison argued that "the
concurrence of each State in the Union would be essential to every
alteration that would be binding on all."[2] It is the Senate and the
presidency that give the system its federal, and by extension
counter-majoritarian, complexion. In the Senate no state has a
veto but, regardless of size, has two senators. This was the result
of the Great Compromise, a struggle between the small and large
states—led by New Jersey and Virginia, respectively—at the Constitutional Convention. The smaller ones argued for a unicameral
legislature based upon the principle of one-state–one-vote, which
was practiced in the existing Continental Congress, while their
more populous counterparts advocated a bicameral institution in
which seats in the lower chamber were distributed to states based
upon the number of their inhabitants and the upper chamber was
handpicked by the lower one. Like many of the decisions made
in Philadelphia in 1787, the Senate was therefore the product of
politics, a concession to New Jersey and its small-state allies.

The Senate's principle of equality among states has important
consequences. With the support of both senators from twenty-five
states and a single senator from a twenty-sixth (or the vice president,
who can break tie votes), a bill can pass the upper chamber. It
matters not that a bill does not require the support of any senators from the top twenty-four states by population who, collectively, represent about 82 percent of Americans. Indeed, with the
Senate's rule that most bills are subject to a filibuster—a parlia-
mentary maneuver that can be ended only when sixty members

desire it—senators representing just over 11 percent of the public can prevent bills from becoming law. Senators representing about 7 percent of the country can block the ratification of treaties and constitutional amendments since the support of two-thirds of the body is needed for the passage of their enacting resolutions.

Individual residents of smaller states consequently have quantitatively greater representation in the Senate than those of larger ones. At its most dramatic extreme, this means that a voter from Wyoming has about 67.5 times as much influence on the body than does a person from California. Indeed, many critics of this system argue the Golden State should be especially aggrieved. Daniel Lazare, for example, has pictured a future in which California, frustrated with a Senate in which it is grossly underrepresented and its interests are continually stymied, succeeds from the Union.[3] Michael Lind has suggested the state be split into eight parts for the purposes of its Senate representation, including areas called "Reagan," "Siliconia," and "Vineland."[4]

Along similar lines, political scientists Frances E. Lee and Bruce I. Oppenheimer argue that, even after controlling for socioeconomic status, unequal representation results in residents of small states receiving more from the federal government per capita than those who live in big states.[5] According to Citizens Against Government Waste, a Washington-based public interest group, Californians received $18.12 of "pork" each in 2004—a showing that placed their state forty-second.[6] California ranked near the bottom with other populous states like Illinois (41st), Florida (43rd), Texas (44th), and New York (45th). The top five were Alaska (whose residents received $809.15 each), Hawaii, New Hampshire, West Virginia, and Montana. The Tax Foundation reported that in 2003 the states that received most federal expenditures as a percentage of the taxes they sent to Washington were New Mexico, Alaska, Mississippi, West Virginia, and North Dakota. At forty-second and receiving $.80 for every dollar was New York; at forty-third and getting $.78 was California; and at forty-fifth and collecting $.73 was Illinois.[7]

Much of the criticism of the Senate's composition comes from the left. Steven Hill, for example, attributes low voter turnout and an unresponsive Congress to a number of things, including Senate malapportionment.[8] He provocatively calls the constitutional design of the Senate an "affirmative action quota for low population states." Constitutional scholar Jack Rakove believes Senate representation is "unjust" and its asymmetrical character makes the upper chamber a "zany institution."[9] Tom Geoghegan argues that unequal representation in the upper chamber is the real cause of the inability of government to push public policy in a leftward direction.[10]

This liberal opprobrium is not particularly surprising because, as I have noted, today the Union's smaller states—largely because less populated ones tend to be rural and situated in the country's interior—generally support the Republicans. Larger states, as John Griffin has shown, have disproportionately greater numbers of liberal voters and racial minorities.[11] And because small states are over-represented in the Senate, this means that the body is predisposed to fall into GOP hands. To be sure, campaigns matter, and Democrats do win statewide elections in states with fewer people. In the 108th Congress of 2003–2004, all six senators from the Dakotas and Delaware were Democrats. But in a time of parity in national party politics, the fact that the Republicans frequently win Senate races in small states is a critical determinant of partisan control of the upper chamber.

There exists sophisticated research to prove the point, as well. Thomas Brunell and Frances Lee and Bruce Oppenheimer show that the counter-majoritarian tendencies of Senate representation have benefited the GOP for most of the post–World War II period.[12] Brunell argues that the population bias inherent in the Senate accounts for a strong GOP advantage, especially since 1978. For Lee and Oppenheimer, the small state bias accounts for Republican control of the body between 1981 and 1987—without the Senate's rule of unequal representation there may not have been a Reagan Revolution.

The federal characteristics of the presidency are less pronounced, but they nevertheless exist. Ostensibly, of course, the Electoral College selects the President of the United States. This institution consists of men and women who cast electoral votes on behalf of their states in their home state capitals on the first Monday after the second Wednesday in December of the election year. The number of electors a state has equals the number of its members in the House of Representatives plus its two senators.[13] As conceived by the Founders, electors were largely autonomous from the popular votes in their states; indeed, it was their names on the ballot, not those of the presidential candidates. As Alexander Hamilton put it in *Federalist 68*, the "election should be made by men most capable of analyzing the qualities adapted to the station, and acting under circumstances favorable to deliberation, and to a judicious combination of all the reasons and inducements which were proper to govern their choice. A small number of persons, selected by their fellow-citizens from the general mass, will be most likely to possess the information and discernment requisite to so complicated an investigation."[14]

The elitist underpinnings of the Electoral College were soon stripped away, however. Fairly quickly, states began to allow their residents—rather than their legislatures—to choose electors. As political parties developed outside of Washington in the early nineteenth century, the states began to effectively couple electors with certain candidates. Today, electors have little, if any, independence. Indeed, in thirty-nine states they are not even on the ballot anymore.[15] In twenty-nine states and the District of Columbia, there exist laws designed to bind electors to the result of the popular vote. In North Carolina, for example, an elector who does not vote in line with the wishes of residents is subject to a $10,000 fine. In New Mexico such behavior is considered a fourth-degree felony, and in Michigan "faithless" electors have their votes voided and alternate electors are drafted. An additional safeguard is the method by which electors are selected. In most states each party's convention or committee chooses a slate equal in number to the state's votes in the Electoral College. The electors are generally party loyalists, contributors, state legislators, county chairs—often political junkies who revel in the constitutional pageantry of it all. The vote frequently takes place in state legislative chambers, is kicked off by a singing of the national anthem, and is accompanied by people dressed as Founding Fathers. The slate of whichever party's candidate wins the popular vote gets to be the state's official electors.

This does not mean that there are not faithless electors. In 1972, for example, Virginia elector Roger MacBride, a Republican, voted for the Libertarian candidate John Hospers rather than Richard Nixon. MacBride, who justified his action as an "attempt to restore to the members of the Electoral College some of the function of independent thinking and action assigned to them by the Federal Convention," then became somewhat of a hero to the Libertarians and their presidential candidate in 1976.[16] In 1984, Margaret Leach from West Virginia voted for Democratic vice-presidential candidate Lloyd Bentsen instead of Michael Dukakis. No one seems to know why.[17] Sixteen years later, District of Columbia elector Barbara Lett Simmons left her ballot blank to protest the circumstances under which George W. Bush became president. In 2004,

Richie Robb, a West Virginia GOP elector and mayor of South Charleston, threatened to vote for another Republican instead of George W. Bush even before the public had cast its votes. A Minnesota elector did actually vote for Democratic vice-presidential candidate John Edwards that year. Still, the rumors flying around the Internet in November and December 2000 that the Gore campaign was seriously planning to persuade Bush electors to jump ship were plainly ludicrous. The rules effectively prevent defection, especially in close contests.

Yet even with bound electors and votes distributed to states based indirectly upon population, majority rule is undermined by the federal principle reflected in the distribution of the electoral votes to each state for its Senate representation. As a result, smaller states have a greater say when it comes to electing the president, although not to the dramatic degree we saw in the Senate. There are about 525,000 Americans per elector. There are, however, around 165,000 Wyomingites for every elector from that state and about 191,000 residents of the District of Columbia per D.C. elector. There are approximately 615,000 Californians, Texans, and New Yorkers for every elector those states get.

This would not be so bad if forty-eight states and D.C. did not use the unit rule—an arrangement in which all of a state's electors vote for the candidate who won a plurality of the popular vote. But, with serious consequences, they do. The first ramification of the unit rule is that citizens who vote for third-party candidates are effectively disenfranchised. Although smaller parties do garner support and once even beat a major party candidate into third place in the popular voting—Teddy Roosevelt did this to Republican William Howard Taft in 1912—it is difficult for them to capture a plurality of the vote in a state. In the winner-take-all system of the unit rule, this means that third parties end up with few, if any, electoral votes. Strom Thurmond and George Wallace, in 1948 and 1968, respectively, were able to pick up electoral votes in the South with their segregationist platforms, but Ross Perot did not get even one electoral vote in 1992 when he won 19 percent of the popular vote or in 1996 when he received 8 percent of it.

Secondly, the unit rule usually exaggerates the winner's margin of victory since the triumphant candidate keeps picking up 100 percent of states' electors for considerably less of the share of the popular vote.[18] This often suggests that a president has a mandate when he really does not. In 1996, for example, Bill Clinton won

70 percent of the electoral vote but less than half the popular vote. In the two knife-edge elections of 1960 and 1968, in which there was less than half a percentage point between the two major party candidates in the popular vote, John F. Kennedy beat Richard Nixon in the Electoral College 303 to 219 and Nixon beat Hubert Humphrey 301 to 191.

A third consequence is that candidates who win the popular vote may lose in the Electoral College. This is, of course, precisely what happened to Al Gore who got over half-a-million more popular votes than George W. Bush in 2000. It happens because you get the same prize—all of a state's electors—if you win a state narrowly or by a handsome margin.

With electors voting in a block, moreover, the counter-majoritarian tendencies of the Electoral College are exacerbated. Lawrence Longley and Neal Peirce have shown that the unit rule benefits the larger states most, especially California, Texas, and New York.[19] Their calculations reveal that any individual in California, for example, had 2.6 times as much of a chance of casting the winning vote for president in the 1990s—by delivering the state's electoral votes to make one presidential candidate victorious—than did a voter in Montana. This approach also reveals, however, that voters in many small states—like Wyoming, Alaska, and Idaho—have more of a chance of determining the outcome than those in states that have six, seven, eight, and nine electors, like Arkansas, Oregon, Connecticut, and Louisiana. It is also true that, as George Edwards has argued, "the relative probability of affecting the election outcomes is outweighed by the extraordinarily low absolute probability that it will occur."[20] Still, if we think that a single individual might determine the result, Andrew Gelman and Jonathan Katz have shown mathematically that any voter in the smaller states has a greater chance in determining the outcome of a presidential election than most people assume. This is because although small states are less likely to make the difference between winning and losing the White House than those with many electoral votes—remember, Bush and Gore wrangled over Florida in 2000, not Iowa, New Mexico, Oregon, or Wisconsin where the outcomes were also exceedingly close—the results of the popular vote within them are much more likely to be tied than those of states that have many voters.[21]

The Constitution does not compel states to use the unit rule. They could plausibly use a system of proportional representation in which a candidate would win roughly the percentage of the state's electors equivalent to the percentage of the popular vote captured—an obvious boost for third parties. In fact, such a proposal was on the ballot in Colorado in 2004, but it was defeated handily—65 to 35 percent—and George W. Bush picked up all of the state's nine electoral votes. I did mention earlier that forty-eight states use the unit rule; two others, Maine and Nebraska, utilize a further possibility, the district system. Here, the states distribute each elector they receive for their House representation to the candidate who wins the popular vote in the corresponding congressional district, granting the two at large electors to the winner of the state-wide popular vote. Neither Maine—which accepted the method in 1969—nor Nebraska—which had it in place for 1992—have ever had to split their electoral vote between the parties. Despite the fact that if the district plan had been embraced nationally in 2000 Bush would still have won (288–250), a systemic adoption of the approach would lessen the possibility that candidates who lost the popular vote would become president.[22]

Interestingly, in the early 1990s some states, including Florida, were seriously contemplating mimicking Maine and Nebraska. Indeed, in 1992 a proposal to adopt the district plan passed the Florida House and a Senate committee. Of course, if Florida had done so, Al Gore—who won ten congressional districts in the state—would have become president in January 2001. Quite presciently, it was the Democrats who pushed for the method back then and Republicans who vehemently opposed it.[23] Analysts list myriad reasons why Gore lost—a "crooked" recount in Florida presided over by Bush's brother Jeb, a conservative Supreme Court, and Gore's failure to win Tennessee. One they do not mention is the Florida Senate's fateful failure to pass the district plan.

If no candidate wins a majority in the Electoral College, the Constitution gives the responsibility of choosing the president to the House of Representatives. Each state's delegation has one vote and must vote as a block. Of course, having the House decide a presidential election is a rare event—it last happened in 1824 when Speaker Henry Clay, having come fourth in the Electoral College and therefore not eligible for the House vote under the Twelfth Amendment, threw his support and considerable influence behind John Quincy Adams so as to defeat Andrew Jackson, the winner of a plurality of electoral votes. As such, we have little to go on in gauging how the House would vote under such circumstances. Presumably, each delegation would canvass its members and cast its collective vote for the candidate with the most support, but how would each individual vote? The party line? For the candidate who won the popular vote in the member's district? One can only imagine the media frenzy and the behind-the-scenes negotiating that would go on. Perhaps we would see things like the purported deal in 1824 between Adams and Clay to make the latter Secretary of State.

The idea that the House could determine a presidential election in the near future is not quite the fantasy it appears. In the spring and summer of 1992 there was a serious discussion about the possibility of Ross Perot winning enough electoral votes to deprive George H. W. Bush or Bill Clinton of a majority and throw the election into the chamber.[24] Even in a two-horse race, it can happen. In the summer of 2004, mathematician Nathan Ritchey computed from contemporaneous polls that there was a 1.4 percent chance of a 269 to 269 tie in the Electoral College.[25] By late October, the *Washington Post* calculated that there were thirty-three scenarios under which the year's battleground states could line up to give us the tie.[26] It sounds like a long shot, but a tie would have happened in 2000 with a Gore (and not Bush) win in Louisiana and a Bush (and not Gore) win in Iowa—a plausible scenario. In 2004 we would have had a tie if Ohio (which, as we remember, was nearly that year's Florida) and Iowa (which Bush won by 13,000 votes) went for Kerry and Wisconsin (which Kerry won by a meager 12,000 votes) fell to Bush. If we do have a tie, the Republicans' small-state advantage means they will fancy their chances. Bush's thirty-to-twenty state advantage in the popular vote of 2000 would have surely made him president if the contest had been decided in the House—and probably in a manner less controversial than the way he ultimately won.

Interestingly, there exists research to show that the Electoral College has a Democratic bias that is unrelated to the small-state tilt of the institution. Political scientists Jim Garand and Wayne Parent have shown, for instance, that from World War II through the 1980s the Democratic candidate should have expected to receive slightly more of the electoral vote than the Republican when popular vote shares were made identical.[27] In 2004, moreover, John Kerry, who received 3.5 million fewer popular votes nationally than George W. Bush, was only 137,000 Ohio votes away from winning in the Electoral College. Still, as I mentioned above, 12,000 more Wisconsin votes for Bush would have made the Buckeye State irrelevant. And clearly, given that Al Gore lost the election but captured a plurality of the popular vote, Garand and Parent's approach shows the Electoral College of 2000 to be biased in favor of Republicans.

What is more, a comparison of the 1996 and 2000 results reveals an increasing Republican edge to the institution. This is highlighted by exploring the swing toward or away from the Democratic and Republican candidates between 1996 and 2000. The swing is the amount, compared to the party's share of the national popular vote, the party's vote increased or decreased in a state between 1996 and 2000. By way of example, Bill Clinton's vote in Alabama in 1996 was 6.08 percent below his national vote, Gore's Alabama vote was 6.79 percent below his national vote. As a result, the Democratic swing in Alabama between the two elections was −.71 percent. If we look at the top states by size— the states which are most handicapped by the federal complexion of the Electoral College—the average Democratic swing between 1996 and 2000 was .66 percent and the GOP's was −.85 percent. But there was a distinct swing toward the Republicans and away from the Democrats in the ten smallest and most advantaged states, a 1.92 percent average for the GOP and a −2.51 percent average for the Democrats. Between 2000 and 2004, interestingly, the Democratic candidate's vote improved more in the ten smallest states than it did the ten largest—mainly because much of Ralph Nader's 2000 vote shifted to Kerry in environmentally conscious states like Alaska, the Dakotas, Montana, and Vermont. As for the ten fastest growing states—those slated to pick up the most electoral votes in the years to come—the swing was again decisively toward the GOP (an average of 1.30 percent for 1996–2000) and away from the Democrats (an average of −1.55 percent for 1996–2000). The situation for Democrats improved in the expanding states between 2000 and 2004, and there was a very slight swing in their favor. Yet these states still on average gave Kerry 6 percent less than his national vote and Bush 5.9 percent more than his.

An examination of the last four presidential races gives us additional insight into how the small-state bias in the Electoral College advantages Republicans. Of the thirty-four states that voted for candidates of the same party on all four occasions, eighteen went to the Democrats and sixteen to the GOP. For the Democrats, the national share of the electoral votes of ten of their states—or 56 percent—was bigger than the state's share of the country's population. For the Republicans, the number was twelve states—or 75 percent.

Not only are Senators Boxer and Enzi from states of different sizes, their homes are located in two different parts of the country. California, on the Pacific coast, is a part of what we might call "Democratic country" or the states generally colored blue on the electoral map, Wyoming a part of "Big Sky" and red "Republican country." Because the geographical constituencies of the two major parties have not really changed much over the last decade or so, we can use recent Electoral College maps as more systematic indicators of where in the United States each party is strongest. Contemporary electoral cartography shows the Democrats to have three strongholds: the Northeast, the industrial Midwest, and the Pacific coast. John Maggs has called the Democratically dominated coasts the "Wall Street–Hollywood Axis."[28] The Republicans control the Southeast, the mountain West, and the rural Midwest. In fact, the geographical divides between the parties are so neat that of the forty-eight contiguous states, only New Hampshire and New Mexico are completely surrounded by states won by the other party in 2000—and, what's more, Bush only won New Hampshire by just over 7,000 votes, and Gore captured New Mexico by 366. In 2004, New Hampshire went for Kerry and New Mexico for Bush, meaning that not a single state was totally encircled by others won by the opposition party. It is interesting that although geographic distinctions are continually being eroded throughout American social and economic life—not least by jet travel, the electronic media, and a national, even global, economy—our party politics retain a peculiarly old-fashioned regionalism.

This geography is quite new. The transformation to it has also been greatly chronicled, but it bears repeating quickly. In the 1948 elections—a year in which the candidates of the two major parties were divided by less than 5 percent of the popular vote— Republican Thomas Dewey did not win a single state in the South but won every state north and east of Washington, D.C., except Rhode Island and Massachusetts. He also lost every state west of the Dakotas except Oregon. After that election two lone Tennesseans were the only Republican members of the House delegation from the old Confederacy, and only twenty members from the industrial heartland states of Illinois, Indiana, Michigan, Ohio, Pennsylvania, and Wisconsin were Democrats.

In 1964, the year of Barry Goldwater's pivotal "states' rights" Republican presidential campaign, the only one of the six states the GOP captured in the Electoral College outside of the deep South was the candidate's home of Arizona. The congressional delegation was changing, too. Of the twenty-two senators representing the old Confederacy's states in the 93rd Congress begun in 1973, seven were Republicans. In the same Congress, only fourteen of the thirty-four senators from the seventeen states completely inside the "L" that is formed by lines connecting Minnesota, Missouri, and Virginia were from the GOP.

Ronald Reagan's electoral successes and the 1994 Republican take over of both houses of Congress for the first time in forty years represented the final stage of this geographical metamorphosis. By 1992, for example, when the GOP was losing for the first time in sixteen years at the presidential level, the only state east of the Mississippi River and outside the South that George Bush could win was Indiana, and yet he beat the all-southern Clinton-Gore ticket in Alabama, Florida, Mississippi, North Carolina, South Carolina, and Virginia. After the famous 1994 congressional midterm elections, a majority of the House delegation from the old Confederate states was Republican for the first time since Reconstruction. Moreover, the Speaker (Newt Gingrich, Georgia), Majority Leader (Dick Armey, Texas), and Majority Whip (Tom DeLay, Texas) of that historic 104th Congress were all southern Republicans and, when Bob Dole resigned from the Senate to energize his presidential campaign in May 1996, so was the Majority Leader of the Senate (Trent Lott, Mississippi). By 2005 only four of the South's twenty-two senators were Democrats—the GOP had picked up five Democratic seats, one each in Florida, Georgia, Louisiana, North Carolina, and South Carolina, the previous fall. Two recent and important books cast serious doubts on the ability of the GOP to dominate southern politics in the future—citing, among other things, the growing importance of the minority vote and the fear national Republicans have of offering southerners the kind of social conservatism they desire.[29] Nevertheless, the pachyderm's current control of large swaths of Dixie cannot be refuted.

A glance at the county-level results in 2000 is equally revealing. It is dramatically apparent that Bush captured more counties—he was the victor in 78 percent of the nation's 3,111—and that these counties were generally larger than average covering 81 percent of the country's territory. The year 2004 brought little change.

Moreover, on closer inspection, you can see that both Gore and Kerry did very well in and around large metropolitan areas and Bush in rural America. In 2000 Bush received only one in four votes in population centers with over half-a-million people, but 60 percent of the vote in centers with less than 50,000 people.[30] Four years later 39 percent of big-city residents went for him; 59 percent of rural dwellers did.

The other geography of current party politics, therefore, has the Republicans in control of rural areas and small towns and the Democrats dominant in the cities. Democrats have had their recent successes in the sticks, as Mark Warner's winning gubernatorial candidacy in Virginia in 2001 illustrated. Warner made dramatic gains for his party in the bucolic southern and western areas of the state but only because he mixed his populist economic message with strong support for the death penalty and gun rights and vocal opposition to gay marriage. These are, of course, generally seen as GOP positions and there are few Democrats today who share them.

The Democrats also used to do better in countrified America. The rural electorate gave only 2 percent more of its vote to Bob Dole than Bill Clinton in 1996. Now the small-town and rural vote is, like that of the South, becoming increasingly Republican. The Democrats seem to focus on cities and have the view, to use John Edwards' words, that "rural America is just someplace to fly over between a fundraiser in Manhattan and a fundraiser in Beverly Hills."[31] As John Kerry's running mate in 2004, the North Carolina senator was dispatched to the hinterlands of the South and Midwest in an attempt to reverse this trend. It was to no avail. Kerry captured only 42 percent of the rural vote.

Reasons for the Democrats' rural exodus are numerous. Michael Barone, for example, has written that voters outside metropolitan areas in the East, West, and Midwest "are more anti-corruption, tradition-minded, and religious than the national average" and that Bill Clinton's personal morality and Al Gore's cultural liberalism greatly hurt Democrats in 2000 in "parts of the West, the farm belt, and eastern coal country."[32] Matthew Dowd, the GOP pollster, sees that white male voters in the South and rural areas have much in common and argues that taxes, national security, and cultural issues are responsible for their overwhelming Republican support.[33] These are the so-called "NASCAR Dads" who, according to political scientist Larry Sabato, are "middle- to lower-middle class males who are family men, live in rural areas, used to vote heavily Democratic but now usually vote Republican."[34] The "NASCAR Dad," in the words of Jeff MacGregor, "may have a Confederate flag stuck to the bumper of his pickup truck—unless he's driving his wife's Subaru, in which case the bumper reads 'Mary Kay' or 'Lose Weight Now, Ask Me How'."[35]

Second Amendment rights are an especially pivotal issue for rural America. As a consequence, Al Gore's anti-gun stance in 2000 devastated his chances in swing states like Arkansas, Tennessee, and West Virginia and has helped place much of Big Sky and Rocky Mountain country out of his party's reach.[36] To illustrate the augmented importance of the gun issue in the heartland, 42 percent of rural voters in 2002 said they supported the National Rifle Association, while only 27 percent of urban voters did.[37] To illustrate a palpable swing against gun control more broadly, Democratic pollster Stanley Greenberg estimated that whereas 37 percent of voters owned a firearm in 1996, 48 percent did in 2000.[38] In 2004, John Kerry recognized all this and talked incessantly about how he hunted—indeed, so as to prove the point, he took a morning off the busy campaign trail and dressed up in camouflage fatigues to shoot geese in Ohio. His reward? Bush won 63 percent of the vote of people who had a gun owner in the household.

With the Democrats maintaining a vice-like grip on urban America—for example, Kerry won 83 percent of the vote in San Francisco, over 80 percent in Philadelphia, about 75 percent in New York City, and well over two-thirds of the vote in Cook County, home of Chicago—the suburbs have become the battleground. The 2000 and 2004 elections were indicative of this competition. The presidential races in the suburbs during those years were a microcosm of the country—essentially the parties were tied with Gore and Kerry winning the coasts and Bush, the interior. The Democrats won the suburbs around New York City like those in Bergen County, New Jersey; Westchester County, New York; and Fairfield County, Connecticut; the bigger suburban counties in Florida; Silicon Valley and the San Francisco area; and Arlington County, Virginia, and Prince George's County, Maryland, around Washington, D.C. In 2000 Gore won the traditional bellwether and older suburban Detroit county of Macomb— tellingly, Kerry lost it narrowly four years later. However, in both elections Bush won rapidly growing suburban counties like Collin and Williamson in Texas (of course); Fairfax, Virginia; DuPage, Kane, and Lake around Chicago; Chester outside Philadelphia;

Wake, home of Raleigh, North Carolina; Orange and San Diego in California; and suburban counties around electorally important cities like Cincinnati and Kansas City.

To be sure, suburbanites sometimes worry about the Republicans' laissez-faire approach to sprawl and its social conservatism, especially the party's stances on public education, race, and abortion.[39] Yet these voters—who include among their number the widely targeted sub-demographic groups like "soccer moms" and "office-park dads"—seem to like Republicans when it comes to economic issues such as low taxes and small government. They also warm to the GOP's traditionally decentralized philosophy about government that argues suburban taxpayers should not pay for the problems of their urban neighbors.[40] Indeed, in recent years there have been concrete efforts by affluent neighborhoods in high-tax cities to formally separate themselves from their jurisdictions. In 1993 Staten Islanders voted to secede from New York City, only for their effort to be blocked by the state legislature. In November 2002 many in the San Fernando valley and Hollywood areas of Los Angeles tried to split off from the city but were defeated in a referendum because of squabbles between the two communities, a wordy and complicated ballot, huge opposition from urban voters, and a deft campaign by Los Angeles mayor James Hahn, who warned residents of the secessionist areas that they would have to pay huge amounts of "alimony" to the city.[41]

Nevertheless, there are those who believe the Democrats are winning this battle, especially in certain types of suburbs. John B. Judis and Ruy Teixeira have written about the "ideopolis"— a physical place in the postindustrial economy where livings are made in the high technology and service sectors, neighborhoods are spacious, and attitudes "tend to be libertarian and bohemian."[42] Joel Kotkin uses the term "Nerdistan" to describe communities like this. Here, livelihoods are made largely in businesses related to the Internet, computer software, biotechnology and health care, telecommunications, financial services, government and higher education, or "soft technology" like architecture, media, and advertising.[43] These places "neither depend on the core city for employment, as many older suburbs did, nor seek to duplicate the traditional functions of the urban core."[44] Their self-containment therefore makes them similar to the communities Joel Garreau was talking about when he coined the phrase "edge city" to describe, in the late 1980s, places like Columbia, Maryland; Framingham, Massachusetts; Schaumburg, Illinois;

Farmington Hills, Michigan; Overland Park outside Kansas City; most of Orange County, California; Bergen County and Cherry Hill, New Jersey; Fairfax, Virginia; and Scottsdale, Arizona.[45] To Garreau, "edge cities" were both new and old, but their defining characteristic was that they had recently and dramatically become self-contained quasi-urban areas with large amounts of office and retail space and a population that increased during weekdays.

Attracted to "ideopolises," "Nerdistans," and, to some extent, "edge cities" are what Richard Florida calls the "creative class"— a distinctively liberal crowd made up of a disproportionate number of gay and foreign-born Americans—and what David Brooks labels "Bobos"—bourgeois bohemians who mix materialism and conspicuous consumption with social liberalism in a gooey apolitical mix.[46] The latter may not be inherently Democratic, but they are certainly repelled by the aggressive style of conservative Republicanism. Stanley Greenberg has argued that they strongly support environmental protection, relaxed immigration, and gun control.[47]

Whether "ideopolises," "Nerdistans," or "edge cities," the physical characteristics of these new kinds of suburbs are familiar to most Americans. They consist of large three- or four-lane roads, strewn with traffic signals and sport-utility vehicles, that are adorned on the sides by office parks, medical-center buildings, and mega strip-malls with their Old Navys, Home Depots, Olive Gardens, and cineplexes, and that lead every half mile or so to a series of subdivisions connected by a maze of sidewalk-less streets that contain three- or four-bedroom single family homes with nicely kept lawns. Places like Kotkin's principal "Nerdistans"—Austin, Salt Lake City, the Raleigh-Durham area in North Carolina—clearly look like this, but so, increasingly, do traditional American suburbs in counties like Norfolk, Massachusetts; Macomb, Michigan; Fairfield, Connecticut; Bergen, New Jersey; DuPage, Illinois; and Nassau and Westchester, New York.

Yet the new suburbia is, in spite of Judis and Teixeira's argument, quite hospitable to the GOP. George W. Bush beat John Kerry by three points in the suburbs. According to an October 2004 Survey USA poll, moreover, in forty-seven states Bush was doing better in the suburbs than he was in the state as a whole— conservative Colorado, Missouri, and Nevada were the exceptions.

The GOP advantage stems from the fact that suburbs are constructed so as to maximize private and family life and minimize engagement in the public sphere. Rural and small-town life has always revolved around critical public institutions like the church, the local Chamber of Commerce, civic groups like the Kiwanis and Rotary club, the town council and mayor's office, the bowling alley and park, and Fourth of July parades, Labor Day picnics, and other community gatherings. It is true that crime rates, migration, and gentrification have likely undermined such institutions in urban areas, but in many cases remnants are still vibrant. In suburbia, however, a variety of factors have conspired to dilute public life.

The first of these is especially evident in the Sunbelt. Building in warmer climates and with generally ample room for development, construction companies in the South and West have erected homes with large lots and fenced-in back yards. With central air conditioning now *de rigueur*, the new homes in the Sunbelt also do not have porches like established ones. Affluence and the availability of home entertainment—which has increased appeal to the large proportion of Sunbelt suburbanites who have young children (6.8 percent of the U.S. population is under five years old; in Phoenix, for example, the figure is 9.6 percent, and in Houston it is 8.2 percent)—also add to the incentive for residents to stay inside or on the deck as a family rather than gather to talk with neighbors. Moreover, the lack of public transportation has made car ownership necessary, and these communities' spaciousness has removed the incentive to build sidewalks.[48] It's much easier to meet people on the street than it is in your SUV.

Geographical mobility into these communities also means that people do not have deep roots and feel little connection with the places in which they live. Residents of traditional suburbs in the Northeast and Midwest are actually less mobile than urban residents, but in many Sunbelt suburban counties, such as Fulton County where Atlanta is, about 55 percent of the population had moved house between 1995 and 2000. Cary, North Carolina, which is next to Raleigh, had 8,707 residents in 1970. By 2001, its size had topped 100,000, and it had long since acquired the nickname Containment (sometimes Concentrated) Area for Relocated Yankees. What is more, the newness of Sunbelt suburbs does not furnish a "narrative tale" or history for the place, the principal connection between people and their hometown.[49] There are no famous houses or historical landmarks, no local heroes to make people proud of where they live.

These characteristics help the Sunbelt suburban GOP because the party's message is generally consistent with this inward focus on self and family. Residents desire low taxes, minimal public services, and private conveniences like yard-waste collection rather than higher taxes to pay for parks, recreation centers, and sidewalks. Local government services are frequently private and involve the construction of infrastructure to assist with commercial development. Many suburban Sunbelt residents—and about 50 million Americans in all—also live in what Evan McKenzie has called "Privatopia," communities where rules are largely dictated by homeowners' associations and not broadly democratic and public municipal governments.[50] Such groups promulgate policies on the color of houses, heights of fences, and the placement of garbage cans, and these decisions become the topics of public discourse in self-contained suburban enclaves. Gated communities particularly encourage an inward-looking approach to life.[51] About 7 million households live in these places that, according to architect Neal Peyton, "are anathema to civic life" since they "isolate individual neighborhoods from each other and from the public realm."[52] Moreover, where there is more conventional public life in the Sunbelt suburbs, it is usually social rather than civic and political. Oprah-esque book clubs, Bunko groups, Pampered Chef parties, and coaching in junior-soccer leagues account for much personal interaction.

In fact J. Eric Oliver has shown that as suburbs grow, political activity, such as contacting public officials and attending public meetings, decreases rapidly.[53] Perhaps the only exception to this lack of public engagement is the interest of many suburbanites in public education. Even this issue, which ought to benefit Democrats, often plays out to the advantage of Republicans. Certainly there are often suburban cries to give the schools more money. Issues such as busing and the racial and ethnic mixing in schools, however, have become prevalent. Suburban parents may not be against diversity in the abstract, but, despite the rise of magnet schools, they regularly and strenuously oppose the reassignment of their children to urban schools with large minority populations because they feel such institutions are inferior.[54]

Oliver's work also suggests that suburban government is detrimental because it splinters regions into a myriad of independent and self-contained political units. It is true that the suburbs are becoming more racially diverse, but it is also the case that they are still disproportionately white and affluent.[55] This all means that suburban communities are organized politically into homogenous racial and socioeconomic groupings in which public discussion surrounding local government policy is sterile and consensual. The mantra is largely "keep taxes low." In large cities where the population is racially and economically diverse, political debate is vigorous. Groups argue on tax rates and the level of public services. To be sure, there are winners and losers and often tumultuous clashes, but participants and their constituents become aware of the political needs and desires of other types of people. Wealthier voters begin to occasionally recognize the virtues of some public services. Indeed, although there is evidence that whites feel a "power threat" and that their prejudice increases as does the proportion of people of other races in their community, there also exists much social science research to show that people have greater appreciation for those of different races and socioeconomic circumstances if they live close to them.[56] This latter theory of proximity—or contact theory, to use Gordon Allport's famous phrase—does not, of course, help the Democrats in the white middle class suburbs, where sometimes the main everyday contact residents have with minorities occurs briefly when Mexican men landscape their yards and African American women ring up their groceries.[57]

The Republican advantage is particularly pronounced in what are often called exurbs—or what have been called "boomburgs" or "sprinkler cities."[58] This is a new type of "suburb" that is growing beyond the "ideopolises," "Nerdistans," and "edge cities," sometimes forming another concentric circle outside of the urban core, sometimes sprawling out from the suburbs like spider's legs. Places like Douglas County, Colorado; Frederick County, Maryland; Forsyth, Gwinnett, and Henry counties outside Atlanta, Georgia; Collin County north of Dallas; Scott County outside of Minnesota's twin cities; Polk County, Florida; and Kane County, Illinois, are quintessential exurbs. Exurbs are sort of suburbs of the suburbs, places where people who work in the offices and stores of new American cities live. They are essentially bedroom communities sought after by people who are looking for more land and cheaper housing and who find contemporary suburban life too hectic and congested. They are populated by the "patio man," a twenty- or thirty-something male who, according to David Brooks who coined the term, takes pride in his souped-up backyard grill, and looks forward to his visits to the Home Depot.[59] They are full of "family-sized subdivisions, outlet shopping malls and booming mega-churches."[60] People who live here are, with the exception of GOP-friendly organized religion, even more cut off from traditional civic and political institutions, even less attached to place, and even less likely to engage in frequent social interaction outside their family and close friends and neighbors. The exurbs, although relatively new to American life, could therefore prove a boon to Republicans. Indeed, they lined up solidly behind GOP candidates in the 2002 congressional midterms.[61] They also went decisively for President Bush two years later—the president carried ninety-seven of the one hundred fastest growing, typically exurban, counties.

The news gets better for Republicans when we look at population growth. It is the newer suburbs, particularly the exurbs, that are expanding dramatically. The proximity of offices, stores, and conveniences; the increased ability because of computers and the Internet for many people to work from home; and the fact that, although they are not always culturally interesting, the suburbs and exurbs often have better public schools and are clean, pleasant, and safe, have stimulated their growth. "If there is an Ozzie and Harriet-ville in America today," demographer William H. Frey contends, exurbia is "where it is."[62] Many of the top twenty U.S. counties by population growth from 1990 to 2000 were exurban. Indeed, five of the top ten, all growing in excess of 90 percent, were in the Denver-Boulder-Colorado Springs area; the others in the top twenty were outside the suburban rings of Atlanta, Washington, D.C., Dallas, and Austin or in the Rocky Mountain states. Even the more traditional suburbs are growing more quickly than the big cities they surround, despite signs of urban renaissance. Cook County, home of Chicago, grew 5.3 percent in the 1990s, but all of the adjoining counties grew at a considerably accelerated rate—DuPage (15.7 percent), Kane (27.3 percent), Lake (24.8 percent), McHenry (41.9 percent), and Will (40.6 percent). Around Philadelphia the trend was similar. While the city lost 4.3 percent of its people, growth was recorded in the surrounding counties of Camden (1.2 percent) and Gloucester (10.7 percent), New Jersey, and Bucks (10.4 percent), Chester (15.2 percent), and Montgomery (10.6 percent), Pennsylvania.

That U.S. population growth benefits Republicans is more systematically illustrated if we look at the country's fastest growing places. In 2004 Bush astonishingly won all of the fifty fastest growing counties measured by percentage change in population between 2000 and 2003. Because of the Electoral College votes involved, it is more important to note that Bush captured eight of the top ten states that added the most people between 2000 and 2003 in both elections he won. To show how the GOP is advantaged by these population shifts, if the 2000 election had been fought using the reapportioned Electoral College votes made necessary by shifting population detected by the census of that year—that is under the rules in place for 2004—Bush would have won 278 to 259 instead of the 271 to 266 by which he was actually victorious.

The new political geography is an important part of the intrinsic Republican tilt to the playing field of contemporary party competition. We should not, however, exaggerate too much the importance of the constitutionally derived advantages Republicans enjoy in Senate and presidential elections. They cannot determine partisan control of governmental institutions when sizable majorities want a certain outcome. Such rules were also unimportant when American politics was characterized by two unequal parties—what Samuel Lubell described as a sun party, which dominates and radiates, and a moon party, which can only reflect the rays of its imperious rival.[63] In these cases, the American public tended to provide the ruling party with a significant mandate to continue its policies—as it did to the Democrats in 1964—or emphatically tossed it out and turned the sun into the moon—as it did to the Republicans in 1932.

However, the Republican slants to Senate and presidential elections are critical today. When the parties are as close as they are now—and Lubell's characterization seems so antiquated—political rules can make a big difference. The small-state bias of the Senate and presidency amplify the influence of significant parts of the Republican's geographical base—the more rural, interior, and generally Western states. Some Founders felt the federal principles that provided the states equal representation were a critical part of the constitutional settlement; others realized they were a political necessity that assuaged the fears of centralized authority held by many of the document's opponents. None could foresee their ideas contributing to Republican rule in the first decade of the twenty-first century. By constructing the U.S. House of Representatives around national principles, however, the Founders did not inadvertently provide the modern GOP with inherent electoral advantages. The number of each state's representatives is proportionate to its population. Still, as we shall see in the next chapter, this has not stopped the Republicans from ending four decades of Democratic dominance over the lower chamber and beginning to exert some considerable control of their own.

3

Elephants in the House: After Forty Years in the Wilderness, Playing the Democrats at Their Own Game

There is no constitutionally derived partisan bias when it comes to the House of Representatives, of course.[1] Whereas the Senate has federal characteristics, the House is distinctly "national" with each state having representation roughly equivalent to the size of its population. For most of the post–World War II era, however, the House has been under Democratic rule. Indeed, the Democrats formed the majority in the body for the entire period of 1955 to 1994, and the Republicans were in control for only the 80th (1947–49) and 83rd (1953–55) Congresses in the roughly three generations between 1932 and 1994. This is somewhat puzzling when we consider that the GOP governed the Senate for three Congresses in the early-to-mid 1980s and controlled the presidency for twenty-six of the forty years they found themselves in the House minority. The Constitution may not have presented the Democrats with an advantage in House elections, but to many, the institution did seem to have an intrinsically Democratic bent.

The explanation for Democratic domination of the post-war House is complex. After the seminal Supreme Court cases of *Baker v. Carr* in 1962 and *Wesberry v. Sanders* two years later, the one-person–one-vote principle was established, and state legislatures were forced to redraw congressional district lines so that all districts within the state were of equal size. Many Republicans claimed that this led to a pernicious, partisan gerrymander in which, after every census, Democratically ruled state legislatures constructed districts so that their party's representation in the House would be maximized. This was done by "packing" the districts of some Republican incumbents with GOP voters so that much of that party's vote would be wasted and "cracking" the districts of other Republicans so that there might be enough Democratic constituents to defeat the sitting member.

There is some evidence to suggest that this did happen, especially in the 1960s when state legislatures—which were generally controlled by the Democrats, especially after the 1964 elections— were first forced to redraw.[2] But the data for other decades are hardly conclusive. The famous "Burton gerrymander" of 1980 in California has been used as a prime exhibit in the GOP's case about Democratic mischievousness. Here, under the supervision of U.S. Rep. Philip Burton, the Golden State's assembly combined the districts of six Los Angeles County Republicans into three new ones and drew a number of other bizarre-looking districts. The new arrangement sent a delegation of twenty-eight Democrats and seventeen Republicans to the House after the 1984 elections, even though the GOP won more of the House vote in the state that year. As J. Morgan Kousser has shown, however, most of the supposedly "pro-Democratic" districts were not reliably so, especially when we examine their voter registration statistics.[3] Moreover, Indiana seemed to be the subject of a GOP gerrymander in the early 1980s, as did Pennsylvania, Utah, and Washington.[4] At the aggregate level then, many see, at best, negligible Democratic bias in that decade.[5] In the 1990s redistricting also conspicuously lacked egregious partisan tampering.[6] Republicans hoped a friendly, state-court drawn plan would assist them in California, for example, but it did not.

The case for a Democratic gerrymander is also undermined a little on two other counts. First, in a revision of the Voting Rights Act signed into law by President Ronald Reagan in 1982, states with traditions of racial discrimination were called upon to aggressively address their pasts and rectify racial malapportionment regardless of the intent of state legislatures. In the 1986 Supreme Court case *Thornburgh v. Gingles*, Justice William Brennan ruled that if a minority resided in an area of racial polarization and the area was sufficiently large and compact, the state legislature should draw districts that provided the minority an opportunity to elect candidates of its choosing. The result was that after the 1990 census many states created so-called "majority-minority" districts in which a majority of the voters were black or Hispanic.[7] This approach not only achieved the explicitly desired outcome of increasing the minority representation in the House, it helped increase the size of the GOP delegation by concentrating, and hence wasting, Democratic votes in such districts.[8] This was especially the case in the South. Take Georgia, for instance. After the 1990 election its delegation consisted of eight, mostly conservative, white Democrats, an African American Democrat, the civil rights activist John Lewis, and one Republican, Newt Gingrich. After the 1994 election, having gained a seat in the intervening redistricting, the state did not have a single white Democratic representative; instead, there were eight Republicans and three black Democrats. By way of showing this transformation more systematically, in the 102nd Congress of 1990–91, the eleven states of the old Confederacy had thirty-nine Republicans, five black Democrats, and seventy-two white Democrats in their House delegation; by the first Congress of GOP control, the 104th, there were sixty-five Republicans, seventeen black Democrats, and only forty-three white Democrats. Although two Supreme Court decisions in the 1990s effectively gutted the "majority-minority" district approach, it is clear that the principle tied the hands of those who drew district lines in 1991 and 1992.[9]

Second, a half-dozen states have decided to extract redistricting from the partisan thicket that is state legislative politics. By employing nonpartisan commissions, states like Arizona and Washington take away the opportunity for any party to manipulate the process. In Iowa, congressional redistricting was given to the nonpartisan Legislative Service Bureau in 1981. The bureau is greatly constrained in how it can draw lines and submits a plan to the legislature, which has an up-or-down vote on the first two designs but can only amend the third.[10] When we add the seats redrawn by commissions to the states that have had only one district and therefore do not reapportion, about 10 percent of all districts have been protected from partisan manipulation in the last fifteen or so years. And this does not include the legislatively drawn plans that have required court resolution.

The Democratic monopoly was therefore not just about gerrymandering. A considerably more significant contribution came from personal favors and the pork barrel. Generally undertaken by the staff that legislators are given—there are over 3,000 members' staff in the House alone—personal favors come in myriad forms, from helping local high schools organize trips to Washington, to having a flag flown over the Capitol on a special day, to recommending constituents for military academy appointments, to requesting a presidential greeting card. More informally, members lean on state and local government officials and private businesses, too. But perhaps the most rewarding type of personal favor—for both the lawmaker and beneficiary—occurs when the member's office represents a constituent's interests in dealings with the federal government. This is called casework. As John Boozman, a Republican from Arkansas, writes about casework on his Web site, "Although I cannot override the decisions made by a federal agency, I can often intervene on a person's behalf to answer questions, find solutions, or just cut through the red tape."[11]

Unsurprisingly, members are quite adroit at solving problems people have with veterans' benefits and records; disputes over Social Security and Medicare payments and eligibility; expedited passport requests; and tax and immigration issues. They vote on the budgets and jurisdictions of the agencies responsible for these programs and can instigate politically damaging oversight hearings if provoked. Indeed, in an influential book written in the late 1970s, Morris Fiorina argued that government bureaucracies were created for the sole purpose of casework. The political scientist posited that legislators, in establishing federal agencies, gave them vague mandates so that "aggrieved and/or hopeful constituents (would) petition their congressman to intervene" on their behalf. Casework would be rewarded "when the congressman lends a sympathetic ear, piously denounces the evil of bureaucracy, intervenes in the latter's decisions, and rides a grateful electorate to ever more impressive electoral showings."[12]

For many decades members of Congress, even Republicans, have been prolific at unraveling the Gordian knot of federal bureaucratic procedures. Former North Carolina Senator Jesse Helms, reviled by many in the Tar Heel State for his social conservatism, was especially revered for his casework. Helms' office did not discriminate when it came to assisting constituents. Indeed, as reported to me by the appreciative recipients, the senator's staff was happy to ask high-ranking IRS officials to advise a politically independent doctor on how to get a tax credit on a public-housing investment; they did not worry about assisting liberal couples from Chapel Hill with the adoption of babies from Asia.

Beneficiaries like casework and have favorable views of their lawmakers as a result.[13] A 1990 NES study revealed that 17 percent of respondents or members of their families had requested help from their representative and that 85 percent were happy with the response they had received.[14] Members of Congress consequently pile resources into the enterprise and unabashedly advertise their willingness and capability to grant such benevolence. Increasingly staff are assigned to the districts where they can do casework unencumbered by the legislative work and political distractions of Washington—during the 1990s, between 40 and 45 percent of House personal staff was assigned to the district.[15] Apart from the district director, just about everyone else outside D.C. works on casework. All caseworkers are generally granted instantaneous access to files and all correspondence between the office and constituent and agency via sophisticated software. Members encourage their constituents to ask for help on the Internet or in newsletters sent free of charge using the infamous congressional frank and can now be quickly and cheaply reached by phone and e-mail. A quick perusal of House members' Web sites illustrates what they are willing to do for constituents. Complete with the necessary release form that allows a member to deal with a federal agency on behalf of a constituent, casework pages are now *de rigueur* and describe in detail what can be done. A *New York Times* survey showed that such information was posted, perhaps not surprisingly, at the expense of details about the member's voting record.[16]

Casework has obvious electoral benefits for incumbents. To be sure, party-line voting dominates in congressional elections—according to NES studies, between 75 and 85 percent of the electorate votes for the candidate of the party with which they identify. Perceptions of presidential job performance, national issues, and general economic conditions also matter.[17] However, because those whose decisions are driven by considerations about the parties are directed by political habit or by the ebb and flow of presidential performance and unemployment, inflation, and economic growth, individual members of Congress can do little to influence their decision. House campaigns therefore often focus on the sizable number of voters who make their decisions outside of partisanship—independents and those whose attachment to a political party is tenuous. These people basically ask themselves the question, Has the incumbent done a good job?[18] An answer in the affirmative is what Bruce Cain, John Ferejohn, and Morris Fiorina call the incumbent's "personal vote" or "that portion of a candidate's electoral support which originates in his or her personal qualities, qualifications, activities, and record."[19] The personal vote may often be very small, but it can make a difference in competitive districts. It has been estimated to be worth about 4 percent to the average incumbent and rose steadily throughout the twentieth century.[20]

Like casework, the pork barrel is integral to the personal vote. Derived from the plantation practice of providing slaves with salt pork from wooden barrels, the term is part of the Capitol's everyday lexicon. It refers to regional, state, or, if done with precision, district-targeted governmental largesse that comes in myriad forms. Jeffrey H. Birnbaum describes types of pork this way, "There is old-fashioned 'green pork' like dams, roads, and bridges, 'academic pork' in the form of research grants to colleges, 'defense pork' in the form of geographically specific military expenditures, and lately 'high-tech' pork, for example the intense fight to authorize research into supercomputers and high-definition television."[21] Federal money also goes to fund courthouses, museums, train services, and subsidize the growing of peanuts. Pork can also be in the form of narrowly tailored tax breaks for certain industries or sectors of the economy.

Pork proliferated on the Hill in the last half of the twentieth century for two reasons. First, it won votes as legislators energetically publicized the granting of goodies to their grateful constituents.[22] The genius of such expenditures is that recipients experience tremendous benefits—$800,000 given to the University of Iowa in a December 2001 appropriations bill to train nurse anesthetists is a big deal in Iowa City—while the costs go virtually undetected, spread as they are among 290 million people and within, what is today, a roughly $2.5 trillion budget. Indeed, Steven Levitt and Jim Snyder have found that a $100 per capita's worth of federal spending translates into approximately an additional 2 percent of the vote.[23] The second reason is that Congress was organized so as to produce pork efficiently. In 1974 Yale political scientist David Mayhew wrote a seminal book on the legislative branch in which he argued that the institution was perfectly designed so as to allow its members to get reelected.[24] A critical part of this was an elaborate and implicit logrolling— a cooperative arrangement in which members would vote for each others' pet projects. To be sure, there were institutions and individuals—parties and committees, Speakers and committee chairs—who controlled Congress, but they were there to make sure the pork was fairly distributed and perpetuate the system. They mediated disputes between individuals and committees and often produced mega-bills bursting with goodies so that there would be something in the legislation for a large proportion of the membership.

Indeed, given the emphasis placed on party conflict by the media, most Americans would be very surprised to discover how much bipartisan work goes on to secure tax loopholes, subsidies, and government dollars for constituents. Members from the same state meet and correspond regularly on matters of interest to the delegation, and there exist on the Hill a large number of regional- and industry-related caucuses that allow Democrats and Republicans to work together on pork-type issues. The Congressional Steel Caucus reaches across the aisle to bring together lawmakers from places like Pittsburgh, Ohio, and upstate New York to increase tariffs against cheap foreign imports. The Congressional Wine Caucus, co-founded by two Californians, Republican George Radanovich and Democrat Mike Thompson, works to protect domestic vintners. The huge Northeast-Midwest coalition, together with an external research institute, promotes sectional interests.

With short two-year terms and 434 other colleagues, committee chairs, majority and minority leaders, a Speaker, a Senate, and president with which to deal, it is not surprising that House members work on pork and often shun the complex and labor-intensive work of building broad coalitions to form national policy. The latter is too time-consuming and exhausting, and besides, members frequently get little credit for it. There may be occasions when it is worthwhile, especially if the president is not pushing the bill since he will always take a bow when he is, regardless of the level of his exertion. Two recent examples include Rep. Jim Leach's (R-IA) tireless ten-year campaign to repeal the Depression-era Glass-Steagall banking law and allow financial houses to offer banking, securities, and insurance services and passage of the Sarbanes-Oxley corporate malfeasance legislation, cosponsored by Senator Paul Sarbanes (D-MD) and Rep. Michael Oxley (R-OH) in the wake of the Enron and World-Com scandals. This work provided these lawmakers with recognition and, indubitably, campaign contributions from affected industries.

However, much national policy making is about as worthwhile to House members as the product Bismarck suggested was ground out of the legislative process: sausages. Take campaign finance, for instance. Before its signing into law in 2002, House sponsors Christopher Shays (R-CT) and Marty Meehan (D-MA) spent about six years working indefatigably to ban soft money—the unlimited donations to the parties—from federal elections. Their bill was twice passed in the House during the late 1990s, despite ferocious opposition from the GOP leadership, and at one stage they were forced to get a majority of their House colleagues to sign a rarely successful discharge petition to extract the bill from an obstructive committee. GOP Majority Leader Dick Armey of Texas publicly described Shays as "arrogant and rude," and Rep. John Doolittle of California summed up the attitude of many Republicans when he told partisan colleagues who had supported the bill, "I do not intend to let bygones be bygones."[25] Shays and Meehan burned many bridges on the Hill and spent countless hours in pursuit of their cause. For what personal political gain? Like most legislation with national reach, their constituents will not really feel direct effects and the legislators' efforts drew the ire of numerous powerful interest groups. The House GOP responded to Shays' behavior by passing over him and making Tom Davis of Virginia chair of the Government Reform Committee in 2002. What is more, the campaign finance law is much better known for its two Senate sponsors, John McCain (R-AZ) and Russell Feingold (D-WI), especially since McCain made it a centerpiece of his 2000 presidential campaign. And President George W. Bush will be linked to the legislation because it was his barely lukewarm assent that, in the end, made reform possible.[26]

Casework and the pork barrel were not the only things on which the Democratic monopolization was built. The raising of significant campaign funds was also critical. Republicans have historically gathered and spent more money than the Democrats because of their strong support among wealthier Americans and their advocacy of business-friendly public policy. In 1896, for example, presidential candidate William McKinley defeated his Democratic opponent, William Jennings Bryan, by spending what for the time was the astronomical amount of $7 million—much of it raised in dubious ways from big business. This state of affairs is reflected today by the money the parties raised in the last few presidential electoral cycles—in 1995–1996 the GOP collected $416.5 million, the Democrats, $221.6 million; in 1999–2000, the

GOP garnered $465.8 million, the Democrats, $275.2 million; in 2003–2004 the GOP raised $330 million, the Democrats, $299 million. Yet, in House elections the Democrats were able to spend as much and, by the mid-1980s, even more than their opponents. Indeed, in 1992 the average Democratic House candidate spent over $100,000 more than the average Republican ($457,994 to $351,880).[27] The advantage is largely attributable to the fact that incumbents raise much more money than challengers in House elections, and Democrats controlled the House.[28] This, in turn, is a product of the fact that House incumbents tend to win reelection at Soviet-style rates—it is generally the case that at least nine of every ten members running again returns to Washington—and that most PACs—the political action committees that contribute money on behalf of interest groups—use their money to gain access to policy makers rather than influence the outcomes of elections.[29] Between 1980 and 1992, for instance, of the money spent in races where there was an incumbent, PACs contributed an average of 19 percent of their money on the challenger. Groups view spending money on those who oppose incumbents, regardless of any congruence on policy preferences, as tantamount to flushing it down the toilet. The loser is no help to you when he returns to his law practice.

During the period of Democratic dominance, GOP challengers were also of generally poor quality.[30] In many parts of the country there was no district party to speak of in the 1960s, 1970s, and 1980s. Individuals just emerged as the Republican candidate, many of them political novices running quixotic campaigns fueled by ideological extremism and little else. As the party of active government, bright and enthusiastic Democrats were quite easily recruited to run for the House because public service appealed to them. Their Republican counterparts, on the other hand, were attracted to the private sector and the creation of wealth and, if they lived in a district in which a Democrat held the seat, deterred by the long odds laid against them knocking off an incumbent.[31] What is more, Democratic domination of state legislatures and municipal offices meant there was a dearth of practical political experience among GOP hopefuls. Whereas, on average, between roughly one in four to one in three Democratic House challengers had held political office in the 1970s and 1980s, just less than one in five Republicans had.[32] The Republicans, in other words, did not have a farm system capable of supplying them with major league players.

In the late 1980s and early 1990s, the GOP slowly and systematically addressed their opponent's advantages in House elections. The principal in this effort was Newt Gingrich, a history professor elected to the House from Georgia in 1978 who had become Minority Whip and the number two Republican in the body by 1989. To many Democrats, Gingrich was a bomb thrower, a conservative *agent provocateur* more concerned with political showmanship than the practical problems of governing. He was perhaps most famous for his emotional and provocative speeches on the House floor during special orders—nightly events in which legislators can speak on anything, generally to the C-SPAN cameras and an empty chamber. He also had several memorable tussles with Democratic Speaker Tip O'Neill, one of which led to the chair reprimanding O'Neill and having the Speaker's words stricken from the record.[33]

But, grossly underestimated by the opposition, Gingrich intelligently and indefatigably set about working for a Republican majority. First, he established the Conservative Opportunity Society (COS) within the House GOP. Assisted by veterans like Bob Walker of Pennsylvania and Trent Lott of Mississippi, Gingrich assembled a group of ebullient young Republican members to develop political and legislative strategy and make contacts with important conservatives in Washington and around the country. COS even had a distinctive vocabulary—it talked of "values," "opportunity," and "competition"—and contrasted its position with what was contemptuously called the Democrats' "Liberal Welfare State."[34]

Next, Gingrich looked to recruit and train strong candidates. His vehicle was GOPAC, an organization created in 1978 by former Delaware governor Pete du Pont. When GOPAC came under Gingrich's vigorous aegis in the mid-1980s, it began to identify and financially support capable candidates, train them at workshops, and supply them with numerous briefing books and audio and video tapes consisting of successful campaign strategies and the same kind of political lexicon COS was compiling on Capitol Hill. After experimenting in Mississippi state legislative races in 1987, GOPAC soon became a sort of grassroots Republican empire, reaching out to GOP state legislators, municipal office holders, and precinct, county, and congressional district chairs all over the country.[35] In doing so, it was among the first to recognize that the key to getting talented people to run for office is inviting and encouraging them to do so.[36] GOPAC was also intricately

connected to a book advance and college lecture series that, ultimately, were to burden Gingrich with a House ethics committee
reprimand and $300,000 fine in 1997. By then more than a third
of the Republican freshman class of 1994 had been trained by the
organization—a historic group of men and women who catapulted
Gingrich to the Speakership and loyally chanted the Georgian's
mantra.

At times, Gingrich seemed obsessed with the Democrats' mis-
management of the House—"corrupt," another of his favorite
words, was nearly always used to describe it. He and his
colleagues maintained a constant and scathing criticism of the
Democratic leadership in an attempt to undermine public confidence in them. In 1985, after a protracted and nasty battle in the
House, the Democratic majority succeeded in having their own
Frank McCloskey seated as the representative from the Eighth
District of Indiana, even though the state's secretary of state had
earlier certified his Republican opponent, Richard McIntyre, as
the winner. After two recounts won by McCloskey—the initial
count had favored McIntyre by seventy-two—both Hoosiers went
to Washington, drew a salary, and watched as their colleagues
became embroiled in a spiteful partisan fight over their political
futures. Gingrich was outraged and organized a series of caustic
special orders speeches for C-SPAN viewers. He also orchestrated
a GOP walkout that received considerable media attention.
Although McIntyre ultimately went home to the Midwest, he had
become a martyr to the cause and, according to Gingrich and a
growing number of incensed House Republicans, another victim
of Democratic turpitude.

Gingrich then upped the ante. He zeroed in on the conduct of
Speaker Jim Wright from Texas, publicizing it incessantly and
demanding an investigation. It was a withering assault. On May
31, 1989, Wright resigned the Speakership rather than fight charges
he had violated House rules on income and honoraria by taking
improper gifts from a Texas developer and, in lieu of speaking
fees, selling a book he had written in bulk.[37] Five days earlier,
Majority Whip Tony Coehlo of California had stepped down over
questions about a junk bond deal involving Drexel Burnham
Lambert, Michael Milken's firm. Gingrich had struck at the heart
of the House Democratic Party. It was no surprise then that his
opponents should strike back at him. Later in 1989, the House
ethics committee was asked to look into Gingrich's failure to report campaign contributions and income correctly, use of official

stationery to endorse businesses, and deal to promote the book he wrote with his wife of the time, Marianne.

Although he was wounded, Gingrich had succeeded in creating the impression, both at the Capitol and across the nation, that the Democrats were mismanaging the House. He continued to speak out against corruption and privilege, often using an ice bucket as a prop to illustrate the custom of twice daily ice deliveries to House offices. He went after the House Administration Committee that he believed gave Republicans cramped offices and inconvenient meeting rooms. He was the scourge of the Democratic patronage machine that hired doormen, House restaurant workers, and elevator operators. Gingrich thought the Democratic majority would die a death of a thousand cuts. He understood that slowly casting the shadow of corruption over the entire House, including himself, would bring down the party that governed it.

In the early 1990s, a confluence of events finally crystallized Gingrich's image in the minds of the public. A realization that federal legislators went ostensibly unchallenged for their seats and that average congressional careers were lengthening—for the House they went from about 4.5 terms in 1981 to about six in 1991—provided fuel for a nascent term limits movement.[38] Stirred up chiefly by U.S. Term Limits, an organization with 70,000 energetic members, approximately 75 percent of the public supported caps on the amount of time their lawmakers could serve. Success at limiting terms for state legislatures in the early 1990s—in California, Colorado, and Oklahoma in 1990; Arizona, Arkansas, Florida, Michigan, Missouri, Montana, Ohio, Oregon, South Dakota, and Wyoming in 1992; and Maine, Nevada, and Louisiana between 1993 and 1995—had proponents aiming their sights at Congress.[39]

Moreover, the federal budget deficit was escalating out of control. In 1990 it reached a record, in current dollar terms, of $221 billion, and by 1992 it was over $290 billion. To many, not least the straight shooting Texas business tycoon, H. Ross Perot, this represented a national catastrophe. Perot was able to focus public attention on the federal government's profligacy during his 1992 presidential campaign with those infomercials, colorful charts, and down-to-earth speeches. In 1988, 8 percent of voters responded to exit polls that the budget deficit was the most important issue in the campaign. In 1992, that figure was 12 percent.

Then, in September 1991, the General Accounting Office (GAO) reported that House members had written 8,331 checks on overdrawn accounts at the institution's bank. The bank had traditionally given members free overdraft protection, but coming at a time of recession, the scandal was ripe for exploitation. Surreptitiously encouraged by Gingrich, who himself was overdrawn twenty-two times, many junior Republicans—whom William Safire described as "banging their spoons against their high chairs"—screamed that the episode illustrated once again the Democratic leadership's innate arrogance and corruption.[40] The story blazed through the media for several weeks; no longer able to withstand the pressure, the Democratic leadership announced there would be an internal investigation. To the embarrassment of many members, individual deadbeats had their names and the number of kited checks publicized. The bank was also closed.

As Gingrich had hoped, public approval of Congress plummeted. To be sure, much of the anger at the political system in the early 1990s found a vehicle in Ross Perot and was rooted in deep concerns about the future of the United States—as one of that year's Democratic presidential hopefuls, Paul Tsongas, put it, "the Cold War is over and the Japanese have won."[41] But almost 3,000 people filed to run for the House in 1992, compared with 1,792 in 1990.[42] Whereas 41 percent of Americans had "confidence" in the institution and 21 percent in its leadership in 1986, by October 1991 these figures were down to 18 and 9 percent, respectively.[43] The Democratic majority was in crisis.

To be fair, Gingrich argued that his opponents across the aisle were wrong on the issues, too. Whenever substantive policy was being discussed, he pulled out the COS song sheet and emphasized the stark differences between the two parties. Nowhere, he believed, were the positions more distinct than on economic policy. Gingrich railed on the Democrats for wanting bigger government and higher taxes; he argued that conservative Republicans would bring smaller government, lower taxes, and greater opportunity and prosperity. In the fall of 1990, he became inexorably linked with this philosophy. After a summit between congressional leaders and high-ranking officials in the administration, Democrats brought a budget agreement to the floor of the House. Explicitly endorsed by Gingrich's boss, Minority Leader Bob Michel of Illinois, Speaker Thomas Foley of Washington, and President Bush despite his "no new taxes" pledge in 1988, the legislation aimed to cut into the burgeoning deficit by reducing spending on social programs and raising taxes. Outraged, Gingrich led a revolt by conservative House Republicans and, with the help of liberal Democrats who opposed the spending cuts, was able to defeat the bill. The response among many newer House Republicans was euphoric—despite the fact that they had given their own president a black eye. "Newt's the new torchbearer," claimed one of them, Jack Buechner of Missouri.[44]

Gingrich therefore suggested the House Republican party present both a policy and ethical alternative to the Democrats. In 1994 the party's issue positions were dramatically and eloquently laid out in the "Contract with America," written by Gingrich and soon-to-be Majority Leader Dick Armey of Texas. The document contained a list of issues that were to be the subject of legislation voted on by the House within 100 days, should the GOP gain a majority in the upcoming election. The position stands included welfare reform, economic deregulation, product liability and tort reform, crime control, tax cuts, term limits, and a balanced-budget amendment to the Constitution and were carved out of the Republicans' "basic philosophy of American Civilization" that Gingrich had unveiled at a conference in February 1994.[45]

As it happened, 1994 was to be the election when Gingrich's dream finally came true. Whether the Contract was a principal reason for the success is highly debatable. The House Republicans did pay for an advertising insertion in *TV Guide*, but the document was central to only a few individuals' campaigns, and a poll done just before election day found that 71 percent of respondents had not even heard of it. A more likely cause was the electorate's basic anger at government and Bill Clinton. Two years of unified Democratic rule had not broken the gridlock in Washington—as the defeat of big health care, economic stimulus, and campaign finance bills revealed. Moreover, to many, especially white Christian lower-middle-class male Perot voters, the Clinton administration seemed to be at war with their values. An emphasis on cultural liberalism—gays in the military, gun control, an expanded role for minorities and women—and the tax increase of 1993 were continually pointed out in the conservative media, most notably on Rush Limbaugh's radio show. Indeed, there is empirical evidence that reveals Limbaugh's program boosted the GOP vote.[46] To many of these disaffected Americans, the new president's style and policies threw gas on the fire that Perot; the deficit; rising crime rates; the economic insecurities of open trade, mass layoffs, and rising health-care costs; and the congressional shenanigans highlighted by Gingrich had set.[47] According to NES, a paltry 21 percent of Americans felt they could trust the government to do what is right most or nearly all of the time.

The Republicans picked up fifty-two seats on November 8, 1994. The American public had given them their first House majority in forty years. They then went to work to keep it. Despite the emphasis on substantive issues highlighted by the Contract and illustrated by important legislative successes on the GOP's watch— the revolutionary overhaul of federal welfare programs, the balanced budget deal of 1997, the massive revision to the nation's banking laws, critical free-trade legislation, large tax cuts, and sweeping efforts to combat terrorism—the Republicans have not maintained their grip on the House through policy. Their continued control is also not an artifact of a new management style. Instead, it is a product of a masterful replication of the strategies and skills the Democrats exhibited in the 1960s, 1970s, and 1980s.

The House GOP's fondness for pork is one example. Despite riding into town with a government-slashing message, the size of the federal budget increased by one-third in the first seven years Congress was under Republican management. In the 2002 fiscal year the government spent over $2 trillion for the first time; in 1995, using the last budget written solely by Democrats, it shelled out just over $1.5 trillion. Fiscal 2004 spending was about $2.4 trillion. The ephemeral balanced budget that was reached after an agreement between the Clinton White House and the Republican leadership in the summer of 1997 did nothing to plug the spending spigot. As former Congressional Budget Office director Robert D. Reischauer wrote at the time, few sacrifices were made in an effort to restrain spending and the budget was balanced largely on the backs of the surging stock market and the productive American workforce.[48]

To be sure, much of the budget increase is the result of augmented spending on entitlement programs like Social Security and Medicare whose administrators send out checks to beneficiaries unless the law prevents them from doing so. Such expenditures do not need explicit congressional blessing. What is more, with Clinton in the White House, the Republican leadership had to create budgets that satisfied the president; they did not have veto-proof majorities. Still, there can be no denying that, especially now they are in the majority, House Republicans love their pork.

Leaders of a number of conservative groups have accused them of spending like "drunken sailors."[49] The National Taxpayers Union has calculated that of the thirty House Republicans who were freshmen in 1995 and served in the 108th Congress of 2003–2004, only two sponsored bills that had a net effect of cutting spending in the latter Congress—twenty-four of them sponsored bills that had the same cumulative effect during their first Congress in Washington a decade earlier.[50] As we shall see in Chapter 6, the party is split over the extravagance, but the profligacy is not necessarily at odds with a basic GOP belief that government should be made smaller, at least not in the long term. Many Republicans hope augmented spending and resultant deficits will force government to shrink down the road. By then, the thinking seems to be, the GOP will be safely established as the House's—and perhaps the Senate's—permanent majority. Cast in this light, the last decade of GOP spending may resemble a fire sale on future government assets.

A good aggregate-level example of the big spending came during the summer and fall of 2001 when Congress was dealing with President George W. Bush's first budget. The Republican-controlled House consistently approved appropriations bills that spent more than the president of their own party had requested. Bush wanted $47.5 billion for the Department of Education, the House, $52.5 billion; Bush wanted $23.0 billion for energy and water development projects—a porker's dream—the House approved $24.2 billion; Bush, $10 billion for military construction projects, the House, $10.5 billion. In the 2003 fiscal year, discretionary spending rose about 12.5 percent—it would still have been 7.9 percent without "emergency" spending on natural disasters and military action in the Middle East—despite the fact that Bush had asked the Republican-controlled Congress to cap growth at 4 percent.

Recent Congresses are replete with more specific examples of juicy pork. In 2001 the House Appropriations Committee reported receiving requests for in excess of 20,000 earmarks and special projects from 420 of the chamber's 435 members.[51] The Congressional Research Service estimates that the number of earmarks incorporated into appropriations bills rose from 4,155 in fiscal 1994 to 10,631 in fiscal 2002—including dramatic increases from 270 to 1,409 in defense and 140 to 1,493 in the area of transportation. Members especially love earmarks because they can be sure that the money goes to its intended recipients in the intended district. General appropriations billeted for more broadly defined programs are often distributed at the state level or open to a competitive grant process.[52]

Fiscal 2004 appropriations bills were no better. Washington watchdog Citizens Against Government Waste (CAGW) detected 10,656 special projects in the year's thirteen spending bills—a 13 percent increase on the previous twelve months.[53] Taxpayers for Common Sense (TCS), a sort of cousin to CAGW, estimated that there were 7,931 earmarks costing $10.7 billion in the single omnibus appropriations bill passed in January 2004. This monster bill included designated bacon such as $2 million for a Florida golf program, $1.8 million for a fruit laboratory in West Virginia, $725,000 for the Please Touch Museum in Philadelphia, $1 million for the Tongass Coast Aquarium in Alaska, $400,000 for the Speed Art Museum in Louisville, Kentucky, $325,000 to build a public swimming pool in Salinas, California, $250,000 for the "Call Me Mister" program at Clemson University, $250,000 for the Lou Frey Institute of Politics at the University of Central Florida, and $200,000 for the Rock and Roll Hall of Fame in Cleveland.[54] House Republican Leader Tom DeLay defended the legislation by saying, "I am not ashamed of the fact that there are earmarks in this bill." Members of Congress, he said, have "the right to direct spending to our districts, rather than wait on some bureaucrat to decide it was a useful project."[55]

The fiscal 2005 omnibus was no different. The 3,320-page bill was passed so rapidly by the lame duck 108th Congress that no one really had time to read all of it. Still, many members were quick to issue press releases touting funds they were able to secure for their constituents. TCS documented nearly 12,000 earmarks in the bill, including $500,000 for the Kincaid Soccer and Nordic Ski Center in Anchorage; $250,000 for the Country Music Hall of Fame in Nashville; $100,000 for a municipal swimming pool in Ottawa, Kansas; and $80,000 for the San Diego Gay, Lesbian, Bisexual, and Transgender Community Center.

Four of the most egregious instances of pigging out under the Republicans are the surface transportation bills of 1998 and 2005, the farm bill of 2002, and the energy bill of 2003. The first, known, without a hint of irony, as the Transportation Equity Act for the Twenty-first Century (or TEA-21), lavished money for highway and mass transit programs on lawmakers.[56] All told the bill authorized $218 billion over six years—a 40 percent increase above existing amounts—with Bud Shuster, the Pennsylvania Republican who chaired the House Transportation and Infrastructure Committee, securing $110 million for his district alone. The 2005 version passed by the House was valued at $284 billion and included, according to TCS, 4,128 earmarks such as $14 million each for I-69 in Indiana and I-40 in Oklahoma, $4 million for a graffiti elimination project in New York, $3 million to renovate the National Packard Museum in Ohio, and $1 million to fund reconstruction of James Madison's home in Virginia. In 2004, a version of the bill did not become law because President Bush, who up until that time had put his signature to all the pork-laden legislation that had come to his desk, took a stand against the spending and threatened a veto. Keith Ashdown of TCS called the earmarking in the bill in 2004, "the worst we have ever seen."[57]

The six-year $249 billion farm bill increased spending 18 percent above that prescribed by extant law. Passed only seven years after the Republicans had created a law to phase out many subsidies, it provided assistance for grain and cotton growers and created new peanut and national dairy programs. It also included $100 million to provide rural dwellers with high-speed Internet access. Many of the beneficiaries of the legislation, of course, came from the type of rural midwestern and southern districts represented by Republican members.

The Bush energy plan that was voted on in 2003 quickly became a Christmas tree, adorned with brightly colored ornaments designed to attract support. Worried that the plan might die because of controversial provisions allowing for oil drilling in Alaska's National Wildlife Refuge, GOP leaders used the bill to lavish pork on their members' constituents. The bill included an $800 million loan guarantee for a coal gasification plant in Minnesota to capture the vote of that state's Senate GOP moderate, Norm Coleman. It also included massive support for an Alaska pipeline at a time when the state's junior Republican senator, Lisa Murkowski, faced an uphill battle for reelection. Controversial legal protections and $2 billion for the producers of the gasoline additive MTBE were folded in to motivate two prominent Republicans, House Majority Leader Tom DeLay and Billy Tauzin, chair of the House Energy and Commerce Committee, for their hard work—the vast majority of MTBE is produced in their states of Texas and Louisiana. There was $5.9 billion for ethanol production designed to win support from members from the Plains states and money for a plethora of local projects, including seemingly unrelated "green bond" proposals—which allow environmentally friendly developers to borrow money from which the interest is not taxable income for the lender—to stimulate tourism in Colorado, Georgia, Louisiana, and New York. The bill was such an egregious example of corpulence that John McCain called it a bill for "hooters and polluters."[58] It took an eclectic bunch of filibustering senators—some of whom, like McCain, objected to the pork-laden legislation—to defeat it. Undeterred, the House approved an almost identical bill in April 2005.

Indeed, the only difference between the profligacy of the 1960s, 1970s, 1980s, and today is that the pig's wearing different-colored lipstick now. Pork is still produced; it just disproportionately benefits Republicans. A recent study revealed that, since the GOP took control of Congress, most of the institutions of higher education earmarked for federal money reside in districts with Republican representation.[59] There has also been a shift from programs that provide benefits to individuals based upon their eligibility in certain groups—we often call these social programs—to contingent liabilities such as loans and federal insurance programs.[60] The latter are more consistent with Republican philosophy and favor GOP-leaning voters like farmers, small businesses, homeowners, and middle-class college students.

CAGW and TCS keep track of government spending and their Web sites and publications continually report examples of the tastiest pork. CAGW also highlights its entertaining "Porker of the Month," a lawmaker who most egregiously pigs out at the congressional trough. He or she is frequently Republican. TCS has its "Weekly Wastebasket," and that is often full of Republican policy. Yet, despite widespread condemnation by the public, interest groups, presidents, and even many of their colleagues, few Republican members seem particularly kosher when it comes to spending the government's money. The fiscal conservative Free Enterprise Fund chair Stephen Moore calls the GOP philosophy "tax cut and spend."[61] The year 2003 in which the Republicans controlled the elected institutions of government was "the most irresponsible year ever," according to Robert L. Bixby, executive director of bipartisan fiscal watchdogs, the Concord Coalition.[62] Indeed, Brian M. Riedl of the conservative Heritage Foundation found that government spending per household in 2003 was the highest, as measured by current dollars, since 1944.[63] As Rep. Bob Inglis of South Carolina sighed after the House passed TEA-21, "We (Republicans) came to change things and we are not. We are participating in the big old trough that has characterized this place in the past."[64]

Nowhere is this more evident than on national security. Not surprisingly, perhaps, many defense contractors have done well out of Republican rule. Terrorist threats and wars in Afghanistan and Iraq, exacerbated by an inherent GOP emphasis on national security, have increased the aggregate defense budget from $294.5 billion in 2000 to over $450 billion today. But it is in the stories of specific programs that the Republican penchant for pork can be seen.

Take missile defense, for instance. The Bush administration and congressional Republicans have continually pushed for an integrated system to protect the United States from attack, even to the extent that the president pulled the United States out of the Anti-ballistic Missile Treaty. It is a matter of partisanship and ideology—Democrats see it as too expensive and unreliable and not the best way to tackle unconventional but immediate threats like terrorism—but the massive program is also a matter of dollars and votes. The first part of the plan calls for the introduction of anti-missile batteries in Fort Greely, Alaska and brings with it a huge boost for the local economy. The state's universally Republican congressional delegation helped secure about $735 million for the Alaska Test Bed Ballistic Missile Defense Organization by the end of 2002.

Or, take the joint strike fighter. A $200 billion contract to build 3,000 new stealth-like supersonic fighters for the air force, navy, Marines, and friendly foreign militaries was won by Lockheed Martin after furious competition with Boeing. Ostensibly, the Pentagon made the decision based upon merit, but lobbying by congressional patrons was intense. A nice political byproduct of the decision for the GOP was that the planes will be built in Fort Worth, deep in their territory, and not in St. Louis, home of then Democratic House Minority Leader and presidential aspirant, Richard Gephardt.

Or, consider the procurement of systems that are not quite so enthusiastically pushed by the Pentagon. Led by former Senate Majority Leader Trent Lott, the increasingly Republican Mississippi congressional delegation has, for a number of years, inserted provisions into defense authorization and appropriations bills for the navy to buy an eighth LHD helicopter carrier from Ingalls Shipbuilding, the largest private employer in the state. This is without an explicit request from the Defense Department for them to do so and despite the fact that it is likely to cost $1.5 billion, about twice as much as the seventh carrier.

Or, take the decision by the air force to lease, rather than buy, one hundred refueling tankers from Boeing for about $21 billion. Boeing, scrambling for military contracts after the bottom fell out of the commercial airline industry, lobbied intensely for the lease deal and recruited a willing Dennis Hastert, the Republican Speaker, to help them. In turn, Hastert worked on House colleagues and the president. He did so despite the fact that the Congressional Budget Office estimated that buying the planes outright—they were basically converted 767s—would cost about $5.6 billion less. After resistance from Senate Armed Services Committee chair John Warner of Virginia and fiscal gadflies like John McCain, the air force was forced to agree to buy eighty of the tankers and lease the other twenty. Boeing's case was not helped when it was discovered that its CFO, Michael M. Sears, had successfully approached Darleen A. Druyun, the air force's deputy procurement director, to work for his company while she was overseeing scores of Boeing's government contracts. The scandal resulted in both individuals being fired and, at least indirectly, in the resignation of Boeing's CEO, Philip M. Condit. Druyun was later convicted on conflict-of-interest charges and assisted in a federal inquiry into Sears' actions. She got nine months. Sears also did jail time. U.S. Air Force Secretary James Roche was forced to resign. The Pentagon promptly suspended the deal but, as if to illustrate the airplane manufacturer's clout on the Hill, then ordered $9.5 billion worth of attack jets and $20 billion in 737 antisubmarine aircraft from the company in 2004.[65]

Republican members have even taken on the Bush administration to protect defense programs that provide precious funds and jobs for their districts. The C-130J transport plane, the V-22 Osprey—a sort of plane-helicopter hybrid—and the Crusader—a $11 billion artillery piece for the Army—have all run into trouble at the Pentagon. Thomas Christie, the Pentagon's chief weapons tester, has stated that the C-130J was "neither operationally effective nor operationally suitable."[66] Made in Marietta, Georgia, however, the plane is vigorously protected by the state's GOP-dominated congressional delegation. The Osprey's problems are largely the product of two accidents in 2000 that killed twenty-three marines and the discovery of a cover-up of maintenance problems. It was also supposed to cost $40 million a unit; the fiscal 2004 budget set aside about $93 million for each aircraft. But the Osprey is watched over by indefatigable Republican House members like Curt Weldon of Pennsylvania, in whose suburban Philadelphia district 1,500 people work on the equipment's fuselages, and Mac Thornberry, in whose Amarillo, Texas, district Bell Helicopter Textron does the final assembly. Weldon so aggressively protects the Osprey that, in his position as head of the House's Tactical Air and Land Forces Subcommittee, he has pushed for increases in government funding for the rotocraft industry generally, even inserting legislative language funding research and development into civilian applications like tilt-rotor helicopters that can be used in urban areas.[67] Despite congressional resistance, the Pentagon is pushing to cut twenty-two units from the original proposal.

In May 2002 the Pentagon announced the termination of the Crusader, the first major weapons system to be killed since the navy's A-12 got the ax in 1991. The big gun was to be built in Elgin, Oklahoma, home to J. C. Watts, who was at the time the fourth-ranking Republican in the House. Despite the price tag and explicit opposition from his president, though, Watts decided to fight hard for the pork and lashed out at the Bush administration's decision calling it "indecent" and "unprofessional."[68] Many speculated that the Crusader incident contributed greatly to the decision of Congress' only African American Republican to retire.[69]

Defense pork will be especially critical to Republican control of the House in the future. As I have hinted at already and shall show in some detail in Chapter 6, many in the party are ready to use the deficit as a scythe with which to slash spending. It is true that the Pentagon will not go untouched—there are already Pentagon plans to slash funding for programs like the F/A 22 fighter and, as we saw, the C-130J. But with a war on terror to fight, national security may be the only part of the economy maintaining financial support from the federal government over the next several years. Indeed, President Bush's fiscal 2006 budget called for a 5 percent increase in defense spending while many domestic departments saw expenditures and programs slashed. The congressional budget resolution generally mirrored this— defense spending was to be just $11 billion shy of the $1/2 trillion mark while Medicaid was cut by $10 billion over four years. As Benjamin Ginsberg and Martin Shefter have written, both the military and the private sector with which it contracts provide critical political support to the GOP—support that is likely only to grow as pork flows to them.[70]

With a burgeoning deficit and, as we shall see in Chapter 6, a large and influential group of Republicans poised to squeeze discretionary spending, the House GOP may not be able to rely on pork—at least not the domestic kind—for much longer. Still, the party has displayed an aptitude for maintaining their majority in other ways. Now firmly in control of the chamber, for instance, House Republicans have learned how to raise campaign money like the Democrats formerly did. From 1978 through 1994, House Democratic incumbents generally raised about the same, if not a little more, than Republican incumbents. In fact, in 1994 House Democratic incumbents were able to spend on average about $145,000 more than their Republican counterparts. This was despite the historical advantage Republicans have enjoyed in raising campaign cash. Since 1994, however, the GOP has raced ahead. In 1996 GOP incumbents outspent their Democratic counterparts by $157,000 on average; in 2004 the figure was about $140,000.

Much of this is attributable to shifting allegiances among corporate PACs. The defense industry, for example, gave Democratic candidates about $800,000 more than Republicans in direct contributions for the congressional elections of 1994 but gave Republicans $4.01 million and Democrats $2.24 million in 2002. Health-care concerns gave in excess of $3 million dollars more to Democrats than Republicans in 1994; in 2002 they gave Republicans about $4.25 million more than Democrats. The pattern is the same for the financial-services industry whose companies gave $1.5 million more to Democrats in 1994 but in 1996 gave the Republicans $21.4 million and the Democrats a comparatively paltry $9.5 million.[71]

Of course, much of this new GOP financial edge is merely the result of being in the majority. The Speaker is a Republican, all committee chairs—with their power to write bills almost single-handedly—are Republicans, and, if they hold together on the floor, Republicans can guarantee the passage of bills. Control over the legislative process in the House is, according to Gary W. Cox and Eric Magar, inherently worth about $36,000 per member in corporate and trade PAC contributions.[72]

Yet, House Republicans have also created an awesome money vacuum. For the 2002 House races, the National Republican

Congressional Committee (NRCC) raised a staggering $179.6 million, $75 million more than the Democratic Congressional Campaign Committee (DCCC). The Center for Responsive Politics estimates that the NRCC raised about $160 million in 2004; this was more than double the DCCC.[73] Under the tutelage of skilled fundraisers and electoral tacticians like Tom Davis of Virginia and Tom Reynolds of New York, the NRCC has created sophisticated procedures, along with other innovations, to extract campaign cash from corporations and wealthy donors. It uses targeted taped phone messages from Republican leaders, elaborate get-out-the-vote systems involving hundreds of activists, and flies around popular Republicans like John McCain and former New York City mayor Rudy Giuliani to help GOP candidates in marginal districts. In the winter of 2002, the NRCC sent out a mass mailing promising briefings on economic and defense policy with Republican congressional leaders and high-ranking administration officials in return for big-dollar donations.[74] In 2003 the organization used telemarketers to call prominent professionals to advise them they had been named, for instance, "businessman of the year." After that subtle bit of flattery came the sales pitch, and the person on the other end of the line was asked if they would be willing to give money to attend a policy seminar or banquet or pay for an ad in the *Wall Street Journal*.[75]

In addition, entrepreneurial Republicans have set up their own PACs to raise money for their partisan colleagues. Of these operations, House Majority Leader Tom DeLay has created the most extensive and influential. As Fred Wertheimer, head of Democracy 21, put it in the summer of 2003, "Tom DeLay is the king of congressional influence-money. In DeLay's world, the operating rule is you have to pay to play."[76] DeLay has had a series of such "leadership" PACs, including one aimed to influence Texas elections. In Washington his Americans for a Republican Majority PAC contributed just under $1 million to GOP House candidates in both 2002 and 2004. To maintain the Republican majority, DeLay plays hard—his fundraising tactics have earned him the sobriquet "The Hammer." He was among the first to see the potential for using "527s"—named so because of the part of the tax code that describes them—as useful fundraising devices because, in the late 1990s at least, they did not have to disclose their contributors.

On more than one occasion the majority leader's reputation for aggressively approaching potential donors has gotten him into trouble. The House ethics committee slapped him on the wrist in 1998 for pressuring the Electronics Industry Association to hire a former Republican House member as its lobbyist, not a former Democratic member. Just before the November 2002 election, DeLay got the NRCC to transfer $1 million to a new group, the Leadership Forum, headed by his former chief of staff, Susan Hirschmann. The organization was to be a clearinghouse for soft money—the nebulous political cash that was unregulated but had been outlawed by the recently passed McCain-Feingold bill. The action earned the NRCC a Federal Elections Commission complaint that was ultimately dismissed.

In the summer of 2003 DeLay was caught up in a minor brouhaha involving Westar, a Kansas-based company that many believed to be donating, on a quid-pro-quo basis, to Republican candidates and PACs for "a seat at the table" during the authoring of a big energy bill. In October 2004 the House ethics committee formally admonished him for this and later the Justice Department began an investigation into whether lobbyists close to DeLay had illegally used gifts and oversees trips to influence lawmakers. Also in 2004, a grand jury began investigating DeLay's Texans for a Republican Majority PAC (TRMPAC) to see if it had been used to launder corporate campaign donations to sidestep a Texas law that prohibits the electoral use of such money. The cash seemed well spent because the GOP gained twenty-six seats in the Texas House, but TRMPAC and its ally, the Texas Association of Business, were accused of investing as much as $2.5 million in the 2002 elections.[77] Three DeLay aides and eight companies were indicted by the grand jury in September. Two months later, the fear that charges would be brought against DeLay himself led the House Republican Party to erase a rule that prohibited a member who had been indicted on criminal charges from holding a leadership post. After widespread criticism, this decision was reversed in January 2005.

A pioneer in the post–McCain-Feingold world of campaign finance, DeLay also ingeniously blurred the lines between philanthropy and politics in an attempt to leverage even more influence. For the 2004 Republican National Convention (RNC) in New York City, the House majority leader planned a variety of events for Celebrations for Children, Inc., a charity for abused children. High-dollar donors were given opportunities to attend private functions with DeLay and other top Republicans. Many critics of DeLay argued that the charity was a façade for part of the majority leader's campaign fundraising empire and that the IRS should deny it tax-exempt status. Under significant pressure, he canceled the organization's presence at the party's convention.

DeLay's aggressive style is not just reserved for Republican clients. As majority leader and, previously, Republican whip, the Texan has worked hard to keep the House GOP together and help it avoid the kind of rancorous internecine battles that accelerated the Democrats' fall from power in 1994. To be sure, the Republicans have had their problems. Observers have also identified a variety of stylistic and substantive factions within the House party.[78] Indeed, they split as it became clear that Bill Clinton was winning the public-opinion war over the government shutdown in early 1996, and they sometimes fractured over issues like the environment and spending. They were also frequently divided over the conduct of Newt Gingrich. In July 1997 DeLay himself was involved in a mysterious and ultimately aborted attempt to overthrow the Speaker. But DeLay has generally been there to keep the party together. His fundraising exploits have garnered loyalty to the collective cause but so have his support for individual members' important projects and his leadership of an efficient and extensive whipping mechanism of more than sixty-five colleagues. Indeed, no detail was left untouched when he was whip. DeLay staffers frequently catered late night meetings and floor sessions, and at the 2000 Republican convention in Philadelphia, they laid on limos for all attending House Republicans and meticulously arranged members' schedules so that they could take advantage of the lavish corporate hospitality.[79]

If anything, as majority leader DeLay has softened his approach, showing a greater appreciation for carrots and less of one for sticks. During the first Congress after his promotion, he claimed, "I don't get up every day and put on my gloves to fight all day long. I get up every day to talk to this person and that person, and sooner or later, we'll work it out."[80] As DeLay's Florida colleague, Tom Feeney, has put it, "Tom knows every member's district, he knows their needs politically, he knows their interests, their policy situations, he almost always understands their family situation."[81] Still, operating closely with his ostensible boss, Speaker Dennis Hastert, DeLay kept the vote on the important Medicare reform bill open in November 2003 for nearly three hours—twelve times as long as is customarily the case—so as to twist a few GOP arms. He was also later rebuked by the House ethics committee for offering an endorsement in a GOP House primary in return for a member's support of the legislation.

DeLay's assertiveness has not been without cost. In addition to the admonitions handed out by the House ethics committee, he has come under increased scrutiny for huge salaries his organizations have provided his wife and daughter and for overseas trips that may have been paid for by lobbyists and foreign agents. By April 2005 vocal critics included Republicans like former Speaker Newt Gingrich, Representative Christopher Shays of Connecticut, and Pennsylvania Senator Rick Santorum. Yet, for the most part, House colleagues rallied around him. They realized just how important DeLay has been to the maintenance of their majority.

To accentuate unity, the new House Republican leadership has also changed party and chamber rules. When Gingrich arrived at the Capitol as the new leader in 1995, he immediately set about undermining the autonomy of committee chairs. Three-term limits were instituted so that committee leaders could not become entrenched. In addition, the GOP's leadership-dominated Steering Committee—the body that makes Republican committee assignments—began somewhat routinely to ignore seniority as the principal qualification to be chair. This allowed the leadership to extract allegiance from prospective committee heads who, because of the term limits, seemed to be emerging at frequent intervals. Christopher Shays' push for campaign finance reform, as noted earlier, cost him the chairmanship of the Government Reform Committee when it became available in 2003.[82] In 2001 Speaker Hastert was able to reward both Michael Oxley of Ohio and Billy Tauzin of Lousiana for their fundraising prowess and steadfastness by making them both chairs. Oxley and Tauzin had been competing to chair the Commerce Committee. Hastert gave the nod to Tauzin but terminated the old Banking Committee and replaced it with the Financial Services Committee. He made Oxley its head and, when the music stopped, Marge Roukema of New Jersey, a moderate who had been in line to lead the Banking Committee, was left without a chair to sit on.

Gingrich, moreover, used ad-hoc, personally appointed task forces to create legislation and bypass traditional committees and often attempted to impose party-approved bills on chairs.[83] Judiciary Committee chair Henry Hyde of Illinois, for example, was forced to bring the constitutional amendment on congressional term limits to the floor despite his deep personal opposition to the proposal. In 2003 the Steering Committee also obtained the right to name the chairs of the thirteen appropriations subcommittees, hence gaining increased leverage over the spending of federal money.

The product of this military-style operation has been an extraordinary amount of solidarity within the party. In the early 1990s, the percentage of House Republicans who voted with their party on party-unity votes—that is those votes on which a majority of Republicans opposed a majority of Democrats—was very high by historical standards. Although majorities are generally more fractious than minorities, this figure averaged 88.7 percent in the 1995-to-2003 period, while the opposition Democrats had a mean annual party-unity score of 82.8 percent. Democratic Rep. Barney Frank of Massachusetts surely exaggerated when he said, after Congress had passed the Medicare reform bill in November 2003, that "the Republican Party in the House is the most ideologically cohesive and disciplined party in the democratic world."[84] But he wasn't too far off.

The Republicans have also quickly learned the art of partisan redistricting. To be sure, in their first reapportionment as the majority, Republicans were generally forced to accept compromises with the Democrats. In many states the post-2000 reapportionment amounted to an incumbent protection plan—after the 2000 redistricting, most pundits believe there are somewhere in the range of only thirty extremely competitive House districts. Holding the majority, however, made this an acceptable strategy. As Tom Davis remarked in the spring of 2002, by greatly reducing the number of seats that can change hands between the parties, "It gives them [the Democrats] a hill to climb."[85]

And the GOP also played some strong offense. The revolution of 1994 had, to some extent at least, permeated state politics, and the party found itself with greater influence in them. By 2001, 48 percent of state senators and representatives—the men and women charged with redistricting—were Republicans. Assisted by sophisticated computers equipped with geographic information system software—such as the GOP's Caliper's Maptitude for Redistricting—they began to work with such precision that they were able to parse apart neighboring streets effortlessly.[86]

In states like Michigan and Pennsylvania, the GOP took the process by the scruff of the neck and its state legislators drew obviously partisan gerrymanders. In Michigan two prominent Democrats, John Dingell and Lynn Rivers, were forced to scrap it out in the same district, and the Republicans turned a nine-to-seven deficit into a nine-to-six advantage. In Pennsylvania, the GOP eliminated two Democratic districts, forced a Democrat into retirement, pitched two Democratic incumbents against each other—in this case squeezing one of them, Frank Mascara, into the new district by drawing the boundary in front of his house— and still had space to draw two new GOP-friendly seats.

In fact, the Republicans seemed to enjoy redistricting so much that they continued to do it after the 2002 elections. In 2003 court decisions blocked reapportionment plans in Colorado and Texas. Emboldened by favorable election results in 2002 and supervised from Washington—as Tom DeLay put it, "I'm the majority leader and I want more seats"[87]—GOP legislators in these states recognized an opportunity to increase their party's advantage in the lower chamber of the federal legislature. In Colorado the centerpiece of the new redistricting plan was the protection of Bob Beauprez, a freshman who won by 121 votes in 2002. The Bush White House acknowledged as much when it admitted that Karl Rove was in communication with Republican legislators during the debate on the new districts in Denver. Unfortunately for the GOP, the courts blocked the plan because, they argued, the Colorado Constitution prohibited redistricting more than once every ten years.

The Texas redistricting provided wonderful entertainment. Incensed by what they considered DeLay's meddling and worried that the new plan could add as many as five Republicans to the state's delegation, Lone Star state legislative Democrats fled to Oklahoma and New Mexico to prevent the presence of a quorum to address redistricting bills. When fifty-one House Democrats skedaddled in May 2003, Speaker Tom Craddick dispatched Texas Rangers to track them down. DeLay's office in Washington asked officials from the Federal Aviation Administration (FAA) and Homeland Security and Justice departments to assist in locating the runaways. The majority leader also spoke to the president and White House senior adviser Karl Rove about the matter. Democrats were apoplectic. Senator Joe Lieberman of Connecticut, ranking member of the Government Reform Committee and presidential candidate at the time requested an investigation, calling the actions of Republicans "a clear abuse of the federal government's resources, and an invasion of privacy, and one that shouldn't happen again."[88] Finally, homesick and under threat of fines, one of the Senate Democrats broke ranks, potentially insuring a quorum and making the self-imposed exile of the others politically meaningless. Yet, still the saga continued. Next, House and Senate Republicans bickered over the exact look of the plan with arguments between agrarian interests in Lubbock and oil interests in Midland. In the end, DeLay coordinated an arrangement that facilitated the capture of six Texas seats from the Democrats in 2004. Initially, and unlike in Colorado, the federal courts found nothing legally troubling with midstream redistricting. The Supreme Court also upheld the principle of partisan gerrymandering more generically. As Justice Antonin Scalia wrote, it "must conclude that political gerrymandering claims are nonjusticiable."[89] The Court was scheduled to revisit the Texas case in 2005, however.

This penchant for partisan redistricting exacerbates the fact that, in Gary Jacobson's words, "Republican voters are distributed more efficiently" across House districts.[90] To put it another way, more Democratic votes are wasted because more Democratic districts are truly safe. Democratic voters tend to be more concentrated, Republican voters more evenly distributed. This is illustrated by 2000 presidential race. George W. Bush won 240 of the 435 House districts that year, even though, of course, Al Gore won more popular votes than the Texan.

Winning House majorities requires a different kind of politics than does capturing the presidency. It necessitates an intense focus on constituency service and local concerns—it is no coincidence that it was a man of the House, former Democratic Speaker Tip O'Neill, who coined the phrase, "All politics are local." It also requires a national organization capable of identifying, training, and funding quality candidates and protecting incumbents during redistricting. Victories are ground out one seat at a time, and battle plans and personnel are molded to suit the political terrain of each district. Candidates are recruited if they have broad appeal in their district and encouraged to talk about the parts of Republican philosophy that resonate favorably with their constituents. The House GOP leadership has come to realize that you do not defend a majority with a national one-size-fits-all message that may not play well in large swaths of the country—and that is a sitting target for Democrats.

National issues can occasionally be important, but they have not really defined a House election since the GOP took over in 1994. Democrats declared 1998 a massive repudiation of Gingrich's

attempt to make the midterm about Bill Clinton's impeachment—
the Speaker ordered a multi-million dollar advertising campaign
about the president's conduct in many swing districts and admitted, after the dust had settled, that "there were no national
issues"[91]—but won only five seats. The GOP declared 2002 an
emphatic stamp of approval for President Bush's execution of the
war on terrorism and his Iraq policy—but won only seven seats.
Indeed, the best measure we have of the extent to which House
elections are nationalized or localized vindicates O'Neill's maxim.
The standard deviation of the change in the vote for a party from
one election to the next in each of the 435 congressional districts
remains, at about 7 percent, high by historical standards—that is,
the Republican vote has not surged or declined particularly uni-
formly across districts. This suggests, in turn, that local concerns
and assessments of incumbent performance are most determina-
tive of voters' choices, not national factors like the state of the
economy or the performance of the president.

Other data illuminate the Republican majority's effort to insu-
late itself from presidential politics and national economic and
political conditions. Incumbent reelection rates have been at historic highs in the five elections since 1994. Ninety-five percent of
House incumbents running in 1996 were reelected; these figures
were 99 percent, 96 percent, 97 percent, and 98 percent in 1998,
2000, 2002, and 2004, respectively.

In short, then, the new Republican majority may be full of
ideas about shrinking government and strengthening America,
but it has held onto the House by employing the same kinds of
strategies that allowed the Democrats to be so successful for so
many years. Even if the party wants to put a squeeze on future
pork barreling, with skillful leadership, hardworking incumbents,
the nurturing of talented challengers, and the continued diminution of the number of truly competitive districts, it should be able
to hold on to the majority for quite some time.

4

Governing Stealthily: Republicans in the States and the Courts

Even more spectacular than the GOP's emergence as Congress' majority party has been the turnaround in its fortunes at the state level. For most of the fifty years that followed FDR's death, state politics were largely unfriendly to Republicans. To be sure, there were enduring and important Republican governors between the New Deal and the Great Society—at the tail end of that period, for example, were Warren Knowles in Wisconsin, Bill Milliken in Michigan, James A. Rhodes in Ohio, Nelson Rockefeller in New York, George Romney in Michigan, Bill Scranton in Pennsylvania, James Thompson in Illinois, and Ronald Reagan in California. But for most of the next couple of decades the party was largely frozen out of the chief executive position at the state level. GOP successes in the 1968 and 1970 gubernatorial elections proved ephemeral—whereas there had been thirty-four Democratic governors in 1964, by 1978 there were thirty-seven. Just after Clinton was first elected president, Republicans still inhabited only eighteen governors' mansions.

The year 1994, however, proved pivotal. In that anti-Democratic year, a slew of new energetic and talented GOP chief executives were elected in the states—George W. Bush in Texas, Frank Keating in Oklahoma, George Pataki in New York, Tom Ridge in Pennsylvania, and John Rowland in Connecticut (another, Christine Todd Whitman of New Jersey, had been elected the year before). Others were returned to their posts for a further four-year term—Arne Carlson in Minnesota, Jim Edgar in Illinois, John Engler in Michigan, Tommy Thompson in Wisconsin, George Voinovich in Ohio, Bill Weld in Massachusetts, and Pete Wilson in California. After that election, fully thirty of the nation's fifty governors were Republican. Although the GOP has subsequently lost control of some of these governors' mansions, the cohort has provided a paradigm for Republican success at the gubernatorial level.

The widely duplicated model exuded pragmatism, an especially important attribute for those executives in states that leaned Democratic. As political scientist Earl Black put it, these were Republicans who were "practical politicians rather than ideologues."[1] They were often termed "problem solvers" who focused "on people and results" rather than ideas.[2] To be sure, economic conservatives lamented that the cohort had made bounteous government spending acceptable, and ardent conservatives often winced at other behavior—as David Plotz of the Internet magazine *Slate* wrote in 1999, these governors exhibited a "softer social policy."[3] Indeed, to David Winston, they looked "upon government not as the enemy but as a tool to help them achieve their political and policy goals."[4] But they also pursued political change that was distinctly Republican. New York's George Pataki, for instance, established the death penalty and called for a $2 billion cut in taxes and spending when he first arrived in office. George W. Bush oversaw the passage of strong tort reform in Texas, and Tommy Thompson of Wisconsin and Arne Carlson of Minnesota indefatigably pursued school voucher programs in their states. Some of the tougher implementations of the federally mandated 1996 welfare overhaul were undertaken in Republican-governed states—indeed, Thompson's program in Wisconsin with its "workfare" requirements and benefit cuts became a model for the bill Congress passed.[5]

This highly regarded group laid the foundations for the current Republican domination of governors' mansions. The GOP currently occupies the top spot in twenty-nine states, including the four biggest by population—California, Texas, New York, and Florida—and the six in which Bush performed most poorly in 2000 and 2004—Rhode Island, Massachusetts, New York, Hawaii, Connecticut, and Maryland. To be sure, Republicans have been repudiated in some of the states they had success in during the 1990s—Illinois, Michigan, New Jersey, and Pennsylvania now have Democratic governors. Moreover, after John Rowland's summer 2004 resignation preempted his probable impeachment in Connecticut, only Pataki in New York—who many Republicans lament has "strayed from the more or less conservative principles that marked his political rise"—is still there.[6] Yet in other states, Republican succession has been secured—notably in Ohio and, after the Gray Davis interlude, California. More critically, the party's reputation for competent leadership has been buttressed by the pragmatic tenures of the classes of 1990 and 1994. The model helped propel moderates like Bob Ehrlich and Mitt Romney to the governorships of two of the most liberal northeastern states—Maryland and Massachusetts, respectively—in 2002. Ehrlich campaigned in the middle of the road; he emphasized his pro-choice credentials, spoke out strongly in favor of public education, and had an African American running mate. At his party's nominating convention, Romney declared himself "a fiscal conservative and social moderate."[7] Both declared they would do their utmost not to raise taxes. Both ran against women who were considered too liberal, even for their left-leaning states.

Republican successes have been even more dramatic in state legislatures. In 1975, when the party was at its Watergate nadir, only 31 percent of state legislators across the country were Republicans. Only sixteen of the nation's state legislative bodies were under GOP control. The California legislature had twice as many Democrats as Republicans, and the GOP had just lost control of New York's lower chamber. Even frequently Republican large and important states like Illinois, Michigan, Ohio, and Pennsylvania had bodies firmly under the Democrats' heel. Perhaps most despondently for the party, Republicans had been obliterated in Dixie, where advances had been made in the wake of the relatively successful southern strategies of Eisenhower, Goldwater, and Nixon. Only 19 of 181 state legislators in Texas were from the GOP, 10 of 170 in North Carolina, 5 of 56 members of the Georgia Senate, and not one single Alabama lawmaker was affiliated with the party.

The surging Reagan and Gingrich tides, however, raised the boats of Republicans sinking in state legislative politics. By 1994 things were very much looking up. After that election, 46.5 percent of state senators were Republicans; 48 percent of state House members were. What's more, Republicans were in command of the California House and New York Senate and both chambers in large and important states like Illinois, Michigan, New Jersey,

Ohio, and Pennsylvania. Today, impressively, the parties are essentially even—there are basically the same number of GOP and Democratic state legislators. Indeed, before the 2004 election, Republicans enjoyed a narrow sixty-four-seat majority. This, in turn, has helped state Republicans collect money for legislative races. Although still out-raised in a number of states, the GOP, now populated by an army of entrenched and powerful incumbents, has expertly tapped funds for legislative campaigns. According to the Institute on Money in State Politics, in 2002 Republican candidates amassed a war chest three times the size of their Democratic rivals in Florida House and Ohio legislative campaigns, twice as much in Michigan, New York, and Texas Senate contests, and about one-and-a-half times more in House races in Pennsylvania and Texas and Senate races in Florida and Missouri.

The gains have been most dramatic in the South. After the historic 1994 election, the GOP took control of four of the region's state legislative chambers—the Florida and Tennessee Senates and North and South Carolina Houses. This was the first time since Reconstruction that any state body in the South had had a Republican majority. Today, at the beginning of the second term of the nation's first truly southern GOP president, the party is in charge of ten of the old Confederacy's twenty-two state legislative bodies, including both chambers in Florida, Texas, and Virginia where they enjoy considerable majorities. It also dominates governors' offices in that part of the country, residing in seven of the eleven executive mansions.

The new GOP dominance of contemporary southern politics is therefore critical to their current hold, however tenuous, on state government in the aggregate. State Republican parties in Dixie no longer consist, as they did in the 1960s, of a small number of disgruntled and provincial white conservative populist businessmen and lawyers who played on racial tensions and highlighted the national Democratic Party's betrayal of southern values. Today they are sophisticated, savvy, wealthy, and well-staffed organizations capable of outmaneuvering the previously hegemonic Democrats. Assisted by in-migration of affluent Republicans from the Northeast and Midwest and the increased liberalism of indigenous Democratic elites, state parties have coupled conservative positions on abortion, race, and religion with a virulent tax-cutting philosophy to attract considerable support in state-level elections in the old Confederacy.[8] They recruit young, eager, erudite, politically connected, and well-financed candidates who are serious about careers in state politics and do not talk or act like good-ole-boys. People like Patrick Ballantine, who was elected by North Carolina Senate Republicans to be their leader when he was thirty-two and became his party's nominee for governor in 2004 at thirty-nine. Florida has Alex Diaz de la Portilla, a Hispanic political go-getter from a connected Cuban Miami family selected to be the president pro-tempore of the Florida Senate at thirty-eight—despite incurring a record fine for campaign violations. It also has a Republican House majority leader, Marco Rubio, who ascended to his position at thirty-three. South Carolina's lieutenant governor is Andre Bauer, thirty-five—he was elected to the state's House at twenty-seven. A former Bush administration official, president of the state university system, and son of Indian immigrants, Bobby Jindal narrowly lost the Louisiana governor's race at thirty-two in 2003. He won a U.S. House seat the following year, however, and joined other young GOP southerners in Washington, including Adam Putnam of central Florida who was first elected to the House in 2000 at age twenty-six and Patrick McHenry who, at twenty-nine, became the youngest member of the 109th Congress when he won an open seat in western North Carolina in 2004.

The Republicans are asserting some considerable control over judicial politics, as well. Comprehensive analysis of the ideology of state supreme-court judges undertaken by Paul Brace, Laura Langer, and Melinda Gann Hall, for example, suggests that many of their courts are currently clustered at the conservative pole of the ideological continuum.[9] Conservatives and Republicans also seem to do very well in the judicial elections that take place in thirty-nine states. Such contests are of two types, election to the court or retention to an appointed position by public approval. In the six states in which candidates for the highest court run with party labels—Alabama, Illinois, Louisiana, Pennsylvania, Texas, and West Virginia—Republicans dominate; they enjoy a nine-to-zero shutout on Alabama's high court, and even in Democratic Illinois they are only down five-to-three. There are several plausible reasons for this GOP success, including the likelihood that voters want the kinds of aggressive law-and-order positions they see in Republicans and that well-financed GOP candidates are exploiting their relationships with the business community and social conservatives to inject unprecedented amounts of money into judicial races. In 2002, for example, victorious GOP top-court candidates—like Maureen O'Connor of Ohio (where parties endorse judicial candidates) at $1.8 million and Harold See of Alabama at $1.6 million—spent oodles of cash. According to Bert Brandenburg of the Justice at Stake Campaign, a judicial reform organization, 2004 was "the year the dam is bursting."[10] Two candidates for a judicial seat in Illinois raised about $10 million between them. What is more, political scientist Melinda Gann Hall has found that party politics, often to the benefit of Republicans, play an important role in formally nonpartisan contests as well.[11]

The federal courts are increasingly friendly to Republicans, too. The Warren and Burger Supreme Courts were famously liberal. Earl Warren, a popular former Republican governor of California, was given the Court's top position in 1953 when sitting Chief Justice Fred Vinson died. The court Warren led revolutionized constitutional law, expanding civil rights and the prerogatives of criminal defendants dramatically. "The biggest damn-fooled mistake" he had ever made, confessed President Dwight Eisenhower of the appointment. The conservative reaction to Warren was so visceral that there was a somewhat serious attempt, energetically led by Robert Welch of the John Birch Society, to impeach him. Chief Justice Warren Burger was not quite as aggressive as his predecessor, but his court antagonized conservatives nonetheless. During his tenure—he followed Warren's retirement in 1969 and was Chief Justice until 1986—the death penalty was placed under moratorium, President Nixon was forced to hand over his Oval Office tapes, abortion was legalized, busing was imposed, the wedge between church and state was driven deeper, and affirmative action was strengthened.

But with Republican domination of the presidency since the late 1960s, the federal bench has taken on a distinctly Republican hue. Seven of the nine current Supreme Court justices were appointed by Republican presidents—only Stephen Breyer and Ruth Bader Ginsburg owe their jobs to a Democrat, in both instances Clinton. In the lower federal courts—the thirteen appeals courts and ninety-four district trial courts—the balance has tilted decidedly in a conservative direction, despite Clinton's eight-year presidency. Much of this can be attributed to President Reagan's attention to the bench and his aggressive recruitment, evaluation, and selling of his nominees. Reagan got to appoint 368 lower federal-court judges, just over one-third of the total. He also

ensured that they would adhere to important conservative juris-
prudential principles by establishing an activist and brazenly
political agency in the Justice Department—the Office of Legal
Policy—and inserting White House personnel such as Attorneys
General William French Smith and Ed Meese into what was previously a more bureaucratic and less ideological process of select-
ing judges. What is more, Reagan was assisted by Republican
majorities in the Senate for six of the eight years he was in office,
and he worked hard on home-state senators who could block
appointments by employing a "blue slip."[12]

When George W. Bush was sworn in, federal judgeships were
evenly distributed among the parties. Largely as a hangover from
squabbles between Bill Clinton and the Republican-controlled
Senate of the late 1990s, however, there were many vacancies.
Bush and his Judicial Selection Committee, headed by White
House Counsel Alberto Gonzales, industriously set about filling
them and others that opened up later. He had already appointed
166 of 665 district court judges and 35 of 179 circuit court judges
by the 2004 election. Returned for a second term, Bush will inevitably make many more. The Bush administration has also made
changes to the selection process. The most radical was to end the
American Bar Association's formal role in the rating of nominees.
To the administration, however, the process was essentially the
same as it had always been; the judges appointed were qualified,
there were no "litmus tests," and senators from both sides of the
aisle were consulted continually.[13]

Many Democratic senators disagreed. They felt left out of the
judicial selection process and, worse still, they and their supporters believed Bush nominations possessed a hard ideological
edge. At the district court level, for example, there have been
vociferous complaints that the Bush administration has ignored
senators and formal bipartisan nominating commissions so as to
get conservatives on the bench. During the 108th Congress of
2003–2004, Democrats pointed to judges like Ken Starr-protégé
John Bates of the District of Columbia; Paul Cassell of Utah, a
law professor and vehement opponent of Miranda rights; and
the demonstrably anti-abortion jurists Leon Holmes from
Arkansas, Laurie Smith Camp of Nebraska, and Jay Zainey from
Louisiana.[14] Ten circuit court appointees were filibustered in the
same Congress. Liberal and influential University of Chicago law
professor Cass Sunstein argued that "it used to be that conservatives believed in judicial restraint—that courts should back off and

let the democratic process work. But the movement conservatives—some of the new right-wing activists—are different. They want to cut back on what government is allowed to do. The new people want to strike down more. It's a radical agenda."[15]

Regardless of the legitimacy of the Democrats' grumbling about Bush and his appointment strategies, it is clear that the federal courts have moved public policy to the right over the past couple of decades. Thomas M. Keck argues, for example, that the record of the William Rehnquist Supreme Court has been mixed but that it has exhibited a discernible conservativism motivated more by politics than legal theory.[16] Andrew D. Martin and Kevin M. Quinn have established a method that allows them to place each Supreme Court justice, year-by-year, on a single-dimension liberal-to-conservative ideological scale. Although the cases the Court deals with change substantively over time, Martin and Quinn have still been able to discern a rightward drift in the median justice since the late 1970s and early 1980s.[17] Bernard Grofman and Timothy J. Brazill come to a similar conclusion. Utilizing an analysis of voting behavior on the Supreme Court until 1991, they have detected perhaps an even stronger movement in the conservative direction.[18]

Lower federal courts have taken this trajectory as well. Ten of the thirteen circuit courts have GOP-appointed majorities and one more is poised to as President Bush fills vacancies in a second term. The Fourth Circuit Court—which encompasses Maryland, West Virginia, Virginia, and the Carolinas—is viewed as especially conservative. Ten of the fourteen judges owe their circuit court jobs to Republican presidents. What is more, under the practice of senatorial courtesy, many Fourth Circuit appointees have needed to be approved by conservative icons like North Carolina's Jesse Helms and South Carolina's Strom Thurmond. Indeed, Thurmond aide Dennis W. Shedd is on the court, and the second President Bush appointed Terrence Boyle, a Helms protégé and district court judge, only to see the confirmation process initially gum up on him.

Even courts consisting of a majority of Democratically appointed judges, like the notoriously liberal Ninth Circuit that covers California and eight other western states, have been unable to stem the tide. Conspicuous because of some of its incongruously liberal verdicts, the Court has more of its decisions overturned by the Supreme Court than any of the other circuit courts. During the 2003–2004 term, nineteen of the twenty-five Ninth Circuit cases decided by the top court were reversed or vacated in whole or in part.

To be sure, in many policy areas this conservatism has made a glacial and often broken advance. This is because the hold Republican appointees have on the federal courts is still nascent and somewhat tenuous. Indeed, despite the seven-to-two GOP majority on the Supreme Court, that body is still dramatically split on many questions. In recent years, there have been a very high number of five-to-four votes—24 percent in the 2003–2004 term, 17 percent in the 2002–2003 term, 28 percent in 2001–2002, 33 percent in 2000–2001, and 27 percent in 1999–2000. In the five or six terms before that, generally at least one of five decisions came down that way. For the most part, although far from always, a "moderate" block of justices made up of Anthony Kennedy, Sandra Day O'Connor, and David Souter split so as to give the Court's either so-called "conservative" wing—made up of Chief Justice William Rehnquist, Antonin Scalia, and Clarence Thomas— or "liberal" wing—consisting of Stephen Breyer, Ruth Bader Ginsburg, and John Paul Stevens—a slender victory.

Still, even a perfunctory examination of federal jurisprudence in important issue areas reveals a palpable conservative evolution in court-made policy over the last quarter century. New doctrines are being established and, in the tradition of judge-made law, nurtured and protected until they can have a real impact on federal and state policy-makers and the everyday behavior of American citizens. Take the area of business regulation, for example. In the past two decades, the Supreme Court has prevented Congress from legislating so as to negate previous deals made between federal regulators and corporations; protected companies under bankruptcy protection from government dismemberment; prevented workers from suing under federal statute if they were contractually obligated to go to arbitration over employment disputes; limited punitive damages in claims made against negligent companies; and consistently upheld firms in their legal tussles with disgruntled employees who have sued under the Americans with Disabilities Act—such as a Toyota assembly line worker with carpal tunnel syndrome, a laid-off employee of a Chevron contractor who had liver disease, a cargo handler at U.S. Airways who injured his back and was looked over for a more accommodating mailroom job, severely myopic twin sisters who were refused positions at United Airlines, and a mechanic at UPS with high blood pressure.[19] Casey Martin, however, got to use his golf cart on the PGA tour.[20] What is more, although federal courts have upheld a ban on "blast faxes," consistently enforced anti-spam laws, and allowed the government to put into operation a "do not call" list to protect members of the public from telemarketers, commercial speech has generally been protected. The Supreme Court has voided bans on the publication of the prices of alcoholic beverages and a Massachusetts ban on tobacco advertising.[21] More importantly for the cigarette companies, in 2000 the Supreme Court undercut the Food and Drug Administration's (FDA's) claims to regulate the golden leaf as a drug.[22]

Where federal courts have supported government, they have done so to promote economic competition—a quintessentially conservative goal. The two most extravagant actions in this regard were the breakup of AT&T by Judge Harold Greene's consent decree in 1982 and the U.S. Court of Appeals' ruling that Microsoft held an illegal monopoly over operating systems software in 2001.[23] In 1999 the Supreme Court continued the assault on consolidation in the telecommunications industry started by Judge Greene by sustaining the Federal Communications Commission's (FCC's) power under the Telecommunications Act of 1996 to open local telephone service to competing interests.[24]

In the related area of property rights, the Court has come a long way since its landmark decision in *PruneYard Shopping Center v. Robins* (1980) that the owners of a shopping mall could not prevent a group of California high-school students from collecting signatures in their building for a petition opposing a United Nations resolution against Zionism. There have been exceptions to the Court finding for private property over public interest in cases arising under the Fifth Amendment's "takings" provision that reads, "private property [shall not] be taken for public use, without just compensation." The Court has sanctioned a moratorium on development in the Lake Tahoe basin and the use of interest on lawyers' trust funds to pay for state-run legal aid programs, for example.[25] But egged on by conservative legal thinkers like the Cato Institute's Roger Pilon, the Court has clearly diluted states' claims to eminent domain and vigorously protected the right of owners to do as they wish with their property. The breakthrough came in *Nollan v. California Coastal Commission* (1987) when it was found that compelling a family to provide a path so that the public could access a beach constituted an unlawful "taking." Later, the Nollan approach freed an Oregon storeowner from having to provide land for a greenway and bike path in exchange for permission to pave a parking lot. It was also used by the Court to permit the development of a private beach club in contravention of Rhode Island wetlands regulations.[26] Tinsley Yarborough, who has written an authoritative account of the Rehnquist era's decisions, argues that it is on this issue that the Court may craft "the most important element of the Reagan-Bush judicial legacy."[27] On this, much will depend on its 2005 decision in *Kelo v. City of London*.

Intellectual property has also been protected. Assailed by what Robert S. Boynton has labeled the "Copy Left" and what Lawrence Lessig of Stanford Law School calls the "free culture movement," owners of recorded music, movies, and books persuaded Congress to add an additional twenty years to copyright protection in 1998.[28] The Supreme Court upheld the legislation in 2003.[29] The federal bench has also assisted in the recording industry's pursuit of file sharers; in February 2001 an appeals court sided with the record companies and ordered Napster to prevent its users from exchanging copyrighted music. Emboldened, the Recording Industry Association of America has gone after other file-sharing software makers and individuals—most are in college and high school—who have transferred thousands of songs over the Internet.

The Supreme Court has recently struck tremendous blows for state power in decisions it has made on federalism. Again, this is precisely the direction most Republicans want to take the country. The watershed decision here was *United States v. Lopez* in 1995 when, for the first time since 1942, the Court ruled for a state in a dispute with the feds over issues related to the commerce clause of the Constitution. In this case, a Texas twelfth grader was prosecuted under a federal statute that banned possession of a gun within 1,000 feet of a school. Indeed, whereas on most issues change has been piecemeal, the nine years that have followed *Lopez* have been nothing short of revolutionary for federalism—Linda Greenhouse argued after the case was handed down that "it is only a slight exaggeration" to suggest that the Court is close to "reinstalling the Articles of Confederation."[30] To expand state prerogatives, the Court has used the commerce clause; a strict interpretation of Congress' enumerated powers in Article I of the Constitution; the enforcement provision of the Fourteenth Amendment; the Tenth Amendment, which states that "the powers not delegated to the United States by the Constitution, nor prohibited by it to the States, are reserved to the States respectively, or to the people"; and the Eleventh Amendment,

which states that "the Judicial power of the United States shall
not be construed to extend to any suit in law or equity, com-
menced or prosecuted against one of the United States by Citizens
of another State, or by Citizens or Subjects of any Foreign State."
As a direct consequence, the Brady gun law provision requiring
states to run background checks on purchasers has been struck
down.[31] Federal age-discrimination legislation has been found to
be inapplicable in state-hiring practices—although states can be
sued for not abiding by federal family- and medical-leave policies.[32] States have been told that they are not obligated to negotiate gaming licenses with Indian tribes under federal guidelines.[33]
The Federal Labor Standards Act cannot, the Court has determined, compel states to authorize private actions against them
in their own courts, and, furthermore, states cannot be forced
against their will to submit to adjudication in a federal regulatory
agency.[34] Congress has also been told that it cannot provide a
federal civil remedy in what is considered a non-economic, intra-
state matter—specifically, the Violence against Women Act does
not permit a purported rape victim to go to the nation's courts
for compensatory and punitive damages.[35]

Change in a conservative direction is also palpable on social
policy. If somewhat haltingly, the courts have moved to erode
the constitutional protections on abortion established by the
Roe v. Wade decision in 1973. In *Planned Parenthood of Southeastern
Pennsylvania v. Casey* (1992), for example, the Supreme Court ruled
that only state abortion regulations that have the purpose or effect
of imposing a "substantial obstacle in the path of a woman seeking
an abortion before the fetus attains viability" are inherently unconstitutional. Here, the Court upheld provisions in Pennsylvania
law such as those that required parental consent if the patient is
a minor and a twenty-four-hour waiting period prior to the procedure. Three years earlier, the Court had sustained a Missouri
statute that prevented the use of state facilities in abortions, forced
physicians to diagnose whether or not a fetus was viable before
utilizing the procedure, and prohibited counseling that recommended abortion.[36]

To be sure, criminal defendants have had surprising victories
at the hands of the Court in the last few years. Execution of
mentally retarded offenders has been deemed inherently unconstitutional.[37] A law allowing judges to unilaterally find facts that
can lead to imposition of the death penalty without jury concurrence has been held unconstitutional.[38] In 2003 the Court ordered

states to grant *habeas corpus* to an inmate who felt that jury selection was egregiously tainted by racial bias and one whose attorney failed to mention during trial that his client had suffered from sexual abuse as a child.[39] The next year it invalidated a police procedure designed to induce confessions both before and after Miranda warnings had been issued.[40] In 2005, it struck down congressionally crafted federal sentencing guidelines designed to dilute the power of "soft" judges.[41]

Yet rightward movement is discernible on many issues concerning the criminal justice system. California's aggressive "three-strikes-and-you're-out" law that allows the imposition of very long sentences on the third offense, even if it is a nonviolent property crime, has been upheld. In these cases the defendants received twenty-five years for stealing two golf clubs and fifty years for shoplifting $150 worth of videos.[42] The Supreme Court also upheld "Megan's Law" sex offender notification provisions that allow application of the statute to people whose convictions occurred prior to passage and photographs and information to be posted on the Internet without the offender having an individual hearing.[43] The Bush Justice Department has added to the push by making it tougher for federal prosecutors to accept plea bargains.[44]

The exclusionary rule provides a further, important, example—the determination of what evidence should be permissible in a legal proceeding is, according to federal circuit court judge Guido Calabresi, the issue that best distinguishes liberals and conservatives jurisprudentially.[45] Here, the line between what can be included and what should be excluded has moved palpably in the direction of the state and the law enforcement community. Again, there have been isolated victories for what we would consider the liberal position. In *Knowles v. Iowa* (1999), the Court held that a "pot pipe" found in a search of a car stopped for speeding, a search conducted with neither the accused's permission nor probable cause, was inadmissible. The next year the Supreme Court found checkpoints employed to catch interdictors of illegal drugs unconstitutional and, the year after that, that agents cannot use thermal imaging to obtain probable cause for a subsequent physical search.[46] Most dramatically of all, the Court upheld the Miranda warnings in 2000 and 2004.[47] Familiar to fans of television cop shows, these inform defendants of their rights to remain silent and to an attorney, even one that is publicly provided, as well as warning them that anything they may say can be used against them.

Still, the general movement has been in the opposite direction. This arguably began in the early 1980s. It was then that the heightened sensitivity to law enforcement's behavior shown during the Warren and Burger Courts was relaxed. The important cases of *United States v. Leon* (1984) and *New York v. Quarles* (1984) provided the real breakthrough. In the first of these, the Court established a "good faith" exception to the exclusionary rule. Here, police officers believed they had sufficient evidence for a search warrant only to discover after they had been granted one and undertaken their investigation that it had been obtained illegitimately. In *Quarles*, the Court argued that a judge had rightly included evidence about the whereabouts of a gun submitted by a suspect prior to him being given his Miranda warnings because immediate concerns about public safety trumped the accused's rights. Since then, the Court has admitted into evidence marijuana seized by a police officer who believed erroneously that there was an outstanding misdemeanor warrant for the apprehended individual's arrest and has allowed evidence gleaned from brief investigatory "stops" of suspects in high crime areas.[48]

There have been legal victories for proponents of religion, too. It is true that early in the 1990s the court handed down decisions that, for example, prevented the offering of prayers at public school graduations.[49] Yet, in 2001 it ruled that public schools had to open their facilities to religious groups—in this case, a national evangelical Christian group was attempting to run Bible clubs for young children.[50] A year earlier the Court had upheld the distribution of federal government funds for educational equipment to private religious schools in Louisiana.[51] Even when decisions have gone against religious interests in recent years, the outcome could be construed as a victory for conservatives. Such was the case in *City of Boerne v. Flores* (1997). In this instance, the Catholic Archbishop of San Antonio believed the local authority's decision to block expansion of a church violated the Religious Freedom Restoration Act. In what, as we have seen, was becoming a pattern in cases concerning the scope of federal power, the Court found that Congress had overreached in creating the statute.

The same pattern has generally been apparent on race. In two critical cases in the mid-1990s, the court moved policy in a conservative direction. The Disadvantaged Business Enterprises program that favored bids for government work offered by minority-owned companies was found to be in potential violation of the Constitution's equal protection clause in *Adarand v. Pena*

(1995). The next year, the Court refused to review a decision made by a circuit court voiding a University of Texas Law School affirmative-action program.[52] In 2003 it struck down the University of Michigan's undergraduate admissions policy of providing African American applicants twenty points on a 150-point scale.[53]

On the First Amendment, the Court has had a surprisingly libertarian bent. In 2004, for example, it blocked the Child Online Protection Act that tried to protect children from pornography.[54] However, this tendency has generally been employed to grant victories to conservative interests. In 2003 the court refused to use federal racketeering and corruption laws to regulate picketing at abortion clinics, and in 2000 it upheld the Boy Scouts' right to prohibit homosexuals from becoming troop leaders.[55] To be sure, Republican Senator Mitch McConnell lost his case against the McCain-Feingold campaign finance reform legislation.[56] McConnell and his attorneys, including Ken Starr, argued that money was equivalent to speech and therefore the banning of certain commercials and soft money contributions to parties amounted to a grievous violation of the First Amendment. Still, as we shall see in Chapter 7, the campaign finance regime the Court's decision protected has greatly benefited the GOP.

Systematic data show, therefore, that the courts have moved in a rightward direction and pulled public policy in a number of important issue areas with them. Yet the public does not generally perceive things that way. To be sure, the Supreme Court's notorious decision in *Bush v. Gore* that effectively ended the contested 2000 presidential election did not endear it to Democrats. A Gallup poll taken a month after the court handed down the momentous decision revealed approval of the institution among Democrats had dropped to 42 percent from the 70 percent it was at in September 2000. By June 2001, however, the organization's figures put Democratic approval back at 54 percent and overall approval back at its pre-decision level of 62 percent. Herbert M. Kritzer has argued that the effects of the decision on the public's evaluation of the court were "essentially nil."[57]

Indeed, where public criticism of the federal courts exists today, it is because decisions are viewed as too liberal. It should be noted that most polls reveal a plurality of respondents approve of the court and its decisions. But a September 2003 Gallup poll showed 31 percent of respondents believed the Supreme Court and "its recent rulings" were "too liberal"; only 15 percent felt that they were "too conservative." In a July 2003 Fox News/Opinion Dynamics poll, 30 percent of respondents replied that the Court's decisions were "too liberal," 20 percent that they were too "conservative." Thirty-three percent of respondents in a CNN/*USA Today*/Gallup poll felt that the federal courts had generally been "hostile towards Christian religions in their rulings," only 16 percent believed they had been "supportive."

The notion of an overly liberal judiciary that is out of step with mainstream America, somewhat tentative though it is, has been gradually enhanced by a series of highly publicized and emotive court decisions. These decisions are ideologically untypical of many of the federal courts' rulings, but they are incendiary and, as such, have a habit of focusing the dominant image in the public's mind. What is more, many conservatives and Republicans do not hesitate to use them as examples of dangerous judicial behavior. The reaction helps mobilize activists and garner sympathy from the much of the public.

Cases concerning polarizing social issues have been an especially effective component of the GOP arsenal. Defending the confederate flag from zealous judges, for example, helped Georgia and South Carolina Republican gubernatorial candidates secure victory in 2002.[58] Flag burning of the stars-and-stripes kind periodically makes an appearance and puts Democrats on the back foot as well. Democratic candidates find themselves hedging in their answer to questions about their views on flag burning because of their concern for First Amendment rights. What is more, the House of Representatives has overwhelmingly approved a constitutional amendment banning the practice on four occasions, frequently with some considerable Democratic opposition. In June 2003, for instance, 113 Democrats voted against the enabling resolution. The issue is a bit of a hot potato for the party because significant majorities generally approve of a constitutional prohibition—63 percent of respondents to a CNN/*USA Today*/Gallup poll did in June 1999. It has brought conservative suspicion on the judiciary because flag burning is protected by a widely reviled 1989 Supreme Court decision.[59]

The pledge of allegiance is a similar issue. In 2003 the Ninth Circuit Court ruled that the pledge was unconstitutional when used in public schools because the words "under God" violated the constitutional principle of separation of church and state. The high-profile decision was met with almost universal opprobrium.

The Senate immediately voted 99–0 to support the "under God" phrase. The day after the court decision eighty senators, an unusually high number, rose early to loudly recite the pledge on the chamber's floor. Ari Fleischer, President Bush's press secretary, called the ruling "absurd."[60] Conservative religious groups were both outraged and astonished. Even the ACLU was silent and the liberal People for the American Way opposed the court's verdict leaving only groups like Americans United for Separation of Church and State and a smattering of vocal atheists to support it. As Republican Edward M. Rogers Jr. who was part of the Republican campaign that used the pledge issue against Michael Dukakis in 1988 sighed, "Gone are the days when the Democrats would walk into a swinging door on something like this."[61] Still, the general disparagement of a liberal decision made by a liberal court did not help Democrats. Although in September 2004 the Supreme Court overruled the lower body by saying that the man who brought the suit—the father of an affected girl—did not have standing because he had insufficient custody of his daughter, the House of Representatives voted to take away the Supreme Court's jurisdiction to rule on cases concerning the pledge's "under God" provision. "We can't let rogue judges redefine our history," explained Republican Steve Chabot of Ohio.[62] It was a position that found support among the public. Eighty-nine percent of those polled by ABC News/*Washington Post* in June 2002 felt that the words "under God" should remain in the pledge.

Decisions on affirmative action have helped conservatives cast the courts as out of step, too. In the summer of 2003, at the same time it was striking down an undergraduate affirmative action plan, the Supreme Court upheld the University of Michigan Law School's admissions policy that provided for an evaluation of race in the processing of applicants' files.[63] The Bush administration immediately and publicly praised both decisions but then went strategically mum on the issue. Although members of the public are conflicted on the merits and justice of affirmative action, they generally oppose it when it comes to college admissions. A Fox News/Opinion Dynamics poll taken just after the law-school decision was handed down at the end of June revealed 63 percent of respondents opposed it.

I have already revealed the palpable, if glacial, move the Supreme Court has made to dilute abortion rights. Yet to many Americans the issue continues to implicate the court as too liberal and outside of the mainstream. This view has been sharpened by a change in the political approach of anti-abortion groups. Wising up to the fact that a dramatic reversal of *Roe* is not immediately in the cards, activists have become, in the words of arguably the most strident pro-lifer in the House, Christopher Smith of New Jersey, "dogged realists."[64] According to University of Virginia sociologist James Davison Hunter they have "adopted a very different strategy" in recent years, "one that is incremental in nature."[65] They want, revealed Southern Baptist Convention leader Richard Land, to end *Roe* by making it "die from a thousand cuts."[66] At the core of this strategy was an attempt to ban "dilation and extraction" or "partial-birth abortion." In control of both chambers of Congress during the late 1990s, conservative Republicans scheduled debates on the issue knowing that Senate Democrats would filibuster and Bill Clinton veto resultant legislation—something the president did twice.

Going after partial-birth abortion brought political rewards for the pro-life movement. Between 1995 and 2003, thirty-one state legislatures passed prohibitions on the procedure. What is more, the congressional proceedings allowed anti-abortion legislators to make emotional speeches and bring graphic pictures of the procedure to the floor where they were broadcast to the nation. Their argument was that, regardless of one's thoughts about abortion, partial birth was different because it happened very late in the pregnancy and the fetus' death occurred outside the womb and hence was not about a woman's sovereignty over her own body.[67] All of this helped persuade many Americans who were somewhat ambivalent about abortion or were soft supporters of choice that a ban on partial birth was reasonable. A July 2003 ABC News poll found that 62 percent of respondents believed dilation and extraction should be illegal. A poll undertaken by CNN/*USA Today*/Gallup the previous January had the figure at 70 percent. As Princeton University's Robert George argued, "It's the only example we have of a pro-life legislative initiative moving public opinion."[68] In November 2003 President Bush seemed to have ended the saga when he signed a federal ban into law.

Yet, right on cue in their role as "liberal extremists," federal courts in California, Nebraska, and New York placed immediate injunctions on the ban. In doing so, they cited a 2000 Supreme Court decision despised by the pro-life movement that found Nebraska's ban on the procedure unconstitutional.[69] The next May the California court struck down the new law. That August U.S. District Judge Richard Casey of Manhattan affirmed the decision.

As far as many social conservatives were concerned, activist liberal judges had once again defied the wishes of democratically elected legislators and blocked policy dear to their hearts.

Some of the same pro-life activists also mobilized over Terri Schiavo, a dying woman in a vegetative state whose husband, Michael, against the wishes of his wife's parents, wanted to remove her feeding tube—an act that would cause her to die. In October 2003, Michael Schiavo, arguing that his wife's condition was permanent—she had been kept alive artificially for nearly fifteen years—won a Florida court's support to have the tube withdrawn. He also seemed to have public opinion on his side. A Fox News/ Opinion Dynamics poll conducted as the story first made national headlines showed 50 percent of respondents believed a patient's spouse should have the final word in situations like the Schiavos', and 61 percent felt the feeding tube should be removed in this particular case.

Again, however, events unfurled favorably for conservatives. Working with Terri's parents—who claimed their daughter still responded to them—religious groups found in the cause the energy to coordinate an intense e-mail and talk-radio campaign that ultimately forced the passage of a Florida law giving Governor Jeb Bush the authority to keep Terri Schiavo alive. As if to confirm social conservatives' suspicions of the bench, the law was struck down by a state judge in May 2004—a decision that was affirmed by the Florida and U.S. Supreme courts. A Florida judge then ordered Terri Schiavo's feeding tube removed in March 2005.

The story did not end there, however. Pressured by religious conservatives, the Republican Congress passed a law designed to get the feeding tube replaced by allowing Terri Schiavo's parents access to federal courts. Responding quickly, several different federal panels refused to hear the parents' case and Ms. Schiavo died on March 31. Again judges felt the wrath of the Christian right. House Majority Leader Tom DeLay roared that the courts had "thumbed their nose at Congress and the president." In somewhat cryptic language he threatened, "The time will come for the men responsible for this to answer for their behavior."[70] Senate Majority Leader Bill Frist denounced Supreme Court justices as "unelected and unaccountable, arrogant and imperious, determined to redesign the culture to their own biases and values."[71]

Pro-lifers did smell success when the GOP Congress inserted language into the fiscal 2005 omnibus appropriations bill that allowed certain health-care providers who received federal funds to refuse to offer abortions on conscientious grounds. In April 2005 the House passed a bill making it a federal crime for any adult to transport an under-age girl across state lines for an abortion without parental consent. Congress also enacted the Unborn Victims of Violence Act in 2004 and, by doing so, joined thirty-one states that already had such statutes. Proponents of the law, which was propelled to passage by the highly publicized murder of Laci Peterson and her unborn son Connor in California, argued that it had nothing to do with abortion and was designed to protect pregnant women. Even though the law applied only to federal offenses, opponents like Senator Dianne Feinstein (D-CA) feared "it will clearly place into federal law a definition of life that will chip away at the right to choose as outlined in *Roe v. Wade*."[72]

Recent judicial determinations on religious cases have helped mobilize social conservatives politically, as well. The Supreme Court's decision in the *City of Boerne* case may have restricted congressional power, but it upset social conservatives because the statute that was voided, the Religious Freedom Restoration Act, was designed to provide exemptions for religious behavior from generally applicable statutes. In February 2004 the court upheld the regulations of a Washington state scholarship program that prohibited students in religious programs from receiving awards.[73] More famously, in August 2003 a federal court ordered a 5,300-pound monument of the Ten Commandments removed from the building that housed the Alabama Supreme Court. The statue was directed there by the state's chief justice, Ray Moore, who refused to allow its transfer, even after a federal court ruled against him and he was reprimand by his associates and the Alabama attorney general. The spat provided good entertainment as the combative and straight-talking Moore joined with hundreds of demonstrative religious activists to protect the monument from removers. More crucially, along with similar incidents involving biblical symbols across the country, it also helped build sympathy for social conservatives. To be sure, Moore and his supporters looked like crackpots to many, but they did not seem particularly harmful. Indeed, in 1999 the House of Representatives comfortably passed an amendment allowing state governments to display the Ten Commandments. The judicial rulings, on the other hand, made federal and state courts seem persnickety and autocratic. An August 2003 CNN/*USA Today*/Gallup poll showed 77 percent of Americans disapproved of the decision against Moore.

School prayer is another issue important to social conservatives that generally elicits broad, if shallow, sympathy among the general public. A September 2003 CNN/USA Today/Gallup poll, for example, revealed that 78 percent of respondents supported "a nondenominational prayer as part of the official program at a public school ceremony such as a graduation or a sporting event." And again the judiciary has issued rulings that have brought controversy. In 2000, for example, the Supreme Court held that the Santa Fe school district's policy that allowed students to lead prayers prior to football games was in violation of the establishment clause of the First Amendment.[74]

The role of religion in public schools especially motivates the fledgling but rapidly growing home-school movement that, according to the Home School Legal Defense Association (HSLDA), is responsible for the education of over 2 million children. HSLDA is active in the religious community—a 1999 National Center for Education Statistics Study reported that nearly 40 percent of parents who home schooled their kids did so for religious reasons—and its political action is a thorn in the side of public education and teacher's unions, two critical components of the Democratic coalition.[75] As Michael Farris, founder of HSLDA, has said, "We are not home schooling our kids so they can read. The most common thing I hear is parents telling me they want their kids to be on the Supreme Court."[76]

Same-sex marriage has provided social conservatives with their most clarion and perhaps effective rallying cry, however. It is certainly true that the public has been increasingly tolerant of equal rights for homosexuals. The General Social Survey (GSS), for example, detected that Americans were becoming discernibly more accepting of gays and lesbians in the mid-1990s. In 1982 only 34 percent of respondents considered homosexuality "an acceptable lifestyle"; by 1996, 44 percent did.

In the summer of 2003, however, the Supreme Court reversed precedent created in the controversial *Bowers v. Hardwick* decision of 1986 and determined that a Texas law prohibiting same-sex sodomy violated the due process clause of the Fourteenth Amendment. Their decision in *Lawrence v. Texas* became immediately notorious. It outraged social conservatives and the religious right. Taking what seemed a highly personal position in dissent, Justice Antonin Scalia called the majority's position a "product of a law-profession culture, that has largely signed on to the so-called homosexual agenda."[77] Former GOP presidential candidate and president of the Christian group American Values, Gary Bauer, fumed, "Once again, an activist Supreme Court has substituted its judgment over the decisions of the citizens of Texas, who, through their elected representatives, had made a moral and legal judgment about behavior."[78] Calling the decision "classic judicial activism arrogance," Ken Connor, head of the Family Research Council, said, "This opens the door to bigamy, adult incest, polygamy, and prostitution."[79]

More worrisome for critics of the ruling, however, was that it would open the door to gay marriage—despite the passage of defense of marriage acts, including one at the federal level, defining marriage as a union between a man and a woman. In November 2003 this fear became alarmingly real. By arguing that its state had "failed to identify any constitutionally adequate reason" that gay couples should not be given the same marital rights as heterosexual ones, the Massachusetts Supreme Judicial Court took a step beyond the Vermont model of civil unions and asked its state's legislature to come up with an equitable resolution to what it considered an inherently unequal situation. Three months later, after the Massachusetts Senate had asked the court for guidance on a bill it was drafting allowing same-sex civil unions but not marriages, the judges responded unequivocally. "The dissimilitude between the terms 'civil marriage' and 'civil union' is not innocuous," they stated. "It is a considerable choice of language that reflects a demonstrable assigning of same-sex, largely homosexual, couples to second-class status."

Again the judges were viewed as radically liberal—evidence of a "runaway judiciary" House Majority Leader Tom DeLay called it.[80] Two months after the Massachusetts court's initial ruling, President Bush warned in his State of the Union address, "Activist judges ... have begun redefining marriage by court order. Our nation must defend the sanctity of marriage." In February 2004, the president officially proclaimed the necessity of a constitutional amendment to restrict marriages to one man and one woman. The fight was on and many Republicans set about protecting conventionally defined marriage. In this, they were supported by large numbers of the American people. Although only a very slim majority regularly expressed opposition to the kinds of civil unions that allowed same-sex couples the same legal rights and access to benefits as married couples—51 percent took this position in a January 2004 ABC News/*Washington Post* poll, for example—a much larger percentage wanted to prohibit formal marriages between homosexuals. A December 2003 CBS News/*New York Times* poll found 61 percent of respondents held this view; a Fox News/Opinion Dynamics poll of a month earlier discovered 66 percent did. This basic sentiment was reflected in the fact that, at the time of the Massachusetts ruling, thirty-eight states had laws defining marriage as a heterosexual institution that joined two people.

For social conservatives, the issue quickly became a mobilizing device, especially after municipal officials in places like San Francisco; New Paltz, New York; and Corvallis, Oregon, began issuing marriage licenses to same-sex couples. In the early fall of 2004, the House passed the Marriage Protection Act that stripped the federal courts of jurisdiction in same-sex marriage cases. Thirteen states moved rapidly to ballot citizens on whether there should be constitutional amendments banning the practice. All thirteen passed their referendums in convincing fashion. In both Michigan and Ohio even a majority of eighteen- to twenty-nine-year-olds voted yes, and the question came closest to defeat in Oregon where it still garnered the support of 57 percent of all voters. "I have never seen anything that has energized and pro-voked our grass roots like this issue, including *Roe v. Wade*," remarked Richard Land, a leader within the Southern Baptist Convention.[81] Tony Perkins of the Family Research Council observed that opposition to same-sex marriage "has unified and created a coalition of organizations that is unprecedented."[82] Paul Weyrich, a long-time conservative leader remarked, "I must say, we ought to have the mayor of San Francisco on our payroll. [He] really energized people in a way that would not have been possible."[83]

As a result, the 2004 Democratic presidential candidate trod softly, especially after two of the ballot initiatives—those in Louisiana and Missouri—passed handily that summer. Indeed, as Bill Clinton had with his "Don't Ask, Don't Tell" policy toward gays in the military a decade before, John Kerry acted as if he was tiptoeing through a minefield. He claimed he was for tradi-tional marriage but said that the matter should be determined by the states. In the final debate, he highlighted the fact that the vice president had a lesbian daughter in an attempt to divert attention from his own position and blur that of the Bush-Cheney ticket. Kerry's contorted stance became especially apparent when Senate GOP leaders brought up a vote on a same-sex marriage ban for the federal constitution. Kerry and his running mate, John

Edwards, did not participate and the amendment failed—it was defeated by a procedural maneuver. For Republicans the episode revealed the dramatic difference between the senator's wishy-washy position—an image that was successfully projected across many of Kerry's postures—and Bush's stalwart protection of traditional marriage. It also fired up social conservatives to come out and vote in the eleven states that had November gay marriage bans on the ballot—including key battlegrounds like Arkansas, Michigan, Ohio, and Oregon. This was because, in the words of Paul Schenck of the Gospel of Life Ministries, "When you toy with the sanctity [of marriage]—as ancient and primordial as it is—you are shaking the core of a community."[84] Liberal writer Thomas Frank suggested another reason the failure of a federal constitutional ban on gay marriage whipped religious conservatives into a frenzy. "Losing," he remarked, "is *prima facie* evidence that the basic conservative claim is true: that the country is run by liberals; that the world is unfair; that the majority is persecuted by a sinister elite."[85]

Religious and social conservatives, then, are using highly publicized judicial decisions on affirmative action, abortion, criminal defendants, homosexuality, and the relationship between church and state as devices to mobilize millions of supporters for political action. They especially have the federal courts in their cross hairs. In the past decade, there have been a series of conservative forums and papers highlighting harmful judicial activism and some concerted efforts to impeach federal judges such as Harold Baer, who suppressed evidence in a 1996 case that revealed that a defendant possessed eighty pounds of cocaine and heroin, and Thelton Henderson, who enjoined California's Proposition 209 that banned affirmative action.[86] More recently, Republican James Sensenbrenner of Wisconsin's House Judiciary Committee has been vocally critical of the sentencing habits of judges like James M. Rosenbaum and William G. Young.[87] Indeed, in 2003 conservatives in Congress were able to force passage of a measure requiring special scrutiny of judges who issue sentences shorter than those recommended by federal guidelines.

After the decision in the *Lawrence* sodomy case, Pat Robertson launched a "prayer offensive" to ask members of his 700 Club to persuade God to retire three Supreme Court justices. There was considerable chatter about impeaching Supreme Court Justice Anthony Kennedy because of his rulings on social issues and embrace of international norms and foreign law in his decisions. When the court handed down its decision on federal sentencing guidelines in January 2005, congressional conservatives threatened a swift response. They were further antagonized after the Schiavo episode. Leaders like Tom DeLay threatened mass impeachments and wholesale restrictions on court jurisdictions. This is all despite the fact that, as I have shown, there exists considerable empirical evidence that the courts are nudging policy to the right anyway.

Although much of this orchestrated vitriol is aimed directly at the courts, social conservatives are acutely aware that the president appoints federal judges who, in turn, must be confirmed by the Senate. Republicans in Washington are consequently exploiting the nexus between the elected and judicial branches to tap the energy of the religious right and its allies. President Bush and Senate Republicans, for example, have expended much time and energy pointing out that the Democratic minority in the Senate had, as of the end of the 108th Congress, filibustered or threatened to filibuster ten federal judicial nominees, including the highly publicized candidates, Miguel Estrada, Priscilla Owen, Charles Pickering, and William Pryor. Late in 2003, leaked Senate memos revealed a coordinated and concerted effort among staffers and liberal interest groups to block the more conservative of Bush's picks. The Senate GOP was outraged and tried to make political hay out of the episode. In November, Majority Leader Bill Frist of Tennessee organized an all-night Senate session to highlight the minority's obstructionist tactics. Just after the 2004 elections, in a furor over whether Arlen Specter of Pennsylvania should ascend to the chairmanship of the Senate Judiciary Committee, Frist suggested that the body's presiding officer might rule that filibusters on judicial nominations were out of order. Indeed, throughout the spring of 2005, the majority leader hinted he was ready to call the Democrats on the so-called "nuclear option." All of this accentuated the importance of strong command of the presidency and Senate to the ideological character of the federal bench.

Social conservatives have skillfully mobilized against the media, too. Groups such as the National Institute on Media and the Family and the Parents Television Council have tapped into a rich vein of public support with their attacks on sex, violence, and obscenity on television and in the movies and video games. A February 2004 Gallup poll revealed that about three in four Americans believed the "entertainment industry needs to make a serious effort to significantly reduce the amount of sex and violence in its movies, television shows, and music." A November 2004 CBS News/*New York Times* poll showed that 70 percent of respondents believed popular culture was "lowering moral standards." Although surveys showed the public was split on whether or not it was offended by singer Janet Jackson's infamous "wardrobe malfunction" during the 2004 Super Bowl half-time show, much of the momentum for the public's growing uneasiness with media content can be attributed to the event. It seems also to have stemmed from the proliferation of violent video games, the "reality TV" craze that hit network and cable programming in the first few years of the new century, and U2 singer Bono's audible expletive at the 2003 Golden Globes. In 2003 complaints to the Federal Communications Commission jumped to 250,000 from just a few hundred two years before.[88] After the Jackson incident the FCC, under pressure from Congress, updated its rules and levied a variety of punishments—especially on "shock jocks" like Howard Stern whose show was pulled by programming directors at Clear Channel Communications where he worked. In March 2004, the House passed a bill increasing maximum fines for the broadcasting of indecencies and vulgarities to $500,000. Unable to come to an agreement with the Senate, it passed essentially the same bill in early 2005. Viacom was ultimately fined $550,000 for the 2004 Super Bowl half-time show. Fox was later penalized $1.2 million for an April 2003 broadcast of *Married by America* that featured whipped-cream-covered strippers and digitally obscured nudity. All of this put the media—which, as we shall see in Chapter 8, a plurality of Americans feel is too liberal—on the back foot and resorting to a defensive self-censorship. An Indianapolis radio station rather ironically deleted the words "urinate," "damn," and "orgy" from a Rush Limbaugh show, for example.[89]

The transformation of judicial politics has brought dual bonanzas for the GOP, then. The courts have delivered the kinds of policy many conservatives want, while simultaneously providing them with a succinct and passionate rationale to persuade the public to vote Republican. Whereas the achievement of policy goals generally sucks the wind out of a party's sails, some highly publicized judicial behavior continues to energize Republican campaigns and mobilize the Republican electorate.[90] A diffuse but highly organized, politically astute, well-funded, and very motivated social conservative movement has, in turn, helped the GOP harness and capitalize upon this feeling about the courts. There are literally hundreds of these groups. They include those concerned directly with judicial appointments and legal issues like the 35,000-member Federalist Society, the Alliance Defense Fund, the American Center for Law and Justice, the Center for Constitutional Jurisprudence, the Center for Individual Rights, the Free Congress Foundation, the Institute for Justice, and Judicial Watch. Also included are those that promote conservative social policy like Focus on the Family, which has annual revenues of about $130 million and a campus in Colorado so large that it has its own zip code, the Alliance for Marriage, the American Family Association, the Center for Reclaiming America, the Christian Coalition, Concerned Women for America, the Family Research Council, the Moral Majority, National Right to Life, Operation Rescue, and the Traditional Values Coalition.[91] Most have multi-million dollar annual budgets and tens of thousands of members with whom they communicate by e-mail, Web sites, and newsletters. Focus on the Family's James Dobson has a daily radio broadcast that is played on several thousand stations across the country. Pat Robertson's Christian Broadcasting Network is shown daily on millions of televisions, as is the religious Trinity Broadcasting Network. These groups lobby vigorously at the state and federal levels. They attempt to mobilize voters, as "The Battle for Marriage" and the Southern Baptists' "I Vote Values" voter registration campaigns in 2004 illustrated. Indeed, they have clearly done it successfully. An energetic voter-contacting campaign by large churches seemed to increase the evangelical vote in 2004 beyond the rise in turnout of the population as a whole—by some estimates 26.5 million evangelicals voted in 2004. This is consistent with extant social-science research that shows that when contacted in their churches, religious Americans are more likely to vote.[92]

These conservative groups are connected by overlapping goals and a large but tight-knit leadership that sets a common agenda—strategy is plotted by an exclusive and regular meeting of evangelical Christian leaders in what is called the "Arlington Group."[93] In 2003 the legal groups galvanized around affirmative action; in 2004, the social groups moved to push the resistance to gay marriage to the forefront; the next year it was the Schiavo episode.[94] Among the leaders of the legal groups are Clint Bolick, Eugene Mayer, Terence Pell, and Jay Sekulow. Among those that head the social groups are Gary Bauer, James Dobson, Wanda Franz, Deal Hudson, Andrea Lafferty, Richard Land, Tony Perkins, Lou Sheldon, Richard Viguerie, Paul Weyrich, and Donald Wildmon.

These groups also have a close relationship with the Bush White House. Tim Goeglein, head of the White House Office of Public Liaison, is well regarded among religious leaders. He led almost weekly conference calls between the administration and the religious hierarchy during the president's first term.[95] The religious right has been especially willing to go to bat for Bush because, in the words of John Micklethwait and Adrian Wooldridge, they see him "as one of their own number rather than as the head of a party that happens to be aligned with them."[96]

It is true that there are equivalent groups sympathetic to Democrats. They include the American Civil Liberties Union (ACLU), Americans United for the Separation of Church and State, People for the American Way, the National Abortion Rights Action League, and the National Organization of Women. They also have big budgets and large memberships—as the massive pro-choice march on Washington in April 2004 revealed. Perhaps because they are often defending status quo policy, however, these groups have not provided Democrats with the level of ebullient grassroots support that their conservative counterparts give the GOP.

It is also true that Americans are not as conservative on social issues as they once were. As Democratic pollsters Stanley and Anna Greenberg observed in early 2004, "It is hard not to be struck by America's growing diversity, tolerance of different lifestyles, social flexibility and openness to change, new roles for women, and skepticism about absolutes and religious truths."[97] Still, as we shall see in Chapter 9, the country is distinctively religious and has a penchant for traditional values that makes it quite unique among rich democracies—polls, for example, regularly reveal about three in five Americans feel religion is an important part of their lives whereas only about 20 percent of Europeans believe that.[98] As a result, while conservatives may not win every battle in the culture war, their attacks on the courts and efforts to move social policy rightward have not met with the kind of backlash that might be expected of the early twenty-first century.

Finally, we need to recognize that the Republicans have frequently exploited a political advantage in attacking another part of the legal community. Since the early 1990s, the party has tightly embraced an ambitious agenda of tort reform designed to protect business and health-care professionals from greedy trial lawyers who exploit tragic mistakes for their own financial self-interest.

The approach began as a reaction to dramatic increases in the cost of medical malpractice insurance and, according to William Haltom and Michael McCann, distorted and obsessive media reports about astronomical jury-awarded compensatory and punitive damages—such as the $2.9 million initially given to a New Mexico woman for burns suffered when she spilled a cup of McDonald's coffee on herself in 1992.[99] In 1994 aggressive tort reform became part of the House Republicans' "Contract with America" only for a watered-down bill—the Senate rejected a House-passed version providing significant legal protection for doctors, drug companies, and makers of medical equipment—to be vetoed by President Clinton. Clinton also put the kibosh on a GOP attempt to limit anti-securities fraud lawsuits in 1995.

In late 2003, tort reform picked up further momentum. It played a central role in George W. Bush's six-part agenda designed to revive the economy. All three components of Bush's plan for legal reform—a bill designed to force class-action lawsuits into more business-friendly federal courts, one written to limit damages in medical malpractice suits, and another to establish a trust fund to compensate asbestos victims and preempt the need for legal action—found themselves stymied by Democratic minorities in the Senate. Acting unilaterally, however, the administration adopted a policy of going to court to stop lawsuits from people who claimed they had been hurt by prescription drugs or medical devices.[100]

After John Kerry picked North Carolina senator and prolific trial lawyer John Edwards as his running mate in the summer of 2004, the GOP was even keener to display its position on the issue. In September, the Republican-led House of Representatives passed a bill sanctioning trial attorneys who file frivolous lawsuits. Republicans also frequently focused public attention on the fact that the North Carolinian made over $150 million for his clients, and possibly as much as $40 million for himself, during his days in the courtroom.

Even after reelection, Bush kept his foot on the gas. In the first weeks of 2005, he traveled around the country imploring the public to support attempts to revise the system of medical malpractice and asbestos-related lawsuits. Tort reform emerged as central to the collective GOP agenda. It was pushed energetically by Republicans at the state level. Moreover, in February 2005, Congress passed legislation forcing class-action lawsuits into the stingier federal court system and out of the states.

The issue of tort reform has therefore become a kind of double whammy for the GOP. First, it has begun to dilute the influence of trial lawyers in American politics. The profession, fueled by multi-million dollar cuts from jury awards, has become a deep-pocketed contributor to Democratic coffers. In 2002, for example, trial lawyers gave nearly $2.5 million to Democratic congressional candidates but only $300,000 to Republicans; in 2004 just about all of the $2.1 million donated by the profession went to Democrats. The GOP, according to Ed Lazarus, a Democrat with the Association of Trial Lawyers of America, is using its tort reform agenda to mobilize affected business groups and simultaneously "defund the Democratic Party."[101] Conservative Grover Norquist agrees. The Bush tort reform agenda, "will defund significantly some of the trial lawyer community, and it rewards the business community, the Fortune 500 guys who have been increasingly supportive of the broad center-right coalition," he has said.[102]

Second, the issue has been used to manipulate public opinion. The message has been that trial lawyers use the personal irresponsibility of citizens to leech off of wealth-creating and socially valuable medical professionals and businesses. Disseminated by groups like the American Tort Reform Association (ATRA), Citizens against Lawsuit Abuse, the Center for Consumer Freedom, and the U.S. Chamber of Commerce-affiliated Institute for Legal Reform, this narrative has been affirmed by stories of multi-million dollar settlements against manufacturers of drugs—such as the $1 billion finding against the makers of the diet pill fen-phen in 2004—and cigarettes—such as the $10.1 billion finding by a notorious court in Madison County, Illinois, against Phillip Morris for fraudulently touting its "light" cigarettes in 2003. Even more compelling have been the stories of people blaming their obesity on fast-food restaurants—McDonald's paid out $12 million for not disclosing that it used beef fat when cooking its fries—and doctors quitting the profession because of suffocating malpractice insurance rates—in 2003 Pennsylvania doctors went on strike because of rapidly rising premiums and the American College of Obstetricians and Gynecologists reported that twelve states faced a shortage of providers as OB-GYNs left their practices.[103] Bottom-line figures—such as the Bush White House's estimation that the U.S. tort system costs the nation's economy about $180 billion annually—also drive the point home.[104]

The public seems sympathetic to the message. In March 2004 the House passed a ban on lawsuits against fast-food restaurants by 276 to 139. Over a dozen states have established laws to the same effect. A January 2003 Kaiser Family Foundation Health Care Report poll found that 74 percent of respondents believed medical malpractice had reached a "crisis" or was a "major problem." Seventy-two percent said they favored putting limits on damages for "emotional pain and suffering." A July 2003 Gallup poll found that 89 percent of Americans opposed holding fast-food restaurants legally culpable for customers' diet-related health problems. A February 2003 ATRA poll found that 83 percent of Americans felt that there are too many lawsuits filed in the United States, and 76 percent believed "excessive lawsuits" result in higher costs for them. Even if ATRA's poll may not be fully reliable, it is true that historically about three-fourths of Americans report to disliking lawyers and three-fifths think they are greedy.[105] A November 2003 Gallup poll reported that only 16 percent of Americans felt that lawyers had "high" or "very high" levels of honesty and ethical standards.

Recent and spectacular Republican gains in state government and the federal judiciary have therefore largely gone unnoticed. The party is governing stealthily from these two platforms and, most notably from the bench, it is moving policy in a rightward direction. Businesses and property owners are generally being protected from government regulation, for example, and federalism has renewed meaning in the American political vernacular.

Despite these important and palpable gains, the public has not tapped the brakes. Instead, its thinking has been influenced by a variety of high-profile judicial decisions that make many believe the federal courts hold values to the left of the American mainstream. This is especially the case on social issues such as abortion, homosexual rights, and the role of religion in public life. These decisions have had the added benefit of mobilizing large and well-funded GOP-allied social conservative groups that have provided considerable grassroots energy for the party. The ultimate effect is that Republicans get the public policy they want while enjoying a critical electoral boost. Interestingly, something similar seems to be occurring on foreign policy. That is the topic of the next chapter.

5

Trapping the Donkey: Foreign Policy as Republican Advantage

In the 2000 election, only 12 percent of voters said that world affairs was the issue that mattered most to them in choosing between presidential candidates. Republican George W. Bush clearly shared the view of many voters, then, when he criticized the Clinton administration for spending too much time on foreign policy. In the second presidential debate at Wake Forest University on October 11, Bush argued that, especially in cases like Haiti and Somalia, the United States had become too involved in "nation building." The country's military, in other words, "is meant to fight and win war" in the promotion of the country's immediate national security interests—it should, by inference, be deployed less frequently. He did agree with the President on his Balkan policy, but the governor's philosophy, at least as it was described that October night, was clear. The U.S. armed forces should not be in the business of overthrowing dictatorships or mediating civil wars. Establishing and nurturing democracies was even more incongruent with their mission.

This Bush campaign's foreign policy was more thoroughly—and perhaps more articulately—sketched out by the Texan's aides throughout 2000. In molding ideas written down earlier in the same year, Condoleezza Rice—who was to become Bush's National Security Adviser and later Secretary of State—and Robert Zoellick—who was to become U.S. Trade Representative and later

Rice's deputy at State—called for a multifaceted foreign policy that had clear core principles and that was at odds with the Clinton administration's extant approach.[1] The first part of this foreign policy consisted of a recognition of American military, political, and economic power and a feeling that the United States should not feel ashamed to project it. As a benevolent, and sole, super-power, appropriate expressions of American strength could be used to uphold international security and law, protect international organizations, and help alleviate poverty and hardship. U.S. military superiority could also be marshaled in technologically advanced synergistic arrangements that unleashed campaigns of "shock and awe" to accomplish goals with minimal bloodshed, cost, and political fallout at home and abroad.[2] From this intellectual soil was to grow the institutionalized acceptance of preemption as a desirable and legitimate military strategy. In 2002, the president's National Security Strategy asserted that, in a world full of terrorists and rogue states that are driven by extremist doctrines, "We cannot let our enemies strike first."[3] This philosophy of preemption, of course, was to justify the Iraq war in 2003—in a speech about the war given to the United Nations later that year, Bush implored countries to "have the wisdom and the will to stop grave threats before they arrive." Even before he became president, then, it seemed to be the case that Bush was not an isolationist, he just advocated a "distinctly American internationalism."[4]

Yet, and this was critical to the second part of the policy, the United States should pursue its direct interests strictly. If world events had only tangential connections with U.S. security concerns and economic and political interests, they should be left to unfold on their own or with the intervention of the powers that inhabited the region where they occurred. When it comes to use of the military, a president should realize that "it is not a civilian police force. It is not a political referee. And it is most certainly not designed to build a civilian society."[5] "The Eighty-second Airborne," Rice once argued, should not be "escorting kids to kindergarten."[6] As Bush himself said during a speech at the Citadel in 1999, "We will not be permanent peacekeepers, dividing warring parties."[7]

Third, the policy asserted that there are people who hate America and wish to do it harm. This was not exactly breaking news—Al Qaeda had devastatingly attacked U.S. embassies in East Africa in 1998 and the World Trade Center had been bombed in 1993—but, critically, the point was delivered in language shrouded in optimism and a dose of self-righteousness. To Bush, Osama Bin Laden and Saddam Hussein were "evil doers"; countries like Iraq, Iran, and North Korea formed what he was later to call an "Axis of Evil." They would undoubtedly be defeated. The United States, on the other hand, stood for freedom and democracy; it was, to use Ronald Reagan's words, "a shining city on the hill." It would be victorious. American motives, then, were beyond reproach and American actions, because of Bush's "soaring conviction that courageous intentions must inevitably produce pleasing results," would ultimately be successful.[8]

Fourth and last, the Bush foreign policy maintained an intrinsic mistrust of international organizations and arrangements. Institutions like the United Nations and foreign powers with interests sometimes different from those of the United States presented barriers to effective policy designed to protect American security. They unfairly and dangerously shackled America. The Bush people clearly believed that the "way to secure America's security was to shed the constraints imposed by friends, allies, and international institutions."[9] To Zoellick, "international agreements and institutions" are "means to achieve ends" and are not, as he thought Democrats viewed them, "forms of political therapy."[10] In the context of military conflict, Defense Secretary Donald Rumsfeld enunciated the approach by arguing that "wars can benefit from coalitions of the willing, but they should not be fought by committee."[11]

Bush's philosophy of foreign policy was, therefore, a strange amalgam—on one hand it seemed internationalist, on the other inward looking. His national security policy was also considered a sort of realist-unilateralist mix.[12] Whatever one wanted to call it, however, the foreign policy was consistent with ideas that were gaining traction in Republican circles. Before the Cold War forged a bipartisan consensus, the GOP had been the party distrustful of things foreign. Between the two world wars many vociferous and influential Republicans—like Senators William E. Borah of Idaho and Gerald P. Nye of North Dakota—demanded the United States extricate itself from international affairs. Republicans were also instrumental in securing the passage of the 1935 Neutrality Act. During the 1976 presidential campaign, Bob Dole called American-involved conflagrations "Democrat Wars."

In the mid-1990s, with the Soviet Union dead, few visible threats, and a Clinton administration keen to exhaust American

military resources in the name of humanitarian missions under
the direction of international organizations, a new breed of conservative Republican resurrected the idea that the United States
should be distrustful of the world and inimical to much internationalist thinking. The first signs of this came during the last few
years of the Cold War, when surveys of elites revealed that
Republicans were more likely to take a hard line with the Soviet
Union, Democrats to be a little more "accommodationist."[13] In
1992 the Defense Planning Guidance document, known to be the
work of then Secretary of Defense Dick Cheney, was crafted.[14]
This stated that the United States should pursue its interests unilaterally and forcefully. Pat Buchanan also ran for the Republican
presidential nomination against President George H. W. Bush on
an "America First" theme. By 1994 the Republicans' "Contract
With America" was calling for the "restricted deployment of
United States troops to missions that are in the national interest
of the United States" and the maintenance of "command and
control by United States personnel of United States forces participating in United Nations peacekeeping operations."[15] An
inication of the isolationist and go-it-alone predisposition of
the new Republican elite could be seen by the fact that two-
thirds of the GOP's new freshman House class did not have a
passport. As Stephen M. Walt has put it, the public that year
"elected a Congress whose disdain for foreign affairs is almost
gleeful."[16] Simultaneously, a broad network of neoconservatives—
that counted Richard Armitage, John R. Bolton, William Kristol,
Richard Perle, Donald Rumsfeld, and Paul Wolfowitz among its
members—was utilizing vehicles like the Project for the New
American Century to mine ideas and pull together a coherent
post–Cold War conservative foreign policy.[17] By October 1999,
when the Republican-controlled Senate rejected the Comprehensive
Test Ban Treaty (CTBT), Bill Clinton believed he had identified
it and spoke stridently about the "new isolationism" of the GOP.

Bush's foreign policy stance may have been part of an evolu-
tionary change within his party then, but it jarred with the kind
of tepid internationalism, multilateralism, and idealism that the
country and its government subscribed to in the 1990s. Indeed,
John Lewis Gaddis has called the president's first-term foreign
policy "the most sweeping redesign of U.S. grand strategy since
the presidency of Franklin D. Roosevelt."[18] Bush presented, to
quote Samantha Power, an "iron fist" that dramatically contrasted
with Clinton's "invisible hand."[19] Clinton used American influence

halfheartedly in his attempts to bring peace and human rights to places like Haiti, Somalia, the Middle East, and Northern Ireland—although, to be fair, he had some significant successes. In the Balkans, where the United States was drawn into the nasty ethnic and religious fighting brought about by the unraveling of Yugoslavia, Clinton expended more energy and resources, but as with the other interventions, it was hard to make the argument that Bosnia and Kosovo directly impacted American strategic and economic interests.[20] The operations in the Balkans were also obviously multilateral.

What is more, Bush's philosophy was somewhat different from his father's who, as vice president, a member of the eastern aristocracy despite his late-in-life residential apostasy, and ambassador to the United Nations and China, was groomed as an internationalist. In the first year of his presidency alone, the elder Bush made 190 phone calls to foreign leaders and met personally with them 135 times.[21] He also led a thirty-four-country coalition to fight the 1991 Gulf War. The justification for Operation Desert Storm came from twelve United Nations resolutions and was the liberation of the Kuwaiti people who, in egregious violation of international law, had been invaded by Saddam Hussein's Iraqi forces. By invading Panama to rid the world of the despot and drug dealer Manuel Noriega, George H. W. Bush invoked, according to conservative columnist Charles Krauthammer, a disconcerting amount of international "legalism."[22] The defense budget was chopped by 11 percent between 1989 and 1991. Despite his pithy "New World Order," the first Bush may not, as many have claimed, had much of an overarching foreign-policy philosophy—he suffered when it came to "the vision thing"—but his actions certainly exhibited fragments of principles more consistent with Clinton than his son.[23]

The dissonance created by the clash of extant and new foreign policies was amplified in the early days of George W. Bush's administration. In 2001 the United States pulled out of the global climate change agreement known as the Kyoto Protocol and the Anti-ballistic Missile Treaty with Russia. In May 2002 it notified the International Criminal Court that it would not live up to its intent to become a party to the treaty that created the institution. The Bush administration also showed no inclination to join the Ottawa treaty to negotiate an end to landmines.

These actions initially threatened to be a liability. Bush's fundamental approach seemed out of step with the positions of most

Americans. The country had for decades rejected the thesis, by roughly a two-to-one margin, that "we should go our own way in international matters, not worrying too much about whether other countries agree with us or not."[24] By about three-to-one, Americans consistently approved of Gallup's statement, first offered to respondents in the mid-1940s, that the United States should play "an active role in world affairs" rather than "stay out of world affairs."[25] In a February 2001 CNN/*USA Today*/ Gallup poll, 54 percent of respondents believed the United Nations was doing a "good job"; only 38 percent of them thought it was doing a "poor job." A June 1999 Gallup poll revealed that 61 percent of Americans wanted the United States to play an active part in world affairs. Even worse news for the president's foreign policy came from an October 1999 Program on International Policy Attitudes (PIPA) poll. It revealed that 56 percent of respondents felt that "it will be increasingly necessary for the United States to work through international organizations" while 39 percent agreed that "international institutions are slow and bureaucratic" and that "the United States should try and solve problems like terrorism and the environment on our own instead." Along the same lines, in a 2000 PIPA poll, 49 percent favored the use of force through the United Nations, 26 percent through NATO, and only 17 percent favored the unilateral use of force when given a choice between the three. To be sure, many polls continued to illustrate that the public felt the United States gave away too much foreign aid and was too quick to try and remedy world problems. A June 2002 *Washington Post*/Kaiser Family Foundation/Harvard University poll revealed that 56 percent of Americans felt too much was spent on foreign aid; 8 percent said too little was being spent. Chicago Council on Foreign Relations surveys have consistently shown a plurality of Americans believe tariffs should be increased.[26] But most public opinion surveys revealed the American public to be at least mildly approving of international organizations and multilateral actions.[27]

On specific issues there was an even clearer repudiation of the new Bush administration's positions. In a 2001 Harris Poll, 70 percent of respondents approved of the Kyoto Protocol, and 46 percent believed that the Bush administration was wrong in pulling the country out of it—only 42 percent thought the president took the correct course of action. In a 1999 NBC News/*Wall Street Journal* survey taken directly after the Senate's rejection of the

CTBT, 46 percent of respondents disapproved of the upper chamber's actions; only 28 percent approved.

Then, on the morning of September 11, 2001, four hijacked commercial airliners were crashed, approximately 3,000 Americans were dead, and an icon of capitalism, New York City's World Trade Center, was destroyed. Much of daily American life was dramatically changed and the sense of tranquility and invulnerability that pervaded the 1990s was shattered. The response to the worst terrorist attack in American history was consistent with Bush's extant foreign policy. As Ivo Daalder and James Lindsay have written, September 11 "did more to reaffirm Bush's view of the world than to transform it."[28] If Bush's policy changed, it did so quantitatively, not qualitatively—in Melvyn P. Leffler's words, the attacks meant that "the administration's threshold for risk was dramatically lowered, its temptation to use force considerably heightened."[29] Less than a month after the strikes, the president was leading a military effort to overthrow the Taliban government of Afghanistan that had sheltered Osama Bin Laden and Al Qaeda. This was an impressive show of American force and resolve justified with moralistic language. A massive air assault, much of it launched from two aircraft carriers, assisted later by a little under ten thousand U.S. troops—all at a cost of about $1 billion a month—quite easily destroyed the Taliban. Bush enveloped the action in emotive words. "Freedom and fear are at war," he said in his famous address to the nation from the House chamber on September 20, 2001. "The advance of human freedom, the great achievement of our time, and the great hope of every time, now depends on us."

September 11 had an additional and critical political ramification, however. It made American foreign policy a crucial part of the elephant's edge. This happened for two reasons. First, the terrorist attacks made foreign policy a vibrant issue again; they gave international affairs a new salience. Prior to September 11, Americans may have held views about foreign policy that put them at odds with the Bush administration. Their views may also have been reasonably stable and rational.[30] But public positions were based primarily on an ignorance of the world. Americans consistently believed, for example, that 20 percent of the U.S. budget went to foreign aid when, in reality, it was less than 1 percent. This was a direct result of a dearth of information readily available to Americans about international affairs.[31] Scholars have shown that the public relies on the mainstream media and presidential attention to international issues to become interested in foreign affairs.[32] If attention is not paid—as Richard Haas argues was the case under the Clinton administration—then foreign policy moves to the edge of public consciousness.[33] A product of the peace and prosperity of the late 1990s was that, according to polls, Americans looked inward. We partied on the stock-market boom, content in the knowledge that the Cold War was over and the United States was the world's dominant power. Foreign policy seemed unimportant—exit polls revealed that 12 percent felt it was the most important issue in 2000; only 4 percent did in 1996.

After 9/11, however, foreign and security issues took center stage in American public life. In a CBS News poll done on the weekend before the November 2002 midterm vote, 47 percent of respondents felt that national security and terrorism should be the country's top priority, 46 percent the economy. There is some disagreement as to what allowed the GOP in 2002 to become only the second presidential party since 1934 to pick up, and not lose, House seats in an off-year election—the Democrats of 1998 were the first. But September 11 and Bush's response were surely critical—as Chuck Todd of *The Hotline*, characterized the election, "Air Force Won."[34] Republicans did well because Bush's approval ratings were, as a direct result of his responses to terrorism, high and because Al Qaeda's strike allowed the GOP to escape blame for a still weak economy.[35]

By 2003 Americans seemed to care about only two things—their economy and the nation's security in a turbulent world. They worried more about international politics than at any time since the Berlin Wall came down nearly a decade and a half earlier. Issues like education, the environment, and health care, traditionally important to them, receded. A January 2003 CBS News/*New York Times* poll revealed 30 percent of respondents to feel issues like Iraq, war, and terrorism were the most important facing the nation, 28 percent the economy and jobs. An NBC News/*Wall Street Journal* poll in June 2004 found that 47 percent believed Iraq or terrorism would be the most important issue to them as they chose candidates in the upcoming election. Thirty-four percent of respondents in the 2004 national exit poll said Iraq or terrorism were the most important issue. Thirty-eight percent of respondents in the Pew 2004 election follow-up poll cited Iraq, terrorism, or foreign policy as the one issue that "mattered most" to them when they voted for president. *New York Times* reporter Adam

Nagourney's informal survey of top Democrats found that the 2004 election was "shaped by the fears and memories of September 11, and memories of Mr. Bush's steely performance in the days after the attacks."[36] Gary Langer, the director of polling at ABC News, argued that the reason Bush won "can be expressed in a single phrase: 9/11."[37] When asked to account for what happened in that election, Democratic Party chair Terry McAuliffe explained, "The die was cast on September 11."[38] John Kerry wholeheartedly agreed in the first television interview he gave—to Tim Russert of *Meet the Press*—after the election.

Second, post-9/11 the public returned to trusting Republicans on foreign and defense policy more than they did the Democrats. During the Reagan years, the percentage of people who generally thought that the Republicans were, of the two parties, "more likely to keep U.S. defenses strong" hovered in the mid-1960s. It had slipped in the mid-1990s, and in 1999 a CBS News/*New York Times* poll recorded the figure at 57 percent. It looked as though the Democrats had shed their "Vietnam Syndrome"—their propensity to equivocate and look squeamish when it came to using military force. The wars on terror and Saddam Hussein, however, reversed that slight GOP decline. In a May 2003 CBS News/*New York Times* poll, 66 percent of respondents chose the GOP in their answer to the question, and in the same poll, whereas 58 percent thought the Republicans were "more likely to make the right decisions when it comes to terrorism," only 18 percent believed the Democrats were. Indeed, the GOP continued to enjoy advantages over the Democrats on all sorts of international issues. A CNN/*USA Today*/Gallup poll in January 2002, taken at the zenith of Bush's popularity, reported 41, 38, and 26 percent more respondents picked the Republicans over the Democrats than vice versa when choosing the party that would do a "better job" on military/defense, terrorism, and foreign affairs. Indeed, even Democrats thought the Republicans did a better job on these issues. In an October 2002 version of the CBS News/*New York Times* poll, 46 percent of Democrats picked the Republican Party—as opposed to 36 percent choosing their own—as the party "more likely to keep U.S. defenses strong." Even when the post-war management of Iraq became unpopular, the public approved of Bush's use of foreign policy at a higher rate than they did his handling of the economy. In an October 2003 CBS News/*New York Times* poll, 44 percent approved of the president on foreign policy, only 37 percent on the economy.

In an attempt to meet this challenge, the Democrats picked John Kerry, a three-time Purple Heart recipient and twenty-year veteran of the Senate, as their presidential nominee in 2004. With Kerry's strong foreign policy credentials and a general feeling that the war in Iraq was not going too well, Democrats seemed to have erased much of the GOP advantage on international issues during the campaign. A July 2004 Pew poll, for instance, revealed that 40 percent of respondents felt the Democrats were the better party on both foreign policy generally and Iraq in particular; 38 percent believed it was the GOP. Yet clearly, when push came to shove, a majority of voters just could not accept the argument that the country was safer with Democrats in charge. Although pluralities frequently disapproved of Bush's job in Iraq when answering polls around election day, Americans manifestly demonstrated more confidence in the president to handle the critical foreign and national security issues. Exit polls showed that 58 percent trusted Bush more when it came to terrorism; only 40 percent trusted Kerry more. In the final ABC News/*Washington Post* pre-election poll, Bush won fifty to forty-one on the issue of Iraq.

This all happened despite many liberal journalists' argument that terrorism would be a liability for the Republican president. Maureen Dowd of the *New York Times*, for example, expressed surprise that Bush's approval ratings remained high in early 2004, "even though Osama and Al Qaeda are still lurking and frothing, even though we couldn't get through the holidays without an orange alert and flights (from Europe and Mexico) being canceled, and even though Iraq is still a free-fire zone after a war to get rid of weapons that may not have existed."[39] She should not have been astonished. For most Americans, this was the way of the post-9/11 world. Primed by that shuddering day in New York and Washington, Americans folded these irritants seamlessly into everyday life. As the British came to live with disruptions and disconcerting scares during the Irish Republican Army's days of terror, so did Americans. Seventy-one percent of the public in a September 2004 CBS News/*New York Times* poll agreed that "Americans will always have to live with the threat of terrorism." Indeed, these regular inconveniences may even have convinced them the government was working to make them more secure. In a January 2004 CBS News/*New York Times* poll, 68 percent thought the president had made the United States less prone to terrorist attacks. According to exit polls that November, 54 percent said they thought the country was safer from terrorist attack than it was four years before. A February 2005 CNN/*USA Today*/Gallup poll showed that 73 percent of respondents had a "great deal" or "moderate amount" of confidence in the Bush administration's ability to protect them from future terrorist attacks. If anything, this figure was an improvement on those gleaned by the poll throughout 2003 and 2004.

Perhaps the fact that the public trusted Republicans more on foreign policy after 9/11 represented a sort of return to normalcy, a reversion to the GOP's domination of the issue in the 1970s and 1980s. Remember how ridiculous Michael Dukakis looked in that tank in 1988? "Rocky the Flying Squirrel" he was derisively called. The fact that Americans strongly supported Bush's distinctive approach to international matters was a little surprising, however. As I noted earlier, Bush's foreign policy directly challenged much of the orthodoxy. How was the president able to reestablish the GOP advantage on foreign policy when his agenda contradicted much of the country's core feelings about the world?

Bush was assisted tremendously by what presidential scholar John Mueller has called the "rally effect" or "the sudden and substantial increase in public approval of the president that occurs in response to certain kinds of dramatic international events involving the United States."[40] As head of state, the president inevitably benefits from the bursts of patriotism with which Americans respond to threats on their country. Such rally effects are often ephemeral and confer political advantages only to the president and not to his party. They rarely move politics.

But in this instance, the rally effect allowed Bush's foreign policy to lay down strong roots and grow a thick trunk before it was buffeted by the winds of political debate. At least in retrospect, it was clear from the 2000 campaign that Bush and his retinue wanted to inject radically new thinking into the Defense and State Departments. Doing so after such a contentious election was perilous, and according to a CBS News/*New York Times* poll in June 2001, only 48 percent of respondents approved of Bush's handling of foreign policy. Little changed in the president's philosophy over the next four months, but by October the same poll found 74 percent did so.

September 11 had given Bush the opportunity to change the direction of the United States' approach to the world because the event represented, according to Christopher Arterton, "the well-spring of his legitimacy."[41]

Moreover, as James Traub has argued, 9/11 "recreated elements of both the psychological and the strategic environment of the '60s."[42] The United States was again a target and Americans felt threatened. This is precisely the kind of environment in which the country desires Republican forcefulness.

Successful application of the Bush policy also helped, of course. Although Osama Bin Laden remained at large, the Taliban was swiftly dispatched, Al Qaeda's leadership decimated, and Saddam Hussein imprisoned; all, it can legitimately be claimed, with minimal fuss and loss of life. Both Afghanistan and Iraq remained unstable for some time after major combat operations and a vibrant insurgency, spiraling costs, the problems organizing the transition to indigenous rule, and the inability of the Bush administration to find weapons of mass destruction (WMD) all cast serious doubts on the economic, military, and diplomatic gainfulness of the Iraqi enterprise. Whereas in April 2003 the CNN/*USA Today*/Gallup poll revealed 73 percent of respondents believed going to war with Iraq was worthwhile; only 50 percent did in its September 2003 version. By early fall 2004, the fruitless search for WMD, a lack of evidence connecting Saddam with Al Qaeda, and the loss of over one thousand American lives caused the figure to slip further—it was 46 percent in a September ABC News/*Washington Post* survey. Still, although the administration was heavily criticized for its post-war actions, it had exhibited the strength and will of the United States, and both wars were generally viewed as military successes.

Polling data illustrate this. In an October 2003 CBS News/*New York Times* poll, taken at the height of worries about the post-war situation in Iraq, 59 percent of respondents claimed the Bush administration had not "developed a plan for rebuilding" the country after the war, and 66 percent felt that the war had cost more than they expected. Yet, 51 percent still felt the war was worth it when they were reminded by the questioner that Saddam Hussein had been removed from power, and 46 percent—a plurality—believed that getting rid of Saddam was the principal *casus belli*. In an ABC News/*Washington Post* poll of the same month, only 47 percent of respondents approved of the job Bush was doing on Iraq, but 54 percent of them felt the war was worth fighting. As Bush faced sharp criticism during the 2004 campaign, majorities still saw the war as valuable. Fifty-one percent of respondents in the 2004 national exit poll approved of the decision to go into Iraq. In the aftermath of what were generally considered successful elections at the end of January 2005, the public felt even better about it. Fifty-three percent of respondents to a March CBS News/*New York Times* poll said they thought the efforts to restore order and stability to Iraq were going "well" or "reasonably well."

In the eyes of many Americans, world events also vindicated Bush's foreign policy. This was not just because the president's central strategy to spread freedom and democracy was demonstrably working—during the winter of 2004–2005 newly acquired political liberties were on display in Ukraine, Iraq, Palestine, Lebanon, and Saudi Arabia. Bush, as I have noted, saw the world with tremendous clarity and believed vehemently in the righteousness and ultimate success of American values. The events of 9/11 dramatically simplified what had become an increasingly complex and unideological world. The fall of the Soviet Union, globalization, and the worldwide expansion of American culture had, for many Americans, blurred international differences and made foreign policy—on the few occasions it was of any import—about issues like trade and aid. The Bush campaign and then his administration's talk of danger and evil seemed at best naïve, at worst destabilizing, but on that fateful day, any obfuscation was removed. Bush's language found tremendous resonance. The United States and its western allies were at war with radical Islam, and the stakes were massive. One side stood for good, the other for evil. The conflagration was to be long, bloody, and to the death.

Immediately principles like international cooperation and friendship were cast in new terms. Instead of a complex world in which most countries worked together within international organizations to solve international problems, the administration viewed everybody with suspicion. A nation was either with us or against us and international institutions could not be trusted to be fair adjudicators of conflicts. At first a pervasive deference to American attitudes and actions emerged from a widespread international sympathy for 9/11, but Iraq split the west, with France, Germany, and Russia vehemently against the U.S.-British position of removing Saddam Hussein by force. This, in turn, ignited vitriolic criticism of Bush and the United States in large swaths of Europe. An October 2003 EOS Gallup Europe poll revealed that in excess of 50 percent of people in Spain, Ireland,

France, the Netherlands, and the United Kingdom felt the United States "presented a threat to world peace." On average, 53 percent of respondents answered the question in the affirmative, and the United States trailed only Israel—but was in front of Iraq, Afghanistan, Pakistan, and China—as the greatest menace.

Much of the anger seemed to be the product of the international media's exaggerated portrait of Bush as some kind of unpolished, uncouth, and unintelligent cowboy—Italy's *La Repubblica* newspaper once reported that the Texan needed to understand "that the world is not his family ranch, full of mustangs to tame with America's lasso."[43] Certainly many foreigners said their current dislike of U.S. policy was based upon antipathy of Bush rather than inherent dislike of Americans. Before 9/11 the president was especially vilified for Texas' aggressive use of the death penalty; French education minister Jack Lang put him on par with a "serial killer."[44] During the Iraq occupation, a March 2004 Pew poll found that the president had an 85 percent negative rating in France and Germany. An Ipsos-Public Affairs poll in December 2004 revealed that these numbers had barely budged, and Bush's reelection had made him no more popular across the Atlantic. Michael Moore's caustic documentary about Bush, *Fahrenheit 9/11*, won the coveted Palme d'Or prize at the 2004 Cannes film festival. Moore's equally acerbic books were bestsellers in Europe, and he became a kind of cult hero to many on the continent. An October 2004 poll conducted by ten of the world's leading newspapers found that a large majority of voters in eight of the ten countries surveyed—Israel and Russia were the exceptions—wanted John Kerry to win the following month's presidential election. Britain's ambassador to Italy, Ivor Roberts, called Bush, "the best recruiting sergeant ever for Al Qaeda."[45]

Regardless of their origins, however, foreign attitudes toward the United States itself deteriorated remarkably. Although the most dramatic disintegration in international approval of the United States came in the buildup to the war with Iraq—57 percent of the French had an unfavorable view of the country in June 2003—dramatic erosion occurred soon after sympathy for the 2001 terrorist attacks wore off.[46] In 1999–2000, for example, 78 percent of Germans had a "favorable" view of the United States; in 2002, 61 percent did, and by June 2003 this figure was 45 percent.[47] A Pew poll in early 2004 found that 61 percent of the French and 65 percent of Germans felt that the U.S. war on terrorism was not "sincere." Poll director Andrew Kohut detected "trends that speak to a more long-term and continuing disconnect between the old allies."[48] Ziauddin Sardar and Merryl Wyn Davies' antagonistic *Why Do People Hate America?* was widely read and met with considerable approval.[49] Emmanuel Todd's vituperative *After the Empire* was a bestseller in France.[50]

Americans came to realize this when they watched pictures of the huge crowds that protested Bush's state visit to Britain in November 2003. They saw it in the attitude of many foreign visitors who were subject to the new fingerprinting and photographing immigration procedures put into place by the United States in January 2004. In response, a Brazilian judge established a reciprocal policy in his country, calling the American procedure, "brutal, threatening human rights, violating human dignity, xenophobic and worthy of the worst horrors committed by the Nazis."[51]

The Democratic foreign policy elite fretted about international attitudes. Robert Kagan argued that, "America, for the first time since World War II, is suffering a crisis of international legitimacy."[52] At the Brookings Institution and Council on Foreign Relations, former Democratic administration aides like Ivo H. Daalder and James M. Lindsay feared Bush's "imperious style" was not only antagonistic but highly dangerous.[53] Former President Bill Clinton and his Secretary of State Madeleine Albright consistently criticized the Bush approach on the lecture circuit.

Yet, the foreign indignation of Bush's policy played into GOP hands. Many ordinary Americans reacted angrily to the criticism and rallied around Defense Secretary Donald Rumsfeld's somewhat condescending assertion that the French and Germans represented the tired "old Europe." Unlike citizens of most other advanced industrialized democracies, Americans are patriotic and do not take kindly to criticism of their country—the World Values Survey of 1999–2000, for instance, found that 72 percent of Americans were "very proud" of their country, while only 49 percent of Britons and 40 percent of the French were.

The split in the West also corroborated Bush's black-and-white view of the world. The French, Germans, and Russians were clearly not with us—the British, Italians, and Spaniards were. An August 2003 Harris poll revealed 43 percent of Americans considered France either "not friendly" or an "enemy"—by way of comparison, 37 percent described Russia in these terms. A summer 2004 Rasmussen survey showed that only 18 percent felt the

French were an ally in the war on terror. Beaujolais was poured down drains, and the House of Representatives famously renamed French fries as "freedom" fries.

What is more, the seemingly futile and interminable process of verifying Iraq as free of nuclear, chemical, and biological weapons, undertaken in the fall and winter of 2002 and 2003 and led by Hans Blix, only contributed to public feeling that the United Nations sided with the French and their crew. So did the decision to drop the United States from the Human Rights Commission in 2001. In the aftermath of 9/11, a February 2002 CNN/*USA Today*/Gallup poll found that 58 percent of Americans felt that the United Nations was doing a "good job." By August 2003 only 37 percent of them did. A summer 2004 Rasmussen survey revealed that only 21 percent of Americans felt the United Nations was an ally in the war on terrorism. To be sure, 68 percent felt the United Nations should supervise the establishment of a new Iraqi government in an October 2003 CBS News/ *New York Times* poll, but that was likely to have been a reaction to the inherent messiness of the exercise and Americans' unwillingness to pay for it all—something illustrated by the fact that 65 percent wanted to give other countries a "major role in making decisions about the rebuilding process" if these countries contributed significant funds for reconstruction.

The public was also attracted to the new GOP foreign policy because it asked relatively little of them. Bush spoke repeatedly about the tremendous challenge the war on terror presented, but he never really asked for broad sacrifice. The war was largely fought by several hundred thousand troops in the Middle East. At home, the costs of protecting airliners, bridges, sporting events, and nuclear power plants from terrorist attack was to be paid in the future as the administration and the Republican Congress drove up the deficit by simultaneously protecting key programs and providing tax cuts and homeland security. As George Packer put it, "Americans were told to go shopping and watch out for suspicious activity. Nothing would ever be the same, and everything was just the same."[54]

Quite simply, therefore, Bush had palpably changed the direction of U.S. foreign policy and given it a discernibly different look to that practiced by his father and Bill Clinton in the immediate post–Cold War years. Americans also generally approved of this foreign policy. Bush's view of the world seemed prescient and his tough demeanor made them feel secure. This all occurred at a time when international affairs and national security were greatly on their minds.

The fact that the Democrats had no real policy of their own added to the nascent GOP advantage on foreign affairs. Out of the White House and in the minority in both chambers of Congress, the Democrats were disadvantaged by the fact that they were on the political defensive and could not speak with one voice. They were extremely reticent to take the Republicans on over the decision to invade Iraq, for instance. Toward the end of the congressional debate about the war, perhaps cowered into acquiescence by GOP claims that opposition to Bush was unpatriotic—Speaker Dennis Hastert asserted that Senate Minority Leader Tom Daschle's complaints "had come mighty close" to "giv[ing] comfort to our adversaries"—they essentially approved the resolutions authorizing presidential use of force.[55]

The power of the president's argument about Iraq and the fear Democrats felt in opposing it are lucidly illustrated by comparing the votes to authorize force against Saddam Hussein in 1991 and 2002. The former, of course, came just before the start of the first Gulf War and the United States' case for military action rested on strong legal and diplomatic foundations. Saddam Hussein had invaded another sovereign country, and there was a large multinational coalition ready to evict him. In 2002 Iraq was only suspected of violating U.N. resolutions relating to weapons inspections, and the United States acted at the head of a small group of nations ready to go to war. Yet, in 1991 only 18 percent of Senate Democrats and 32 percent of House Democrats supported the resolution to use force. In 2002 these figures were 58 and 40 percent, respectively.

The Democrats did become a little more assertive as the postwar occupation of Iraq seemed to descend into chaos. Frequent guerilla attacks on U.S. personnel, astronomical costs, and no sign of Saddam's weapons of mass destruction emboldened some of its presidential field. Former Vermont governor Howard Dean and retired general Wesley Clark were, of those deemed to have a reasonable chance of winning the nomination, the most critical of Bush's execution of war. Both candidacies seemed to gather momentum by attacking Bush's policy; Dean was perhaps the biggest winner—he questioned the decision to go to war itself. Yet to many in the Democratic establishment, the more pro-war positions of Senators John Edwards, John Kerry, and

Joseph Lieberman presented a better platform from which to launch the operation to retake the White House. Kerry and Edwards, of course, went on to form the party's presidential ticket, but the popularity of Dean's anti-war message within many Democratic constituencies ensured the party would remain conflicted on Iraq.

Liberal intellectuals were also split—on human rights grounds many of them believed that dealing with the post-war pain was worth the trouble of getting rid of Saddam—and many continued to support the American occupation well after the main fighting had stopped.[56] Democratic members of Congress were also divided. Despite the howls of protest about Bush's post-war policy, the Democrats could not muster a united front in the face of the president's request for $87 billion to rebuild Iraq and Afghanistan in the fall of 2003. On original passage of the bill, eleven of forty-eight Democrats voted no in the Senate—the Senate version included some loans and was therefore a little more palatable for opponents—118 of 205 in the House went against the president. In the end the money was appropriated as a grant with nary a whimper of protest—the Senate passed the legislation by voice vote. Ultimately, then, fractured over Iraq, the Democratic Party chose not to take Bush on directly and adopt a contrasting position on national security policy. Instead, it fought Bush largely on his terrain and with a muddled message. In November 2004, of course, it also paid the price.

There was a fifth part to Bush's foreign policy we have not examined but should. This is trade. Bush considers himself a staunch advocate of free trade, and on this particular issue, he differed little from his Democratic predecessor who had helped craft the World Trade Organization (WTO), cleared up the final details regarding the North American Free Trade Agreement (NAFTA), and signed the Permanent Normal Trade Relations (PNTR) with China bill that was to greatly liberalize trade with the world's most populous nation. Bush secured fast track or trade promotion authority (TPA) for the chief executive— something Clinton was unable to achieve—and, as a consequence, went about signing free-trade deals without congressional interference. In 2003 he had agreements with Chile and Singapore ratified and began his pursuit of a U.S.-Middle East free-trade pact, giving the parties a 2013 deadline to get it done. Bush also breathed new life in the Doha free-trade talks meant to further push down tariffs and other barriers to economic interaction and continued the United States' pursuit of a Free Trade Area of the Americas that is designed to make the thirty-four countries of the western hemisphere the largest single market in the world. In 2004 the administration formalized the Central American Free Trade Agreement (CAFTA) that included the United States, five Central American Nations (Costa Rica, El Salvador, Guatemala, Honduras, and Nicaragua), and the Dominican Republic. It also announced open-trade arrangements with countries like Australia and Morocco.

Yet the Republican president could pragmatically bend his philosophy when necessary. In March 2002, in order to win support for TPA and egged on by a Karl Rove worried about political repercussions in states like Pennsylvania and West Virginia, Bush increased tariffs on steel imports by between 8 and 30 percent to protect domestic industry from dumping by competitors such as South Korea and Japan—a policy that was declared illegal by the WTO in November 2003 and, as a consequence, was then reversed after the European Union and others proposed punitive tariffs on American goods. Nudged by congressional Republicans, Bush also began to try to get the Chinese to devalue the yuan—the Chinese currency being seen as a principal cause of the United States' annual $162 billion trade deficit with the Asian country. In November 2003 the administration placed quotas on certain types of Chinese textile exports. In addition, Bush signed into law the farm bill of 2002, which, among other things, provided $40 billion per year in subsidies to help American agriculture in the global marketplace.

This dual approach has benefited Republicans. Americans tend to support free trade in the abstract—a February 2000 Pew poll found 64 percent felt "free trade with other countries" was good for the United States, and a May 2002 *Investors' Business Daily* (IBD)/*Christian Science Monitor* (CSM) poll found 52 percent thought it good for the American economy. They worry greatly about its effects on jobs, however. The same IBD/CSM poll found that 45 percent of respondents believed free trade loses more jobs than it creates; 24 percent believed that it creates more jobs than it loses. Sixty-one percent said they supported "restrictions on imported foreign goods to protect American jobs." Still, despite the incessantly bad press trade received as a result of the decline in manufacturing and the outsourcing issue in 2003 and 2004, a July 2004 Pew/Council on Foreign Relations poll revealed that

47 percent of respondents felt that free trade agreements like NAFTA and WTO were good for the United States; only 34 percent thought they were generally a bad thing.

Occasionally, the issue has Republicans tying themselves in knots. The Carolinas provide a good example of this. In the 1990s and early 2000s, the states' manufacturing base, especially its textile and furniture sectors, took a pounding in international markets. North Carolina's manufacturing sector lost over 200,000 jobs—shrinking by about 25 percent—in the decade between 1993 and 2003. As a result, Republican candidates in U.S. Senate races— Elizabeth Dole in 2002 and Richard Burr in 2004 for North Carolina and Lindsey Graham in 2002 and Jim DeMint in 2004 for South Carolina—distanced themselves from a basic free-trade approach. In August 2003 Dole and other members of the North Carolina Republican congressional delegation remonstrated against the administration after Pillowtex, a textile giant headquartered in Kannapolis, shut down, leaving over 6,400 without jobs. The company blamed cheap foreign imports.

During the December 2001 House TPA vote, Republicans Robin Hayes from the south-central part of North Carolina and Jim DeMint from Greenville-Spartanburg in South Carolina were strong-armed into voting for the presidential power. DeMint actually switched his vote after acquiring promises from the House GOP leadership that U.S. textile companies would receive protection from cheap imports from other countries in the hemisphere. Both were therefore able to demonstrate their concern for constituents and yet back the president. Both were reelected in 2002, DeMint by 39 percentage points.

The Senate Republican candidates in the Carolinas—including DeMint—were also elected in 2002 and 2004, all in competitive open-seat races. Sympathy for laid-off workers and anger at foreign countries and its own administration—Charlotte Republican Representative Sue Myrick called Bush "out of touch" when it came to trade—seems to have been enough, at least so far, to obfuscate the GOP position and inoculate many of the party's members of Congress from any backlash on the issue.

Despite the political gymnastics, there is considerable political vulnerability in the Republicans' fundamentally free-trade position. The Democrats, however, have been unable to take advantage of the GOP's liberal stance. The party is irrevocably split, with "New Democrat" types advocating trade liberalization and old-fashioned liberals a more protectionist position. During the Clinton years, the schism was highly visible. When PNTR for China was debated in the spring of 2000, for instance, the Democratic administration worked feverishly to persuade the American public and many skeptical Democrats that granting China a normalized trading relationship would open it up to democracy and freedom—"We will have more positive influence with an outstretched hand than with a clenched fist," Clinton argued—and be good for the American economy—"Chinese farmers cannot keep pace with their own consumers," the president said during a swing through the Midwest to promote the bill, "but American farmers can."[57] On the other side of the debate were a smattering of anti-communists and evangelical Christians but an army of union workers, environmentalists, and human-rights activists. The three Democratic groups contended, among other things, that trading freely with China would cause a hemorrhaging of American jobs—according to Michael E. Mathis, director of government affairs for the Teamsters, 817,000 within a decade—represent a disaster for nature—Carl Pope, executive director of the Sierra Club, predicted PNTR would boost China's black market for parts of animals on the endangered species list—and provide encouragement to China's dictatorial leadership—House Democrats like Nancy Pelosi and Sherrod Brown argued vehemently that China's leaders should not be rewarded for clamping down on political dissidents like the Falun Gong.[58] In the end, the May 2000 vote in the House divided the Democrats 73 in favor, 128 against. With the game up, the Senate vote in September split them thirty-seven to seven.

Democrats have become more united on the issue in opposition. This consensus is no doubt largely attributable to a desire to oppose President Bush and embarrass Republicans. The House Democrats' TPA vote in December 2002 was 21 in favor, 189 against, for example. But the basic rift within the party still exists and is deep enough to prohibit it from using the issue to its advantage. Research on trade politics reveals that support for protectionist and free-trade positions fluctuates between industry- and class-based explanations—that is advocates for the two policies break down along the lines of industrial sector or socioeconomic status. Michael Hiscox has shown that in the current post-1970 era divisions on trade are reflected by intra-industry battles, between agriculture and manufacturing to be specific, and not class ones.[59] Clearly, if trade politics were all about class, this would help bring clarity to the Democrats' position and might allow them to take advantage of doubts Americans have about the global marketplace. Instead, they have set Democrats against each other.

This internal schism was on display in the 2004 race for the party's presidential nomination. On the trade liberalization side were, especially, John Kerry and Joe Lieberman. Kerry, for example, took the free-trade position on all major Senate votes in the 1990s—including NAFTA, PNTR, and fast track. On the protectionist side were John Edwards, Howard Dean, and Richard Gephardt. Dean, according to the *New York Times*, "flipped back and forth on trade," although he frequently argued that, in order to trade freely with the United States, other countries had to bring their labor and environmental standards in line with American ones.[60] This, according to Kerry, would mean "we would trade with no countries." Gephardt and Edwards focused on jobs. The "trade policy we need," the former said, "globalizes with fairness and standards around the world so work, wherever it's performed, is given a fair wage."[61] Edwards, when he finally reached his stride late in the nomination contest, suggested that it was the Bush administration, and not the jobs of American workers, that should be "outsourced."[62] As if to underscore the Democrats' difficulties on the issue, Kerry went on to make a tortuous U-turn on trade and sounded much more like a protectionist in the general election.

Foreign and security policy are, therefore, important parts of the Republicans' edge. The public believes the party's moral clarity, deep suspicion of international organizations and many foreign governments, minimalist conceptualization of the national interest, and willingness to deploy America's military might are the best ways to meet the challenges of the contemporary world. As a result, and for all the Bush administration's failings on Iraq, it feels safer with the GOP in charge. The Democrats, most Americans seem to be saying, do not have a discernible policy. When they are able to articulate basic principles, these seem to be too soft for a world full of danger and evil.

This state of affairs shows little sign of changing any time soon. National security and foreign affairs will form a critical part of American public discourse as long as terrorism casts a shadow over aspects of everyday life. The Democrats are therefore ensnared. They would like partisan battles to be fought on terrain that is favorable to them—education, health care, the environment—but if they do that they will be accused of neglecting the security of Americans. When they do address the dangers of today's world, though, they provide a pale imitation of Republican strength. If someone like John Kerry cannot reassure Americans that the Democrats have what it takes to protect them, what member of his party can?

6

Trapping the Donkey Again: Domestic Policy as Republican Advantage

The Democrats also find themselves caged in on domestic policy. At the center of a Republican strategy designed to ensnare their opponents is an ambitious—if so far patchily successful—plan to cripple the federal government. How, exactly, is of constant debate in GOP circles. In fact, some in the party are even agnostic on the issue of the government's health. Irving Kristol has argued that neoconservatives, the group of intellectuals who provided much of the intellectual firepower for the conservative shift of the 1980s, do not feel much in the way of "alarm or anxiety about the growth of the state in the past century, seeing it as natural, indeed inevitable."[1] Others actually want to bulk up government for the long term and have argued that a strong government is essential for "American Greatness." Without powerful government the United States would not be able to project the inherent superiority of its values, it would not be able to construct magnificent buildings, it would have a harder time exporting its culture.[2] David Brooks has argued for a kind of "Progressive Conservatism" that follows in the footsteps of the statist traditions of Alexander Hamilton, Henry Clay, Abraham Lincoln, and Theodore Roosevelt—all of them Republicans or members of parties that are ancestors of the modern GOP.[3] Government, according to this line of thinking, should vigorously protect the United States from foreign terrorists and furnish economic opportunities at home. Indeed, the dramatic increase in federal spending during the Bush years suggests Republicans who do not loathe government have some influence—David Broder has argued that "big government is back, with a Republican label."[4] George Will actually believes that, "regarding the post–New Deal role of the federal government, the differences between the parties have narrowed."[5]

Still, I will suggest that a significant number of powerful Republicans are pushing a strategy to bring about the long-term goal of an emaciated federal government—at least on the domestic side—even if short-term tactics do not betray this essential fact. If aggressive and ineluctable cuts in government occur, not only will public policy be more congruent with traditional Republican philosophy, the GOP will benefit hugely from two important political byproducts.

The first of these is that when Democrats get to occupy positions of power and are capable of shaping policy, there will be little in the way of public resources with which they can reward core constituencies. There won't be much money for the kinds of programs on issues such as social welfare, health care, and education that the lower-middle class, organized labor, and racial minorities want. There also won't be the agencies and bureaus to implement such programs quickly and effectively. President Bill Clinton has already experienced what this Republican strategy can do to the Democrats. As a result of the Reagan tax cuts and a recent recession, Clinton spent much of his first two years in office focused on the huge annual deficit—historically very high at $255 billion or 3.9 percent of gross domestic product in 1993—rather than stroking his party's principal voters by passing a middle-class tax cut and bolstering domestic programs. He quickly realized that the fiscal emergency rendered many of his plans to expand the scope of government captive to inherently conservative financial markets.[6]

With scarce resources, Clinton also expended a disproportionate amount of political capital on regulatory policy—family and medical leave, the protection of the California desert, direct lending of educational financial aid, affirmative action, health-insurance portability, a minimum-wage hike, and safe drinking water legislation were all successful components of his agenda. He did this, it has been argued, because regulatory policy is generally welcomed by Democratic groups—environmentalists like it when nature is protected, workers like the minimum wage raised, and

African Americans like anti-discrimination policy—and incurs minimal costs on government but large ones on the businesses that have to abide by the new rules.[7] Indeed, Clinton's big legislative failure, the attempt to radically overhaul the delivery of health care headed by Ira Magaziner and Hillary Clinton in 1993 and 1994, was essentially regulatory policy and not a new program. It did not really involve the redistribution of wealth or the creation of large new government agencies. Operating within budget constraints Clinton proposed to, among other things, cut Medicare and Medicaid and provide incentives for the private sector to reduce its health care spending. The plan was also intrusive, not least in that it compelled employers to provide coverage for workers.[8]

Clinton was never in a position to create the kind of programs that palpably extend the reach of government and get core Democratic constituencies truly excited. Bearing the cross of huge deficits, he was able to enact the relatively small program called Americorps—the national service policy that allows mainly college students to receive aid in return for working on educational, health-care, and environmental projects—but there was little liberal policy beyond the regulations discussed above. Indeed, Clinton even presided over the death of federal guarantees to support welfare recipients. In 1996 he signed into law a bill ending Aid to Families with Dependent Children (AFDC)—a program that had provided assistance to poor families since the New Deal—and shifted much of the responsibility for welfare to the states.

The result of all this was political repudiation. The first Democratic President since FDR to serve two full terms lost both chambers of Congress for his party—the Democrats hadn't been the minority in the House since 1954—and could not get his vice president elected to succeed him. He also left the Democratic National Committee (DNC) bereft of funds and a party organization in no better shape than he found it. As Robert Kaiser assessed the Democrats at the beginning of the new century, "They seem as divided, feckless, and undisciplined as they were before Clinton ran for president."[9]

The second and related benefit to the Republicans' plan for the federal government is that if Democrats do want to endow their most loyal supporters, they will have to increase federal revenues or, to put it more bluntly, raise taxes. Republicans can sometimes get away with doing this. To be sure, George H. W. Bush's domestic presidency began to unravel when he went back on his "no new taxes" pledge and signed a $137.2 billion tax increase in 1990. Ronald Reagan, however, signed into law three tax increases—the $98.3 billion Tax Equity and Fiscal Responsibility Act (at the time the largest in U.S. history) in 1982, a 1984 increase that raised taxes $50 billion over three years, and in 1987 a hike of $79 billion over five years. His reward was to be permanently enshrined in the pantheon of presidential history as a great tax cutter. As Clinton and Walter Mondale discovered—Jimmy Carter's vice president admitted in the 1984 presidential campaign that revenues needed to be increased—Democrats, on the other hand, should wear goggles and thick rubber gloves when handling tax policy.

The Republican effort to weaken government is underway. It has several dimensions. The first is, of course, an aggressive tax-cutting strategy. Between his inauguration and the 2004 election, President George W. Bush had ensured the enactment of five large tax cuts totaling just over $2 trillion. The Economic Growth and Tax Relief Reconciliation Act of 2001 was at the center of the 2000 campaign and became Bush's signature issue prior to September 11. Among other things, it cut marginal rates, expanded the child tax credit, sent most taxpayers $300 rebate checks, reduced the "marriage penalty" in the tax code, and phased out the estate and gift tax. The 2002 Job Creation and Worker Assistance Act also provided tax relief for corporate America—something conspicuously missing from the 2001 legislation—including expanding the depreciation deduction and increasing the amount of time businesses could claim retroactive net operating losses. A 2003 law accelerated reductions in marginal income-tax rates, cut the long-term capital gains and dividend rates to 15 percent (Bush wanted the latter rather controversially eliminated entirely), protected more individuals from the dreaded "alternative minimum tax" (AMT) designed to make sure itemizers pay enough, provided parents with rebate checks, and expanded the permissible expensing of business equipment. In 2004 Congress passed a $1,000 per child tax credit, expanded the lowest 10 percent income tax bracket, checked the growth of the AMT, and provided tax relief for middle-income married couples. As the November election approached it also ratified a $136 billion corporate tax cut. At the end of Bush's first term, federal revenues were 16.2 percent of GDP, their lowest since the 1950s.

The push, moreover, continues. Although some Republicans started to get a little squeamish as the deficit exploded after 2002, many conservatives and tax-cut crusaders—such as Daniel Mitchell at the Heritage Foundation, Stephen Moore at Cato and formerly of the Club for Growth, and Grover Norquist at Americans for Tax Reform—urged the President to keep his foot on the gas. Moore sees an overarching goal for Bush's tax-cutting efforts. It is "to eliminate all taxes on saving and investment" so that there will be "no capital-gains tax, no dividends tax, no estate tax, no tax on interest."[10] For Ernest Christian of the Committee for Strategic Tax Reform, there is still much to be done in what had become the tax-cutters' master five-piece plan—marginal rates need to come down even more, taxes on dividends have to be eliminated altogether, the speed with which business can write off expenses needs to be accelerated further, tax-free individual retirement accounts (IRAs) have to be applied to all saving, and the foreign income of American corporations has to be excluded from taxation.[11] The House responded by approving a permanent repeal of the estate tax in April 2005.

Two facts assist those who wish further tax reductions. The first is that the recent cuts have been aimed largely at capital and not labor. As a result, the tax burden is being slowly shifted to income gained from work and the middle class. The GOP approach is therefore as much qualitative as it is quantitative and, if it becomes entrenched, will be difficult to alter. In the future, if personal income taxes are where most revenue comes from, there will be huge political costs to expanding the federal government's financial resources.

The second is that many of the provisions of these laws have sunset requirements—that is, they will expire at some point in the near future. The AMT, initially created to make sure that wealthier Americans with many itemized deductions paid at least some tax, has begun to creep up on middle-income filers. To relieve them, the 2004 bill contained just a short one-year AMT "fix." The AMT is therefore assured to emerge as an important issue in the near future. The estate tax is being slowly phased out until it expires completely in 2010. Then, in 2011, it will be reestablished at 2001 levels with a top rate of 50 percent and only the first $1 million exempt. As Paul Krugman has written, this provides heirs with "some interesting incentives" as elderly parents look like they will live past New Year's Eve, 2010. Ever the critique of Republican economic policy, Krugman suggested that the 2001 tax cut would have been more appropriately termed the "Throw Momma from the Train Act of 2001."[12]

There are four basic motivations for the sunset approach. First, for accounting reasons, sunsets allow legislation to come in under cumulative limits set for tax cuts by preceding budget resolutions that, under congressional rules, must constrain lawmakers. In 2003, for example, Bush's proposal for $726 billion in cuts over ten years could not be accommodated because the House and Senate had only created room for $350 billion in their prior facilitative agreement. Second, the Senate's Byrd rule—named after the Democratic senator from West Virginia, Robert Byrd—means that anything enacted in budget bills can only be in effect for a maximum of ten years. Sunsets therefore make sense for legislative reasons. Third, there is an economic rationale. By frontloading the tax cuts, the Republicans have argued they could get maximum stimulative effect at a time when the country was hurting. Finally, there seem to be political reasons. Although these motivations are hard to definitively determine, it is likely that Republicans wanted to use the issue of renewing the tax cuts in future presidential and congressional campaigns. Indeed, in his last budget before the 2004 campaign, President Bush asked Congress to make permanent many of the sunset-restricted cuts made to personal income taxes during the previous three years. Fearful of facing angry middle-class voters, Congress, just six weeks before the 2004 elections, approved an extension of a number of personal and business tax cuts that were set to expire early the next year. Only sixty-five House members and three senators—just one of whom was a Democrat—voted against ten-year extensions for marriage penalty relief, the $1,000 per child tax credit, and the expansion to the lowest 10 percent tax bracket.

Faced with *de facto* tax increases as, to use former Congressional Budget Office (CBO) director Robert Reischauer's metaphor, these "Cinderella" provisions turn into pumpkins, it is quite likely that presidents and lawmakers will be forced to extend them *de jure*. As Reischauer expounded, "When the sun sets in nature, you know it is going to rise again. And when you sunset a piece of tax legislation, you know full well that the political process will bring it back to life."[13] Voters will feel the reversion back to old marginal rates and the ending of larger deductions directly and, deaf to the intricacies of partisan fiscal politics, will wonder who took their money away. If in power, Democrats will be faced with a Hobson's choice: they either extend the cuts in some way or allow Republicans to continue to portray the party as one of higher taxes. Extending all of the tax cuts would enhance their deleterious effect on the Treasury dramatically. In 2002 the liberal Center on Budget and Policy Priorities (CBPP) calculated that a successful attempt to make all expiring tax cuts included in the 2001 legislation permanent would cost $2 trillion through 2012.[14]

As the GOP cuts taxes, however, it is presiding over large increases in expenditures. It is this behavior that leads many to argue the party is increasingly one of not small but big government. Indeed, annual federal spending increased from just over $1.5 trillion in 1995 to about $2.5 trillion in 2005. What's more, this is not completely attributable to the relatively "uncontrollable" mandatory spending on things like Social Security, Medicare, and servicing the national debt. In fiscal year 2002, "discretionary" spending—that is on items that require annual approval from Congress in the form of an appropriations bill—was $734.4 billion, up from $544.9 billion in 1995. In 2003 it rose spectacularly to $825.7 billion—a 12.5 percent increase from 2002, itself a 13 percent increase on 2001—not least because of a $87 billion appropriation for Iraq and Afghanistan. The figure in 2004 was above $900 billion. With an emphasis on defense and fighting wars on terrorism and in Asia, President Bush was perhaps expected to increase spending, but as Veronique de Rugy and Tad DeHaven of the Cato Institute reported in 2003, expenditures under Bush also accelerated spectacularly in domestic areas. In the first three years of his administration, for example, spending for the Department of Education increased 60.8 percent, for the Department of Labor 50.6 percent, and for Interior 23.4 percent.[15]

The spending continued even in the face of conservative criticism. Since 2003 a drumbeat of discontent has resonated through the community of GOP fiscal gadflies. David Hogberg complained in the *American Spectator* in December of that year, for example, that the president "has vetoed no appropriations bill and has actually encouraged profligacy by his eagerness to sign budget busters."[16] Ramesh Ponnuru of the *National Review* criticized what he saw as a new "big government" conservatism.[17] Stephen Moore of the Cato Institute labeled Bush a "big-government Republican," adding that "there's no longer even the pretense that he's for smaller government."[18] House Republicans like Jeb Hensarling from Texas and Paul Ryan of Wisconsin angrily introduced bills— ultimately soundly defeated—intended to cap spending and the Senate's fiscal 2004 budget resolution called for lower expenditures than the president had requested. Edward H. Crane, president of the Cato Institute, lamented that "it's safe to say that there is a tremendous dissatisfaction and a kind of dawning on people that Bush is not interested in smaller government."[19] The conservative House Republican Study Committee and think tanks and interest groups like the Heritage Foundation and the National Taxpayers Union grumbled mightily.

As a result of the tax cuts and spending, the annual deficit seems to be careening out of control. It reached a record, at least in raw dollar terms, of $374 billion in fiscal year 2003. In 2004 it came in at $413 billion, and the White House calculates it will be about $427 billion in 2005. By 2011 the CBO estimates the publicly held debt of the federal government will be over $6.5 trillion. And that's not all. These calculations do not include costs for our ongoing commitments in Iraq and Afghanistan—Congress passed an $82 billion appropriation for these two operations in just 2005. More critically, if we took away the surplus that the Social Security trust fund is running—it really should be kept aside for the program's beneficiaries and not used for other government functions—and accounted for future obligations to the mammoth public-pension program—that is, hold it to the same accounting standards as are private companies—the federal government would be about another $8 to $10.5 trillion in the hole.[20] Folding in these obligations, the deficit, which was a little under 3.5 percent of GDP in 2003, would, according to the Concord Coalition, reach double digits by the mid-2020s.[21] The CBO has reported this figure to be about 22 percent by 2050.[22] Trustees for Medicare and Social Security have recently estimated that the gap between promised benefits from the two programs and the revenues available to pay for them could be as much as $50 trillion over the next seventy-five years.

Many Republicans seem ambivalent about the deficit. As we discussed in Chapter 3, congressional Republicans see federal pork as a way of maintaining their majority and, as former Treasury Secretary Paul O'Neill recounted in Ron Suskind's exposé of the Bush presidency, Vice-President Dick Cheney extinguished nagging concerns about fiscal problems arguing, "Reagan proved deficits don't matter."[23] Many others, however, are not disinterested. For them the fiscal indiscipline is precisely the opposite, a concerted attempt to reduce revenues and hungrily consume present and future resources through voracious spending so that government lives way beyond its means in a manner that is impossible to sustain for any length of time. If these Republicans get their way, the likely result of large deficits is a catastrophe after which spending would have to be slashed dramatically and indiscriminately. Indeed, whether for philosophical reasons or gripped by tightening fiscal constraints, President Bush said immediately that he wanted to start cutting domestic spending in his second term.[24] Despite being chock-full of earmarks, the increase in domestic discretionary spending in the fiscal 2005 omnibus appropriations was a paltry 1 percent. The administration's fiscal 2006 budget made some large cuts in domestic programs in policy areas like agriculture, education, the environment, and transportation. The president's "No Child Left Behind" (NCLB) education initiative was targeted for a $11.5 billion cut over five years, Head Start by $3.3 billion, and community development programs by $9.2 billion.[25] Congress' budget resolution for fiscal 2006 cut Medicaid by $10 billion. If the "starve the beast" Republicans get their way, the federal government will look as though it has been put on an Oprah-like regimen, bloating up until it reaches crisis point and then crash dieting into a size four.

For some Republicans the ultimate goal of such a strategy is to alter public policy. As Barry Goldwater put it forty-five years ago, these conservatives "have little interest in streamlining government or making it more efficient" because they want to "reduce its size."[26] Grover Norquist puts the sentiment in even harsher terms: "I don't want to abolish government. I simply want to reduce it to the size where I can drag it into the bathroom and drown it in the bathtub."[27] For others in the GOP the aim is clearly political. As Nicholas Lemann characterizes Karl Rove's view of all this, emaciating government is tantamount to "fundamentally changing the social compact." Doing so will "enthrone the Republican party as firmly as possible for as long as possible."[28]

Interestingly this is not a particularly new GOP approach. Conservative economist Friedrich von Hayek was persuaded in the 1980s that "Reagan thinks it is impossible to persuade Congress that expenditures must be reduced, unless one creates deficits so large that absolutely everyone becomes convinced that no more money can be spent."[29] David Stockman, the Gipper's director of the Office of Management and Budget (OMB), argued it was time to "starve the beast" that is the federal government.

It seems that during the Bush years many Republicans have finally and fully rejected the party's policy of fiscal discipline that was so prominently displayed in Eisenhower's time and now look upon large deficits as both philosophically desirable and politically useful. As we noted above, by the mid-1980s the Reagan administration had been forced to engage in deficit reduction and even accept tax increases. What is more, two of the chief architects of the 1985 legislation designed to bring the budget into balance by 1991 were Republicans—Senators Phil Gramm of Texas and Warren Rudman of New Hampshire (the Democrat was Ernest Hollings of South Carolina). Now, however, only a handful of moderates and conservatives protest the growing mountain of debt. In 2003 former Oklahoma GOP Rep. Tom Coburn published a scathing critique of the Republican leadership and their spendthrift ways.[30] Another prominent conservative and chair of the Republican Study Committee, Sue Myrick of North Carolina, wrote fretfully in a letter to Speaker Hastert sent in late 2003, "As the majority party, we do not have the luxury of delaying tough decisions and practicing the politics of instant gratification."[31]

In 2004 and 2005, Senate Republican moderates like John McCain of Arizona, Susan Collins and Olympia Snowe of Maine, and Lincoln Chafee of Rhode Island, worked to block the GOP's budget by insisting that future spending increases and tax cuts needed to be offset by savings elsewhere. "I fondly remember a time when real Republicans stood for fiscal responsibility," McCain lamented. "Apparently, those days are long gone for some of those in our party."[32]

Instead, many Republicans seem to share the position of the eminent economist Milton Friedman, who argued in the *Wall Street Journal* in January 2003 that "deficits will be an effective—I would go so far as to say, the only effective—restraint on the spending propensities of the executive branch and the legislature."[33] John F. Cogan, a top Reagan administration budget official, put it slightly differently when he said, "It is wrong to allow surpluses because they invariably lead to higher spending."[34] This argument has gushed—not trickled—down to GOP members of Congress. Rep. Patrick Toomey of Pennsylvania argued in early 2003 that a good case can "be made that the deficit will force spending down."[35] His Keystone State Senate colleague, Rick Santorum, pithily asserted, "Deficits make it easier to say no."[36]

Another dimension to the Republicans' strategy toward government can be seen in the federal workforce. In 2002 there were approximately 1.82 million civilian employees, a figure that excludes the postal service. This is down noticeably from 2.25 million employees in 1990. According to Paul Light, political pressure is the main reason for the erosion of the federal workforce, with Republicans calling for the devolution of tasks to the states and private sector and Democrats, especially Bill Clinton, looking to "reinvent" the federal government or "downsize" it but allow it to continue to perform core functions.[37] Indeed, the Clinton years were ones of modest yet accelerated contraction as Vice-President Al Gore took the reigns of the National Performance Review and looked to cut agencies and positions.

Of course, government still does a lot. It's just that, as Light points out, there is a "shadow" government workforce that is employed in the private and nonprofit sector but that works on contracts and grants from the feds or that serves state and local governments by helping them perform tasks mandated to them by Washington. In 1996, for example, Light estimates that 332,000 private-sector employees were making fixed-wing aircraft for the government and 519,000 corporate workers were servicing government facilities. This federal "shadow" civilian workforce was, in 1996, nearly eight times larger than the "official" directly employed version.[38]

President Bush wants to continue moving workers out of the public sector. In 2002 the administration identified more than 800,000 federal jobs it considered essentially commercial. In May of the following year, OMB revised its Circular A-76—a document that, for purposes of classifying government work, defines the boundary between public and private—and effectively opened up 425,000 of these jobs to what is called "competitive outsourcing." The jobs, which included repairing trails and working in gift shops for the Park Service, staffing veterans' all-purpose stores, and maintaining buildings and computer systems throughout government, would move into the private sector. Although GOP members of Congress—especially those who have many federal workers as constituents—have opposed the plan, it has considerable momentum.[39] Bush's reelection will only enhance the administration's effort. As political scientist Donald F. Kettl has said, "I expect they will be pushing harder at privatization and contracting."[40]

Even war making, a quintessentially governmental task, has been somewhat privatized. As P. W. Singer writes, "The debate about the public and private sectors has moved farther than it ever has before—to military services themselves."[41] By 2000, about half of all people engaged in defense related work, including many in the research, development, and testing of weaponry, were employed by private contractors.[42] A small number of private military contractors even provide military training, logistics, and intelligence to the armed forces—David Issenberg calls them the "new mercenaries."[43] During the Iraq war in 2003, about 10 percent of Americans in the combat zone were working for private contractors.[44] By the spring of 2004, 20,000 of the 150,000 armed Americans in that country were working for private security firms—some, allegedly, were involved in the notorious abuses of Iraqi detainees at Abu Ghraib prison.[45] David Passaro, working for a private contractor, was indicted in the death of an Afghan detainee in the other foreign theater of the Bush administration's war on terror.

Another part of the strategy was revealed in 2002 when Bush persuaded Congress to strip civil-service protection away from about 170,000 employees at the new Department of Homeland Security. In 2004 the White House announced that thousands of the department's workers would be transferred into a performance-based pay system.[46] A year earlier Congress approved the National Commission on the Public Service's recommendation that many other federal workers be subject to a new pay-for-performance system. The ostensible purpose of these initiatives was to get more out of the government and give the president flexibility to deal with national emergencies. A political byproduct is the further erosion of the morale and privileges of many in the federal workforce.

The shrinking of the traditional public sector will be made increasingly easy because about one-half of all federal workers will reach retirement age by 2008. It is not as difficult to leave positions unfilled as it is to remove real human beings. Moreover, as Paul Light has argued, the pool of future government workers is shrinking as young Americans envision federal "dead-end jobs where seniority, not performance, rules."[47] A smaller government also means fewer Democratic voters and less zip to Democratic campaigns. The participation by federal and state bureaucrats in campaigns is circumscribed by the Hatch Act—legislation enacted in 1939 to "prevent pernicious political activities" by government employees. However, amendments to the law in 1993 relaxed constraints on political action for most civil servants and allowed government workers, generally thought to be big supporters of

Democrats, to engage freely in away-from-the-workplace political advocacy.

Public-sector employees are important to the Democrats because, as Elizabeth Corey and Jim Garand have argued, they turn out in demonstrably higher numbers than other segments of the population.[48] They do so because, in Benjamin Ginsberg's and Martin Shefter's words, "The career employees of the federal social and regulatory agencies have an enduring commitment to public sector programs championed by the Democrats."[49] Government workers are also four times more likely to be unionized than their private-sector counterparts and have organized effectively at all levels of government. The conduits for government worker political activity are the 600,000-member American Federation of Government Employees and, more importantly, the 1.3 million-member American Federation of State, County, and Municipal Employees (AFSCME) that regularly organizes large electoral and lobbying campaigns. In the 1999–2000 electoral cycle, AFSCME's political-action committee lavished $8.5 million on Democratic campaigns making it the fourth biggest spender. In 2001–2002 it again spent $8.5 million. In 2003–2004, it again spent $14.7 million. AFSCME also provided much of the organizational acumen and campaign ebullience to Howard Dean's shot at the Democratic presidential nomination in 2004—this was especially so in Iowa, where, armed with Palm Pilots, hundreds of members knocked on doors to drum up support for the former governor of Vermont.

That government workers are energetic Democrats is not particularly surprising since GOP philosophy is generally to give many of them pink slips, and the party's rhetoric on the stump, as Paul Light has noted, is generally about "bureaucracy" and "waste, fraud, and abuse" as opposed to the Democrats' "public service."[50] Indeed, it was a Democratic Congress that passed and Bill Clinton who signed the easing of the Hatch Act three years after George H. W. Bush had vetoed a similar bill.

The GOP effort to wither the federal government has had deleterious effects on the states. State budgets have been shellacked by an economic downturn—in 2003 the fifty of them had a cumulative deficit of about $50 billion despite the fact that most budgets are subject to constitutional and statutory requirements that they be balanced. They have been undermined further by Washington's fiscal policy, though. To be sure, only Rhode Island bases its state income tax directly on an individual's federal liability, but twenty-five states and the District of Columbia link their tax collections to federal adjusted gross income, an amount that the Bush tax policy has generally reduced.[51] On the spending side, CBPP reported that President Bush's fiscal 2006 budget called for a $10.7 billion cut in grants, with the exception of Medicaid, to states and localities. What is more, the states are still on the receiving end of unsubsidized federal dictates, despite the passage by the congressional Republican revolutionaries in 1995 of the Unfunded Mandates Reform Act. After the Florida debacle in 2000, for instance, Congress passed the Help America Vote Act to insure the abolition of punch-card ballots and lever voting machines. The feds also gave the states $1.5 billion to pay for it all, but this was generally considered to be well short of the costs for new sophisticated voting equipment like touch screens. As Denise Lamb, the president-elect of the National Association of State Election Directors, said as Congress was acquiescing to the president's request for $87 billion to help stabilize and rebuild Iraq and Afghanistan, "The states were promised the money, and I find it ironic that we're spending money to develop democracy elsewhere and very little here."[52]

Passed in 2001, NCLB, legislation that required widespread testing of students and called for smaller class sizes and higher teacher quality, will also be expensive for the states. A study by the New Hampshire School Administrators' Association in 2003 estimated that the state would, as a result of the law, have to shell out $575 per student and in return receive only $77 from Washington.[53] A 2004 analysis commissioned by the Ohio General Assembly found the law would cost the state $1.4 billion a year.[54] The General Accounting Office (GAO) reported that costs for student testing alone could range from $3.9 billion for short answer or objective tests to $5.3 billion for essay tests. Of this only about 69 percent would be paid for by the federal government.[55] In 2005 these burdens motivated school districts in some, even Republican, states to go to court or reject federal funds so as to free themselves from the requirements of NCLB. The Utah legislature passed a bill ordering local officials to ignore parts of the legislation.[56] The National Conference of State Legislatures (NCSL) issued a report that vehemently criticized the law and suggested that it was "unconstitutional." As David Shreve, senior committee director for the NCSL said, "There's a grassroots rebellion brewing."[57] For the most part, though, the Bush administration has been able to quell much of the revolt.[58]

According to a study by the NCSL, local and state costs for federal homeland security mandates have greatly exceeded federal assistance as well. The out-of-pocket expenses for states and municipalities are estimated at between $6.5 billion and $17.5 billion.[59] The federal government has called for states to, among other things, train and buy expensive equipment for first responders, ready their public-health systems, and protect critical infrastructure like nuclear power plants, bridges, and water-treatment facilities.

The elephant in the room, however, is Medicaid. Exempt from the unfunded mandates legislation and resourced jointly by the federal and state governments, its costs have been spiraling out of control as the number of participants grows and drug and medical expenses inflate.[60] The National Association of State Budget Officers estimates the program represented 21.4 percent of total state spending in 2003—that is, it cost states $122 billion and is projected to have cost $133 billion, or 21.9 percent of budgets, in 2004. They also calculate that it is about to overtake education spending as a proportion of state budgets for the first time ever.[61] In the five years prior to 2005, federal and state Medicaid expenditures increased by about 63 percent, and CBO estimates spending will rise by nearly 8 percent a year in the coming decade. It does not take a math wizard to realize that if this growth continues, the hit to states will be crippling.

Indeed, with federal assistance not forthcoming—the Bush administration has suggested allowing greater flexibility in return for fewer dollars from Washington—the states have already begun to manage the Medicaid crunch in controversial ways.[62] A Kaiser Commission on Medicaid and the Uninsured report in early 2004 revealed that thirty-nine states were restricting payments to health-care providers and forty-three were controlling drug costs.[63] This was a slight improvement on 2003—when all fifty states reduced or froze provider payments and took action to control drug costs—but was nevertheless indicative of the continued pressures exerted by the program.[64] Some states have begun to think about market solutions to the crisis—in 2005 Florida and California began to consider allowing recipients to purchase their own coverage from managed-care operations.[65] Other states moved to put a lid on paralyzing Medicaid costs. In 2005 New York Governor George Pataki proposed slashing $1 billion from his state's program and Tennessee Governor Phil Bredensen took 323,000 residents off the state's TennCare rolls.

Some cost-containment was of dubious legality. In 2004 Congress' GAO argued that, "States have used various financing schemes to generate excessive federal Medicaid matching funds while their own share of expenditures has remained unchanged or decreased."[66] The next year the Bush administration named fifteen states it believed had used improper accounting techniques to defraud the federal government of Medicaid money.[67]

All of these demands have sucked tremendous resources from the services the states traditionally and unilaterally provide. It looks like some long-lasting damage has been done to public education, for example. In 2003 California reduced its budget for community colleges by $161 million.[68] The NCSL reported that in 2004 that Massachusetts cut spending on higher education by 21.5 percent, California by 8.9 percent, Michigan by 6.2 percent, and Virginia by 5.7 percent. According to the National Association of State Universities and Land Grant Colleges, these budget problems forced tuition to rise at member institutions by 9 percent in 2002–2003, 14 percent in 2003–2004, and 10 percent in 2004–2005. More critically, the governors of Colorado and South Carolina proposed privatizing their public colleges and universities.[69]

The pain has been felt at other levels, too. Elementary and secondary schools have been closed and teachers laid off in numerous states—Illinois, Massachusetts, Missouri, Nebraska, New York, Oregon, and South Carolina being among the worst hit. According to the National Education Association (NEA), cuts in the summer of 2003 created four-day weeks; longer summer vacations; the elimination of arts, English-as-a-second-language, music, and sports programs; the doing away with field trips; the cutting of bus routes, janitorial staff, teachers aids, and nurses; and the delaying of much-needed building maintenance and supplies— including in Texas where social studies books still listed Ann Richards as governor.[70] In New York City, overcrowding became so acute in 2003 that at John F. Kennedy High School in the Bronx lunch hour lasted about five hours and began at 9:21 a.m., while four miles up East Fordham Road at Columbus High School, most freshmen had to attend classes from 12:30 p.m. until 5:46 p.m.[71]

And public education was generally protected. Corrections departments and law enforcement were hit hard across the country. In many states prisoners' food was cut; Texas inmates saw their calorific intake drop from 2,800 a day to 2,500 in 2003.[72] In

2003 Michigan repealed its aggressive mandatory minimum sentences for drug offenders, Colorado limited the amount of time nonviolent criminals can be sent to prison, and Missouri shortened the period after which people convicted of property crimes could apply for release.[73]

In Texas, state budget cuts meant that the state children's health insurance program (SCHIP) was trimmed and the coverage of about 275,000 kids was affected.[74] Florida stopped providing SCHIP to new applicants, effectively blocking 44,000 children from enjoying the benefits.[75] Indeed, according to the CBPP, between 1.2 and 1.6 million people were cut from Medicaid, SCHIP, and other health-care program rolls as a result of state budget cuts in fiscal years 2003 and 2004.[76] Twenty-three states were also forced to cut child-care subsidies for low-income families between 2001 and 2003, a program that had previously been protected because it is seen as central to the effort to get people off welfare.[77] As David Broder reported in November 2003, hardly a day went by without news of deep cuts in state programs somewhere in the country.[78]

There will be no immediate respite, let alone a turnaround, either. On the surface, the budget picture brightened slightly for the states in 2004 and 2005 as revenues rebounded a little—according to the NEA, for instance, spending on schools rose by 3.6 percent in 2004. Still, state spending, at 4.6 percent of GDP was still well below 1990s averages in 2004 and spending increases were projected to be much lower than the 6.2 percent quarter-century average.[79] Moreover, in the three years before that time states had collectively closed $200 billion in budget gaps.[80] To absorb steep declines in revenues during those years, seventeen states increased sales taxes and ten increased income taxes. Political expediency also forced many to exhaust rainy-day funds, tap funds that were in surplus, increase user fees and excise taxes, lay off workers, and utilize payments from the national tobacco settlement to ease the pain.[81] These strategies are largely one-offs and make a future recovery that much harder to achieve.

The crisis in state budgets is important because it is at the state level that the public sector delivers many of the services that sustain Democratic constituencies—education, health care, social services, and public transportation. When they are cut back many Democratic groups—public-sector unions, the elderly, the poor—become demoralized. Cognizant of this, Republicans continue to pile on the pressure. Many in Washington want to make more domestic programs block grants, for example. Darlings of the party since the Nixon years when that president accelerated the General Revenue Sharing "no-strings" attached program, block grants allow states greater flexibility in the administration of programs but call for them to increase their share of the costs. They therefore put additional financial strains on the states. There are currently block grants in all types of programs—law enforcement, economic development, job training, and, after the 1996 welfare reform legislation, the Temporary Assistance for Needy Families program that replaced the old AFDC and allowed the states considerable latitude in determining eligibility and benefit levels. In the fall of 2003, the Bush administration circulated a proposal to establish six additional block grants, including grants within Medicaid and Head Start.[82] Later the House passed bills that would convert Head Start, food stamps, and the Department of Labor's main job-training program into block grants. Given that Medicaid currently consumes $160 billion of the federal budget and $100 billion of state budgets, turning the program into a block grant would represent a major shift in American public policy.

Republicans salivate at block grants because the programs are consistent with the party's desire to see power devolved. As Jonathan Walters puts it, block grants assume the "federal government's organizational chart ... should be smaller, and what better way to shrink it than to give whole chunks of it away."[83] Although some conservatives worry about relinquishing authority—Robert Rector of the Heritage Foundation, for example, believes the feds should use money to insure that welfare programs encourage marriage—many realize that fiscal realities will cause states to cut programs they are given.[84] As Walters writes, "The most effective strategy for killing off those pesky liberal social programs" is to give "them to state governments that can't afford to pay for them."[85] If Republicans in the nation's capital are able to couple block-grant expansion with large reductions in federal financial support for the states and their core functions, they will have effectively scythed programs Democrats cherish without leaving their fingerprints on the blade.

To be fair, Republican policy in the domestic arena is more than a crude assault on the resources and people of government. The GOP has forwarded imaginative solutions to real problems. These approaches frequently contrast dramatically with tired, old reflexive Democratic defenses of the New Deal and Great Society.

To be sure, if successful, they will generally assist in the basic task of enfeebling government, but they are important illustrations of why many Americans are attracted to the freshness and verve of much Republican philosophy.

Take Medicare, for instance. Numerous Republicans have been pushing for several years to at least partially privatize the government policy that provides health care to the elderly. In the 1997 Balanced Budget Act, they were able to establish the Medicare + Choice program that, at its height in 2000, had over 6 million seniors enrolled in private plans after they had opted out of traditional fee-for-service Medicare. Soon afterward Republicans were pushing to expand privatization and allow plans to compete with conventional Medicare across the country—hence exposing the program to market forces. Called "premium support," this approach would initially require private plans to bid against each other to offer health-care services to the elderly in geographic regions—not unlike a core principle of the Clinton health-care plan of the early 1990s. The three lowest bidders would then offer preferred provider organization (PPO) type services and Medicare beneficiaries would have to choose between the three private entities and Medicare. Starting in 2010, traditional Medicare would compete directly on price and benefits against the PPOs, and the federal government would calculate a weighted average of all costs to establish a schedule of payment rates. Traditional Medicare would have to provide service at these rates, and, if the cost of the plan—public or private—exceeded them, the beneficiary would make up the extra out of her pocket. The post-2010 part of the process was endorsed in 1999 by a bipartisan commission on reforming Medicare, co-chaired by now House Ways and Means chair Republican Bill Thomas and then Senator John Breaux, a Democrat from Louisiana.

To liberals, offering choices outside Medicare is anathema because, the basic argument goes, it would weaken the foundations of the program. In the words of the head Democrat on the House Budget Committee, John Spratt, "Managed care plans have a record of designing and marketing benefit packages that appeal to healthy beneficiaries. As private plans 'cherry pick' healthier beneficiaries, traditional Medicare will be stuck with sicker, more expensive beneficiaries."[86] This, in turn, would leave the program buckling under the weight of demanding affiliates.

Spratt and his Democratic allies might be right, but Medicare faces an impending crisis. In 2003 Medicare trustees projected the fund that supports the program would start spending more than it takes in from the public by 2013 and would run totally dry in 2026. Medicare, therefore, presents an important public policy problem in search of a fix.

In 2003 another significant reform effort was launched in the form of the Prescription Drug and Medicare Improvement Act. For several years spiraling drug costs had moved seniors to push for a prescription-drug benefit within Medicare. Many were crossing into Canada and Mexico for medicines, and states like Illinois were seriously considering drug importation, despite conflicts with the federal Food and Drug Administration over safety. What's more, there was gathering pressure to alter the rules that provided lengthy protection for brand-name drugs from competition with generics. The Democrats mounted an offensive for the drug benefit and Republicans were swept along in the public outcry.

House Republicans, especially, saw an opportunity to couple partial privatization with the prescription drug benefit. Many of them argued that a $400 billion expansion to Medicare—this was the amount set aside for prescription drugs in previous budget bills—was too much and could only be stomached if swallowed simultaneously with significant reform. In order to prevent a filibuster in the Senate, however, the conference committee created to reconcile the differences in the House and Senate versions of the bill watered down the legislation so that it exhibited only the most minimal characteristics of privatization. Still, the bill that passed called for the government to sponsor, starting in 2010, experiments in six metropolitan areas in which private plans would enter into head-to-head price competition with traditional Medicare.

In many ways the legislation was a Frankensteinian monstrosity that included a $12 billion fund to induce private insurers into the program, $25 billion to rural hospitals and, in order to stay within budgetary constraints, an extremely complex and somewhat illogical calculus for determining how much of a drug benefit a retiree would receive—there existed, for example, a "doughnut hole" in which there was no coverage for annual expenses between $2,250 and $5,850 a year. Sprawling bills like it generally become malformed as they wind their way through the labyrinth that is the lawmaking process. Still, ugly though it was, the legislation represented a political masterstroke and a triumph of policy for the GOP. It nudged government out of the health-care sector a little, and it is predicted that by 2009, 32 percent of Medicare beneficiaries will be in private plans.[87] The partial privatization may end up, as Democratic opponents argued, filtering healthy, and by extension, more affluent seniors out of the traditional program. This will undermine political support for Medicare and make future attempts to erode it easier. A major reason the massive program has survived withering attacks from conservatives in the past is that, unlike what we generally consider conventional welfare programs, it has a very broad constituency—it serves every American who reaches retirement age.

By adding a prescription-drug benefit, moreover, the Republicans earned plaudits from those who generally opposed them—sixteen House Democrats and eleven Senate Democrats voted for the bill and the 35 million member AARP, a usually reliable Democratic ally, launched a $7 million lobbying campaign to support it. They also shored up their traditional weakness on the program—Newt Gingrich and his colleagues were hammered by Democrats for "cutting" Medicare during the 1996 campaign—and took the pivotal prescription-drug issue, a valuable one for Democrats, out of public debate. John Feehery, a spokesman for Speaker Dennis Hastert suggested his boss thought that the bill "will keep us in the majority for a while."[88] Former Clinton aide Harold Ickes lamented that the Medicare issue was "a big piece of political real estate to give up."[89]

The GOP appeared as the problem solvers; it was they who showed imagination. Endorsing the prescription-drug plan also made them seem moderate. As Bill McInturff, a GOP pollster said, "This is the equivalent of what welfare reform did for Clinton."[90] The Democrats did try to land some counter punches on Republicans, however. They embarrassed their opponents by highlighting the heavy-handed way in which the GOP House leadership had assured passage of the bill. To allow for some vigorous arm-twisting, members were given three hours to vote instead of the usual fifteen minutes and Republican Rep. Nick Smith of Michigan initially reported his son's campaign to succeed him in the House had been offered $100,000 in return for his vote in favor of the bill. Given that the proposition had taken place on the House floor, it conceivably constituted a bribe—something the FBI began to investigate. The House ethics committee ultimately admonished Majority Leader Tom DeLay for his role in the incident. In addition, the chair of the House committee largely responsible for the bill, Billy Tauzin of Louisiana, soon resigned from Congress and apparently pursued a $2 million-a-year job at the pharmaceutical industry's trade association before political pressure put him off the idea. The Bush administration also increased its estimate of the new prescription-drug benefit's cost by a spectacular $134 million barely eight weeks after the bill had passed—by early 2005 its estimate for the ten years after 2006 had reached $724 billion. Its chief Medicare administrator was accused of threatening to fire Medicare's chief actuary if he told Congress the true cost of the legislation when it was being debated—an action that theoretically violated federal law.

These jabs did not really connect. But others aimed at the GOP's Medicare policy did. John Kerry and congressional Democrats campaigned in 2004 that the bill was a giveaway to the big drug companies. This had some impact. In most polls surrounding the election a plurality of respondents felt they could trust Kerry to do a better job on health care—a representative October *Washington Post* poll, for example, gave a Kerry a forty-eight to forty-one advantage on the issue. What is more, millions fewer seniors initially signed up for the drug discount cards than were predicted because the program was extremely complex.[91]

Still the Democrats' advantage on the issue has narrowed. The 2003 legislation illustrated that the party has no real solution to the considerable problems that face Medicare. There is little talk about cutting administrative costs, trimming benefits, or increasing payroll taxes, even incrementally. The party was associated with the status quo; it appeared as though it wanted to block progress. The Democrats' creativity was the prescription-drug plan, a proposal ultimately attributed to Republican ingenuity and one with an admirable goal but that, of course, only adds to the fundamental resource problem Medicare faces. Indeed, the plan that became law contributed to a reassessment of the projected date for Medicare's bankruptcy. In 2005 the program's trustees were calculating the fund would be completely empty by 2020, six years earlier than they had estimated two years before.

A similar scenario is unfolding on Social Security. Referred to historically as "the third rail of American politics," the public pension program has been a notoriously bad issue for Republicans. Although the actual figures fluctuate a little, CBS News/*New York Times* polls over the last decade have consistently found that about half the public thinks the Democrats are more likely to make the "right decisions" about Social Security, roughly one-third feel the Republicans will. The traditional public skepticism regarding the GOP's position on the issue probably extends from the party's opposition to the creation of the program in 1935 and its frequent resistance to benefit expansions in the 1950s, 1960s, and 1970s. In 1983, on President Reagan's watch, a bipartisan commission recommended significant changes to Social Security that were adopted by Congress. The alterations included an increase in the retirement age to sixty-seven by 2022, treating one-half of benefits as taxable income, delaying cost-of-living adjustments for six months, and bringing forward already scheduled increases in the payroll tax. The legislation did little to revise perceptions of the parties' positions on the issue, however.

Still, the gap is narrowing now. A May 2002 CNN/*USA Today*/Gallup poll revealed only 43 percent of respondents felt the Democrats in Congress would do a "better job" on Social Security; 33 percent felt congressional Republicans would. A December 2000 *Newsweek* poll that sought to see which party the public had more "confidence" in on the issue separated the two parties by only four points—38 percent chose the Democrats, 34 percent the GOP. Perhaps sensing this, and armed with chilling statistics that reveal that, like Medicare, the program is on the actuarial ropes—recent estimates state its trust fund will be insolvent by about 2041—Republicans began to float the idea that Social Security should be "modernized." President George W. Bush propelled the issue toward the top of the nation's agenda during his first year in office. In December 2001 the bipartisan President's Commission to Strengthen Social Security proposed workers be allowed to invest significant portions of their payroll taxes into voluntary accounts that "improve retirement security by facilitating wealth creation and providing participants with assets that they own and that can be inherited, rather than providing only claims to benefits that remain subject to political negotiation."[92]

A focus on more pressing issues and the precipitous decline in the stock market, corporate financial scandals at places like Enron, WorldCom, Tyco, Global Crossing, and Adelphia, and the discovery of shenanigans among financial analysts at big investment houses like Credit Suisse First Boston and Merrill Lynch and those who run mutual funds at places like Putnam Investments, Janus, Strong Financial, and Prudential conspired to persuade Bush to put Social Security reform on the back burner. Members of Congress were also frightened to approach the program. Conservative policy wonks and Republican operatives continued to work on the idea's behalf, however. Individuals such as Peter J. Ferrera, James K. Glassman, Daniel Shaviro, and Michael Tanner at think tanks like the American Enterprise Institute and Cato Institute kept the flame alive.

On the Hill, supported by groups like Jack Kemp's Empower America, Senator Lindsey Graham (R-SC) proposed a bill to allow about 2.7 percentage points of the 12.4 percent payroll tax to be placed in private or personal accounts. A partial privatization plan that called for the Treasury to borrow money to cover the transition to the new system was pushed by Republicans like Senator John Sununu of New Hampshire and Rep. Paul Ryan of Wisconsin. Slowly, the public warmed to the basic idea. It is true that some polls—especially those that suggest, in their question wording, that the stock market may be unpredictable—showed continued wariness toward private or personal accounts. A December 2002 *Los Angeles Times poll*, for example, found that 55 percent of respondents disapproved of the approach. A February 2003 poll by the same newspaper that excluded references to the stock market's weaknesses and explicitly associated George W. Bush with the policy, however, found 54 percent in approval. A CNN/*USA Today*/Gallup poll in October 2003, moreover, found that 62 percent of respondents favored allowing individuals the choice to invest a part of their Social Security taxes in their own accounts. A November 2004 CBS News/*New York Times* poll found that 49 percent thought it was a good idea to allow individuals to invest portions of Social Security into such accounts. Much of the nascent acceptance is probably attributable to the stock market rebound of 2003–2004 and the fact that many people are beginning to believe that, in its current state, there will not be any Social Security left for them to receive when they retire. A November 2002 CBS News/*New York Times* poll showed that 55 percent of the public did not feel Social Security benefits would be available to them after they quit working.

By late 2003, advisers were arguing strongly that Social Security was no longer the "third rail"—pointing to victories in the previous year's Senate races by GOP candidates such as Norm Coleman in Minnesota, Elizabeth Dole in North Carolina, and Sununu in New Hampshire, all of whom favored at least partial privatization.[93] As a result, Bush gained the confidence to stick by his position on retirement accounts during 2004. In the presidential campaign that year, he talked a lot about an "ownership society"—one that, among other things, has control over its own retirement savings. In his acceptance speech at the Republican National Convention, the president said, "We must strengthen

Social Security by allowing younger workers to save some of their taxes in a personal account." Two days after John Kerry conceded the election to him, he placed partial privatization of Social Security at the top of his second-term agenda. The president iterated this in the first State of the Union address of his second term. In the first few months of 2005, the media and Washington insiders were fixated on the issue.

As with Medicare, the Republicans' position on Social Security has been frequently received as an imaginative approach to a big problem. Once again, the Democrats are reflexively protecting status quo policy and seem unwilling to address an impending crisis. If the GOP is able to establish personal or private accounts— and that is a big if, Social Security reform faces considerable opposition, not least from some GOP members of Congress, and polls began to show the public turning its back on Bush's proposal in the spring of 2005—the accomplishment will also generate far-reaching political advantages. With such accounts, millions more Americans will be sensitized to the vicissitudes of capital markets and have a stake in the public policy that facilitates the growth of investments within them. The "investor class" that, as we shall see in Chapter 9, is important to the Republican Party will grow and another pillar of the New Deal—that set of policies that provides the Democratic Party with direction, cohesion, and conviction—will start to erode.

Even if personal or private accounts don't fly, the Bush administration may persuade Congress to accept "progressive indexing." This was the president's "olive branch" to Democrats in his negotiations with them. Over time progressive indexing reduces payments to wealthier beneficiaries. As a result, the policy would wean richer and, by extension, more politically active Americans off of Social Security. This would greatly dilute political support for the program. Either way, then, fundamentally altering Social Security may lead to further policy breakthroughs for conservatives. This is important because, as Stephen Moore puts it, "Social Security is the soft underbelly of the welfare state. If you can jab your spear through that, you can undermine the whole welfare state."[94]

The GOP is going after the Byzantine tax code, as well. Republicans like House Majority Leader Tom DeLay have advocated consumption levies like a sales tax or value-added tax. The White House and Fed chair Alan Greenspan lean toward this type of tax, too. Others, like former Majority Leader Dick Armey and presidential aspirant Steve Forbes want a flat income tax. President Bush made revision and simplification of federal taxes a central part of his 2004 reelection campaign and has placed it at the center of the agenda of the 109th Congress—the president named former Senators Connie Mack, Republican of Florida, and John Breaux, Democrat of Louisiana, to head a commission to scour various options. It is a Herculean task fraught with political risk, but at least Bush appears to be working hard for change. With the exception of people like House Minority Whip Steny Hoyer, Democrats have responded largely by praising the virtues of the status quo.

Republicans seem to have more vision when it comes to social issues, too. I mentioned earlier that NCLB has taken a lot of flack, but something has happened on education to significantly reduce the Democrats' advantage on the issue. An October 2004 ABC News/*Washington Post* poll found that George W. Bush enjoyed a forty-seven to forty-four edge over John Kerry when it came to whom prospective voters trusted to do a better job on the issue. NCLB, as the most visible legislative change to federal education policy in quite some time, is a likely cause.

The GOP has other new ideas about education. In response to a widespread perception that standards in the nation's public schools are poor—a perception that is based largely on a breakdown in discipline and schools' overwhelming size, their obsession with racial diversity, and their insensitivity to the concerns of parents—many in the GOP have suggested vouchers be provided to pay for education at private schools. The argument for vouchers is multifaceted but is based on the fact that, as John E. Chubb and Terry M. Moe have argued, educational performance and innovation are currently stifled by bureaucracy, markets generally work better than governments, and that children with disadvantaged backgrounds who attend under-performing schools should be given the opportunity to go elsewhere.[95]

Voucher programs have been adopted—most notably in Milwaukee in the early 1990s, Cleveland, and Florida—but their success has been ambiguous and the momentum of the movement has been slowed. A major reason for the stuttering advance is that vouchers are highly controversial. The 2003 Phi Delta Kappa/Gallup poll on public attitudes about public education revealed that 56 percent of Americans opposed vouchers. An April 2000 ABC News/*Washington Post* poll showed 51 percent in opposition.

Yet the issue is not dead. Privately funded voucher programs have proliferated—the Children's Scholarship Fund, which as of late 2004 had given about 62,000 scholarships for children to attend private schools, is probably the largest. Congress gave approval to a small District of Columbia program early in 2004. Utah created one for special education students in 2005. Moreover, the courts have provided constitutional legitimacy. In 2002 the Supreme Court decided a Cleveland program that allowed vouchers to be used on religious as well as unaffiliated private schools did not violate the constitutional principle of separation of church and state.[96] Although a federal judge deemed Colorado's fledgling program unconstitutional in 2003, the ruling was seen as specific to the case at hand. So was the Supreme Court's decision in 2004 that prevented the use of public scholarship money for education in a theology program.[97] Public acceptance of vouchers also seems to be increasing. In Milwaukee the voucher program has generally been met with enthusiasm.[98] When the public is asked whether it would support vouchers for low-income families specifically, a majority has demonstrated approval for the idea—an Associated Press poll in July 2002, for example, revealed 51 percent of people endorsed it.

What is more, although the Bush administration has backed down from whole-hearted acceptance of the policy, it has pushed, in an alliance with Republicans at the state and local level, programs that move education toward the voucher model and the idea of school choice. Six states—Arizona, Florida, Illinois, Iowa, Minnesota, and Pennsylvania—provide tuition tax credits to parents who want to teach their children at home or send them to private or parochial schools. A controversial provision of NCLB allows parents to move their children out of schools that repeatedly do not perform to standards as revealed by student testing. Republicans have also supported charter schools. Although authorized by local and state governments and prohibited from having a religious affiliation, these schools have considerable autonomy from public oversight and raise money from foundations, corporations, and individuals. The charter-school movement has flourished despite some academic problems. As of December 2003, forty states had charter-school laws, and there were about 3,000 such schools across the country.

As a result, Republicans are again seen to be promoting policy that challenges the orthodoxy in an avant-garde fashion. Democrats are again left to say no, this time because teachers' unions stand fast in their vehement opposition to all things voucher. On this issue, however, we are witnessing cracks in the Democratic opposition. The black community is stirring as it sees many public schools in poor neighborhoods fail its children. Led by Howard Fuller, former superintendent of Milwaukee schools, influential African Americans have created the Black Alliance for Educational Options. *The New Republic* and *Washington Post* have run editorials complimentary of vouchers, and prominent Democrats like former vice-presidential candidate Joseph Lieberman and labor secretary Robert Reich have publicly expressed support. Encouraged by this, conservatives are beginning to push harder. Groups like the Milton and Rose D. Friedman and Bradley foundations are funding a comprehensive campaign to promote school choice. Sam Walton's Walton Family Foundation is underwriting work enhancing the charter-school movement. Policy success on this issue would help the GOP politically by undermining the influence of another important part of the Democrats' constituency, the powerful, coast-to-coast 2.7 million-member NEA.

Bush's faith-based initiative has the potential to do similar political damage to the Democrats. The micro-idea is to permit religious organizations to compete for public money that will facilitate their engagement in important social projects such as assisting at-risk youth, the homeless, drug abusers, and ex-cons. The more general philosophy is to allow churches and other religious organizations access to the implementation of social policy because, it is argued, their values and assiduous personnel equip them well to perform the task of improving the lives of unfortunates. Off to a rocky start when, in August 2001, the first head of the president's Office of Faith-Based and Community Initiatives, John J. DiIulio Jr., left because of suffocating political control, the policy has had modest beginnings. Although it passed the House in July 2001, a watered-down version of Bush's plan—Joseph Lieberman and Rick Santorum's Charity Aid, Recovery, and Empowerment (CARE) Act—stalled in the Senate. Moreover, the executive's in-house faith-based initiative has to await legal decisions as to its potentially dubious constitutionality. "There are a number of issues that will have to play out in court," DiIulio's successor, Jim Towey, admitted in early 2004.[99] David Kuo, former deputy director under DiIulio and Towey, argued in early 2005 that the president was not really interested in the program.[100]

But there are signs the policy is increasingly important to Bush. In 2004 faith-based organizations were awarded $2 billion, according to the White House, and the president reiterated his commitment to the approach in his 2005 State of the Union address. Faith-based initiatives can also hurt the Democrats in several ways. They are popular—a 2002 Pew poll revealed 70 percent approved of churches obtaining federal funds to "provide social services such as job training or drug treatment," and a September 2003 CNN/*USA Today*/Gallup poll revealed 64 percent approved of government money going to Christian organizations who wish to run "day care and drug rehabilitation" programs. Like school vouchers, the faith-based initiative is popular in many black neighborhoods where churches are at the center of community life. It also illustrates the GOP's innovative approach to solving problems.[101] It could, if expanded beyond its current relatively modest role, also undermine public-service unions and replace them with apparently benign and apolitical religious agencies. Indeed, expansion attempts are under way. Both chambers in the 108th Congress passed versions of CARE only to see a compromise get bogged down in conference committee.

Jonathan Rauch argues that Bush's positions on Medicare, Social Security, school vouchers, and philanthropy are at the core of his political philosophy. Bush, Rauch posits, is not simply a reflexive "small government" conservative.[102] The president wishes to emphasize individual choice. For Americans, choice, being a close cousin of liberty, is intuitively appealing. It can also be equated with empowerment. In Rauch's words, "Conservatives have been obsessed with reducing the supply of government when instead they should reduce the demand for it; and the way to do that is by repudiating the Washington-knows-best legacy of the New Deal. Republicans will empower the people, and the people will empower Republicans."[103]

What is more, the emphasis on choices gives Bush's policy prescriptions their freshness—he is not just an old-fashioned, anti-government Republican. It also appeals to traditional Democratic constituencies—such as those who do not have them. Many minorities, for example, support school vouchers and faith-based initiatives—60 percent of Hispanics support government funding for private schooling, according to a 2002 Tomas Rivera Policy Institute poll, and 81 percent of blacks and Hispanics but only 68 percent of whites support faith-based funding, according to a 2001 Pew Research Center poll. The young seem to support the idea of personal accounts in Social Security—61 percent of those between eighteen and twenty-nine approved of such a policy in a January 2005 CBS News/*New York Times* poll, 68 percent in an ABC News/*Washington Post* poll two months later.

Choice also provides political benefits. In the areas where Bush has pushed to give people options, the status quo provides sustenance to important Democratic constituencies. To the left, Medicare, Social Security, and strong public schools are worth fighting for. Undermine them greatly and Democrats will become dispirited. Provide numerous choices and the parties will also be unable to take simple and clear positions for or against programs—in the way the Democrats successfully framed the Medicare issue during the 1996 congressional campaign. Instead, partisan disagreements will become blurred and technical; they will become, for instance, ones over an array of retirement investment strategies and seniors' health plans. These will not mobilize blue-collar Americans like a solid and clearly defined defense of New Deal and Great Society programs.

As on foreign policy, then, the Republican governance of the first few years of the twenty-first century has placed the Democrats in a trap. President Bush and the GOP-controlled Congress have been promoting imaginative and appealing policies designed to undercut the kinds of programs that galvanize Democratic supporters. By doing so, they have portrayed their party as forward looking, the Democrats as protecting a problematic status quo. As Service Employees International Union (SEIU) president Andrew Stern puts it, the Republicans are "vibrant" in creating "twenty-first century ideas" while the Democrats are "defending sixty-year-old ideas."[104] The GOP has also been voraciously cutting taxes, consuming the public's future resources, and eroding federal government authority. When Democrats do get to make policy again, they will face the same dilemma Bill Clinton did. He tried hard to give core Democrats the policies they wanted and was at least somewhat successful in expanding government regulation. The president, under political pressure from a Republican Congress and within the policy constraints of a huge budget deficit, however, also presided over some cuts in spending, the establishment of block grants to states, and the shrinking of the federal workforce. If a Democratic president has to do this again, the party will truly be demoralized. As a consequence, any Democratic rule will be ephemeral, and, at least when it comes to domestic policy, small-government Republicans can then continue their push to decrease the size, resources, and reach of the state. They can also resume their dismantling of crown-jewel domestic programs—the protection of which is critical to the mobilization of Democratic voters. If the aim is to roll back time to, say, 1960, before the Great Society, the federal budget, measured as a percentage of GDP, must be cut by roughly one-eighth. Medicare must be privatized and Medicaid done away with or perhaps handed over entirely to the states. If Republicans aspire to go back to 1930 and before the New Deal, the budget must be cut by about one-half and the federal civilian workforce, if measured as a percentage of the total population, by somewhere around 60 percent. Social Security must also be turned into private or personal investment accounts. That's a lot of work many in the GOP would still like to see done. If they were to go about it as they are doing so now—by gorging on future resources, eroding the public sector, shifting burdens to other levels of government, and offering interesting and imaginative policy proposals—these may not be unattainable goals.

7

The Well-Oiled Machine: The Republican Party Organization, Allied Interests, and Political Money

Compared to their European counterparts, American political parties are feeble entities, weakened by the separation of powers and federalism that fragments government and impaired by state and national rules that permit the public to select their candidates for office and that facilitate the giving of campaign money from private sources. Emasculated, they collapse into one another and the rest of public life. American parties are not, therefore, easily delineated and robust private associations but "public utilities."[1] Party members are difficult to identify, know, and direct. Leaders are hard to control. What is more, voters, who now receive most of their information about politics from the media, are often unimpressed by the parties' philosophies and candidates, and many frequently vacillate in their support of the Democrats and Republicans. Organizing for the party's *raison d'être*, winning political power, presents a gargantuan challenge.

Yet the contemporary Republican Party has masterfully addressed these problems. It is, today, a mammoth institution made up of myriad interlocking parts each consisting of diligent and motivated activists led skillfully by a cadre of savvy and sometimes-inspirational elites. It has efficiently formalized beneficial relationships with many politically muscular, private allied interests and created highly effective voter mobilization practices.

The party's organization is, put succinctly, a well-oiled machine that is critical to the elephant's edge.

Although President Bush and House and Senate GOP chiefs in effect lead the party—their words and actions, for example, establish in the voters' minds the party's positions on issues—the Republicans are guided on a day-to-day basis by the Republican National Committee (RNC). The committee has been doing this adroitly for the most part since Bill Brock, a former senator from Tennessee, took its helm in 1977. Brock revitalized Republican state party organizations, began a successful fundraising organization motored by direct mail, and helped coordinate and modernize the GOP's message by exploiting existing, and establishing new, outlets in the print and broadcast media.[2]

Today, eleven committee chairs and more than a quarter of a century later, the RNC, directed from the Bush White House, is at the core of the Republican machine. It has created and institutionalized important relationships and lines of communication between itself, the White House, and the congressional party. Indeed, it is as if the three components of the national Republican Party had seamlessly merged. The Bush agenda is pushed relentlessly by what Michael Deaver, a top Reagan administration official, calls "the most disciplined White House in history."[3] It has been dutifully enacted by House and Senate Republicans who, as we saw in Chapter 3, have been largely unified. Annual mean member presidential support scores have generally been over 90 percent in the Bush years—that is, on every vote the president takes a position he can expect the support of at least nine of every ten GOP members of Congress.

The RNC projects this message of unity and strength to the American public. It sends high-ranking administration officials and congressional leaders on the Sunday morning political talk shows. It also communicates a powerful indivisibility through numerous daily e-mails sent to tens of thousands of party activists and opinion leaders. Popular moderates like Governor Arnold Schwarzenegger, Senator John McCain, and former New York City mayor Rudy Giuliani are sagaciously employed to stump for conservative Republican congressional candidates and President Bush all across the country. During the Florida saga of 2000, as local officials recounted ballots and big-shot lawyers for George W. Bush and Al Gore made their cases in front of judges from Tallahassee to Miami, Republicans in Washington realized they needed to win a public-relations battle. Operating out of then Majority Whip Tom DeLay's office, over 500 people—including many Republican congressional staffers—were enlisted to go to the Sunshine State and protest the recounts. Wearing "Sore-Loserman" t-shirts and chanting "voter fraud" they were transported to and from venues by buses paid for by the RNC. The party reportedly ponied up for plane tickets and hotel rooms as well.[4]

The RNC, with the guidance of White House political operative Karl Rove, has also aggressively recruited candidates that it feels can win. South Dakota Rep. John Thune was tapped to win a Senate seat against shaky Democratic incumbents Tim Johnson in 2002 and Tom Daschle in 2004. He triumphed on the second occasion. Successive Senate races in North Carolina also featured Rove-anointed GOP nominees, Elizabeth Dole and Richard Burr. Both of them won. What's more, the party in Washington has not been reticent to adjudicate what it feels are injurious primary battles. In 2002 Tim Pawlenty was advised to step aside and allow Saint Paul mayor Norm Coleman to run for a Senate seat in Minnesota. In 2004 the president and other party mandarins campaigned energetically—and successfully, it turned out—for Pennsylvania Senator Arlen Specter in his primary against conservative House member Pat Toomey.

Still, it is at the grassroots that the formidable organizational acumen of today's national Republican Party is most clearly visible. An entire army of partisan activists has been successfully mobilized and trained to do political battle. Its soldiers communicate through e-mail, listservs, and Web sites and meet at periodic conventions and workshops. They are taught how to assist candidates, run campaigns, and speak the language of politics. Honed by focus groups and polling, GOP strategists like Frank Luntz furnish elected officials, candidates, and activists with a vocabulary that can help them to be successful.[5]

They are often trained young. Conservative and Republican groups for Generations X and Y, both on- and off-campus, are rapaciously recruiting and organizing activists. College Republican (CR) and Young Republican groups are growing rapidly—the CRs increased their membership threefold in the three years following the 2000 elections.[6] These junior activists are also increasingly tied in with well-financed and politically sophisticated groups like the Leadership Institute—which dispatches conservatives to Washington each year and enrolls them in courses such as "campaign leadership," "Internet activist," and "public speaking"—the Young America's Foundation—which runs annual conferences and bankrolls a network of conservative speakers to send to campuses—and the Collegiate Network— which funds dozens of independent conservative-thinking campus newspapers all over the country.[7] Historically, the CRs, especially, have proved to be a crucial part of the party apparatus. Karl Rove, Bush senior's 1988 campaign manager and former RNC chair Lee Atwater, and powerful conservative activists Grover Norquist and Ralph Reed each served as chairman or executive director of the group.

This attention to grass roots extends to voter mobilization as well. In 2004 especially, the GOP established extensive and sophisticated organizations at the state, county, city, and precinct levels in critical swing states or marginal districts across the country. The Bush campaign, for example, recruited for each county in fourteen target states an overall chair, a chair for volunteers and voter registration, and an "e-chairman" whose responsibility it was to communicate with supporters over the Internet.[8] In Ohio, a particularly pivotal state, the campaign organized over 69,000 volunteers and appointed a captain for each of the state's 12,000 precincts. Journalist Matt Bai compared the GOP's 2004 operation there to a "multi-level marketing scheme" like Tupperware that "broadens to include more and more recruits with each descending level" and uses a sort of word-of-mouth or viral method at its base "to get one volunteer to recruit several other volunteers, and so on, so that the organization is constantly growing, feeding off itself."[9] The networks used included local party organizations, gun clubs, and churches. Bush 2004 campaign chair Ken Mehlman called the sales people within these networks "influentials"— individuals who, because of their knowledge, aggressiveness, and personal appeal, could persuade others by talking to friends and neighbors and writing op-eds and "blogs" (Web logs). The way you get through the "cacophony of information" that's out there, argued Mehlman is by using people others "trust."[10]

Much of the GOP's voter mobilization effort is dazzlingly high-tech. It has developed from its direct-mail childhood—political entrepreneur Richard Viguerie was clearly the midwife—into a sophisticated and comprehensive analysis of Americans' demographic characteristics, economic means, and cultural tastes. The RNC, for example, has a database called "Voter Vault"—the Democrats have a similar one called "Datamart," and others exist outside the parties—that holds information about 168 million people constructed from data on voter registration, magazine sub-scriptions, mortgages, and product warranties. It is regularly updated as volunteers go door-to-door with hand-held computers capable of transmitting the demographic characteristics and pol-icy interests of voters immediately to the central database.[11] This information allows strategists to identify the politically relevant traits of strong supporters, opponents, and swing voters. They can decode what Jon Gertner has called a voter's "political DNA" to see to what electoral cues they may respond.[12] They can deter-mine whether a voter is, to use the conservative Club for Growth's description of Howard Dean in a 2004 presidential campaign ad, "a latte-drinking, sushi-eating, Volvo-driving, *New York Times* reading" liberal and, consequently, ascertain whether she is worth expending precious time and resources on.

The Republicans also have data, collected by Scarborough Research, about the choice in automobiles, recreational activities, television sports viewing, and a host of other pursuits of Republicans, Democrats, and independent voters. This allowed the 2004 Bush campaign to micro-target advertising appeals to certain media outlets and programming. It even discovered that a good way to reach young GOP and swing voters was to get them at their health clubs; the campaign subsequently bought time on a cable channel that is piped into gyms across the nation.[13] The information leveraged by this technology is not, to use poll-ster Geoff Garin's words, a "magic bullet,"[14] but it does enable more effective campaigning.

The Internet, of course, is an important part of this techno-logical revolution. It has not, however, provided the kind of paradigm-shifting political effect initially ascribed to it. Howard Rheingold, for example, argued that it would "challenge the exist-ing political hierarchy's monopoly on powerful communication media, and perhaps thus revitalize citizen-based democracy."[15] This was illustrated during the brouhaha over Trent Lott's racially tinged remarks about Strom Thurmond at the South Carolinian's one-hundredth birthday celebration in 2002. It was an army of liberal "bloggers" that forced the mainstream media to pursue the story.[16] Anthony Corrado suggested that the Web would usher in a "revitalized democracy characterized by a more active informed citizenry."[17] But it has done none of these things. As Bruce Bimber and Richard Davis found in their research, "Web sites and e-mail communication serve as supplemental tools rather than replacements for traditional campaigning."[18]

The Internet has brought opportunities, however. Both parties, for example, have realized the Internet's potential when it comes to raising money. Candidate and party Web sites are easy-to-use and allow people to donate by typing in a credit-card number and clicking their mouse. The Web is particularly useful at reaching large numbers of small-dollar contributors. John McCain and Howard Dean were the trailblazers in their failed presidential bids—McCain trawled in over $30,000 an hour the day after his shocking New Hampshire primary win in 2000, and Dean's biggest one-day haul in late 2003 was $820,000. Now the Web is mainstream. John Kerry raised about $82 million via cyberspace and purportedly took in $3 million on just one day, June 30, 2004. Kerry's sophisticated Internet fundraising machine—with its carefully worded, timed, and placed pitches—is likely to become a model for future campaigns.[19]

Campaigns have also discovered that the Internet can be helpful in reaching voters—and not just in the obvious way of steering surfers to your party, candidate, or advocacy group Web site. In the 2004 campaign, the Republicans, for instance, bought Internet video ads featuring Laura Bush, rather than her less-appealing husband, on sites popular with women such as Foodtv.com and InStyle.com. The RNC bought pop-up ads on 1,400 sites that spring to attack John Kerry for his vote against spending on Afghanistan and Iraq.[20] The Bush campaign also e-mailed attack ads to targeted voters with some frequency. By compartmentalizing the electorate, the Internet allows campaigns to create special appeals to niches of voters. It also furnishes a low-risk forum in which to trial run ads before broadcasting them to a wider television audience. Internet ads have the added attraction of being cheap and exempt from the new federal requirement that the beneficiary appear in them.

When it comes to politics, the Internet, mobile phones, and other small wireless devices have added the most value, however, as a tool of communication among activists—enhancing "human networks" as political scientist Michael Cornfield puts it or creating almost spontaneous groupings or "smart mobs" in the words of Howard Rheingold.[21] The Kerry campaign exploited cyberspace to get thousands of supporters to e-mail the mainstream media so as to reinforce the impression that their candidate had won the first presidential debate of the 2004 campaign. Liberal activists in groups such as Still We Rise and United for Peace and Justice used the Internet to orchestrate large demonstrations in New York at the 2004 Republican National Convention. The use of the Internet in this manner was particularly evident in the Dean presidential campaign during 2003. That year, the former governor of Vermont used his intense opposition to the war in Iraq to mobilize a grassroots organization of hundreds of thousands of largely young supporters. This was far from a virtual campaign, but its workers communicated largely in cyberspace, writing "blogs" about the candidate and his ideas or hastily arranging face-to-face get-togethers using existing Internet resources like MoveOn.org—a liberal group initially formed on the Web to oppose the Clinton impeachment—and Meetup.com—a site that generally helps hobbyists and singles find others with similar interests. Ultimately, Dean fizzled and then screamed in Iowa, but he left as a legacy lessons about how to use the Internet as a political tool.[22] As legal and political theorist Cass Sunstein put it, "The intensity of Dean's support came less from his own personal efforts than from the fact that Dean supporters were in pretty constant touch with each other, whereas geography would normally isolate them and spread them out."[23]

The GOP has realized this about the Internet, too. The 2004 Bush campaign regularly sent messages to the e-mail accounts of 6 million supporters. Republican activists and supporters have their fair share of "blogs" to disseminate ideas and can receive literally dozens of daily e-mails from the RNC, state and local parties, candidates, and activists such as Bobby Eberle and his GOPUSA site, BushCountry.org, and FreeRepublic.com. During the 2004 election, hundreds of Bush "house parties" were organized across the country "meet-up" style.[24] The RNC now has its GOPTeamLeader.com concept in which cyber groups of activists compete against each other for GOPoints—good for Republican gear like leather PDA covers—by contacting the media, expanding their group, and forwarding e-mails to each other. RightMarch. com, although not part of the party machinery, is a conservative imitation of the liberal MoveOn.org that brings Republican sympathizers together in a virtual meeting place.

The Republican mobilization of voters has a distinctly old-fashioned and personal flavor as well. Voters need to be registered, and the best way to do that is to have a live person hand them a form and help them fill it out. As a result, party activists went to GOP-friendly places to find the unregistered during the 2004 campaign. Sporting events with a distinctly conservative feel—such as NASCAR races and Southeastern Conference college football games—were visited by volunteers who set up tables and handed out the necessary paperwork. In New Hampshire, new homeowners were sent a welcoming postcard by the state party reminding them of the GOP's traditional hostility to property taxes and encouraging them to register as Republicans.[25] Throughout the country, religious conservatives were encouraged to talk to fellow congregants and organize voter registration drives within their churches.[26] "Reggie the Registration Rig" drove around the country in search of unregistered Republicans. Much of this attention to registration has clearly paid off. In the twenty-seven states that allow people to register by party, the Republicans have increased their ranks by 8 million voters since 1987, the Democrats by only 4.8 million.[27] The GOP registered 3.4 million voters in the sixteen months prior to the 2004 election.[28]

This labor-intensive approach has also been used to "get out the vote," or GOTV as political commentators call it. In 2002 the Republicans bused volunteers to work in twenty swing House districts across the country in a program started by Tom DeLay called STOMP—Strategic Task Force for Organizing and Mobilizing People. The RNC also ran the "72-Hour Project," a thirty-state, 130,000-volunteer effort to contact pivotal voters, often in three stages. Canvassers knocked on doors early in the year to find out what targeted voters felt about certain issues. Later, these individuals were told about favorable GOP positions on these issues and then were mailed, phoned, or, because caller ID is now pervasive, more effectively visited personally by a party activist in the critical last hours. Millions of dollars were poured into the project, and although evidence is anecdotal, many argue that it helped the GOP to a famous, if narrow, victory in that year's election.[29] Indeed, recently, for the first time since record-keeping began, more respondents to the National Election Studies' biennial election survey said they had been contacted by the Republicans than by the Democrats—the GOP touched base with 30 percent in 2002 and 25 percent in 2000, the Democrats 28 percent in 2002 and 22 percent two years before. In 2004, despite the fact that the Democrats had huge independent organizations like America Coming Together (ACT) and MoveOn.org working on their behalf, exit polls revealed that 26 percent of voters had been contacted by Kerry people and 24 percent by Bush's. The Republicans made a total of about 3 million voter contacts in the five days before the election in Florida alone.[30] All of this kind of activity is crucial because experimental research has revealed that being subject to canvassing increases the chances that a person will go to the polls.[31]

In 2004 Democrats beefed up their ground game and were able to register hundreds of thousands, if not millions, of new voters in neighborhoods presumably sympathetic to them.[32] They were also able to get many of them to the polls—Kerry received 7 million more votes than Al Gore and 53 percent of the first-time voters. But the GOP was clearly not outdone. Once again the 72-Hour Project's targeted person-to-person approach seemed instrumental. Directed by Blaise Hazelwood, the project contacted about 1.2 million prospective voters in Ohio, for instance. It also organized people into coalition groups depending on their interests and got them to talk to co-workers, neighbors, and friends, and it sent targeted "robo-calls" or automated phone messages from prominent GOP figures that would appeal to the recipient.[33] Compared to 2000, the Bush vote was up 19 percent in Ohio and 36 percent in Florida. Against conventional wisdom that increased turnout benefits Democrats, a Republican president was reelected in a year in which a larger proportion of voters went to the polls than at any time since 1968.

The GOP also seemed to have more committed volunteers. It was estimated by many, for example, that in pivotal Florida there were about twice as many Republican precinct workers as their Democratic counterparts—about 109,000 to roughly 40,000. As evidence of its entrepreneurship, the Bush campaign swapped invitations to front-row seats at the president's campaign rallies for several hours working the phone banks.[34]

Underneath the national party organizations are similarly effective mature and sophisticated state and local parties that complement the RNC and the GOP's elected officials. These include rapidly developing parties in important southern states like Texas. Just a couple of generations ago there was no GOP to speak of in the Lone Star State; now it dominates. Its ascendancy began when Bill Clements won the governorship in 1978 and reached its zenith in November 1998 when Republican gubernatorial nominee George W. Bush led his party to a clean sweep of state-wide offices. Now, the Texas GOP benefits greatly from the energy of Christian conservatives who have built a sophisticated organization and really run the party on a day-to-day basis.

The GOP also gains from established suburban machines like the Nassau County Republican Party on Long Island, New York.

This organization practices a rather pragmatic type of politics—as recent political success stories like Rep. Rick Lazio and Senator Alphonse "Pothole" (called that because of all the federal pork he pulled in for New York) D'Amato illustrate. The Nassau County party is also organized hierarchically under boss Joseph Mondello and distributes patronage as a reward for effort and fundraising and vote-delivering performance.[35] Although the Nassau County GOP has fallen on hard times—the Democrats have made gains in county-wide elections—it remains formidable and a model for other GOP organizations in places like DuPage County, Illinois, and Delaware and Montgomery counties in Pennsylvania.

Today's Republican Party has seamlessly integrated supportive but disparate groups into its machinery. It has built, in the words of Democratic strategist Simon Rosenberg "an unbelievably mature array of institutions that are partisan but not of the party" and that provide critical manpower and financial support.[36] In Chapter 4 we discussed many of the myriad social and legal conservative groups that have been, for the most part, successfully folded into the GOP. Indeed, according to Kimberly Conger and John Green, in 2000 the Christian Right had "strong" influence over eighteen state Republican parties—these mergers are especially pronounced in the South, the rural Midwest, and mountain states.[37]

But the party has worked industriously to absorb other groups as well. A critical partner is a large and energetic group of small government populists led by the National Federation of Independent Business (NFIB). GOP congressional staff has long provided the talent pool from which the NFIB recruits its personnel.[38] The group also gave 98.4 percent of its campaign contributions to Republican candidates in federal races in 2004 and has provided priceless grassroots infrastructure to numerous GOP campaigns. Unlike many economic groups, the NFIB does not hedge its bets and supports the GOP almost exclusively. As long-time Texas Democrat Charlie Stenholm put it, the NFIB and its 600,000 members "have become a total arm of the Republican Party."[39]

The National Rifle Association (NRA), with about 4 million members, has had its ups and downs. A fairly large majority of the public consistently supports stricter laws on gun ownership, and highly publicized events like the Columbine High School killings in April 1999 have not helped the organization's cause.

Still, the NRA is another tremendous resource for the GOP. Its Political Victory Fund was the biggest spending PAC in the 2000 elections, splashing out $16.8 million and, in congressional races, giving five times more to GOP candidates than to Democrats. In 2004 it gave nearly 85 percent of its federal contributions to Republican candidates. Its members are assiduously trained as political activists and disproportionately inhabit key presidential battleground states like Ohio, Pennsylvania, and West Virginia. It utilizes an extensive and decentralized nationwide network of clubs to penetrate the grass roots of politics. It is also famously aggressive and innovative—in the spring of 2004, it announced a unique plan to create a news company to produce programming for the Internet, satellite radio, and television.[40]

Of all its associates, however, none has been more important to the GOP than big business. This was not always the case. Through the early 1990s, the Democrats held tight rein over congressional policy-making and, in a careful attempt not to upset House and Senate leaders and powerful committee chairs, corporate America generally gave as much, if not more, of its political money to Democratic candidates. Businesses conscientiously hired lobbyists with connections to both parties. That this was not an exercise in holding its nose—Democrats were thought of as less liberal in the 1970s and 1980s—made the strategy a little more acceptable to executives.

By the mid-1990s, however, Republican leaders, exercising their new congressional majority status, had lassoed the business community and pulled it forcefully into the party's fold. In Chapter 3 we saw how corporate campaign contributions gushed into congressional Republican coffers after the party took control of the House and Senate in 1995. Led by Newt Gingrich and Tom DeLay, Republicans in Washington also undertook a strategy to make the lobbying community GOP-friendly. Called the "K-Street Project," the ongoing effort involves identifying the partisan affiliation, Hill experience, and campaign contributions of lobbyists. Senator Rick Santorum of Pennsylvania also presides over weekly meetings in which aides identify important openings in the lobbying industry and GOP-approved candidates for them.[41] After processing the data, congressional Republican leaders then pressure corporations and trade associations to hire Republicans in open slots. In 1998, as if to suggest what might happen to recalcitrant groups, the House Republican leadership postponed a vote on an intellectual-property bill to protest the Electronics Industry

Association's decision to hire a Democrat as its head. In October 2004 a $1 billion credit for movie and television producers was dropped by GOP leaders from a corporate tax bill because, it was claimed in some quarters, the Motion Picture Association of America had decided to hire Clinton administration Agriculture Secretary Dan Glickman as its chief lobbyist.[42] Two years earlier, House Financial Services Committee chair Michael Oxley had reportedly leaned on the Investment Company Institute, a group of mutual-fund companies, to fire Julie Domenick, a Democrat, as its top lobbyist. According to the *Washington Post* and Democrats, Oxley's staff had offered to relax a congressional investigation into the mutual-fund industry in return for the granting of their request.[43]

The project has had marked success. With tight control over agenda setting and floor votes, congressional Republican leaders, according to strategist Marshall Wittmann, have lobbyists "shaking in their boots because K Street lives on access, and DeLay can shut off their oxygen."[44] Turning the screw on big business has also had more indirect and perhaps unintended but nevertheless beneficial consequences for the GOP. Command over K Street, it is argued, will help recruit candidates for elected office. According to Republican activist Grover Norquist, the party can now "go to young people at Harvard, Yale, and UMass and say ... 'We're not just offering you low paid service jobs. There's a rainbow at the end of the tunnel.'"[45]

With GOP guidance, moreover, trade-association resources have been utilized in an electoral setting—on issue advocacy, polling, issue ads, and other forms of voter outreach. In the 2004 elections, the Chamber of Commerce used 215 people to campaign for candidates it supported in thirty-one states. To the same end, it posted 3.7 million pieces of mail, made 5.6 million phone calls, and sent over 30 million e-mails.[46] Indeed, the Chamber has even acquired newspapers to get its message out.[47] That same year, businesses also began to provide electoral services directly to their workers. A Business Industry Political Action Committee (BIPAC) voter program—called the Prosperity Project—created Web sites that made it easy for employees to download voter registration materials and apply for absentee ballots. Users were then pointed to sites that compared candidate positions with those of their company.[48] Voter registration information was provided in newsletters and on paycheck envelopes. In addition, BIPAC used the corporate-communications infrastructures of about 700 companies in battleground states to persuade workers to vote for pro-business candidates.[49]

Tying the party to these groups is a cadre of Republican political operatives who work like beavers in rather murky political waters. These people seem to do many chores, often simultaneously. They have numerous formal titles and informal responsibilities. Ralph Reed provides a good example. As a twenty-eight-year-old doctoral candidate at Emory University, he was picked by Pat Robertson to head the Christian Coalition. Reed beefed up the organization's finances and, most notably, fertilized its grass roots—in the first seven years of the 1990s he added around 1,900 chapters and 1.9 million members.[50] "In some areas of the country," according to political scientist Lyman Kellstedt, "the Christian Coalition's local operations were (under Reed) the equivalent of the old Mayor Daley organizations in Chicago."[51] In 1997 Reed quit to form his own political consulting business and assist GOP candidates. Century Strategies quickly became a major K-Street player with high-dollar corporate clients.[52] In 2001 Reed was also made head of the Georgia Republican Party and conducted the wildly successful 2002 campaign in which the GOP defeated an incumbent Democratic governor and senator and the Speaker of the state House. In 2004 he was running the Bush campaign's southern operations and the next year launched his bid to become Georgia's lieutenant governor.

Grover Norquist, the conservative jack-of-all-trades, is another example of this phenomenon. Today Norquist heads the interest group Americans for Tax Reform, is a point man for the K-Street Project, sits on the board of the NRA, leads a weekly organizational meeting of conservative activists from across the country, and seems always available to reporters for an interview or quote. Using these roles he has become, in the words of Karl Rove, "an impresario of the center-right."[53] The political scientist John Pitney describes Norquist's work this way: "To the extent that there is a conservative network, Grover is at the switchboard."[54] Norquist works diligently with Republican candidates across the country, especially in state legislative races. Bush administration higher-ups attend his Wednesday meetings—labeled the "Grand Central Station of the conservative movement" by *Wall Street Journal* columnist John Fund.[55] Norquist, however, is not formally of the party. He pugnaciously pushes a small-government agenda and has been vocal in his criticism of federal spending on Bush's watch. In return, some Christian conservatives have attacked his political alliances with Muslims.[56]

To be sure, the Democrats also do these kinds of things. Sometimes, in fact, they do them better. During the 2004 presidential campaign, for example, John Kerry out-raised George W. Bush over the Internet by nearly six to one. Affiliated groups like ACT, led by prolific fundraiser Ellen Malcolm and former AFL-CIO political director Steve Rosenthal, focused on an intensive voter mobilization project in seventeen swing states. The group, financed greatly by billionaire George Soros, came out of nowhere to successfully coordinate with left-of-center organizations and register and mobilize millions of voters. Still, in contemporary party politics, the Democratic machine does not whirr quite as mellifluously as its Republican counterpart. This is because the GOP organization possesses several critical advantages.

The first of these is unambiguous leadership. The Republican Party is directed from the White House. The current chair, Ken Mehlman, and his predecessor, Ed Gillespie, are both close to President Bush. Often through the RNC, the administration enunciates GOP policy and, for the most part, the rest of the machinery falls in line. We have already seen how wholeheartedly congressional Republicans, led by Speaker Dennis Hastert in the House and Majority Leader Bill Frist in the Senate, have supported the Bush agenda. The RNC also spreads the word to the grass roots.

The Democrats' chain of command, on the other hand, is not quite as distinct. Some of this can be explained by the party's minority status in government. When Bill Clinton was in the White House, chief domestic policy adviser Bruce Reed explains that "a single voice could define the debate and drag the rest of the establishment along behind him." The White House, moreover, provided "a table to sit around" when it came time to hashing out strategy and policy.[57] Now, the minority leaders in the House and Senate, Nancy Pelosi and Harry Reid, respectively, can both legitimately lay claim to being the party's leader. So can the DNC chair Howard Dean. During the 2004 presidential campaign, the party's nominee, John Kerry, was surely the Democrats' leader—witness the Kerry love-fest at the Democratic National Convention—but this was largely an artifact of a peculiar presidential campaign in which the party was gelatinized by its hatred of George W. Bush. The president, of course, will not be at the top of the Republican ticket again.

Much of the Democrats' organizational incoherence, however, is attributable to historic and entrenched differences within the party. Such differences largely fall on one dimension so as to form a single and deep, frequently unbridgeable, chasm between two discernible factions. The divide is both substantive and stylistic. The first bloc consists mainly of central tenets of the party's New Deal coalition, organized labor, white ethnic Catholics, and older African Americans. It is distinctly liberal in its economic philosophy but often pragmatic in its approach to electoral politics and perceives winning office as paramount. The other group is more vehemently liberal, is greatly interested in social policy, and believes ideas and principles are critical. It is largely white and is noticeably middle class and young.

The seeds of this schism were sown in the massive upheavals—centered around the war in Vietnam, civil rights movement, and quest for gender equality—that took place in the 1960s. Out of this ground came a new type of Democrat willing to challenge the party's aging elite—politicians and labor leaders who had come of age during the New Deal. In the early 1960s, James Q. Wilson wrote an influential book in which the emerging group, the so-called "amateur" Democrats, were first characterized.[58] They were white, educated, and middle class. They were also stridently liberal and dedicated to intra-party reform that would democratize the party machinery. In 1968 during the Democrats' presidential nomination process, they split the party asunder by undertaking a concerted and energetic attempt to snatch control from the elite. That year, ostensibly because of his policy on Vietnam, President Lyndon B. Johnson was challenged for his party's nomination by, first, Minnesota Senator Eugene McCarthy and then former Attorney General and New York Senator Robert F. Kennedy. Both opponents attracted support from the nascent faction, but it was McCarthy whom it embraced most tightly. He was the more vehement anti-war candidate, and it was he who allowed the new groups to run his campaign—youngsters like Seymour Hersh, who is now a heralded investigative journalist, and Curtis Gans, from the "Dump Johnson" movement, were in charge. Indeed, to many young, white, middle-class liberals, RFK was not to be trusted. After all, he got into the race just as McCarthy, fresh from his near upset of President Johnson in New Hampshire, was reaching a full head of steam. As one of McCarthy's student army put it to Theodore White, "We woke up after the New Hampshire primary, like it was Christmas Day.

And when we went down to the tree, we found Bobby Kennedy had stolen our Christmas presents."[59]

Kennedy was assassinated that June, hours after winning the California primary. Johnson had dropped out of the race in the spring. This left the contest for the 1968 Democratic presidential nomination to McCarthy and LBJ's vice president, Hubert Humphrey. Humphrey worked hard to cultivate the business and labor supporters of his boss and avoided public confrontation with the anti-Johnson candidates in the primaries by skipping the contests entirely. McCarthy kept up the anti-war rhetoric and galvanized an army of young liberal supporters.

At the Chicago convention, the struggle came to a violent denouement. Humphrey's behind-the-scenes lobbying for delegate votes saw him somewhat comfortably (he won over 68 percent of the vote) into the nomination. That, however, did not stop thousands of McCarthy supporters from protesting what they considered to be the illegitimacy of Humphrey's victory. There were scuffles and punch-ups on the convention floor and more dramatic and bloody clashes between demonstrators and the Chicago police throughout the city.

Nearly forty years after Chicago, the old New Deal faction has lost ground.[60] Organized labor may still help determine electoral outcomes with its important endorsements and get-out-the-vote activities, but it is internally divided.[61] A new generation of union leaders, such as Bruce Raynor, president of the Union of Needletrade, Industrial and Textile Employees (UNITE); Andrew Stern, president of the Service Employees International Union (SEIU); and John Wilhelm, former president of the Hotel Employees and Restaurant Employees International Union (HERE), frequently talk about labor's permanent interests and how they are more important than the traditional alliance with the Democrats.[62] Stern, especially, has rankled older labor bosses with his outspoken style, calls for revolutionary reorganization within organized labor, and apocalyptical view of the future.[63] He has threatened to bolt the AFL-CIO. Others in the movement—like the Brotherhood of Carpenters' Doug McCarron and the Teamsters' James P. Hoffa— flirt with Republicans. The GOP, they realize, appeals to many of their members on cultural issues and often fights energetically for the interests of industry against environmentalists.[64]

The 2004 presidential nomination process illustrated how the labor movement is changing. The unions representing workers in the manufacturing sector generally supported House Minority

Leader Richard Gephardt of Missouri—an old friend who vehemently assaulted the free-trade policies of the Republican administration and his Democratic rivals—but the SEIU and the powerful American Federation of State, County and Municipal Employees (AFSCME) endorsed Howard Dean. The former Vermont governor worked the leadership and rank-and-file of these service sector unions. Perhaps because they have larger numbers of minorities and women, he also won them over with his populist and liberal positions, not a more closely cropped message about labor issues, jobs, and pay.[65]

Equally worrying for the traditional faction is that the old urban machines have eroded substantially. Until the 1960s, many large cities in the Northeast and Midwest were governed by Democratic mayors who presided over giant patronage organizations that showered largess on the voting public and hounded them to the polls on election day—Richard J. Daley's "machine" in Chicago was perhaps the most famous. But for numerous reasons these organizations are no more. Today northern cities are as likely to be ruled by Republicans—like Rudy Giuliani and Michael Bloomberg in New York—and African Americans—like Dennis Archer and Kwame Kilpatrick in Detroit, David Dinkins in New York, John F. Street in Philadelphia, and Mike White in Cleveland— who were frozen out of the machines that ethnic blue-collar whites ran for their own. Federal and state civil-service laws have crippled patronage, white flight has ravaged the tax base needed for the machine's benevolence, and the growth of federal welfare programs diminished the demand for it anyway. Even in the Windy City, where Daley's son, Richard M., is still the mayor, the machine is a mere shadow of itself. Broken by the mayoralties of Jane Byrne and African American Harold Washington, it can no longer control Democratic voters. In March 2004 little-known state legislator Barack Obama rolled to victory in the party's U.S. Senate primary by crushing the machine-backed candidate, state comptroller Dan Hynes, who could not even win his well-heeled, north-side suburban Chicago precinct.

Yet the Democrats still remain divided, essentially along a fault line close to the one that emerged in the 1960s. On no recent occasion has this cleavage been better displayed than during the contest for the party's 2004 presidential nomination. Long-time members of Congress, Richard Gephardt and John Kerry, represented the old wing of the party. Gephardt, as I have mentioned, promoted issues dear to the heart of traditional labor—a faction that, according to political scientist Taylor Dark, maintains considerable influence within the national Democratic Party.[66] Gephardt also pushed to compel employers to provide health insurance for workers and greatly reinforce two beams of the New Deal-Great Society edifice, Medicaid and Medicare. Kerry, with his Vietnam War service and vote to authorize President Bush to go to war with Iraq, showed he was not weak on defense— something old-school Democrats appreciated when the country faced down communism during the Cold War. The newer faction was personified by Howard Dean. Stylistically, Dean echoed the discontents of 1968 as he railed against the "Washington Democrats" and the "Democratic Establishment"—even as he picked up endorsements from members of Congress and Al Gore. He claimed to represent the "Democratic wing of the Democratic Party." He raised copious amounts of cash in small increments and ran an insurgent grassroots campaign manned by devoted young people connected through the Internet. His fervently anti-war message resonated at a time when American soldiers fighting abroad was topic number one in public discourse. Even doyens of the Washington press corps like R. W. Apple Jr. and David Broder could not help making comparisons with Eugene McCarthy.[67] Certainly Dean appealed to the same kinds of Democrats the Minnesotan did. He won 34 percent of the eighteen- to twenty-nine-year-old vote in New Hampshire, beating Kerry among that cohort. He was the only top-tier candidate who did better among college graduates than those who did not have a degree in New Hampshire and Wisconsin. What is more, in New Hampshire he won 41 percent of those who considered themselves "very liberal" and was the only candidate who did perceptibly better among non-union households than households that contained a member of a union.

In fact, it could be argued the party is even more fractured today than it was in the 1960s. Out of the ashes of the disastrous presidential elections of the 1970s and 1980s emerged a further faction, this one of mainly southern moderate Democrats who wished to push the party in a more conservative direction. Galvanized under the Democratic Leadership Council (DLC) and fed ideas by the Progressive Policy Institute, these "New Democrats" sought what was later to be called the "Third Way." In the words of Kenneth S. Baer, the DLC's philosophy "endorsed a strong military and an interventionist foreign policy, advocated a de-emphasis of the party's stance on many contentious issues, and made a call ... for an egalitarianism in both social and economic policy based on equality of opportunity, not equality of outcome."[68] Its most famous son, Bill Clinton, signed the bill that ended about sixty years of federal guarantees to welfare recipients and announced in his 1996 State of the Union address that "the era of big government is over." Although this faction saw the presidential campaign of one of its leaders, Joe Lieberman, fizzle in 2004, it still has many important acolytes. The New Democrat Coalition claims about ninety-five members on Capitol Hill; it has been led in the House by Jim David of Florida, Ron Kind of Wisconsin, and Adam Smith of Washington and in the Senate by prominent members like Louisianans John Breaux and Mary Landrieu, Evan Bayh of Indiana, John Edwards of North Carolina, and Bob Graham of Florida. It is also backed by a wealthy PAC, the New Democrat Network.

It is true, as we shall see again in Chapter 10, that the GOP also suffers from internal fissures. In the House delegation alone, Douglas Koopman has identified seven distinct, if not equally large and strong, factions—the socially conservative "moralists," the economically conservative "enterprisers," plain old "moderates," socially liberal "patricians," the party loyalist "stalwarts," the pragmatic pork-barreling "provincials," and the moderately liberal and constituency-oriented "placeholders."[69] Off the Hill, the Log Cabin Republicans, the party's gay organization, has clashed with the Bush administration over a constitutional amendment to prohibit same-sex marriage. In 2004 the group ran commercials in a number of swing states opposing the president's support of the change.[70] At the 2004 GOP National Convention, social conservatives complained vehemently about prime-time speaking slots for opponents of the marriage ban—moderates like Rudy Giuliani, John McCain, and Arnold Schwarzenegger. There also remains significant disagreement on the abortion issue. The Republican Majority for Choice works hard to change the party's generally pro-life position—according to a CBS News/*New York Times* poll in January 2003, only 29 percent of Republicans felt abortion should be "generally available." It includes among its advisory board four current senators, eleven members of the U.S. House, and three sitting governors.

There are even internal disputes over the party's generally less controversial stances on economic issues. The Club for Growth works to purge the GOP of "RINOs" or "Republicans in Name Only" who do not pass its former leader Stephen Moore's litmus test: "You've got to be for school choice, and you've got to be for cutting taxes, and you've got to be for smaller government."[71] It has supported a number of avidly anti-tax challengers to GOP lawmakers in party primaries, including Rep. Pat Toomey's quest to unseat Senator Arlen Specter of Pennsylvania in 2004. Pushing more moderate and what it considers fiscally responsible economic policies is the Republican Main Street Partnership (RMSP). Although it packages itself as a grassroots organization, RMSP has fifty-five members in the House, nine in the Senate, and counts several governors, including Arnold Schwarzenegger, among its numbers. As we saw in the last chapter, its adherents, like John McCain, have gone head-to-head with the Bush White House and congressional leadership on taxes and spending.

Yet the present internal divisions within the GOP do not seem quite as injurious as those that afflict the Democrats. Some of this might be explained by the party's desire to support a sitting president. What's more, and as we saw in Chapter 3, it is clearly a function of the unusual assertiveness of the current crop of congressional leaders. Congressional scholar John Pitney has characterized bickering within the House GOP this way: "The fights may be fierce, but the fights are over marginal things."[72] But there seems to be something else. Republicans, for whatever reason, don't like to allow internal disputes to fester. Take the two parties' presidential nominating processes, for instance. Political scientists like Martin Wattenberg have argued that the Democrats' reliance on proportional representation in primaries allows losing candidates to gather delegates for the national convention—giving them a stronger pitch to potential donors, motivating supporters, and offering them a rationale for remaining in the race.[73] The Republicans, on the other hand, have winner-take-all states—sixteen of them in fact in 2004. Other scholars, like William G. Mayer, reject these institutional explanations and say that the ideological fissures within the Democratic Party make its nomination process more competitive than the Republicans'.[74] Either way, there is empirical evidence to show that the combative contest for the quadrennial Democratic presidential candidacy greatly weakens the eventual nominee for the general election.[75]

The latest competitions for "open" nominations provide good examples. In 2000 the Republican contest broke quickly into a two-way race between George W. Bush and John McCain. The candidacies of social conservatives Gary Bauer and Alan Keyes and economic conservative Steve Forbes rapidly melted away as conservatives mobilized behind Bush. In 2004 the various factions within the Democratic Party were all strongly represented in the race—Kerry as the liberal establishment candidate, Dean and Rep. Dennis Kucinich as the insurgents, Gephardt representing much of organized labor, Lieberman and Edwards from the DLC, General Wesley Clark as a moderate, and Al Sharpton and former Senator Carol Moseley-Braun emblematizing African Americans. Devastating bloodshed was only prevented because a uniquely strong desire to unseat the president galvanized Democratic voters and DNC chair Terry McAuliffe deliberately condensed the process so as to have twenty-seven states hold their delegate-selection contests by March 2.

The second Republican advantage is financial. "Money," as the California politician Jesse Unruh famously put it, "is the mother's milk of politics." It buys all the necessities of the successful modern campaign—staff, media, polling, and, because it is so essential for victory, yet more money from donors looking to back a winner. Historically, the Republican Party, with its strong backing from the business community and wealthy individuals, has enjoyed a sizeable advantage when it comes to fundraising. Through the 1990s, however, the gap narrowed a little. In 1992 the GOP raised $315 million to the Democrats' $200 million. In 2000 the Republicans' advantage in dollar terms increased to about $195 million—approximately $715 million to $520 million—but shrunk from about 37 percent to around 28 percent of the money they had garnered. This slight convergence was almost entirely attributable to a spectacular increase in the amount of soft money—the unlimited and generally large contributions made for "party-building activities"—raked in by the parties. In hard dollars—contributions capped prior to 2003 at $20,000 per donor per year and that can be used directly for campaign activities—the GOP out-raised the Democrats $267 million to $178 million in 1992 and around $466 million to $275 million in 2000. However, when it came to the soft kind, both parties raised within a hair's breadth of one-quarter of a billion dollars in 2000—a little over five times as much as they had each collected eight years earlier.

Two legal facts brought about the explosion in soft money. The first was the prohibition of privately raised candidate funds in presidential general elections. Since the 1970s, the government has given the nominees of the two major parties lump sums for their campaigns and compelled them not to accept outside finances. As a result, the candidates have leaned heavily on the parties for resources. The second was the Federal Election Commission and courts' gradual relaxation of the definition of "party-building activities." Over time regulators allowed soft money to be used for more than just staff salaries, operating budgets, and the maintenance of facilities. Mixed with hard money, it was permitted in voter-registration drives, get-out-the-vote activities, and even issue advertising—that is political ads that do not "expressly advocate" the election or defeat of a candidate but that can criticize or praise their actions or positions.

As a result, the floodgates opened, most dramatically for the Democrats. In the 2000 election cycle, for example, the AFSCME and SEIU donated $5.95 and $4.26 million, respectively, to Democratic Party committees. Deep-pocketed corporations also wrote big checks, but not exclusively to the GOP. AT&T, a particularly generous giver, contributed $1.76 million in soft money to the Republican Party in 2002 and $1.39 million to the Democrats. In 2000 and 2002, Microsoft gave 35 percent of its $5 million to Democrats. Perhaps more spectacularly, soft money ushered in the era of the "fat cat"—a wealthy individual capable of writing a single check for hundreds of thousands of dollars. The GOP has had many of these, including San Diego Chargers owner Alex Spanos and Cincinnati financier Carl Lindner, but, interestingly, it was the Democrats who attracted the real high rollers. In the 2002 cycle, Democratic Party committees received several payments of over $1 million from trial lawyers like Texan John O'Quinn and media moguls Stephen Bing, Fred Eychaner, Robert Johnson, and Haim Saban—in January 2002 Saban, the children's television programmer, wrote one check for $7 million to the DNC. Whereas in 1992 soft money constituted 18 percent of Democratic Party receipts, in 2000 it made up 47 percent of the total, and in 2002, a non-presidential year, the Democrats raised more soft than hard money. The GOP, on the other hand, did not rely on soft dollars as much. In 1992, such funds were 16 percent of their treasure chest; in 2000 and 2002 they were just over 35 percent.

On March 27, 2002, President Bush signed the Bipartisan Campaign Reform Act—more popularly known as McCain-Feingold for its two Senate sponsors—and effectively banned soft-money donations to the national political-party committees as of the 2004 election cycle. No longer could the DNC, RNC, and House and Senate parties receive these huge checks.

McCain-Feingold restricted them to tightly limited hard dollars. Although the new law increased the hard-money donation limits to parties to $25,000, the parties would be compelled to cast their nets much further if they were to trawl in the kind of money they had in the previous decade.

Throughout an interminable legislative journey—begun in earnest after the abuses of the Clinton-Gore campaign in 1996—McCain-Feingold generally met resistance from Republicans. In 1998, for instance, House Republican leaders blocked floor debate on Shays-Meehan, the lower chamber's version of the bill, and it finally came to the floor after Democrats and a few renegade Republicans signed a rarely used discharge petition to extricate it from committee. The legislation also met with numerous GOP filibusters in the Senate, and it was a Republican senator, Mitch McConnell of Kentucky, who put his name to the legal challenge to the bill that was ultimately rejected by the Supreme Court. In the end, 176 House Republicans voted against McCain-Feingold, and in the Senate, the GOP voted eleven for, thirty-eight against. Democrats, on the other hand, supported the legislation. Only twelve House Democrats and two Senate Democrats opposed the bill on final passage. The motives of opponents were somewhat obvious. Republicans viewed soft money as the most effective way labor union financial resources could influence the political process.[76] Many Democrats saw it as the principal way by which Republicans offset inherent Democratic advantages in grassroots organization.

Yet McCain-Feingold has generally hurt the Democrats, not helped them. Somewhat presciently, the party was admonished by members of the Congressional Black Caucus during the bill's legislative journey, African American Democrats worried that without soft money they would have few means to get out the vote in their generally poor neighborhoods. In fact, according to political writer Seth Gitell, the bill "could hardly be more devastating to the Democrats if it had been drafted by the right-wing talk-show host Rush Limbaugh and the House Majority Leader, Tom DeLay."[77]

McCain-Feingold has been bad for the Democrats for two reasons. First, the soft money prohibition came at a time when, as we have seen, these unregulated dollars had helped the party close on the Republicans and comprised a significant part of the party's treasury. To be sure, Democrats have been extremely innovative and have quickly found outlets for unlimited contributions away from their formal national party organizations. Political activists sympathetic to Democratic causes have established "527s," groups—named for the section of the tax code that gives them tax-exempt status—that engage in voter mobilization efforts and run issue ads that laud or criticize a candidate's positions. As the parties did pre-McCain-Feingold, Democratic-leaning 527s also take large checks—Bush-nemesis George Soros gave in excess of $18 million during the 2004 election cycle, insurance executive Peter B. Lewis and Hollywood producer Stephen Bing each donated over $10 million. Among the big spending Democratic-friendly 527s are ACT, the Media Fund, and the MoveOn.org Voter Fund—ACT spent just over $55 million in 2004, the Media Fund about $46.5 million. According to the Campaign Finance Institute, 527s supportive of the Democrats received about $321 million during the 2004 campaign.[78]

What is more, there are some veteran party activists on these 527s' staffs—Harold Ickes, Stan Greenberg, and Jim Jordan, Kerry's first campaign manager, played prominent roles in all three mentioned above. Yet these groups can have no contact with the Democratic Party and its candidates and have proved difficult to corral.[79] Early in the 2004 race they proved useful at coordinating a broad assault on George W. Bush—they were, like most Democrats, galvanized by opposition to the president. In an organized ad campaign several 527s divvied out media markets in battleground states among themselves and America Votes, an umbrella under which many of these groups stood, was created, to quote Deb Callahan of the League of Conservation Voters, as a kind of "traffic cop" to ensure efforts were not duplicated and tasks did not go undone.[80] The 527s also took up Kerry's simple foreign policy messages of "strength" and "alliances" in the late summer when the Massachusetts senator had to rely on public financing given to him after he received his party's nomination.[81] By the fall, however, when Democratic presidential candidate John Kerry had to convey a complex and multifaceted message, the 527s' status outside of the formal party proved problematic. MoveOn.org ran a television ad questioning Bush's military service that was denounced by the Kerry campaign.

Some Democrats fear more long-term damage as 527s move the party to the left. There is also a grave concern that the groups will balkanize a weakened party incapable of arbitrating disputes. As Andrew Stern, the president of SEIU put it, "This is like post-Yugoslavia. We used to have a strongman called the party. After

McCain-Feingold we dissolved the power of Tito."[82] It is true that the emergence of groups like ACT has allowed the DNC to outsource voter mobilization. The result, however, is that a crucial function of the Democratic Party organization has withered. What is more, the centrifugal forces exerted by 527s will surely be greater when the Democrats are not running against such a galvanizing figure as Bush. By 2008, predicted Joe Cari Jr., the national finance chairman for the DNC in 2000, "these groups will have mushroomed into their own little primaries, with candidates competing for their money and grassroots organization—all to the demise of the DNC."[83]

At first, Republican supporters were slow to form and fund 527s. David French, a lobbyist for the International Food Services Distribution Association, synopsized a central concern, that of control, this way, "You give your money over to some entity that is loosely affiliated with a particular political purpose and loosely regulated."[84] After the FEC refused to criminalize 527 soft-money activities in May 2004, however, Republican-affiliated organizations started to catch up quickly. Early and influential GOP-friendly 527s included Citizens United, the Progress for America Voter Fund, The Leadership Forum, American Resolve, Americans for a Better Country, and the Chamber of Commerce-financed November Fund.[85] Another important group, Swift Vets and POWs for Truth, was famous for its ads questioning John Kerry's Vietnam service. Despite the sluggish start, GOP-friendly groups raised and spent millions. Important big dollar contributors included Alex G. Spanos, Texas oilman T. Boone Pickens, Ameriquest Capital's Dawn Arnall, and Amway co-founder Richard M. DeVos. The Swift Vets went through about $13.75 million and the Progress for America Voter Fund about $28.8 million, including $14 million on one ad alone—the story of the President and a young girl who lost her mother in the World Trade Center attacks. As a result, these 527s neutralized their opponents somewhat, especially late in the campaign. Indeed, a month before the election they were outspending their Democratic rivals six to one on television and radio.[86] As Brian McCabe from the Progress for America Voter Fund put it, "We got a late start and had to play some catch up. But once we got started, we were aggressive, focused and determined to level the playing field."[87] His group poured money into battleground states, and the November Fund went after Vice-Presidential candidate John Edwards and trial lawyers. As McCain-Feingold's great nemesis,

Mitch McConnell, had presciently forecast the day the Supreme Court upheld the law's soft-money ban in December 2003: "Soft money is not gone, it has just changed its address."[88]

The second problem posed to the Democrats by the new campaign-finance regime is the changes made to hard-money limits. As part of the deal to get enough Republican votes for McCain-Feingold, reform proponents agreed to a doubling, to $2,000, and an indexing for inflation of the limit to the contributions of individuals to candidates. This was in addition to an increase in the hard-money limit of annual donations to parties to $25,000. The compromise benefits the GOP because, although the Democrats may have more supporters willing to sign checks of $1 million or more, the Republicans have many more partisans willing to give between $1,000 and $2,000. In 2000, for example, Bush had 59,279 $1,000 donors; Al Gore had 19,298. Indeed, empirical work undertaken on a survey by researchers at the Campaign Finance Institute suggests that it is GOP donors who are most likely to take advantage of the new hard money limits and give more to their party and candidates.[89]

True to form, the Republicans have done a tremendous job identifying top-dollar hard-money contributors and getting them to give generously. Much of this is attributable to incumbency—many donors are "access" donors who prefer to use money to influence policy-makers rather than elections—and the star power of the president who can fill convention halls with people willing to pay a couple of thousand dollars for a sandwich and a twenty-minute speech. On several occasions Bush has raised over $5 million in a day doing this. Bill Clinton was similarly adept. But there is more to the GOP's hard money outreach than incumbency. The Bush campaigns in 2000 and 2004 built an impressive fundraising infrastructure designed to reach as many high-dollar donors as possible. This was done by recruiting "bundlers"—essentially conduits who are able to pull disparate contributions together for a candidate. The Bush campaign called them "Pioneers," "Rangers," or "Super Rangers," depending on how much they were able to generate—for 2004 designees roped in over $100,000, $200,000, and $300,000, respectively. These bundlers, because of their motivation and professional and social connections, were first recruited, cultivated, and extolled. They responded by making calls, organizing luncheons, and holding fundraisers. They were next "maintained." They were continually thanked and invited to get-togethers with the president and administration higher-ups. They became a special class of donors who could then be easily identified and rewarded.[90] In 2000 twenty-one Pioneers were rewarded with ambassadorships, including to such desirable spots as Madrid and Paris, and three got into the cabinet—Elaine Chao at Labor, Don Evans at Commerce, and Tom Ridge at Homeland Security.[91] Most of the rest were regularly invited to the White House and Bush's Crawford ranch. The outreach was so successful that in 2000, 60 percent of the money Bush received was in maximum-allowed $1,000 increments. According to a *Washington Post* study, the 2000 Pioneers came mainly from Bush's connections with Texas; the Republican Governor's Association; the oil business; major-league baseball; his brother Jeb, governor of Florida; and his father.[92] Mercer Reynolds III, financier and soon-to-be ambassador to Switzerland, was the top bundler bringing in about $600,000. He became the president's national finance chairman in 2004. In 2004 Stan O'Neal, CEO of Merrill Lynch; lobbyist Thomas Loeffler; and Carl Lindner were among Bush's Super Rangers.

The GOP has also ingeniously discovered new ways to exploit hard-money advantages. In the waning weeks of the 2004 presidential campaign, for example, the party realized that it could use hard money to supplement the federal dollars the Bush campaign had received after the president's nomination at Madison Square Garden in early September. As long as the money was used to convey a broad message shared by Republican candidates, as well as Bush, it was okay for the GOP to channel funds from the RNC's overflowing hard-money account to bolster his reelection effort.[93]

The new hard-money reality is not all bad news for Democrats. As Anthony Corrado and Thomas Mann of the Brookings Institution reported throughout 2004, the Democrats kept pace with the GOP and insured that the election would not "be determined by a disparity of resources."[94] Indeed, in 2004 the party tripled its hard-money total of 2000 and raised $389.8 million— even surpassing the GOP by $4.5 million. The party also has its own bundlers—that year the Democrats' presidential candidate had 266 "Vice-Chairs" who each raised at least $100,000. Kerry garnered money at an unprecedented clip in the spring of 2004— over $1 million a day between March and June—and all the Democratic presidential candidates in 2004 raised about $143 million more than Bush. Moreover, and as we mentioned earlier, the party has, up until now at least, better exploited the opportunities provided by the Internet. The 2004 campaign delivered thousands of new Democratic donors, many of whom gave through cyberspace. The Internet is a particularly useful fundraising tool because it facilitates "impulse" donations—in the words of political scientist Michael Cornfield, "You can give two moments after you've seen something that motivates you to give."[95] However, when we consider that about 90 percent of those earning in excess of $100,000 are not giving now, new rules, technologies, and methods that allow the exploitation of previously untapped resources of campaign money can presumably only help the GOP.[96] I also think 2004 provided a poor test of BCRA's effects on Democratic fundraising capabilities. The soft-money ban and hard-money contribution increases are likely to hurt the party when someone less polarizing than George W. Bush is at the top of the GOP ticket.

Third, Republicans have largely overcome intrinsic Democratic advantages in voter mobilization. Getting people to the polls used to be a labor-intensive enterprise well suited to the Democratic Party's capabilities. It could rely on the organization and manpower of organized labor, the urban party machines, the civil-rights movement, and African American churches to contact its core supporters and get them to the polls on election day. Now the party is largely what Daniel Shea calls "base-less," it is elite-led and relies less on a readily available, quasi-permanent, and committed army of grassroots volunteers.[97] In turn, this top-down approach exacerbates an emaciation of Democratic affiliates' organizational capabilities that was begun by dramatic and pervasive social, economic, and political changes. Unions provide a good example of this deterioration. In 2003, 15.8 million workers—or 12.9 percent of the labor force—were in a union. Only 8.2 percent of private-sector workers were in a union. The aggregate membership rate was 20.1 percent of the labor force in 1983 and around 30 percent in the mid-1960s. The decline in membership and a concomitant diminution of political influence is attributable, in varying degrees, to several factors including the shift from manufacturing to service industries, increased foreign competition, government-mandated benefits that unions traditionally secured for their members, and inimical public policy created largely during the Reagan years.[98] As unions declined, moreover, they also lost the ability to turn out all types of voters—Benjamin Radcliff's empirical work has revealed a connection between union strength and political participation within a geographical area.[99] In turn, Democratic elites feel less beholden to labor interests. During the Clinton years, the White House pushed for a series of trade-liberalization measures—the creation of the World Trade Organization, fast-track negotiating authority for the White House, and permanent normal trade relations with China—that were vigorously opposed by the labor movement. A Democratic president less encumbered by obligations to the unions did not feel compelled to reward them. The result is a vicious cycle and a union movement increasingly less capable and willing to work for the Democrats.

Clinton certainly aroused black voters. He was comfortable with them, and they respected his upbringing and empathized with him as he defended himself during the impeachment process, but like organized labor, and as we shall see in Chapter 9, African American institutions critical to mobilizing the black vote are in decline.[100] Indeed, although black turnout in recent presidential elections seems to be increasing slightly, the reason is a widespread cynicism with politics—chariness among whites, curiously, depresses voting—and not organization.[101]

As we saw in Chapter 4, the GOP, on the other hand, still has a highly motivated labor force, the Christian right. As former RNC chair Rich Bond said in 2004, "Republicans have refused to concede the ground game to the Democrats. The Republican Party under these guys is as well equipped as labor ever was."[102] Perhaps more importantly for the Republicans, however, is the fact that, as Robert Putnam has put it, "Financial capital—the wherewithal for mass marketing—has steadily replaced social capital—that is, grassroots citizen networks—as the coin of the realm."[103] Put another way, voter mobilization can be paid for these days. Notwithstanding the importance ascribed to grassroots, get-out-the-vote efforts described earlier, campaigns are, as political scientist John Green puts it, becoming more "capital-intensive."[104] Money has traditionally been important in campaigns—it buys media advertising, direct mail, and automated phone messages, for instance. These days it increasingly buys help as well. The GOP, then, is in a better position to secure the assistance of the skilled professionals who jump from candidate to candidate, moving from presidential races and an office in Des Moines to a senatorial one headquartered in Raleigh. It can even hire the type of blue-collar people the Democrats have relied on for volunteers to collect signatures in voter-registration and petition drives—campaigns paid $.75 to $1 per signature during the California gubernatorial recall in 2003, for instance. In a political world of free agents with few loyalties, the Republicans' financial advantage will only become more critical.

Money has also become increasingly important as electoral processes have become more diverse and complex. A significant number of states, for example, are turning to mail-in ballots and are allowing people to vote early at special sites rather than submit to a complex absentee procedure. Indeed, 14 percent of the electorate is said to have taken advantage of such early voting in 2004. The mail-only system in Oregon does not seem to benefit any party particularly, but the expensive exercise of tracking those who have voted and continuing to target those who have not surely helps the GOP.[105] To be sure, both parties have exploited early voting procedures by helping people to collect the appropriate form and to fill it in correctly so as not to have the vote disqualified. Both parties cross reference lists of people who have requested mail ballots or utilized early voting procedures and then, according to a Bush-Cheney 2004 campaign official, "chase the vote all the way through the process."[106] Indeed, the Democrats' efforts to take advantage of Arizona's liberalized absentee rules during the 2002 gubernatorial election are seen as a kind of model.[107] But J. Eric Oliver argues the GOP has generally organized its supporters to better take advantage of the new processes.[108] In 2004, for example, BIPAC facilitated early voting among employees sympathetic to Republican candidates. Trade associations and corporations also formed "Helping America Vote" to advise their members how to take advantage of absentee voting rules in various states. Even those, such as Jeffrey Karp and Susan Banducci, who do not believe new procedures provide Republicans with an inherent advantage recognize the way we will vote tomorrow is better exploited by well-financed party organizations that can use expensive technologies to cull lists for those who have yet to vote.[109] What is more, R. Michael Alvarez and Thad E. Hall, in one of the first serious and in-depth analyses of the subject, argue that Republicans are most likely to benefit from the spread of Internet voting.[110]

It is surely true that both political parties have strengthened as organizations since the tumultuous politics of the 1960s and 1970s. Although splits remain, the Democrats have certainly recovered since they were ripped apart by internecine warfare in the

1960s and demoralized in the 1980s. In 2004 they were particularly energized and galvanized by an intense desire to defeat George W. Bush. Yet, today the party is intrinsically weaker than the GOP. The Republicans have more money and a more unified leadership. They seem to paper over ideological cracks better. In addition, they have overcome inherent disadvantages at the grass-roots level and have exploited technological advances in politics at least as well as have their opponents.

The GOP has, it could be said, organized proficiently to win the hearts and minds of much of the American electorate. In this they have been assisted greatly by the information industries. The war for hearts is being won on the battlefields of talk radio, cable-television news, the Internet, and bookstore shelves. Sophisticated Republican ideas are winning minds today, too. Conservative and libertarian thought now pervade the world of think tanks, social science, and policy research, long bastion of liberalism. These developments are the subject of the next chapter.

8

Winning Hearts and Minds: The Media and the Republican Ideas Industry

That the American mass media are incorrigibly liberal has been an enduring axiom of conservative thought. It is true that since the Depression on only three occasions—1964, 1992, and 2004—have more newspapers around the country endorsed the Democratic presidential candidate than his Republican opponent. Yet, to many conservatives, most small-town papers, rooted as they are in middle-American culture, have minimal influence compared with the mammoth New York, Washington, and Hollywood media establishment, which cunningly pushes liberal-policy prescriptions and Democratic philosophy and candidates onto an unsuspecting public. It is true that columnists like Robert Novak, William Safire, and George Will, as well as the late Robert Bartley's *Wall Street Journal* editorial page, have steadfastly promoted Republican positions over many decades. Yet, as far as many Republicans are concerned, theirs are lonely voices in the press. Indeed, for much of American conservatism media executives and journalists are generally arrogant blowhards who look down their noses at the cultural attitudes of most of the country. To former CBS News executive Bernard Goldberg, "sophisticated media elites don't categorize their beliefs as liberal but as simply the correct way to do things." They don't just disagree with conservatives but see them as "morally deficient."[1] It was this kind of thinking that left Mel Gibson's *The Passion of the Christ* off of the nomination list for best picture in 2004. To Ann Coulter, a particularly aggressive member of the conservative punditocracy and a participant in what Eric Alterman derisively calls the "right-wing blond fashion craze," "the left's media dictatorship" keeps conservatives from being heard.[2]

There is something to these charges. In 2004, for example, *Editor and Publisher* calculated that about fifty more newspapers endorsed John Kerry than did George W. Bush. Journalists are also notoriously Democratic in their personal politics. A 1996 Roper Center/ Freedom Forum poll found that 89 percent of Washington journalists voted for Bill Clinton in 1992, but only 7 percent voted for George H. W. Bush. A May 2004 Pew Research Center for the People and the Press poll found that 34 percent of journalists considered themselves liberal; only 7 percent thought of themselves as conservatives. This does not necessarily mean that pro-Democratic bias seeps into stories, of course, but observers sometimes do detect it. A 2000 Pew poll discovered that 47 percent of the public believed the media were rooting for Al Gore in the presidential election, while only 23 percent felt they were pulling for George W. Bush. Interestingly, even 36 percent of Democratic respondents said that journalists seemed to be hoping for a Gore win, 6 percent more than those who thought the press wanted Bush to be victorious. The Center for Media and Public Affairs found that in the 1996 presidential election 50 percent of nightly newscast stories about Bill Clinton were positive, while only one-third of those about Bob Dole were. In 1992 these figures were 52 percent of those about Bill Clinton and only 29 percent of those about George H. W. Bush. What is more, press coverage of the economy during that election was more negative than macroeconomic indicators suggested it should be.[3] Others found different kinds of demonstrable pro-Clinton media bias in the 1992 campaign.[4] Using more recent data, political scientists Tim Groseclose and Jeff Milyo have created ideology scores for several news outlets based upon the think tanks they cite and found a majority of their sample—especially the CBS Evening News, the *New York Times*, and *USA Today*—to be well to the left of the median member of the U.S. House of Representatives.[5] Wilson Mixon, Amit Sen, and E. Frank Stephenson have even shown what they call "bias" in the calling of the 2000 presidential election. They reveal that, when controlling for margin of victory and other conceivable influences, CNN called results in states that went to Gore about fifteen minutes before they did those that went for Bush.[6]

The evidence exists on issues, too. Kenneth Dautrich and Thomas Hartley reveal that journalists are overwhelmingly pro-choice.[7] Paul Maurer detected a liberal bias in the media's treatment of those individuals who accused Bill Clinton during the presidential scandals of the 1990s.[8]

Yet on the other hand, there are also many systematic and empirical analyses of the media that have found no real ideological or partisan bias. Using twenty years of newspaper coverage of governors, for example, David Niven could not find any demonstrable aggregate favoritism.[9] He also found no bias in coverage of presidents, members of Congress, and mayors of different parties.[10] David Domke and colleagues' large content analysis of the 1996 presidential campaign did not detect discernible bias.[11] David D'Alessio and Michael Allen's meta-analysis of newspaper coverage of presidential campaigns since 1948 came up empty-handed as well.[12] This has all led prominent scholar Kathleen Hall Jamieson to conclude that, "Content analysis has failed to demonstrate a systematic liberal bias in press reports on politics."[13]

Indeed, it seems Republican ideas are well represented in the mainstream media today. Talk radio is an especially friendly arena. In a 2003 *Talkers* magazine survey of the top twenty-five national talk-radio shows by audience, not one host could reasonably be considered liberal.[14] Most were incontrovertibly conservative. They included Sean Hannity, Laura Schlessinger, Michael Savage, Glenn Beck, Mike Gallagher, G. Gordon Liddy, Bill O'Reilly, Michael Medved, and Laura Ingraham. These national stars have, in turn, spawned an army of clones on local radio stations across the country. People like Jerry Agar, formerly in North Carolina and now in Kansas City, Marc Bernier in Florida, Bill Cunningham in Cincinnati, Mark Davis in Dallas, Dave Elswick in Arkansas, Dom Giordano in Philadelphia, Bob Grant in New York, Roger Hedgecock in San Diego, Tom Marr in Baltimore, Bob Mohan in Phoenix, Mike Rosen in Denver, Tom Sullivan in Sacramento, and Kirby Wilbur in Seattle attract millions of listeners everyday.

The king of conservative talk radio, though, is Rush Limbaugh. Limbaugh is essentially a performer who worked his early days in radio in Kansas City, Pittsburgh, and Sacramento before hitting it big with the political format in New York. In fact, one of his former producers, Kitty O'Neal, told Paul Colford that she did not think it was Rush's "intention at all to become this big, conservative icon for so many people. A lot of it was just shtick—still is shtick."[15] In the early 1990s, however, Limbaugh began to effectively push "a body of beliefs that strikes terror into the heart of even the most well-entrenched liberals, shaking them to their core."[16] Credited with almost single-handedly ending forty years of Democratic rule in Congress in 1994, Limbaugh began to team up with Republican politicians and activists to broadcast a daily tirade against all things liberal. Today, he reaches about 15 million people on over 650 radio stations around the country—despite his celebrated addiction to prescription drugs and his unceremonious firing from ESPN's Sunday Night Football in 2003 for making racially charged remarks. It is certainly true that many listen to Rush for entertainment and many others to vindicate beliefs they have long held—a 2004 Gallup poll showed that 77 percent of those who tuned in to the show considered themselves conservative. There exists research, however, that shows listening to Limbaugh can have a palpable effect. Social scientist David Barker has illustrated that the show motivates conservative listeners into political action while turning liberal listeners into shrinking violets.[17] He has also demonstrated that Limbaugh's show helped increase the GOP vote in the 1994 and 1996 elections.[18]

The influence of Limbaugh and his compadres would not be so important to the GOP's edge if there was a meaningful liberal equivalent, but of the 22 percent of Americans who, according to a 2002 Gallup survey, listen to talk radio on a daily basis, very few hear voices like those of Jack Ellery, Thom Hartmann, Randi Rhodes, and Ed Schultz—that is, from the left. Air America Radio, a recent attempt by liberals to broadcast their views on a single network, has met with little success. In the summer of 2004, three months after its launch, the network was still playing on only fifteen stations—including three in Hawaii and others in places like Anchorage; Chapel Hill, North Carolina; and San Luis Obispo, California. Clear Channel Communications tried later to give it a go in liberal hotbeds like Ann Arbor and Portland, Oregon and by early 2005 it had two million listeners and fifty-one affiliated stations. Yet liberals are still scarce on the A.M. dial.

Republican elites understand the power of talk radio. Elected officials and party activists regularly call in or get themselves invited to shows hosted by conservatives. Not only does this allow them to quickly and easily reach their party's base, but it motivates the radio personalities who are doing important leg work for them. Phil Valentine, a conservative host from Nashville who interviewed Karl Rove and White House chief of staff Andy Card in 2003, said of the party's willingness to give him access to its stars, "It shows people like me that we're on the radar screen and they care about us. That makes a big difference."[19]

When it comes to the printed word, however, the Republican advantage is not so clear. Three of the top five selling newspapers in the country probably have a liberal hue—the *New York Times*, the *Washington Post*, and the *Los Angeles Times*. Indeed, the *Times* even admits to it.[20] The new giant in the generally shrinking newspaper market, *USA Today*, provides its roughly 2.6 million readers with an editorial page that is "decidedly moderate and nonideological, taking up issues on a case-by-case basis, never veering far from the center."[21] Still, Republican thought is effectively passed along by the print media. There is an army of conservative syndicated columnists—among the most prominent are Charles Krauthammer and George Will. The Bush administration even put three columnists—Margaret Gallagher, Michael McManus, and Armstrong Williams—on the government payroll. This was ostensibly for government work, but it may be that the White House was hoping to influence their writing as well.

Moreover, the country's second-largest circulating paper, the *Wall Street Journal*, has an unabashedly conservative editorial page to which it exposes its roughly 1.8 million readers. *Journal* editorials, the paper's former editor Robert L. Bartley once said, "are always advocating free markets and free men."[22] Other Republican-leading newspapers are also gaining market share and influence. Foremost among these is the Reverend Sun Myung Moon's *Washington Times*, Rupert Murdoch's *New York Post*, and Hollinger International's *Chicago Sun-Times*. More importantly, perhaps, is the fact that these outlets disseminate conservative ideas more aggressively than do their more liberal counterparts. In a 2003 study Michael Tomasky revealed that the editorial pages of the *Wall Street Journal* and *Washington Times* were far more critical of Bill Clinton than the *New York Times* and *Washington Post* were of George W. Bush.[23]

Republicans and conservatives must also battle it out for supremacy in the land of opinion magazines. Here, conservatives have had several outlets, including the sixty-year-old *Human Events*, the *Public Interest*, and the influential *American Spectator*, but the big two are William F. Buckley's *National Review* and Bill

Kristol's *Weekly Standard*. The former steadfastly took conservative positions when doing so was widely unpopular—Buckley and his publisher, William Rusher, vigorously promoted Barry Goldwater in the mid-1960s, for example. Founded in 1995, the *Standard*, on the other hand, has enjoyed a more salubrious political climate, even though it has yet to make money. Still, it is read closely by members of the Bush administration and seems to have had some influence on policy.[24] In 2002 the *National Review* and *Weekly Standard* together had a per-issue circulation rate of about 220,000—20,000 more than their liberal equivalents, the *New Republic* and the *Nation*.[25]

Bookstore shelves are also deeply divided along partisan lines. Democrats and liberals, for example, have recently hit the bestseller lists with scathing attacks—some witty, some sophomoric, others just plain nasty—on the right. As I discussed in Chapter 1, most of these recent titles take aim at George W. Bush, but there are other works of character assassination like Al Franken's number one *New York Times* bestsellers, *Rush Limbaugh Is a Big Fat Idiot and Other Observations* and *Lies and the Lying Liars Who Tell Them: A Fair and Balanced Look at the Right*, which skewers Fox News channel's Bill O'Reilly. There have also been popular and truculent swipes at conservatives more generally, such as Michael Moore's *Dude, Where's My Country?* and Joe Conason's *Big Lies*. Conservatives, however, are not to be outdone. Among recent mega-sellers on the right are Ann Coulter's *Slander, Treason*, and *How to Talk to a Liberal (If You Must)*; Mona Charen's *Useful Idiots*; Hugh Hewitt's *If It's Not Close They Can't Cheat*; Michael Savage's *The Savage Nation* and *Liberalism Is a Mental Disorder*; John E. O'Neill and Jerome R. Corsi's *Unfit for Command: Swift Boat Veterans Speak Out against John Kerry*; and from Fox's talking heads, O'Reilly's *Who's Looking Out for You?* and Sean Hannity's *Let Freedom Ring*.

Indeed, this market is so lucrative that publishers have been falling all over themselves to put writers into print. Book publishing has long been an activity of conservatives wishing to influence the nation's discourse—Henry Regnery Sr. released classics like William Buckley's *God and Man at Yale* and Russell Kirk's *The Conservative Mind* in the 1950s. But funded by sympathetic deep-pocketed foundations like Bradley and Olin and led by entrepreneurial editors frustrated at established houses, Regnery and others boosted their output dramatically in the 1980s. Large mainstream publishers also created new imprints—such as Random

House's Crown Forum—as a vehicle for conservative titles and organizations.[26] It seems just about anyone can make money by selling books to the conservative faithful. Fourteen-year-old Kyle Williams' *Seen and Heard* and his contemporary Ben Ferguson's *It's My America, Too* are in the now tried-and-trusted recipe of vitriol. Perhaps the most telling evidence that the publishing industry is increasingly welcoming conservative voices, however, can be found in the larger market for fiction. Max Lucado and Randy Singer, for instance, have sold hundreds of thousands of copies of books aimed at a Christian audience. So have Tim LaHaye, Jerry B. Jenkins, and Joel Rosenberg.[27] Ostensibly thrillers, many of these books—LaHaye and Jenkins have the "Left Behind" series, Rosenberg *The Last Jihad* and *The Last Days*—present an apocalyptical future and sell a conservative message of American virtue that is under constant attack by ruthless enemies.

Republican and conservative positions have fought liberals close to parity in the electronic media, as well. The Web is a sprawling mass of news sites and Web logs belonging to thousands of liberals, conservatives, and any other political persuasion one can think of. Liberal blogs—like MyDD, Daily Kos, and Eschaton—have certainly created a buzz and have raised money for the Democrats,[28] but there are also individual conservative-tilting news sites with above average influence like the Drudge Report, Townhall.com, Andrew Sullivan, FreeRepublic.com, and InstaPundit.[29] Indeed, the army of conservative bloggers has scored notable victories—it has recently created pressure significant enough to force Dan Rather of CBS to step down after airing a story using falsified documents about President Bush's military record and Eason Jordan of CNN to resign for alleged comments about how U.S. military personnel in Iraq target journalists. Moreover, many liberal bloggers feel their conservative counterparts do a better job disseminating their message. As left-wing blogger Bob Fertik lamented, "The way we perceive it is that right-wing bloggers are able to invent stories, get them out on Drudge, get them on Rush Limbaugh, get them on Fox, and pretty soon that spills over into the mainstream media."[30] Still, the blogosphere, as the virtual space in which bloggers operate is known, seems to belong to no party or philosophy.

Republican influence is expanding on television, however. The networks used to have a monopoly on TV news, but the last twenty years have seen the emergence of cable stations whose *raison d'être* is current affairs. The king was Ted Turner's Cable

News Network or CNN that was baptized as "America's news channel" on June 1, 1980.[31] Today, however, CNN has been usurped. Of cable news prime-time viewers in the summer of 2004, 56 percent watched Rupert Murdoch and the GOP media consultant Roger Ailes' Fox News channel—only 32 percent tuned into CNN. During the three nights the networks broadcast live coverage of the 2004 Republican National Convention, more people watched Fox than any other station, including ABC, CBS, and NBC. On election night 2004, Fox had 8.1 million viewers, about the same as CNN and MSNBC combined. Nielsen Media Research estimates that CNN had an average nightly audience of 775,000 viewers during the 2004–2005 season, Fox about two million. Indeed, in eight years, Fox has not only become the leader it is now the model for CNN and its other main rival, MSNBC. The two trailing networks have imitated Fox's talk show format and the bottom-of-the-screen "crawl" that became ubiquitous after September 11. CNN even duplicated the whooshing sound Fox uses to introduce breaking news.

Fox's rise to the top has come not from covering hard news in a better or revolutionary way. Instead it appeals to the many who feel the American media are biased. It has long considered itself an underdog and outsider; Murdoch and Ailes felt they were different from the media establishment from the beginning.[32] Fox implicitly takes shots at the liberal-media elite when it argues that "we report, you decide" and that its presentation is "fair and balanced." It also lacks, according to media critic Gene Veith, "the sense of out-of-touch elitism that makes many Americans, whatever their politics, annoyed with the news media."[33]

Moreover, Fox programming is ebullient, edgy, and opinionated. This makes it entertaining. As *New Yorker* writer Joe Klein put it, "Television is all about energy and Fox has a lot more energy than its competitors."[34] Bill O'Reilly, Fox's star and the host of cable news' top-rated show, attributes the network's success to the fact that it is "daring."[35] Ailes quickly realized that people provided this oomph, and he rejected CNN's early mantra that the news should be the star.[36] He now has a stable of proven winners—O'Reilly, Sean Hannity, Alan Colmes, Shepard Smith, Brit Hume, and Greta Van Susteren—to animate the news.

Fox is indubitably conservative. A quick glance at its on-air talent provides evidence of this. Moreover, you did not need to be convinced of the *New York Times'* objectivity to agree with its reporter Jim Rutenberg's assertion that the network had aggressively supported the Bush administration's decisions during the Iraq war.[37] Together with its entertaining packaging, this stance has hurt it with many viewers—according to a May 2004 Pew poll, only 24 percent of Democrats "believe all or most" of the information they get from Fox, and only 29 percent of Republicans do. Still, Fox's philosophy helps it attract like-minded viewers— according to the Pew survey, 35 percent of Republicans get their news from Fox, compared to 19 percent who regularly watch CNN. It also makes the network a critical component of the new, more GOP-sympathetic media.

   This all begs the question: Why have the media, long thought to be inhospitable to Republican and conservative positions, become more GOP-friendly in the past decade or so? A number of reasons are regularly offered. First, many argue that Democrats and their philosophy are not particularly well suited to the fiery format of increasingly popular talk-radio and television punditry. Former CNN chief Walter Isaacson argues that liberals are "more timid and easily cowed" and that when they "have strong beliefs, they act as if they were not quite sure they actually agree with them."[38] As Democratic consultant Bob Shrum put it, "It's probably a weakness that we're not real haters. We don't have a sense that it's a holy crusade. We don't have a sense that it's Armageddon."[39] On the other hand, Democracy Radio Inc.'s head Tom Athens has argued that liberals have a communication problem of a different sort. In his words, they "sound too erudite, it's like egg-heads talking at you."[40]

   Others think the dearth of liberals in these formats is more a lack of demand. Hendrick Hertzberg has written that Democrats do not think of politics as entertainment. Indeed, "they wouldn't think it was fun to listen to raw expressions of contempt for conservatives."[41] Political scientist William Mayer has argued that conservatives dominate talk radio because their potential audience is bigger. In turn, this is largely the case because liberals have long had Tom Brokaw, Peter Jennings, Dan Rather, and National Public Radio and do not need the medium.[42]

   Still, that liberal filmmakers do a pretty good job packaging vit-riol into documentaries suggests Democrats are perhaps not quite so soft and quiet. So does the fact that audiences eat their work up. Michael Moore's sulfurous critique of George W. Bush, *Fahrenheit 9/11*, took in over $100 million at the box office—much more than the conservative retort, *Celsius 41.11: The Temperature at Which Your*

Brain Dies. Moore's *Bowling for Columbine*—which examined gun violence—is the second-highest-grossing documentary of all time. Although not so obviously anti-conservative, other films in this genre have been successful recently, including Morgan Spurlock's parody of McDonald's food, *Super Size Me*, and *Control Room*, a study of the Al-Jazeera network critical of the U.S. war in Iraq.

Second, these days aggressive investigative journalism often works against Democrats. Since Bob Woodward and Carl Bernstein ushered in a new era of reporting with their uncovering of the Watergate scandal in the early 1970s, ambitious journalists have aspired to replicate their administration toppling work. When Clinton was president, for instance, we read and heard thousands of stories about Monica Lewinsky, Travelgate, Vince Foster, FBI files, and Whitewater. Indeed, many began to feel that the media were going too far, that they were contributing too much to the rise of cynicism and the erosion of trust in American public life. As a result, we might have witnessed a backing off in the last few years. To be sure, much ink has been spilled on Dick Cheney's "secret" energy task force, the veep's connections to Haliburton and the corporation's securing of government contracts in the reconstruction of Iraq, and the murky nexus between the administration and the Swift Vets and POWs for Truth—the group that ran television ads accusing John Kerry of lying about his Vietnam service. But the generally liberal *New York Times* and *Washington Post* feel that they gave the Bush administration a free pass during the build-up to the Iraq war by, among other things, mistakenly taking its word for it that Saddam Hussein possessed weapons of mass destruction.[43] Moreover, when Dan Rather went after Bush's service in the Air National Guard, the veteran CBS anchor based his story on forged documents and created an event that boomeranged in the president's favor.

That the media fancy themselves as advocates for the public interest has had other consequences that can help the Republican cause. The massive budget deficits of the past quarter-century have motivated hundreds of investigative reporters to uncover profligacy in Washington. NBC, for example, has run the "Fleecing of America" segment on its nightly news for many years. ABC News' "Your Money" also looks at government waste. The preoccupation with this type of coverage has, in turn, perpetuated the notion that the government is at best incompetent and at worst a thief—a message that, of course, is consistent with the GOP's general outlook.

A third reason for the emergence of a media climate more hospitable to the GOP is the rapid concentration of outlets into the hands of a small number of huge corporations. The trend has been facilitated by a loosening of ownership restrictions permitted by the 1996 Telecommunications Act. That same year, for example, Disney bought Capital Cities/ABC in a $19 billion deal. Also in 1996, Westinghouse/CBS's acquisition of Infinity Broadcasting equated to a huge consolidation of the radio industry. In 1999 Viacom bought CBS for $36 billion, and the following year, the largest media merger ever, between Internet giant AOL and Time Warner, took place. In August 2003 NBC absorbed the French company Vivendi Universal. After these and other mega mergers, most of the American media found itself in the hands of just five massive conglomerates. The largest, Time Warner, owns, among other things, CNN, TBS, TNT, twenty-four magazines, the second-largest cable company in the country, the second-largest publishing house, and Warner Brothers' studio. The other four are Disney—which now includes ABC and ESPN and was nearly bought by cable giant Comcast in 2004—Murdoch's News Corp.—which owns the *New York Post*, the *Weekly Standard*, and HarperCollins, in addition to Fox—Viacom—which has CBS, Paramount Pictures, UPN, MTV, Infinity Broadcasting's radio stations, and Simon & Schuster—and Bertelsman—which dominates European media and controls Random House.[44] A sixth corporation, Clear Channel Communications, owns over 1,200 radio stations and 35 television stations in the United States. Moreover, the concentration may be intensified if the Federal Communications Commission (FCC) gets its way. Although a federal court overturned the commission's 2003 ruling relaxing ownership limits in individual media markets, the FCC, even without the forceful leadership of former head Michael Powell, may continue to push to allow companies to accumulate television and radio stations.

Much the same has occurred in the newspaper industry. Whereas papers were locally owned and most cities generally had more than one, today most belong to a large conglomerate. Among today's newspaper behemoths are Gannett—which owns about one hundred U.S. dailies, including *USA Today*—the Tribune Company—which holds both the *Chicago Tribune* and the *Los Angeles Times*—Knight Ridder, and Newhouse Newspapers.

This dramatic consolidation has placed tremendous top-down commercial pressures on news people. Mergers and acquisitions have motivated owners and managers to make reporters, editors, and news directors acutely aware of the economics of covering politics. Increasingly, the bottom line drives media coverage—Walter Cronkite has observed that "it's a dollars-and-sense-issue with the ownership."[45] Martin Gilens and Craig Hertzman, for example, have shown that newspapers whose parent companies stood to gain relatively more from the loosening of ownership restrictions in the 1996 Telecommunications Act tended to provide the legislation with more favorable coverage.[46] The economic pressures, in turn, create a tendency to endear yourself to broad audiences, be uncontroversial, and, in the words of Eric Alterman, "turn away from what journalists like to term 'spinach,' or the kind of news that citizens require to carry out their duties as intelligent, informed members of a political democracy toward pudding—the sweet, nutritionally vacant fare that is the stock in trade of the news outlets."[47] Pudding, or soft news as it is generally called, includes coverage of health, crime, and popular culture. It has proliferated spectacularly in all forms of media in recent years.[48] An increased reliance on soft news does not make the media more GOP-friendly, of course, but it does make them less predisposed to the type of public-journalism-cum-social-activism that many conservatives point to as evidence of liberal bias.

Pressures from the commercial side of media enterprises have been felt in other ways, too. Many in the industry worry about the "crumbling wall" between advertising departments and the newsroom at television stations and newspapers. A 2001 study by the *Columbia Journalism Review*, for example, found that 53 percent of television news directors felt pressure from advertisers and marketing departments "to kill negative stories or run positive ones."[49] A 2004 survey by the Pew Center for the People and the Press found that 66 percent of news people felt "the effect of bottom-line pressure" was "hurting" news coverage—an increase from 49 percent on a similar study done in 1999. Again, none of this is *prima facie* evidence of a conservative tilt, but it does suggest a media less free to pursue the kinds of political interests in the way it could in the past.

A fourth reason, forwarded by conservatives Richard Viguerie and David Franke, is the end of the "fairness doctrine."[50] Established by the FCC in 1949, the policy was supposed to make sure media coverage was politically balanced. By the mid-1980s, however, there was a widespread feeling that it had had a "chilling effect" on political coverage and had outlived its usefulness. The FCC subsequently dropped it. Unshackled, many media outlets were able to present popular conservative messages in an undiluted format.

Finally, the fragmentation of the consumer, especially when it comes to television, has assisted the GOP. There may be fewer owners in the industry, but there are many more new outlets. Cable and satellite have brought a whole host of channels that have eaten into the broadcast networks' audiences—according to Nielsen Media Research, ABC, CBS, and NBC were watched by 71 percent of prime-time viewers in 1992; by early 2004 the big three, along with Fox, UPN, the WB, and Pax, were watched by only 52 percent. Reaching individual voters through television advertising has therefore become more expensive as campaigns must buy from more outlets.[51] And, as we saw in the previous chapter, Republicans are advantaged when elections cost more.

The GOP, then, can only benefit from this more genial media climate. Even better for the party's prospects is the fact that—as we saw with judicial politics in Chapter 4—a palpable movement to the right has not met with public backlash. Americans have long believed that, in Newt Gingrich's words, "The national press has become the most powerful arm of the left."[52] In 1971, for instance, Edith Efron catalogued media bias against Richard Nixon's 1968 presidential campaign.[53] They still do. A September 2003 Gallup poll revealed that 45 percent of Americans felt the media were "too liberal," while only 14 percent thought they were "too conservative." In the same poll taken exactly a year later, 48 percent of respondents felt the media were "too liberal." And just to make sure the public continues to feel Republicans and conservatives are battling a liberal head wind blown by the media, there exist influential individuals and organizations who chronicle and disseminate examples of reporters' left-wing bias. These include Reed Irvine's Accuracy in the Media and L. Brent Bozzell III's Media Research Center.

Even if the media are still predominantly liberal, their influence on the public seems to be waning somewhat. A May 2004 Gallup survey revealed Americans spent seven minutes a day less consuming news than they had a decade earlier. Moreover, by just about all accounts, Americans are increasingly distrustful of the press.[54] In 1985, 80 percent of respondents greatly "believed" newspapers, by 2002 this figure was 59 percent.[55] Scandals involving plagiarism and fabricated stories at the *New York Times* and *USA Today* seem to have hurt newspapers' reputations even more. The May 2004 Gallup poll revealed that only

30 percent of respondents had "a great deal" or "quite a lot" of confidence in newspapers. To make the print medium feel better, however, an identical proportion felt the same way about television news, too.

Conservatives have also made strides in the battle of policy ideas. It used to be the case that think tanks—those institutes and centers staffed by scholars whose job it is to formulate policy-relevant ideas and have them injected into the political blood-stream through seminars, papers, books, and newspaper articles—were a particularly left-leaning phenomenon. The New Deal through to the 1970s was what David Ricci called the "lib-eral age" of think tanks.[56] To be sure, most policy centers of the era were, in the words of R. Kent Weaver, "universities without students."[57] Yet encouraged by Democratic dominance of govern-ment, funded by government activism, and peopled by scholars who drifted in and out of successive administrations, policy insti-tutes also produced work that generally supported the liberal establishment.[58] The oldest Washington-based think tank, the Brookings Institution, led the way, but it was not alone. The RAND Corporation, fundamentally a contractor for Defense Department research, had a cozy relationship with the Kennedy and Johnson administrations. The stridently liberal Institute for Policy Studies was formed in 1962, and in 1968, with the encouragement of LBJ, the Urban Institute was created to focus on domestic issues.[59]

There were conservative voices in this era. The Hoover Institution was established at Stanford University, although it was viewed more as an academic entity than a classic think tank involved in the dirty business of day-to-day ideological combat. The American Enterprise Institute (AEI) for Public Policy Research was founded in 1943 by Lewis H. Brown to give business a voice in the policy arena and counteract the liberal elite. But it was not until the Nixon years that GOP-friendly think tanks really imposed themselves on the policy process.

The big breakthrough came in 1973. It was in that year that, with $250,000 from the Colorado brewing magnet Joseph Coors, the Heritage Foundation—or, to use its original name, the Analysis Research Corporation—was established by two congressional staff-ers, Paul Weyrich and Edwin Feulner. It took time for this new right-wing think tank to gain its footing, especially since Watergate helped make conservative ideas unfashionable. But during the 1980s Heritage flourished. It was at the vanguard of what the journalist Sidney Blumenthal called a conservative "counter-establishment" revolution.[60] In 1980, for example, Heritage composed *Mandate for Leadership*, a 1,100-page report that furnished policy guidelines to the incoming Reagan administration. It began aggressively to enlist donors so as to ensure a broad funding base. Generally young and energetic conservatives were recruited to staff the organization. Indeed, Heritage has been particularly successful at identifying bright prospects and providing them with the tools and reputation necessary to gain leverage in the policy process.[61]

Today Heritage is vigorously pursuing its mission "to formulate and promote conservative public policies based on the principles of free enterprise, limited government, individual freedom, traditional American values, and a strong national defense." It has nearly 200 staff and in 2002 enjoyed revenues of $52.29 million, over one-and-a-half times those of Brookings and three times those of AEI. It has a sleek new addition to its original building on Massachusetts Avenue in Washington in which its interns can lodge and has built a state-of-the-art 250-seat auditorium. It disseminates a variety of products, such as the magazine *Policy Review*, the weekly electronic *PolicyWire*, issue-specific "Backgrounders" that provide essential and concise information for policy-makers, and the annual agenda publication—which it calls its "policy playbook." It also works assiduously to get its people in the media. Heritage experts are quoted in national and local newspapers everyday, and many write op-eds that are distributed across the country by the wires. Experts like Peter Brookes, James Carafano, and Nile Gardiner also regularly appear on the radio and network and cable news—according to the foundation's 2003 annual report, Heritage people were on television 1,100 times that year.

Heritage blazed a trail for a number of other GOP-friendly think tanks. In 1977 the Cato Institute was founded by Edward Crane, the former head of the Libertarian Party. It was initially funded by oil and gas tycoon Charles Koch, but today counts a number of multinational corporations among its broad base of donors and in 2002 had $17 million in revenues. The institute produces a number of influential publications like the *Cato Journal* and *Regulation* and, like Heritage, has aggressively and successfully placed its people—such as Doug Bandow and David Boaz—in the mainstream media. Cato does not always advocate positions Republicans are particularly comfortable with—it was very critical of the war in Iraq—but on economic policy its libertarian ethos is welcomed by the GOP. Cato has been a vocal supporter of the privatization of Social Security, for instance.

Indeed, Heritage's influence is such that it has been cloned repeatedly. The Manhattan Institute for Policy Research, for example, has worked for just over a quarter of a century to turn New York to the right. Founded in 1978 by Reagan CIA director William Casey, it has continually promoted ideas close to the heart of Republican philosophy. In the early 1980s it promoted controversial conservative critiques of welfare policy like George Gilder's *Wealth and Poverty* and Charles Murray's *Losing Ground*. It has an influential publication, *City Journal*, and its associated scholars—individuals such as Brian Anderson, Tamar Jacoby, and Abigail Thernstrom—write prodigiously for academic audiences and in the mainstream media.

There are many others. The twenty-year-old Chicago-based Heartland Institute works to "promote parental choice in education, choice and personal responsibility in health care, market-based approaches to environmental protection, privatization of public services, and deregulation in areas where property rights and markets do a better job than government bureaucracies." FreedomWorks—which was formed from the merging of George H. W. Bush adviser C. Boyden Gray's Citizens for a Sound Economy (CSE) and Bill Bennett and Jack Kemp's Empower America—was created in 2004 to "broaden the national fight for lower taxes, less government, and more economic freedom." Formed just as Reagan was sworn into office, the Family Research Council "champions marriage and family as the foundation of civilization, the seedbed of virtue, and the wellspring of society." In 2002 it had revenues of $9.73 million. The Hudson Institute that embraces "free markets, individual responsibility, the power of technology, and a determination to preserve America's national security" had $7 million in revenues in 2002. The Project for the New American Century, created in 1997 by *Weekly Standard* editor Bill Kristol and *Washington Post* columnist Robert Kagan, promotes neoconservative foreign policy. So does Frank J. Gaffney Jr.'s Center for Security Policy. Controversial conservative social commentator, David Horowitz, has his own Center for the Study of Popular Culture. The Reason Foundation publishes the influential *Reason* magazine about "free minds and free markets" out of Los Angeles. Indeed, the surge in conservative thought has even invigorated staid, old AEI and moved it perceptibly to the right. In the late 1970s large parts of corporate America realized it needed assistance in disputes it had over policy with labor unions and numerous public interest groups that were emerging to fight for consumers and environmentalists. Many companies turned to AEI, and by 1981 600 of them were contributing to its coffers.[62] AEI was also embraced by the Reagan administration and became an important cheerleader for supply-side economics. As evidence of its new conservatism, it has recently listed among its scholars Dinesh D'Souza, Bush speechwriter David Frum, Newt Gingrich, Jeane Kirkpatrick, Irving Kristol, Charles Murray, and Richard Perle.

There are also dozens of right-leaning think tanks outside of Washington and the other major centers of American business, culture, and politics. They generally crop up in state capitals, underwritten by local business people and conservative philanthropists who are eager to shape public policy at lower levels of government. They often have multi-million dollar budgets and produce interesting and quality research packaged in ritzy publications and Web sites. They include the Discovery Institute, the eclectic Seattle-based organization that has been at the vanguard of the movement to push "intelligent design"—the argument that Darwinism must be wrong and that there was clearly a hidden hand involved in the creation of mankind.[63] There is also the Commonwealth Foundation in Pennsylvania, the James Madison Institute in Florida, the John Locke Foundation in North Carolina, Ohio's Buckeye Institute for Public Policy Solutions, the Pioneer Institute for Public Policy Research in Massachusetts, and the Texas Public Policy Foundation. The efforts of these institutes are coordinated in a number of ways. The American Legislative Exchange Council (ALEC) is based upon "Jeffersonian principles" and supports limited government by providing government officials and activists with research and information about policy at the state level. The State Policy Network is a valuable resource for conservative state-level think tanks. It links right-leaning experts with one another and assists small think tanks with the basics of establishing, running, and marketing a local or regional policy institute.

All of these organizations have benefited considerably from a deep pool of financial support generated by a small number of enterprising donors. The Coors Foundation, as I have noted, was instrumental in getting Heritage up and running. It has become, in the words of liberal journalist Russ Bellant, "a powerful, wealthy, highly-organized force for social change" and a "return to Darwinian political and economic morality" and "traditional family values."[64] Richard Mellon Scaife, heir to the Mellon banking empire, distributes funds to right-wing causes through three foundations, the Allegheny, the Carthage, and the Sarah Scaife. He reportedly supported conservative think tanks and other organizations to the tune of $340 million between 1960 and 2000.[65] Scaife has given generously to the *American Spectator* and underwrote the magazine's infamous "Arkansas Project" of the 1990s that delved deeply into Bill Clinton's past in an attempt to discredit him. Scaife also publishes the *Pittsburgh Tribune-Review*— the paper whose reporter was famously told to "shove off" by Teresa Heinz Kerry at the 2004 Democratic National Convention. To many conservatives, he is "nothing less than their financial archangel."[66]

The Koch family foundations, which helped make Cato possible, have invested in libertarian causes. "My overall concept," co-owner of Koch Industries, David Koch, has said, "is to minimize the role of government and to maximize the role of private economy and to maximize personal freedoms."[67] The foundations have given generously to Cato and CSE. The Milwaukee-based Lynde and Harry Bradley Foundation distributed $44 million to conservative causes in 2000. It has been especially generous to research activities at the University of Chicago and George Mason University. Under William Simon, the Olin Foundation was a particularly magnanimous conservative philanthropy until it decided to shut up shop in 2001. It gave hundreds of thousands of dollars annually to AEI, Heritage, and Manhattan and funded research and programs at universities like Chicago, George Mason, Princeton, Stanford, and Yale.

It is true that left-leaning think tanks have been founded in the past quarter century, too. The Center on Budget and Policy Priorities—that has revenues very similar to those of AEI—was founded in 1981 to influence policies that affect low- and middle-income groups. The Economic Policy Institute was established by liberal economists Jeff Faux, Robert Kuttner, Ray Marshall, Robert Reich, and Lester Thurow in 1986. The Democratic Leadership Council's Progressive Policy Institute (PPI) provided many of the ideas that propelled Bill Clinton to the presidency in 1992. In 2003 former Clinton chief of staff John Podesta became the first president of the Center for American Progress. Funded largely by billionaire George Soros and Infoseek founder Steven T. Kirsch, the center will have an attention-grabbing Web site, issue daily briefings, send out regular responses to conservative arguments, book left-leaning commentators for media appearances, and re-search new policy ideas. It will be, according to Podesta, a "think tank on steroids."[68] The venerable Urban Institute still has a huge budget and in 2002 raked in just over $79 million. Yet it seems clear that Brookings, PPI, the Urban Institute, and the others have disappointed Democrats by being too academic and pedestrian. Tom Daschle, the then Democratic leader in the Senate, lamented in 2003 that the GOP has "a dozen think tanks, and we have none."[69]

What is more, there often seems to be greater creativity and energy emanating from the center than from the left. The New America Foundation brings bright and talented young thinkers to Washington where they grapple with policy problems and come up with "outside-the-box" sort of solutions that defy con-ventional liberal-to-conservative understanding—the foundation's head, Ted Halstead, co-authored a well-received book titled *The Radical Center*, and its mission claims there is "a dearth of new thinking on both sides of the political divide." The foundation has been heralded in many circles, but its success and attacks on Democrats and liberals have made many on the left bitter. Robert Kuttner believes the foundation is scared to take on conserva-tives.[70] Eric Alterman believes liberal donors were duped into supporting it.[71]

This conservative ascendance matters. It is true that research has shown congressional staff and journalists find non-ideological think tanks most credible, but as Donald E. Abelson has written, the United States' uniquely decentralized system of separation of powers and federalism, coupled with weak parties, allows American think tanks to be especially influential.[72] What is more, Republicans are very willing to furnish right-leaning institutes a soap box.[73] This is no small thing given that the GOP's nearly uninterrupted decade-long control of Congress has them in charge of committees and capable of setting agendas. As a direct conse-quence, Heritage, Cato, and other Republican-friendly think tanks have their policy papers discussed in meetings of the powerful majority party and their experts invited to give testimony to con-gressional committees. Moreover, political scientists Andrew Rich and R. Kent Weaver have found that their generally larger bud-gets have helped thrust conservative think tanks into the spotlight and, in turn, get them cited more frequently by the news media.[74]

The ebullience, organization, visibility, and resources of right-leaning policy institutes have made them the apple of the GOP's eye. As a result many are now connected seamlessly to the Republican establishment at all levels of politics. They provide policy ideas and do research for Republican politicians—whether it be in the form of real social science or a snappy polemical one-pager that a legislator can take to the floor with her when she is to give a speech. They also supply personnel—top Reagan advisers included Hoover's Martin Anderson and Richard Allen, Heritage's Norman Ture, AEI's Arthur Burns and Murray Weidenbaum, and Casper Weinberger from the Institute for Contemporary Studies; top lieutenants to George W. Bush have included Gale Norton of the Mountain States Legal Foundation, Mitch Daniels of the Hudson Institute, Condoleeza Rice of Hoover, and Lawrence Lindsay of AEI. In return, the GOP gives these think tanks legitimacy. By recognizing their work, the party has been the conduit through which Heritage, Cato, Manhattan, and others have been absorbed into mainstream public discourse. This is where Brookings and AEI have been all along. The GOP also supplies these think tanks with influence. Heritage president Edwin Feulner estimated that about 60 percent of the roughly 2,000 proposals outlined in a Mandate for Leadership report were adopted by the Reagan administration.[75] The more recent conservative thoughts about welfare, social security, race relations, education, and the role of religion have all bubbled up from conservative policy institutes. In some form or another, these ideas are now part of public policy.

Since the 1980s, conservatives and libertarians—often tightly allied with Republican politicians and activists—have undertaken a pincer-like assault on the hearts and minds of the American electorate. With trenchant and emotive language and images, an argumentative style, and colorful personalities, new right-leaning media outlets have attempted to capture hearts. Funded generously by conservative foundations, right-wing think tanks have moved on minds by recruiting bright and creative people and then undertaking imaginative and sometimes sophisticated research that is astutely and doggedly promoted. The result, according to Democratic activist Rob Stein, is "perhaps the most potent, independent institutionalized apparatus ever assembled in a democracy to promote one belief system."[76] That may be stretching things a bit, but it is clear that the media and ideas industry are immensely more receptive to and reflective of Republican thought than they were twenty-five years ago. If anything, it's the Democrats who are now playing catch-up.[77]

Still, as James Glassman has written recently, political supremacy is determined not so much by ideas, but "demographics, economics, and sociology."[78] It is to Republican advantages uncovered by such fundamental components of American life that I turn to first in the next chapter.

9

Social, Economic, and Attitudinal Change as Republican Advantage: Public Opinion and the Partisan Politics of Wealth, Work, Faith, and Race

In 1973 influential sociologist Daniel Bell wrote a book called *The Coming of Postindustrial Society*. His thesis was that "industrial society" or "the coordination of machines and men for the production of goods" was being replaced by a "postindustrial society" that is "organized around knowledge."[1] To Bell and other social scientists, this postindustrial society would have significant economic and social consequences. These ramifications included a workforce employed increasingly in the service sector rather than heavy manufacturing, a decentralization of corporate power and the rise of dynamic, smaller, and more egalitarian businesses, the importance of technology, the emergence of a new middle class, and the fracturing of traditional social institutions.

These fundamental changes in the way Americans live and work have had knock-on political effects. Most dramatically, I argue, the postindustrial economy has placed a thumb on the Republican side of the partisan scale. The new economy's recessions, for example, are shallower than those Americans used to experience. We had some fairly deep downturns between World War II and the 1990s. At the end of the Eisenhower presidency, the economy took an especially shuddering jolt. In April 1957, the unemployment rate was 3.9 percent; by July the next year it had raced up to 7.5 percent. The oil crises of the mid and late 1970s came with something called "stagflation"—simultaneous inflation and low growth. Escalating energy prices in an economy heavily reliant on oil helped prices through the roof. In the decade between January 1972 and January 1982, the indicator generally used to measure the cost of living for Americans, the Consumer Price Index or CPI, rose by 129 percent. Normally, such a rise in prices is illustrative of a booming economy, but unemployment climbed from about 5 percent at the beginning of 1974 to 9 percent in May 1975 and then spiked again in the early 1980s when it rose from 6.3 percent in January 1980 to 10.8 percent in December 1982.

During the postindustrial age, however, economic downturns have not been nearly as stomach churning. Median income dropped less in the 1991 and 2001 recessions than it did in the two previous ones—according to the Census Bureau it declined 3.4 percent in 2001, 4.7 percent in 1991, 4.8 percent in 1981, and 5.7 percent in 1973–1974. At the height of the recession of the early 1990s, unemployment reached only 7.8 percent, prices were hardly growing, and the economy barely shrunk. We then had to wait a decade for the next downturn. Before then came what Clinton administration economist Joseph Stiglitz calls the "Roaring Nineties"—a time of meteoric returns from the stock market, unemployment below 4 percent, flat prices, and annual growth rates in excess of 6 and 7 percent. Even when it came, the first recession of the twenty-first century might not have even been one. The National Bureau of Economic Research, which the government has named as the official designator of these things, has not formally labeled the slump in 2001 a recession. For that to happen, the country's economy would have to experience two consecutive quarters of contraction in gross domestic product (GDP). In 2001 the economy was rooted to the spot rather than in retreat.

Still, the question remains: Why should the cursory economic downturns of the new economy benefit the GOP? After all, the historically mild recession of the early 1990s cost George H. W. Bush his job, and the patchy economy on his son's watch nearly put a second family member out of the White House. They do so because they do not create the kind of fundamental and serious economic problems only a comprehensive deployment of governmental resources can solve. In other words, mild recessions do not beg for Democratic Party policies. We all know, of course, that the Depression brought in with it a massive Democratic majority and New Deal programs that revolutionized the federal government, but the downturns of 1958, 1973–1974, and 1981 had similar consequences, even if they were on a much smaller scale. On the electoral side, Republicans were repudiated the next time voters went to the ballot box. Much of this, to be sure, had to do with the usual midterm slump experienced by the president's party, and 1974 coincided with Watergate. But on the first two occasions the GOP lost a massive fifty or so House seats, and only after 1981 did it recover quickly enough to win the next presidential election. On the policy side, the recessions forced politicians of both parties to look to governmental solutions. Public-works programs were accelerated dramatically after the 1958 recession, especially in housing. President Gerald Ford, after initially suggesting revenues should increase, pushed for an anti-recession tax cut that was aimed at enticing demand by providing tax rebates. Even Reagan looked to Democratic Party philosophy to pull the country out of the 1981 recession. Despite ballooning deficits, he was forced to push for a massive public-transportation bill in 1982.[2]

The response to the recession of the early 1990s was a "New" Democrat with moderate and "Third Way" solutions to economic problems. Bill Clinton did have some statist answers to economic questions, as his health-care proposal illustrated, but, as we saw in Chapter 6, he quickly realized that if the recovery needed help it ought to be more in the form of deficit reduction than the kind of fiscal stimulus Democrats were famous for.

The causes of the 2001 downturn are opaque—it may have been brought about by the equities bubble and exacerbated by terrorism. Yet it is clear that the rough patch's deleterious effects were felt minimally and evenly across the population—the latter quality gave rise to Harvard economist Lawrence Katz's moniker, "the egalitarian recession."[3] Moreover, its shallow downward trajectory and light bump off the floor suggested to many economists that, after the initial tax cuts, no additional stimulus was needed—it may have been a similar assessment that cost Larry Lindsey his job as head of Bush's National Economic Council in 2002.[4] Indeed, as if to show the recession to be quite forgettable, the Republicans actually won a handful of House seats in 2002.

Another reason the postindustrial economy helps the Republicans is that it brings with it relative prosperity. To be sure, for many the postindustrial economy is no picnic. As left-leaning economists like John Kenneth Galbraith, Paul Krugman, Robert Kuttner, Robert Reich, and Lester Thurow have argued, the middle class is being "squeezed" somewhat. Some data suggest Americans are increasingly "outsourced" and their jobs sent to China, India, or Mexico. Others reveal that as middle-class incomes have stagnated, the costs of a middle-class lifestyle—especially in the areas of health care, child care, and education—have grown.[5] Just about all the data show, quite unequivocally, that income disparities between the rich and poor have widened dramatically—in current dollars, the average real family income of the bottom fifth was 9.2 percent of that of the top twentieth in 1980; it was 5 percent of it in 2002. The new jobs created by the postindustrial economy also generally do not provide the health and pension benefits of the manufacturing ones they have replaced.

Still, numerous indicators point to a basic and palpable improvement in the economic situation of the average citizen. Whereas it used to be the case that wealth was inherited, in today's postindustrial economy, as Cornell economist Robert Frank says, "It's possible to become a wealthy person just by what you earn for doing your job."[6] W. Michael Cox and Richard Alm have shown that it took the typical American about sixteen weeks to work off the cost of one hundred square feet of new home in the mid-1950s; today it takes fourteen weeks. These days, as they have also highlighted, the average American can buy a McDonald's cheeseburger for about three minutes of work, whereas it cost half an hour of toil fifty years ago.[7] Using 2002 dollars, 14.1 percent of American households had income in excess of $100,000 that year, up markedly from 3.1 percent in 1967. As a result, more than just a few Americans have "Luxury Fever" and are snapping up boats, Mercedeses, the huge cookie-cutter houses that are often called "McMansions," Cuban cigars, and massive outdoor grills.[8] Journalist Gregg Easterbrook calls the dramatic and pervasive improvement in the standard of living "The Great Story of Our Era."[9]

This new affluence has not always translated into emotional well-being. Wealth can bring health and social problems.[10] It can also cause psychological stress because ubiquitous affluence makes the relative position of high-earners less desirable—when all do well, individuals feel their efforts and abilities are less valued.[11] Yet, as Everett Ladd wrote over thirty years ago, such affluence helps the GOP because it turns the poor, a critical Democratic constituency that looks to the government and not the market to solve its problems, into a "minority."[12]

As Ronald Inglehart famously described a quarter of a century ago, prosperity also causes people to worry less about their economic security and concern themselves more with "postmaterial" values.[13] Some of these have certainly benefited the Democrats, as the vibrant bourgeois environmental movement illustrates, but others help the Republicans. It is surely the case, for example, that the fixation on moral and social issues exhibited by many lower-income Christian conservatives could only survive in the context of a pervasive sense, mild though it may be, of economic comfort.

The new affluence has also given birth to a huge "investor class." Millions of Americans have taken much of their surplus income and decided to put it in mutual funds, stocks, and bonds. This class is important because it now forms a majority. According to an August 2003 *Washington Post* poll, 58 percent of respondents have some money in financial markets. A 2002 Zogby poll revealed that 66 percent had a 401(k) plan or IRA. An Investor's Action exit poll taken on election day 2004 found that 70 percent of voters held stock of some kind. Grover Norquist has gone as far as to argue that "the biggest demographic shift in the past thirty years is not the number of people who speak Spanish; it is the number of Americans who own stocks."[14]

The growth of the investor class should help the GOP in many ways. Most obviously, investors tend to be Republicans. Of those who own individual stocks and were surveyed by the August 2003 *Washington Post* poll, 50 percent said they "always" or "mostly" voted for the GOP. These investors undoubtedly supported Republicans for a number of reasons, but clearly the party's approach to financial markets had something to do with it. The *Post* survey found 46 percent of respondents felt the GOP's policies were better for the stock market, compared to only 32 percent who believed the Democrats' were. Indeed, despite the dismal returns under George W. Bush—the Dow Jones Industrial Average (DJIA) stood at 10,587 the day before he was inaugurated, and it was at 10,035 the day before the 2004 election—history bears this out. Of the top five post-war administrations by mean annualized returns of the DJIA, only one was Democratic—Bill Clinton's, which topped the list at a heady 26 percent. Positions two through five were filled by Reagan at 16 percent, Eisenhower and George H. W. Bush at 13 percent, and Ford at 12 percent.

The big question for GOP strategists, though, is: Does investing make you more Republican? Here, the data are pretty sketchy, but there exists empirical evidence that shows this to be the case. GOP pollster Matthew Dowd has argued that RNC polling in 2002 revealed investors increased their support for Republicans between January and June of that year while non-investors turned away from the party.[15]

There are also theoretical reasons to suggest that investing makes you more Republican. John Hood has argued that savings and investments augment personal property and wean individuals from their dependence on the state. This, in turn, lessens their interest in government activism and instills in them a motivation to protect their property from forcible redistribution.[16] *National Review* editor Ramesh Ponnuru has written that stock ownership "has the potential to connect the direct interests of a mass of voters with the broad health of the economy."[17] Voting is no longer just a response to one's pocketbook, then. Instead, stockholders worry about the kinds of economic gauges that seemed, before they had invested, tangentially related to their personal economic circumstance. Critically, voters have frequently felt the Republicans are better at looking after the macroeconomy.

Richard Nadler has posited that this affinity for GOP policy gets stronger the longer one owns stocks.[18] He also states that the investor class is particularly attracted to Republican positions such as those emerging in support of partial privatization of Social Security and tax-advantaged education and health-savings accounts. In the words of Cato's Stephen Moore the argument reads, "The dividend tax cut, expanding IRAs, and private Social Security accounts are all examples of President Bush and Karl Rove understanding that the more people we can lure into the 'investor class' with private pools of private capital, the better it is for Republicans and Republican issues."[19]

Moreover, a burgeoning investor class helps Republicans because investors are extremely sensitive to their tax bills. Stockholders pay capital gains and, at least in years when returns are good, see discernible slices of their investments returned to the government.

With similar effects, the postindustrial economy is characterized by massive increases in homeownership. Fueled by the new affluence and, in recent years at least, record low interest rates and dramatic increases in property values, homeownership has risen from 63.7 percent of the population in 1993 to 69.2 percent in mid-2004. Buying a home makes a person more sensitive to that great nemesis of conservatives—the property tax.

Finally on the topic of the postindustrial economy, the GOP has benefited greatly from the new emphasis on information and services. The U.S. manufacturing sector has shrunk to about 15 percent of the private workforce from nearly 30 percent in 1979 while services account today for nearly 40 percent of Americans who work outside of government. The heavy industry that was America's hallmark in the thirty years after World War II has been replaced by health care, computers, financial services, education, and other types of work in which the labor force does not get its hands dirty. This has important ramifications for party politics because the shift has devastated a critical Democratic constituency, the unions. Although, as we saw in Chapters 6 and 7, labor has recruited well among government and other non-manufacturing workers, the unionization rate within the service sector as a whole is a measly 6 percent. This compares miserably with the 15 percent of those in manufacturing who belong to a union. It is no surprise then that organized labor is hemorrhaging members—in 2003 alone it lost 369,000. Indeed, today the movement has resorted to organizing outside of the work place in an effort to increase its political clout. The AFL-CIO, under President John Sweeney and his "new voices" team, has looked to promote the advocacy of progressive policies more generally.[20] The union has established the labor-community affiliate "Working America" in ten cities. The goal is to bring together hundreds of thousands of labor-sympathizers.[21] The outcome is likely to be a large but disparate liberal interest group.

Even though there have been successes like SEIU's mobilization of custodians through the Janitors for Justice campaign on the West Coast and HERE's organization of casino workers in Las Vegas, the service sector remains barren terrain for unions. There are several reasons for this. Service-sector workers are not, in the words of Max Green, "subjected to anything like conditions within dark satanic mills."[22] There is no real shop floor; there is no need for special gear. There is a less lucid demarcation of class and professional lines. Many people wear a jacket and tie, and there is greater everyday contact between people at the bottom of the company hierarchy and those above them. What is more, many of the most rapidly expanding parts of the service sector—like technology—are highly competitive. Workers are also well paid and geographically mobile.

Indeed, in the few instances it has been successful, the organization of the service sector has helped drive a wedge into the union movement. Traditional blue-collar members believe that the public-sector unions are really just professional associations. They also have a hard time identifying with the largely female, immigrant, minority, and poor members of service-sector unions like the United Food and Commercial Workers, SEIU, and UNITE-HERE.[23] I discussed the pernicious effects this disunity has had on the Democrats in Chapter 7.

With a postindustrial economy, the United States has evolved into a quintessentially modern society. Americans, for example, are geographically mobile, increasingly live outside of the traditional nuclear family, and use numerous high-tech gadgets on a daily basis. There has also been a related acceptance of liberal positions on cultural and social issues. Take homosexuality, for instance. As I mentioned in Chapter 4, the public has become increasingly tolerant of homosexuals and their lifestyles. A Gallup poll in 1977 revealed that 43 percent of Americans felt that homosexual relations between consenting adults should be legal; by May 2003, 60 percent felt this way. In the same poll, 56 percent felt that gays and lesbians should be given "equal access to job opportunities" in 1977; 88 percent did in 2003. We have even seen some dramatic liberalization on the question of civil unions for same-sex couples since the mid-1990s. In an April 1996 Gallup poll, 67 percent of respondents opposed such an institution; by May 2003 Gallup was reporting that only 49 percent were against them.

We have seen similar liberalization or modernization on other issues. Data collected by sociologists Paul Burstein and Susan Wierzbicki show a dramatic increase in the public's acceptance of sexual equality. A Gallup poll in 1945, for instance, revealed that only 33 percent of respondents would vote for the presidential candidate of their party if she was a woman. By 1969 the figure had reached 54 percent; by 1994 it was at 92 percent. In 1945 only 18 percent approved of a woman earning money in business if "she has a husband capable of supporting her." By 1953, 21 percent of men claimed it made no difference if they worked for a man or a woman, and thirty-four years later 57 percent said they had no preference with regards to the gender of their boss.[24] The same trends can be seen on the issue of racial diversity. In 1972 Gallup found that only 25 percent of whites approved of inter-racial marriages; by 1997 the figure had reached 61 percent. Gallup also discovered in 1958 that 80 percent of whites would move if African Americans came into their neighborhood in large numbers, but only 18 percent said they would in 1997.

For most of the Western world, modernity has brought secularization with it. According to a 2002 Pew Global Attitudes Project Survey, only 33 percent of Britons, 30 percent of Canadians, 27 percent of Germans, 21 percent of Italians, and 11 percent of the French claim that religion plays a "very important" part in their lives. The 1995–1997 World Values Survey revealed that 25 percent of Spaniards, 16 percent of the Swiss and Australians, 4 percent of Swedes, and 3 percent of Japanese attended religious services on a weekly basis. In the United Kingdom, creeping secularization is illustrated by the fact that, according to Mori polls, 76 percent of Britons believed in God in 1980, whereas only 60 percent of them do today.

Curiously, however, modernization has barely diluted religious attitudes and practices in the United States. To be sure, in the words of researchers Andrew Kohut, John C. Green, Scott Keeter, and Robert C. Toth, "Traditional practices have declined."[25] Still, they have done so only marginally. The 2002 Pew global poll found that 59 percent of Americans still say that religion is very important in their lives. A May 2004 Gallup poll showed that 90 percent of Americans believe in God and 42 percent attend church at "least once" or "nearly every" week. Forty-six percent of respondents to a December 2002 CNN/*USA Today*/Gallup poll considered themselves "evangelical" or "born again." Sixty-one percent of respondents to a February 2004 ABC News poll said they thought the biblical story that the world was created by God in six days was literally true. This is not a belief we would generally attribute to a wealthy and high-tech society. In fact, when the nations of the world are plotted on a graph with religious attitudes and per capita income forming the two axes, the United States represents a striking and lonely outlier. Generally, it is poor countries that are religious—in the 2002 Pew survey 92 percent of Indians, 84 percent of Ghanaians, and 80 percent of Guatemalans said religion was very important to them.

For many Americans, religion and politics should be like oil and water. By way of evidence, sociologists Michael Hout and Claude S. Fischer have argued that a rise in the number of Americans who consider themselves religious but do not formally affiliate with a particular church or denomination reveals religion as increasingly personal.[26] Similarly, a 2000 Pew Research Center for the People and the Press poll found that 64 percent of respondents felt that clergy should not discuss politics. These Americans believe religion is a private thing. They share John Kerry's sentiment that, in words he used to accept the Democratic Party nomination for president in 2004, "Faith has given me values to live by" but "I don't wear my faith on my sleeve."

For many others, however, religion does and should penetrate public life. Kohut, Green, Keeter, and Toth have revealed a "diminishing divide" between religion and politics.[27] This is not always markedly apparent, to be sure. In May 2004, for example, a CBS News poll showed that 50 percent of respondents thought it appropriate and 47 percent felt it inappropriate for candidates to talk about personal religious beliefs in a campaign. A 1998 *Washington Post*/Kaiser Family Foundation/Harvard University poll found that the public was evenly split—48 percent in favor, 47 percent against—on whether "the government should take special steps to protect America's religious heritage." Yet, the same *Post* poll discovered that 61 percent of respondents agreed with the idea that "Christians should get involved in politics to protect their values." In 2000, what's more, a Pew survey revealed that 70 percent of Americans felt that it was important for a president to have "strong religious beliefs." In 2003, 41 percent of respondents said there were too few references to prayer and faith by politicians; just over half that number—21 percent to be exact—felt that there were too many. Along similar lines, polls have consistently found that Americans would solidly reject an atheist who ran for the nation's highest office. A 2000 Gallup poll undertaken shortly after Democratic presidential candidate Al Gore selected Joseph Lieberman to be his running mate discovered that 92 percent of Americans would vote for a Jew for president, 92 percent for an African American, 79 percent for a Mormon, and 59 percent for a homosexual. A shade less than half—49 percent—said they would cast their ballot for a nonbeliever.

The prominent role millions of Americans want for religion in public life is generally a boon to the GOP. Although religion may drive more liberal and Democratic policy positions on issues like welfare and the death penalty, research has shown that it overwhelmingly leads committed Christians to support Republican philosophy on issues like prayer in school, same-sex marriage, and abortion.[28] Moreover, the public generally feels that the Republicans do a better job at protecting religious values—in the 2000 Pew religion survey cited above, 39 percent of respondents felt this way, with 30 percent arguing for the

Democrats. As a result, it is not surprising that religious voters tend to support Republicans by large margins. In 2004 the exit polls showed that of the 42 percent who went at least weekly to church, 61 percent voted for the president. Republicans are acutely aware of all this. The Bush-Cheney campaign came close to crossing the line on issues of politics and religion in their courting of churches and their congregations in 2004.[29] They knew—as Clyde Wilcox and Lee Sigelman have shown—that Americans who worship regularly are much more likely to vote Republican.[30]

The Democrats understand the role of religion in partisan politics, too. During the summer of 2004 the DNC created the post of Director of Religious Outreach. Despite John Kerry's remarks about the personal nature of religion during his acceptance speech at the Democratic National Convention, he did indeed wear his faith on his sleeve—and his chest, back, and legs, too—during the 2004 presidential campaign. Kerry did not so much emphasize his Catholicism as his intense attachment to moral and religious values. He constantly reminded attendees of his rallies that he was "a person of faith" who was "surrounded by people of faith."[31] In the third debate he quoted from the Bible—as he did frequently in his many Sunday mornings spent in African American churches—and talked about his days as an altar boy.[32] By mid-October, *Washington Post* reporter Jim VandeHei observed that Kerry had changed from "a reserved Catholic reluctant to discuss faith in the public square into a Democratic preacher of sorts who speaks freely and sometimes forcefully about religion on the hustings."[33]

The fact that, according to the exit polls, 22 percent of voters in 2004 said "moral values" were the most important issue to them only heightened Democratic sensitivity to religion. The new leadership of Harry Reid in the Senate, Nancy Pelosi in the House, and Howard Dean at the DNC suddenly started quoting the Bible and emphasizing Christ's compassion for the poor.[34] Reid is known for his opposition to abortion rights and even Hillary Clinton suggested that the Democrats needed to bend their virulently pro-choice position a little. Jim Wallis, an evangelical left-leaning Christian and influential author, started getting invited to all the important Democratic pow-wows.

Yet there is no doubt that a "God gap" remains. Although he argues that cultural polarization is greatly exaggerated, Stanford political scientist Morris Fiorina recognizes that religious differences have had a dramatic—and, interestingly, a relatively recent—impact on how Americans vote.[35] Consultants Jeffrey Bell and Frank Cannon pointed out a month before the 2004 election that "values voters"—or those who were primarily motivated by moral and family issues—were supporting Bush by as much as ten to one in Ohio and twelve to one in Missouri.[36] So long as Americans' religiosity continues to weather the storms of the modern age, it is likely the GOP will reap important electoral advantages up and down the ticket.

There are demographic trends that do get Democrats excited, however. Perhaps most prevalent among these is that the Spanish-speaking population continues to grow by leaps and bounds. In 2000, 12.6 percent of America's 282 million people were Hispanic. This proportion is projected to grow to 15.5 percent by 2010 and a startling 24.4 percent by 2050. Hispanics are already key voters in crucial presidential-battleground states like Arizona, Nevada, and New Mexico and make up about 15 percent of the electorate in California and 17 percent in Texas, the nation's two largest states.

Hispanics also seem to be siding with the Democrats. In 1992 Bill Clinton won 61 percent of the Latino vote. Then in 1994, led by California and its GOP Governor, Pete Wilson, conservatives pushed for policy change that directly and adversely affected the Hispanic population. Wilson vigorously and successfully promoted the state's Proposition 187 that banned state aid to illegal immigrants, the vast majority of whom were from Mexico. He also handily won reelection by associating his campaign with the tough anti-immigration message of the proposition, and the GOP did well up and down the ballot. The next year, the new Republican majority in Congress passed aggressive immigration reform designed to restrict illegal immigrants' access to welfare programs and force legal ones to have jobs or financial sponsors.

At the same time, there were concerted efforts across the country to formally establish English as the nation's language. During the mid-1990s, eight states—Alaska, Georgia, Missouri, Montana, New Hampshire, South Dakota, Virginia, and Wyoming—passed English-as-the-official-language laws. In 1996 the House of Representatives passed Missouri GOP Congressman Bill Emerson's bill declaring English the official language of the federal government; 223 Republicans voted for the bill, but only 36 Democrats did. Two years later Republicans pushed hard to support

Proposition 227 that sought to outlaw bilingual education in California. It passed with 61 percent of the vote.

As a direct consequence, Latino support for the Democrats seemed to grow. Clinton won 71 percent of the group's vote in 1996. Hispanics, angry at Proposition 187 and what many of them perceived as other anti-immigrant GOP attacks, helped give the Democrats solid majorities in both chambers of California's state legislature. In 1992 there were 3.4 Hispanics registered as Democrats to every one Hispanic who registered as a Republican; in 1998 this ratio increased to 3.88 to 1.[37] Today, according to the Congressional Hispanic Caucus, nine out of ten of the nation's roughly 5,000 Hispanic elected officials are Democrats. This ethnic group, in the words of the party's pollster Stanley Greenberg, is "very much a part of the Democratic world."[38] Even against a Republican candidate who speaks Spanish and is from a Hispanic state, Al Gore managed to get 62 percent of the Latino vote in 2000.

There is evidence to show that Latinos are considerably more ambivalent about party politics, however. Typical among surveys of the Hispanic community is a July 2004 *Washington Post/Univision/Tomas Rivera Policy Institute* (TRPI) poll that revealed that although only 19 percent of Hispanic registered voters felt "closer" to the GOP than the Democrats, nearly a third—32 percent—answered that they felt closer to "neither" party. The 36 percent who picked the Democrats was five percentage points lower than an ethnically neutral national sample. Hispanics often feel detached from both parties because the appeal of the Democrats on economic issues is neutralized by the Republicans' conservative stance on social issues. As *Economist* writers John Micklethwait and Adrian Wooldridge argue in their recent book about conservatism in America, Hispanics are perhaps the most "family-oriented" constituency in the country.[39] Seventy percent of Hispanics approved of organized prayer in public schools in a 2002 TRPI poll, for instance. In the same poll, 66 percent felt that abortion should never be permitted or only in cases of rape and incest, and 65 percent said that "sexual relations between two people of the same sex is always wrong."

As a result, Republicans have sometimes done well among Latino voters. In his dramatic victory in the California gubernatorial recall election in 2003, Arnold Schwarzenegger won one-third of the Hispanic vote. This was an impressive performance given that Schwarzenegger was going up against the state's most powerful Latino politician, Lieutenant Governor Cruz Bustamante, in a multi-candidate field. A year later, George W. Bush won around 40 percent of the Hispanic vote—a sharp increase over 2000. Bush's share of the Hispanic vote in 2004 was up 16 percent in Texas and 12 percent in New Mexico. The performance was surely indicative of the innate conservatism of the nation's Spanish-heritage voters. As Adam Segal, director of the Hispanic Voter Project at the Johns Hopkins University observed, "The Bush campaign used moral values, and specifically the national discussion over gay marriage and abortion rights, as wedge issues within the Hispanic community to try to break off a conservative religious segment."[40]

Surveys have also shown that Hispanics do not experience the kind of prejudice and economic distress that would likely make Democratic Party philosophy appealing. A 2003 CBS News/ *New York* Times poll found that 64 percent of Latinos had not experienced a specific instance when they felt discriminated against. The figure for African Americans was 25 percent. In the same poll, only 15 percent of Hispanics believed they had a worse chance of getting ahead than people with other ethnic backgrounds.

Moreover, the fragmented nature of the Latino community exacerbates the problem the parties have packaging messages that will appeal to large numbers of Hispanic voters. There is no monolithic Spanish-speaking voting bloc. Mexicans focus on border control and immigration issues. Puerto Ricans are interested in their island's governance. Cubans, of course, fixate on Fidel Castro and U.S. policy toward the dictator. Mexicans and Puerto Ricans tend to be Democratic, but Cuban Americans, who reside primarily in the critical presidential state of Florida, are still ardently Republican. In 2004, for instance, Bush won 56 percent of the Sunshine State's Latino vote. Hispanics who are not immigrants tend to be more Democratic, newcomers a little more for the GOP.

Perhaps more critically, much of the Latino electorate is not particularly engaged with the basic political process. Only 57 percent of eligible Hispanic voters are registered, while more than 70 percent of the rest of the eligible voting population is.[41] As a consequence, Hispanics turn out less—in 2000 only 45 percent of eligible Hispanics voted. The language barrier is clearly an obstacle. Many Latinos struggle to understand and identify with candidates and policies. Parties and interest groups find them costly and difficult to activate. This is especially problematic in midterm elections—where there is no visible and important presidential race to bring out voters naturally.[42] In recent years, what is more, Hispanic immigrants have moved to burgeoning agri-business and manufacturing plants in small towns scattered across the Southeast and Midwest. Between 1990 and 2000, for example, the Hispanic population of North Carolina grew by 394 percent; in Georgia it grew by 300 percent, in Tennessee by 278 percent, and in Arkansas by 337 percent. Many of the new immigrants are therefore isolated from the assimilation infrastructure that exists for many Hispanics in big cities. Roberto Suro, director of the Pew Hispanic Center, has noted that "the process of learning about the United States is different in the new settlement areas than when somebody lands in a place with a lot of robust institutions that have helped millions of prior immigrants go through the process."[43]

Exacerbating this disconnect is the fact that many Hispanics are transient and feel little connection with the United States. Louis DeSipio, for example, has shown empirically that Latinos are slower to naturalize than other immigrant groups.[44] Four out of ten Hispanics currently living here are not yet citizens. Even those who naturalize tend to feel strong connections with their homeland and expect to return to it one day.

On top of this, Hispanics have not always joined with blacks to form tightly knit synergistic coalitions that can help Democratic candidates. Indeed, in a number of cities across the country, the two groups have worked at cross-purposes as they jostle for political office and the prestige and patronage that come with it. During the 2001 mayoral race in New York City, for example, rivalries between blacks and Hispanics are said to have cost Bronx Borough president Fernando Ferrer and the Democrats city hall. The same year, James Hahn won about 80 percent of the black vote in defeating Antonio Villaraigosa for the Los Angeles mayoralty. In 2005 Villaraigosa won the rematch, but the city's blacks and Hispanics still squabble. This competition is not isolated. Nicolás Vaca argues that African Americans and Latinos will never be politically comfortable with one another because they will compete for scarce jobs and different types of benefits from government—Latinos will want more in the way of bilingual public education, for instance.[45] Blacks also fear being eclipsed by the continued waves of Hispanic immigration.

It is difficult, then, to be as sanguine as journalist Jorge Ramos who has recently written the book, *The Latino Wave: How Hispanics Will Choose the Next President*—especially since, as Suro has noted, an "underlying structural problem of the Latino vote is that so much of it is concentrated in states [such as California and Texas] that aren't in play."[46] Today, Latinos are a heterogeneous group somewhat disconnected from American politics and with little immediate prospect of creating the kinds of institutions necessary to activate and coalesce their members. They are still some distance from being a club with which the Democrats can beat the GOP.

Among minority groups, however, the Democrats do have such a weapon. It is the African American community. Despite being the party of Lincoln and emancipation, the GOP has seen blacks sneer at it from the other side of the partisan divide since the mid-1930s when, drawn by the New Deal, more blacks voted Democratic than Republican in a presidential election for the first time. In 2000 only 9 percent of African Americans voted for George W. Bush. Four years later Bush did just two percentage points better among blacks. Only 12 percent voted for his father in 1988. With Oklahoma Rep. J. C. Watts' retirement in 2002, there are currently no black Republican members of Congress—just as was the case in the dozen years between Massachusetts Senator Edward Brooke's defeat in 1978 and Connecticut Rep. Gary Franks' victory in 1990. According to the Joint Center for Political and Economic Studies, of the 9,040 black officials elected at all levels of government in the United States in 2000, only fifty were Republican.

Still, the support of a monolithic black community is far from unequivocally beneficial to the Democrats. It is true that voter turnout among African Americans has increased a little in the last half-a-dozen-or-so years. In 1996, 79 percent of registered blacks voted. In 2000 the figure was 87.7 percent—only one percentage point below the amount of registered white voters. According to exit polls, African Americans made up about 11 percent of the electorate in 2004, up from 10 percent in 2000.

But the political infrastructure required to connect African Americans with the political process—something Hispanics have never really had—is rapidly deteriorating. The civil-rights generation of African Americans was the first to be able to exercise their vote thoroughly. As a result, the black community in the 1960s and 1970s created sophisticated and efficient institutions designed to mobilize its members and get them to the polls. One of these institutions was the church. The other was the organizations—like the National Association for the Advancement of

Colored People (NAACP), the Southern Christian Leadership Conference, the Student Non-Violent Coordinating Committee, and the Urban League—that had worked long and hard for the rights of black people and collectively, if rather loosely, were known as the civil-rights movement. After the passage of the Voting Rights Act in 1965, these organizations turned to the task of getting more black voters registered and to the polls. In 1982 alone, the NAACP registered 850,000 voters.

African Americans needed these institutions to connect them to the political process because, for the most part, the Democratic Party was not doing it. By the 1970s, blacks were, in the words of political scientist Paul Frymer, "captured" by the Democrats— that is, with the GOP ambivalent about the black vote and Democrats complacent about it, the African American community was ignored by party elites.[47] What is more, given the fact that blacks went to the polls in smaller numbers than other groups, the Democrats were loathe to expend precious resources getting them there. This had important ramifications because, as Peter W. Wielhouwer has shown, blacks are more likely to participate when contacted by the Democratic Party.[48] Maurice Mangum has revealed that political engagement and contact are the most robust determinants of black turnout.[49]

These African American institutions are not what they were, however. The NAACP, for example, has seen its membership stuck at about half a million for a number of years. As Theda Skocpol has argued, moreover, political-advocacy groups in general may have proliferated over the past several decades, but, nudged along by Washington-centric elites, they have transformed into "professionally managed organizations able to gain immediate access to government and the national media."[50] The grass roots, as a direct consequence, have been neglected. Groups no longer see the value in mass membership. As Skocpol puts it, "civic energy" has been redirected to "professional advocacy, private foundation grant making, and institutional trusteeship."[51]

To make matters worse, younger African Americans are neglecting the church and ignoring civil-rights groups. Indeed, young African Americans seem to eschew all sorts of formal civic and political organizations for more informal groupings and private pursuits. This may largely be a result of limited opportunities—there are fewer soccer leagues and Jaycee clubs in black communities. Regardless of causes, Rodney Hero has shown a strong negative correlation between the size of a state's minority population and its "comprehensive social capital index"—a measure, taken from Robert Putnam's influential book *Bowling Alone*, of the citizenry's propensity to engage in civic activities like working with philanthropic and community groups and attending community meetings.[52] Hero also shows that the political effects of young black men and women's disengagement from formal civic life are important. He finds a positive, if slightly weak, relationship between social capital in minority communities and voter turnout.[53]

There have been attempts to reverse this trend. The Active Element Foundation attempts to build cultural and business networks for young people in low-income and minority communities. The Hip-Hop Summit Action Network, established in 2001 by former NAACP director Benjamin Chavis and Russell Simmons, founder of Def Jam Records, has produced a concerted effort to use music to involve primarily young African Americans in public life. It claims, rather pompously perhaps, to be "dedicated to harnessing the cultural relevance of Hip-Hop music to serve as a catalyst for education advocacy and other societal concerns fundamental to the well-being of at-risk youth throughout the United States." During the 2004 campaign, the group called for a distinctly liberal "Nu America" and held rallies across the country with some of hip-hop's biggest stars. Rap star P. Diddy's 2004 "Citizen Change" campaign with its dramatic "Vote or Die" message had the same intention. Such efforts, however, tend to draw young people who are more interested in the music than the proselytizing.[54] In fact, in the end, building social capital in young black communities may not be worth the effort. Getting African Americans angry seems to be more fruitful. Priscilla Southwell and Kevin Pirch have shown a strong positive relationship between distrust in government and the propensity of blacks to vote.[55]

Even when blacks are engaged, their loyal support for Democratic candidates can be problematic. Many African Americans push the party to adopt liberal policies that antagonize white voters. Slave reparations are a good contemporary example. Rep. John Conyers of Detroit, the senior Democrat on the House Judiciary Committee, has spent about fifteen years pushing a bill to have the federal government study whether or not the descendants of slaves should be formally apologized to and financially compensated. Conyers and his allies have consumed time and resources attempting to making the issue a subject of public debate.

In 2002 the advocacy group, Millions for Reparations, organized a march on Washington and the Reparations Coordinating Committee orchestrated a series of lawsuits designed to extract payments from corporations whose histories are intertwined with slavery. They are encouraged by support that pervades the black community. According to a January 2002 CNN/USA Today/ Gallup poll, for example, 57 percent of blacks want money for descendants, and 68 percent feel that corporations who made profits from slavery prior to the Civil War should apologize. Yet 62 percent of whites don't think they should have to resort to what amounts to symbolic penitence, and 84 percent feel that these corporations should not have to give money to the descendants of slaves. It's not surprising that the Democrats are uncomfortable on the issue.

Affirmative action and school busing are certainly less controversial, but they are nevertheless disapproved of by large swaths of the white population. Busing has always been energetically resisted—the General Social Survey found that 79 percent of respondents opposed the policy in 1974; 66 percent did in 1994. Even in 2000, only 34 percent of respondents to the National Election Studies (NES) survey said that Washington should see to it that black and white children go to the same schools. As for affirmative action, it is true that respondents often seem warm to the policy in the abstract, but a 2003 Gallup poll found that while 49 percent of blacks believed that race and ethnicity should be taken into consideration when evaluating college admissions, only 22 percent of non-Hispanic whites felt this way. What is more, a *Time*/CNN poll from the same year discovered that 54 percent of respondents disapproved of admissions policies at law schools and colleges that gave preferences to minority applicants. Both busing and affirmative action are issues to which the Democrats are committed—the party explicitly supported the latter in its 2004 platform.

In recent decades, the GOP has ruthlessly exploited the doubts whites have about the Democratic Party's racial policies. Historians and political scientists have argued that Richard Nixon, using Barry Goldwater's states' rights rhetoric as political cover, campaigned against quotas and busing and failed to implement affirmative action and voting rights laws as he should. The approach was so electorally successful that it was adopted again by Ronald Reagan who timidly administered federal race policies—he placed school desegregation cases on hold, weakened the Voting Rights Act, and tamed the Civil Rights Commission, for instance.[56] In 1988 an independent group sympathetic to the Bush campaign took the GOP a step further. Republicans began to realize the value of fusing race with exploding crime rates when the group aired commercials about Willie Horton—the black convicted murderer who disappeared during a weekend furlough allowed by a policy approved by Massachusetts governor and Democratic presidential candidate Michael Dukakis, only to resurface and commit a heinous crime in Maryland. The subtext was that Democrats were soft on crime because they did not want to offend African Americans with tough law-and-order policies.

In response, Democrats have sometimes tried to distance themselves from the African American community and show whites that they are not captured by black interests. During the 1992 campaign, Bill Clinton famously chastised rapper Sister Souljah for song lyrics suggesting that blacks might want to kill white people. In 2001 the DNC selected Terry McAuliffe to be its chair. The action seemed to signal an intention to show the party could distance itself from its black constituency—McAuliffe beat out prominent African American Maynard Jackson just after many black Democrats accused him of racial insensitivity by using the term "colored people."

Such actions may assuage white fears about the Democrats, but they also provide Republicans with political opportunities. Many in the GOP are working to prize away black voters by highlighting the fact that Democrats take their allegiance for granted. As George W. Bush rather optimistically put it, "Blacks are gagging on the donkey but are not yet ready to swallow the elephant."[57] Still, conservative black organizations like the Center for New Black Leadership and the Black America's Political Action Committee relay the message that right-wing ideas and African American interests need not be antithetical. There are increasingly more prominent black Republican officials—such as current and former Bush administration members Condoleeza Rice, Colin Powell, Rod Paige, and Alphonso Jackson and Maryland Lieutenant Governor Michael S. Steele. Republicans are also running ads on black radio stations; in August 2004 one campaign attacked John Kerry as "rich, white, and wishy-washy."[58] In 2002 the ads tended to highlight parts of GOP philosophy that might appeal to black voters. One ad said, "Democrats say they give us more. Ain't that the truth. They give us more sales tax. They give us more gas tax. They tax my home, they tax my phone, they tax my smokes. They even tax my dog. I've got a new program for you Democrats: Stop attacking me with your taxes. Let me and my family keep more of the cash I work forty hours a week to earn. In the meantime, I'm voting Republican."[59]

The approach seems to have gained a little traction with younger African Americans, the group less tethered to the social and political institutions within the black community that are enmeshed with the Democratic Party. A 2002 poll by the Joint Center for Political and Economic Studies found that about 35 percent of blacks aged eighteen to twenty-five considered themselves independents, a proportion almost twice that for blacks over thirty-six.

It seems unlikely, however, that the GOP is going to win dramatically more black votes in the near future. Still, the party can begin to show that it has at least a modicum of acceptance in the African American community. This, in turn, provides some legitimacy to the argument that the Republicans are a diverse and accommodating bunch. The image makes the GOP more appealing to white, often female, voters who want to vote for a warm party, not one that seems harsh and exclusive. A strategy of modest appeals to African Americans, moreover, has the added advantage of not altering the party's positions on core issues so as to anger other constituencies.

Subtle changes in American attitudes about policy and government are assisting the Republicans, too. For example, although the public seems to want to protect Social Security and Medicare more than they desire tax cuts—a November 2002 CBS News/*New York Times* poll found that 69 percent felt that shoring up the two programs would have been a better use of the budget surplus—President Bush's plans to lessen the intrusion of government and roll back taxes have won widespread applause. Despite ballooning deficits and a series of tax cuts, a January 2005 *Los Angeles Times* poll found that 46 percent of respondents opted for lessening taxes and 45 percent for reducing the debt as the best prescription for an under-the-weather economy. In the same spirit, a July 2003 Pew Research Center for the People and the Press survey found that 54 percent of respondents approved of the Bush income tax reductions. Such systemic approval is interesting given that wealthier Americans have done disproportionately well from the president's policies—according to a report by the liberal

Center on Budget and Policy Priorities, the cuts increased the average annual take-home income for the middle 20 percent of earners by $647, for those in the top 1 percent by $34,992.[60] Americans' ignorance of public policy and innate optimism may also explain this support for the tax cuts. Political scientist Larry Bartels has written that the public's general support for estate-tax repeal—almost 70 percent took this position in the 2002 NES survey—is based upon the fact that a majority of them inaccurately believe that most Americans have to pay it, a sort of "unenlightened self-interest" to use his words.[61] It might also be the case that many feel that one day they themselves will be among the top few forced to pay estate tax. John Micklethwait and Adrian Wooldridge of the *Economist* report 2000 poll figures that show 20 percent of Americans believe that, at some point in their lives, they will be in the top 1 percent of earners.[62]

Similarly, when presented with a choice of a smaller government with fewer services or a bigger government with increased services, more Americans plump for the former. A November 2003 CBS News/*New York Times* poll revealed that the public preferred a smaller government with fewer services over the alternative by a 45 to 42 percent margin. A June 2004 ABC News/*Washington Post* poll had the gap in favor of reducing the scope of government at 50 to 46 percent—it was 54 to 41 percent in January 2002.

Americans are increasingly distrustful of government as well. According to NES, the proportion of the public that felt they could trust the federal government to do what is right most or just about all of the time declined precipitously from 76 percent in 1964 to 21 percent in 1994. It rose dramatically after September 11, 2001, reaching 56 percent in NES's 2002 study but quickly fell back—a CBS News/*New York Times* poll had the figure at 36 percent in July 2003. Intuitively, a pervasive wariness of government works well for the Republicans because they wish to weaken the state.

When it holds the reins of power in Washington, however, skepticism about political institutions may work against the GOP. Yet when we investigate the probable causes of this lack of faith, we see that it is an expression of feelings consistent with core Republican values. According to the 2002 NES, for example, 48 percent of Americans feel the government "wastes a lot of money," a significant number but down from the 70 percent of 1994 when the White House and Congress were both in Democratic hands.

Even the populist roots of this distrust do not necessarily hurt Republicans. The proportion of respondents to NES indicators of the belief that "government is run by a few big interests," "public officials don't care what people think," and "quite a few government officials are crooked" reached periodic highs in 1980 and 1994, times when the Democrats had control of the federal government.[63] It would seem, therefore, that Americans are as apt to believe that labor unions and ethnic minorities run government as much as big corporations and, even after Watergate, that Democrats can lie, cheat, and bribe as much as Republicans. As political scientists John Hibbing and Elizabeth Theiss-Morse put it in a recent analysis of Americans' feelings about their government, "People see both parties steeped in an aloof and isolated process, motivated only by inside-the-beltway minutia, money, and malarkey and not by the valid concerns of real people."[64]

The public is especially wary of the feds—the Republicans' chief governmental nemesis. A 2000 National Public Radio/Kaiser Foundation/ Kennedy School of Government poll found that 51 percent of respondents had a lot or some confidence in the federal government's ability to solve a problem, but 64 percent had the same level of confidence in their state government's capacity to do so. This has only helped the GOP. Since the Nixon presidency, the party has been pushing a "New Federalism" designed principally to provide states with greater latitude in administering programs crafted and funded by Washington.

In the aggregate, however, comprehensive studies by political scientists like William G. Mayer and Jim Stimson have shown American public opinion has not moved demonstrably and consistently to the right in the past quarter century.[65] Where we have seen movements in one ideological direction or the other, they have been quickly and fully reversed. Indeed, the NES survey reveals that there has been very little change in the difference since 1964 in the feelings Americans have toward conservatives on a zero to one hundred thermometer scale—the score has fluctuated from a low of 53 (in 1970 and 1982) to a high of 62 (in 1980). Still, the current period seems to be a good one for Republicans. The NES study reveals a palpable uptick since the early 1990s in the proportion of people who identify themselves as "conservative" or "extremely conservative." Twelve percent of respondents put themselves in these categories in 1990, whereas 25 percent did in 2002—the number of people who think of themselves as "liberal" or "extremely liberal," on the other hand, grew from 8 to 14 percent over the same period. Along similar lines, a February 2005 *Economist*/YouGov poll found that 30 percent of respondents felt that they had become more conservative over the previous decade, while only 19 percent believed they had moved to the left.

What is more, there is considerable evidence that standard measures of party identification—the concept political scientists use to describe an individual's fundamental allegiance to the Democrats or Republicans—overstates the extent to which the electorate thinks of itself as Democratic. Traditionally, scholars have understood partisanship to be cognitive—that is, people think about their party affiliation. Recent research, however, shows that voters also have "feelings" about the parties and that they frequently act upon more emotive evaluations. Individuals understand the parties to consist of an array of constituent groups, for example, and they ally with one depending upon how they feel about its components.[66] Barry Burden and Casey Klofstad have shown empirically that when respondents are prompted to express their feelings—rather than their thoughts—about party politics, they are more likely to consider themselves Republicans.[67]

The elephant's edge is therefore sharpened by the social, economic, and attitudinal trends of the last couple of decades. Despite the prognostications of some practitioners and academics, the Democrats have not converted their support among professionals, women, and ethnic minorities into political power. I have argued in this chapter that there is little evidence such a development will unfold any time soon, either. Instead, economic changes have furnished affluence and opportunities that have made Republican ideas about government and freedom more appealing to large swaths of the citizenry. The country's postindustrial economy has also weakened labor unions, and GOP strategies have undercut any advantages Democrats might see in the country's increasing diversity. To make matters worse for the Democrats, the GOP's embrace of many traditional values resonates in much of the country where people stubbornly adhere to their faith despite the modernization that is occurring in most other facets of their lives.

10

The Republicans as a Ruling (Not Majority) Party

The elephant, therefore, has an edge. Some of this edge has roots in the Constitution; some of it is created by statute and electoral rules. More important advantages come about because of social and economic change and are the function of central issues and the way Americans feel about them. Yet others are caused by the organizational acumen and superior resources of the GOP and groups affiliated with and sympathetic to it.

This edge has made the Republicans a ruling party. They control the two elected branches of the federal government and the lion's share of governorships. The party holds its own in state legislatures. Yet, the edge has not brought with it real majority status. Today, only about one-third of Americans consider themselves Republicans. As a result, the GOP's hold on the reins of government is quite ethereal. Even a small disruption to the current state of party politics will neutralize many, if not all, of the Republicans' advantages and pull us back to a true state of parity.

This state of affairs is quite novel. For most of American history, one of our political parties has had the consistent and largely unwavering support of the majority of voters. As was the case under the Jeffersonian Republicans and Jacksonians in the first forty years of the nineteenth century, under the Republican Party of McKinley, Roosevelt, Taft, Harding, Coolidge, and Hoover, and under the New Deal Democratic hegemony of 1932 through 1968, this results in persistent periods of unified government—when a single party occupies the White House and enjoys majorities in both chambers of Congress. There may be brief interregnums in which the other party grabs control of one or both branches, as the Democrats did under Woodrow Wilson in the 1910s, but for the most part, the majority party is able to govern aggressively, comfortable in the knowledge that the American public has given it a mandate. Concomitantly, the majority party receives the acclaim for the country's successes but the opprobrium for its failures.

By contrast, the lack of a durable and reliable electoral majority for any one of the two major parties has generally resulted in frequent divided government—a situation where the Democrats control one elected branch at the federal level and the Republicans the other. This was the case in the dozen or so years after 1840 when the Democrats and Whigs exchanged control of the presidency and Congress. The country also experienced an almost continually divided government between 1969 and 2000. The epoch was punctuated only by brief interludes of unified Democratic rule under Jimmy Carter and for the first two years under Bill Clinton.

Divided government is frequently characterized by legislative gridlock as Congress refuses to pass bills on the White House's agenda and the president vetoes legislation that comes down from Capitol Hill—witness the paltry output under George H. W. Bush of which a deficit-reduction package, clean-air bill, a minor adjustment to civil-rights law, and the Americans with Disabilities Act are about all that's worth mentioning on the domestic side. When this happens the parties point fingers at each other and maneuver to avoid blame. They also try to deflect criticism for economic problems and foreign crises. But sometimes good things can happen under divided governments. They can be productive. The legislative record of the Nixon years, at least according to David Mayhew's seminal work on divided government and lawmaking, was quite spectacular. Major laws passed included sweeping expansions to Social Security and programs for food stamps, job training, unemployment benefits, public transportation, and health care; increases in the minimum wage; revisions to the tax code; the emergence of revenue sharing and a new kind of relationship between the states and the federal government; and the establishment of the Supplemental Security Income program, the Environmental Protection Agency, and the Occupational Safety and

Health Administration.[1] When Bill Clinton worked with the GOP congressional majority in the late 1990s, the deficit was wiped away, welfare was reformed in a historic overhaul, and the farm, telecommunications, and banking sectors of the economy were radically changed. When these kinds of things happen both parties work hard to claim credit.

The problem with divided government is not therefore one of inevitable gridlock. Instead, the public has a torrid time assigning blame when things go badly or don't get done and credit when the opposite occurs. In contrast with unified government, divided government makes it easy for the parties to evade accountability.

Periods without a discernible majority party also mean that congressional majorities are often small and precarious. This was the case in the late 1940s and early 1950s when control of the House switched between the parties five times in a dozen years. Today's GOP majorities are certainly slim. In the 109th Congress of 2004–2005, only 53 percent of House members and 55 percent of senators are Republicans. This is the largest majority the GOP has had in the House since it took over the lower chamber in 1995—the 1994 elections meant that 230 of the House's 435 members were Republicans. The Senate has had no more than 55 Republicans in any one Congress since that time. Still, GOP control is not shaky. Although the defection of Senator Jim Jeffords of Vermont in May 2001 did put the upper chamber in Democratic hands for a year and a half, both congressional bodies seem tightly in the GOP's grip.

There is some evidence, therefore, that we have entered a new and almost unique period in American history. With the exception of an eighteen-month Democratic majority in the Senate, we have witnessed constant unified government under a now two-term Republican president. Unusually, this government is not built on the support of a majority of the population but an edge that the party has in its competition with the Democrats. Naturally, the edge cannot on its own furnish decisive electoral victories for the GOP, but it does provide a platform, however rickety, for Republican governance. It explains two consecutive narrow wins at the presidential level and decade-long, wafer-thin majorities in both chambers of Congress.

I say the current period is almost unique because there exists an instructive historical parallel. During the Gilded Age from 1877 to 1893 the Republicans managed, for some of the time at least, to govern with minority presidents—Rutherford Hayes (1876),

James Garfield (1880), and Benjamin Harrison (1888) all failed to win a majority of the popular vote—and slim congressional majorities. During much of those sixteen years, the GOP acutely understood its situation. It realized that partisan competition was fierce and the electoral foundations of its governing status cracked.

As a result, the party set about feverishly exploiting the advantages it had. It enjoyed allies in the editorial offices of influential newspapers. Men like Joseph Medill of the *Chicago Tribune* and Whitelaw Reid of the *New York Tribune* used their pages to energetically promote GOP candidates and policies. The Republicans, assisted by business icons like John Wanamaker, also put tremendous pressure on large corporations to contribute to party coffers and enjoyed significant financial advantages over the Democrats. Even before Cleveland businessman Mark Hanna raised over $6 million for William McKinley's 1896 campaign, Republican presidential candidates had oodles of cash at their disposal—in 1888 the Harrison campaign leaned on business for about $3 million.[2] In the early part of the period, Republicans who held federal offices also utilized patronage to perpetuate their power—senators like Roscoe Conkling of New York and Matthew Quay of Pennsylvania used the appointment power to leverage loyalty and financial assessments from civil servants under their aegis. Then, when the political winds turned and there was public outcry against this spoils system after the assassination of President Garfield by the disgruntled office seeker Charles Guiteau in 1881, the GOP pushed what was essentially a Democratic bill, later to be known as the Pendleton Act, that removed many government positions from the patronage ranks and set up a Civil Service Commission to administer a system based on merit rather than political connections.

The Republican Party was not alone in its fervent attempts to win political power, of course, and the Democrats did not lie down and die. They held on to many large industrial cities with an iron fist. The Democratic machines in places like Chicago, Boston, and Boss Tweed's New York cultivated several million votes for Democrats running for federal office by liberally sprinkling patronage and public services on immigrants and the working class. But the Republicans did seem to have some critical advantages.

The GOP of the time also knew it had an opportunity to move policy in a conservative direction and it understood that, given its general control of the White House and Congress, especially the Senate, the party would be held directly accountable for government performance. Baldly pushing policy out in front of public opinion without upsetting a divided electorate would be difficult given the party's tenuous hold on power. As a result, there were attempts to centralize authority and streamline procedures so as to keep the party cohesive and, in turn, increase the government's productivity and effectiveness. In 1890, for example, the House instituted changes named after its Republican Speaker, Thomas Brackett Reed of Maine. Reed's rules empowered the Speaker to reject dilatory motions and ended the disappearing quorum—the comic and obstructionist practice of members refusing to acknowledge themselves present even as they stood on the House floor. This period also witnessed a palpable uptick in the number of attempts—many of which were pushed by Republicans—to reform the Senate's practice of unlimited debate.[3] Harvard political scientist Eric Schickler shows that Reed's principal motivation for establishing the new rules was a fractured Republican caucus.[4] Similarly, GOP leadership efforts to curb filibustering in the upper body were at least partially brought about by the large fault line running through the Senate party—Republicans in that chamber were split with "Stalwarts" supporting New Yorker Roscoe Conkling and "Half Breeds" affiliating with James Blaine, "The Man From Maine." Still, at least the congressional Republican leadership was in a position to corral its members. As reporter O. O. Stealey put it in the 1870s, congressional Republicans were "an organized well-disciplined army" compared to the "headless undisciplined force," that was the House and Senate Democratic Party.[5]

Consequently, and despite only muted support from the American public, manufactured Republican unity moved policy to the right. According to Herbert Croly, Republicans saw the nation's economy as "a vast cooperative productive enterprise, in which the social or the public economic interest was promoted by energetic and promiscuous stimulation of productive agencies in private hands."[6] They also worried about a fragile social harmony that was threatened by waves of immigrants from eastern and southern Europe and even China. To be sure, a pervasive deflation and pressure from Democrats and third-party gadflies forced the enactment of legislation facilitating the free coinage of silver, but most major laws were clearly consistent with Republican philosophy. The tariff was raised, immigration rules were tightened, and the navy was strengthened.

As I have shown throughout the preceding chapters, today's GOP has behaved similarly. It has recognized the advantages it enjoys and acted ruthlessly to exploit them. It has also centralized procedures so as to make sure it governs effectively. George W. Bush has aggressively used the appointment power to provide ideological coalescence and ensure loyalty to his administration. At the beginning of the second term, appointments of confidants like Alberto Gonzales as Attorney General, Condoleeza Rice as Secretary of State, and Margaret Spellings to head the Department of Education only hardened this impression. Tight control has also been exerted. Bush has emphasized a corporate management culture in which loyalty to the organization is paramount and political appointees are expected to rein in civil servants.[7] More specifically, there are increased White House controls of agency rule-making, new "pay-for-performance" procedures that make it easier for managers to supervise civil servants, tighter restrictions on the public release of government information, and stricter vetting processes for prospective appointees.[8] The White House has even packaged video segments for television news so that the media project the administration in a positive light.[9] As a result of all this, in the first term, "Leaks generally were few in number and controlled, overt dissent was unusual, and the capacity to stay 'on message' was striking."[10] Strengthened by the public deference generated by the reaction to September 11, this remarkable coherence allowed a president elected without even a plurality of the popular vote to, in the words of journalist Alexis Simendinger, flex "all the muscles the Constitution gave him and, some would say, a few it didn't."[11]

Centripetal forces have been experienced at the other end of Pennsylvania Avenue, too. Under the vigorous leadership of Newt Gingrich and then Tom DeLay, House Republicans have been marshaled into a cohesive unit. The leadership has tremendous control over appointments to standing committees and has frequently ignored seniority to install loyalists as chairs—Bob Livingston of Louisiana, the "Speaker-in-waiting" who resigned his seat after he admitted to an extra-marital affair during the Clinton impeachment, became the first example of this when, as the fifth most senior Republican on Appropriations, he was made the committee's chair in 1995. Moderates like Marge Roukema of New Jersey and Christopher Shays of Connecticut have been passed over for chairmanships because of their purported infidelity to the party. What is more, committee leaders in both chambers are now limited to serving six years. In the Senate, Majority Leader Bill Frist has been given greater power to assign GOP members to committees and has been working—although until now unsuccessfully—with his party to do away with the minority's prerogative to filibuster judicial nominees. After initially delivering on a promise to allow rank-and-file members to offer more amendments during the floor debate on bills, moreover, House GOP chieftans have reversed themselves and greatly restricted the ability of members to revise legislation after it has left committee. This move prevented Democrats and Republican moderates from watering down conservative proposals crafted in committee. In the 104th Congress of 1995–96, for instance, 43 percent of important bills had rules that restricted the offering of floor amendments; by the 107th Congress of 2001–2002 the figure had risen to 63 percent.

This has all helped move policy to the right—indubitably, in a shift more comprehensive than that of the 1877-to-1893 period. Strewn throughout the book are examples of recent conservative policy-making in the areas of taxes, regulation, education, health care, abortion, and foreign affairs.

In contrast to the 1890s, however, I think it is unlikely that the Republicans will be able to translate their edge into a lasting electoral majority. After clinging to power by their fingernails for several years, the GOP lost control of the House in 1890—there were only eighty-eight Republicans in the chamber after the disastrous elections of that year. In 1892 it lost the Senate and Grover Cleveland captured the White House for the Democrats. But two years later the GOP was back with vengeance. The American public, miserable after a particularly nasty recession—unemployment is estimated to have reached between 15 and 20 percent—evicted 125 Democrats from the House and handed over control to the Republicans. The GOP also emerged with a plurality of the Senate. The election was, it turned out, a realigning one. The Republicans went on to form the majority in the House in all but three of the next eighteen Congresses; in the Senate it was only in the minority for two Congresses during the period. When William McKinley was elected with nearly 61 percent of the popular vote in 1896, he ushered in a thirty-six-year epoch in which only Woodrow Wilson—albeit on two occasions—was able to wrest the White House away from the GOP.

Karl Rove has suggested he believes that today's Republicans can forge a similar electoral majority from their current ruling status. Indeed, his favorite president is McKinley precisely because the Ohioan changed party politics so dramatically in the GOP's favor. I disagree with George W. Bush's political guru for five reasons. First, in stark contrast to the elections of a hundred years ago, the campaigns of today—even Democratic ones—have tremendous resources, information, and expertise at their disposal. Excluding the cash poured into the race by parties and 527s, nearly $720 million was spent by candidates in the 2004 presidential election. Coupled with technology, such money can leverage all sorts of valuable information. Chapter 7 revealed, for example, that the parties have built and are maintaining vast databases about the electorate. Their strategists can quickly access information about the demographic characteristics, political proclivities, and even commercial tastes of an individual. Geographical information systems permit efficient deployment of voter registration and get-out-the-vote efforts. Sophisticated polling yields rich data that are analyzed using high-powered statistical techniques. All of this, in turn, exposes the messages, candidates, and issue positions that attract or repel voters. The electorate and its habits and desires are rendered extraordinarily, and perhaps creepily, transparent.

Political scientist John Geer outlined a similar argument in his 1996 book, *From Tea Leaves to Opinion Polls: A Theory of Democratic Leadership*.[12] Geer stated that polls have provided candidates with so much information about the electorate that they can rapidly and effectively shift issue stances if their extant positions are alienating voters. One consequence is that the type of realignments that made the Republicans the majority party in the early years of the twentieth century and the Democrats the majority from the New Deal to the Great Society are a thing of the past. In light of the dramatic differences in the positions of the Bush and Kerry campaigns on abortion, same-sex marriages, gun control, health care, and taxes during the 2004 campaign, it may be difficult to agree with Geer's assertion that the well-informed candidates and parties of today avoid taking polarized positions on critical issues. Still, his main point on the continued competitiveness of partisan politics is well taken. The great scholar E. E. Schattschneider once said, "A political party is first of all an organized attempt to get power."[13] If this is the case, purposive parties with ambitious candidates are unlikely to hold obdurately to positions a majority of voters find unpalatable. Today, since they can cull detailed information about the electorate, they do not have to be so ignorant as to have to.

The tendency to adopt vote-winning policy positions is exacerbated by candidates' reliance on political consultants. In the past few decades, elections for federal office have spawned a massive and often lucrative industry. Having raised pocketfuls of cash, candidates set about purchasing assistance because parties are of minimal help. Professional expertise is available for the construction of a campaign message—in both its substantive and stylistic forms—advertising, polling, and yet more fundraising. This, in turn, contributes to victorious campaigns. David A. Dulio and Stephen K. Medvic have shown that hiring the right help can add to the votes you get on election day.[14]

Because electoral victories burnish their reputations and fill their bank accounts consultants are innately cautious. This is not to say they are all mercenaries—Dulio has shown that most are driven by ideology, partisanship, and the thrill of the political game.[15] Still, they clearly like money—profit margins are routinely boosted to 25 percent and a 2000 American University survey showed that over one-fifth of consultants earned at least $200,000 a year.[16] Since their livelihoods depend on assisting successful candidates, they tend not to recommend temerarious strategies. They are also likely to reprise winning formulae from elections past. As a result, the parties and candidates for federal and top state offices, acting on advice from their army of risk-averse consultants, will run campaigns that blunt ideological edges. This, in turn, makes it likely that elections will be tight.

A second reason not to believe the emergence of a new Republican majority is that today's Democratic Party is adaptable; it will continually transform itself to meet the wants of the electorate. Some of this flexibility can be explained by the developments I've just discussed—the emergence of sophisticated polling techniques and political consultants, for example—but most of it is the product of the party's long and painful march from the political Siberia of the 1970s and 1980s. During those decades, the Democrats' chances of controlling the presidency and moving public policy to the left were fatally undercut by liberal messages that rang discordant in the politics of the time. George McGovern, Walter Mondale, and, to a lesser extent, Michael Dukakis proposed the kinds of policies that won over Massachusetts and Minnesota but not much else. Jimmy Carter captured the White House by a narrow margin in 1976 because the Republicans were still reeling from Watergate, and, as a southerner and newcomer to national politics, the peanut farmer from Georgia did not seem to share the values of the national Democratic Party. Congress, although ostensibly under Democratic control, was run, at least until the late 1980s, by a coalition of Republicans and conservative southern Democrats who, because of their seniority, were able to head up many important committees.

Desperate for success and armed with new policies, many influential members of the party began the trek back toward the ideological middle. Moderates and modernizers like James Blanchard, John Breaux, Al Gore, Joe Lieberman, Sam Nunn, and, of course, Bill Clinton were helped along the way by organizations like the Democratic Leadership Council. They were finally rewarded in 1992 when the "New Democrat" Clinton won the party's presidential nomination and then the White House.

Of course, not every Democrat shared Clinton's moderation. The president was frequently criticized for a lack of strong principles and for being too poll-driven—the arrival in the White House of his old consultant, the survey-obsessed triangulator Dick Morris, was too much even for chief of staff Erskine Bowles and top aide George Stephanopoulos.[17] High-ranking Clinton-appointed Department of Health and Human Services officials Mary Jo Bane, Peter Edelman, and Wendell Primus resigned after the president approved the 1996 welfare overhaul bill—legislation that ended the New Deal Aid to Families with Dependent Children program. Liberals in Congress also despaired over the policy change—165 House Democrats voted against the bill in its original form when it passed the lower chamber in July 1996. Still, Clinton connected with millions of Democratic voters on a personal level. As I suggested in Chapter 9, nowhere was this attraction more evident than in the president's relationship with African Americans. Blacks related to his poor southern upbringing and his underdog status, and they appreciated the ease with which he interacted with them.[18]

Not only was Clinton likeable, he was a winner. In 1993 Democrats realized how wonderful it was to govern. Campaign workers and policy wonks salivated as they leafed through the "Plum Book," the directory of thousands of government jobs available for presidential appointment. Democratic consultants and lobbyists soon caught on that they would have access to the executive branch and its colossal influence over what was then about a $1.5 trillion budget.

In 2000 the Democrats lost the White House in a bitterly contested election. They paid a big price for Al Gore's failure.

Democratic consultants, policy advisers, and lobbyists were frozen out, and public policy moved rightward. George W. Bush's swagger only heaped on the misery. Four years later then, as they went to the polls to select a candidate to oppose Bush, they chose someone they believed could recapture the White House for them. Many Democrats were initially attracted to former Vermont governor Howard Dean and his anti-Iraq war message, but they soon came to realize that victory in November was the paramount goal. At the Iowa caucuses in January 2004, entrance polls revealed that 26 percent of respondents felt that beating the sitting president was the most important "quality" they were looking for in a candidate. Of these people, 37 percent picked John Kerry, 30 percent John Edwards. The next week 20 percent of New Hampshire primary voters felt the most important quality was the ability to unseat Bush—as opposed to 13 percent who looked for a "positive message" and 12 percent who wanted the nominee to "care about people"—and of these, 62 percent voted for Kerry. By the time we got to Wisconsin in mid-February, Kerry was winning 69 percent of the vote of those who looked primarily for a candidate who could evict Bush from the White House.

To be sure, the contest for the 2004 Democratic presidential nomination reopened old divisions within the party. We discussed this earlier. But the general election campaign of that year also provided plenty of evidence that winning now largely trumped ideology for the Democrats. There was, of course, talk about protecting Medicare and Social Security and of raising taxes on people who earned more than $200,000 a year. Yet even though many strategists believed the key to victory would be turning out the base, Kerry generally eschewed liberal policies. He emphasized his service in Vietnam, his strength as a leader, his interest in foreign policy, and a program that, he claimed at least, would bring fiscal discipline to government. Kerry campaigned as if he'd never heard of Massachusetts and never met Ted Kennedy. He looked nothing like the senator who has a ninety-two lifetime vote score from the liberal Americans for Democratic Action—for the sake of comparison, Kennedy enjoys a ninety lifetime rating. Kerry hunted and windsurfed; he was macho and mean. The campaign's attacks on the president were very aggressive and often personal, especially after it hired much of Bill Clinton's old team—Joel Johnson, Joe Lockhart, Mike McCurry, and Doug Sosnik. What is more, its approach did not alienate the Democratic base. To be sure, it seemed as though many were voting more

against Bush than for Kerry—70 percent of the one-fourth of voters who selected a candidate primarily because they were repelled
by his opponent went for Kerry—but Democrats still heartily
embraced the Massachusetts senator's meticulously crafted moderate positions and acerbic style.

Even the choice of Howard Dean as party chair is not the
strategically disastrous move some have claimed it to be—in the
2004 presidential contest, Dean showed himself to be a master
motivator, organizer, and fundraiser. What is more, the Democrats
have pulled together in opposition to President Bush's plan to
create personal or private accounts in Social Security. As an opposition party, the Democrats look positively galvanized, motivated,
and businesslike compared to some of their counterparts in other
corners of the industrialized world. Fifteen years after Margaret
Thatcher's resignation, the Conservative Party in Britain, for
example, still cannot make up its mind where it stands on the
pivotal issue of the country's role in Europe. With a diminishing
and graying membership and a series of lightweight leaders—the
nonentities William Hague, Iain Duncan-Smith, and Michael
Howard have served in opposition—it seems incapable of solving
crucial internecine disputes that impede its efforts to reclaim
power. The French Socialists, hung up on protecting France's
antiquated welfare state and outflanked by conservative President
Jacques Chirac's vitriolic criticism of the Bush administration's
decision to invade Iraq, are still reeling from crushing defeats in
the 2002 National Assembly and presidential elections—in the
latter, the socialist candidate, Lionel Jospin, received fewer votes
than the quasi-fascist Jean-Marie Le Pen. The Socialists have made
a small comeback recently—in the fall of 2004 they won a few
more seats in the parliament's upper chamber—but they, like the
Conservatives across the Channel, are split on the future of
Europe.

A third source of Democratic solace is that the contemporary
Republican Party has a tendency to overreach—a bad habit that
the GOP, if it misreads the 2004 election as realigning, may well
fall back into.[19] The attempt to outlaw the Senate filibuster on
judicial nominations might become an example of Republican
intemperance. So could questions surrounding the behavior of Tom
DeLay. The House Majority Leader's ethical troubles are the kind
of thing that smell of the abuse of power and that allowed Newt
Gingrich to bring down the old Democratic majority. The business
over Terri Schiavo may already have done some lasting damage.

Although Republican leaders won applause from the party's conservative base, majorities within the general public consistently approved of what Mr. Schiavo and the judiciary were doing and disapproved of what was considered the interference of the president and congressional Republicans.

There is precedent for the GOP pushing too hard. With an ignorance of congressional procedures and the system of checks and balances that belied the incoming Speaker Newt Gingrich's career as a professor of American history, the new House Republican majority attempted to bulldoze their agenda through the Senate and over President Bill Clinton in 1995 and 1996. It came out of the period looking particularly extreme and incapable of governing responsibly and effectively. The infamous government shutdown during the winter of 1995–1996—when a stopgap spending measure was held hostage to partisan disagreements over the basic direction of federal fiscal policy—did much to create this impression. Republicans strutted around the House floor allowing Clinton to look reasonable and moderate and sympathetic to the plight of those affected by the shutdown. A mid-January 1996 CBS News poll revealed the public largely shared this view. It found that 51 percent blamed the congressional GOP for the episode; 27 percent blamed Clinton. There seems little doubt that what happened helped focus an image of the Republican Party that the president used to haunt Bob Dole with to great effect the following November. Dole, a patrician Republican, was ruthlessly tarred with the same brush as Gingrich, the strident conservative.[20]

The Clinton impeachment furnishes another example. In 1998 the Democrats became the first presidential party to gain seats in House midterm elections since 1934. As a direct consequence, Newt Gingrich resigned as speaker. Yet, the GOP pressed on within its germinal attempt to get Bill Clinton out of office. The House Judiciary Committee continued its hearings and proposed the president be impeached on four counts in mid-December. Then, despite growing evidence that the public felt Clinton's conduct was a personal matter and he should remain president, the full House impeached on two counts the week before Christmas.[21] In the end, the Senate went through the motions of a trial when it was quite clear the two-thirds vote required for conviction and removal was not there. Congressional Republicans were ultimately left to deal with an aggrieved and emboldened Clinton.

Then, of course, there is Iraq. Counter-factual history is generally a fruitless exercise, but it is hard to believe that the 2004 presidential election would have been so close had the successful invasion not been marred by a violent and chaotic occupation. The bloody aftermath allowed Americans to focus on President Bush's zealous embrace of the war. With a feeble and small international coalition Bush preemptively struck the Iraqis. To many, this illustrated poor judgment. Worse still, the absence of weapons of mass destruction meant that either the administration misled the public or was overseeing an incompetent intelligence organization. That there was no real evidence of a Saddam Hussein–Al Qaeda relationship served to reinforce this impression. By the time of Bush's second inaugural, a CBS News/*New York Times* poll found that 75 percent of Americans feared the president had no clear plan for getting out of Iraq. By the end of April 2005 a CNN/*USA Today*/Gallup poll discovered that 57 percent felt that it was "not worth going to war." Continual reports of American deaths and a well-organized ruthless insurgency contributed to an increasingly pervasive impression that the United States was in a Vietnam-like quagmire.

Fourth, many of the GOP's foot soldiers are motivated to protect the status quo, not promote change. They become engaged politically when they are, to use Thomas Frank's lovely phrase, "performing indignation."[22] Christian conservatives, for example, have gone to the polls when they feel their traditional values are under fire. They turned out in 1994 to protest Bill Clinton, his gays-in-the-military policy, and his reverence for the 1960s. A decade later they voted *en masse* against same-sex marriage and John Kerry's cultural cosmopolitanism. If Republicans continue to enjoy electoral and policy victories, therefore, the enthusiasm of much grassroots support will wane. If, let's say, the federal bench continues to fill up with conservative judges and advocates of same-sex marriage beat a strategic retreat, will evangelicals stay at home in 2008 as Karl Rove believes they did in 2000?

A final reason to suspect that the Republican advantage will not transmute into an enduring majority any time soon is that the party is experiencing internal tensions that could, quite plausibly, open into debilitating fault lines. To be sure, and as I explained earlier in the book, the GOP has not had to deal with the kinds of intrinsic divisions that the Democrats have, but that does not mean the party is monolithic and immune to fracture. I discussed fissures among the House GOP in Chapter 7, for instance. In fact, a number of political scientists and pundits have suggested the Republicans are on the verge of domestic unrest that, if the circumstances are right, could evolve into the kind of civil war the Democrats experienced in the 1960s and 1970s.

Splits are on view everywhere.[23] William Safire talks about five conflicting parts of his "Republican brain"—it has, he says, "economic conservative," "social conservative," "libertarian impulse," "idealistic calling," and "cultural conservative" components.[24] *New York Times* reporter Adam Nagourney identifies the following factions: "libertarian Republicans, Christian conservative Republicans, moderate Republicans, Wall Street Republicans, balanced-budget Republicans, tax-cutting Republicans, cut-the-size-of-government Republicans, neoconservative Republicans supporting global intervention, and isolationist Republicans who would like to stay at home."[25] As John Judis has written, the rise of the southern and moralist wing of the party—personified by people like Texan George W. Bush and North Carolinian Jesse Helms—has marginalized and antagonized the western and libertarian wing that embraced Arizonan Barry Goldwater and Californian Ronald Reagan.[26] Norm Ornstein saw a number of the GOP senate primaries in 2004 as an illustration of an establishment-populist cleavage in the party—Arlen Specter versus Pat Toomey in Pennsylvania and David Beasley against Jim DeMint in South Carolina being prime examples of the phenomenon.[27] As we noted earlier, many Senate moderates like John McCain, Lincoln Chafee, Susan Collins, Olympia Snowe, and George Voinovich are at loggerheads with supply-siders and pork barrelers over the deficit.[28] Liberal journalist Frank Rich has predicted a "civil war" within the party caused by conflicting views on homosexuality.[29] The GOP has even fractured on its forte, foreign policy. Bush's bold and aggressive approach has drawn criticism from GOP midwestern isolationists and realists like Senators Chuck Hagel of Nebraska and Richard Lugar of Indiana.[30] "America-Firsters" like Pat Buchanan despise Bush's trade policy and immigration.[31] All of this suggests a free-for-all over the party's presidential nomination in 2008. Mavericks like Hagel and McCain, conservatives such as Senate Majority Leader Bill Frist and his Pennsylvania lieutenant Rick Santorum, and moderates like Rudy Giuliani and Mitt Romney—all possible candidates—will at least make it a spectacular fireworks show. After that, it's plausible that the winner will have to lead a shattered party in that fall's election.

Still, one cannot help but conclude that it is generally better to be a Republican these days. Although the presidential race will be for a vacated White House in 2008, the GOP will be the incumbent party and it has a tight grip on both chambers of Congress. The party also controls twenty-nine governorships and fifty of the ninety-eight state legislative bodies that have partisan elections. Public policy will continue, if frequently slowly or jerkily, to move palpably rightward. This will please GOP constituencies and, as we saw in Chapters 4, 5, and 6, undermine the Democrats. Constitutional and statutory rules that protect Republican advantages in elections will—with the possible exception of campaign finance—remain unaltered. In control of the bully pulpit and with the assistance of many media outlets and think tanks, the ruling party will continue to frame public debate so as to influence attitudes. It will also work to exploit social and economic trends that are glacially shifting large and important segments of the electorate its way. The elephant's edge may not, therefore, be a platform for Republican realignment, but there is enough circular logic to it that it will be of comfort to GOP government officials, candidates, activists, and supporters for a number of years to come.

Notes

PREFACE

1. Quoted in John F. Harris, "Was Nov. 2 Realignment—Or a Tilt?" *Washington Post*, November 28, 2004, p. A1.

2. David R. Mayhew, *Electoral Realignments: A Critique of an American Genre* (New Haven, CT: Yale University Press, 2002).

CHAPTER 1

1. Kevin P. Phillips, *The Emerging Republican Majority* (New York: Anchor Books, 1970). Chapter 1 of John B. Judis and Ruy Teixeira's, *The Emerging Democratic Majority* (New York: Scribner, 2002) begins the same way. This is a testament to the importance of Phillips' book and, I hope, not to my inability to think of an original beginning to mine.

2. Walter Dean Burnham, *Critical Elections and the Mainsprings of American Politics* (New York: W.W. Norton and Company, 1970).

3. The late Everett Ladd named an essay about the supposed Republican realignment after Beckett's play. See Everett Carll Ladd, "Like Waiting for Godot: The Uselesssness of 'Realignment' for Understanding Change in Contemporary American Politics," in *The End of Realignment? Interpreting American Electoral Eras*, ed. Byron E. Shafer (Madison: University of Wisconsin Press, 1991).

4. Phillips, *The Emerging Republican Majority*, p. 25.

5. Nebraska has a nonpartisan unicameral legislature.

6. Quoted in Michael Janofsky, "Rove Declares Nation Is Tilting to Republicans," *New York Times*, November 14, 2002, p. A27.

7. Quoted in Liz Marlantes, "Where Republicans Invaded Democratic Turf," *Christian Science Monitor*, November 21, 2002, p. 3.

8. Quoted in Dan Balz, "Challenges on Agenda, Leadership," *Washington Post*, November 7, 2002, p. A1.

9. Jeffrey Bell and Frank Cannon, "The Beginning of the Bush Epoch? Handicapping 2004," *The Weekly Standard*, December 9, 2002, pp. 18–19.

10. Adam Nagourney, "Bush, Looking to His Right, Shores Up Support for 2004," *New York Times*, June 30, 2003, p. A17.

11. Jim VandeHei and Juliet Eilperin, "Targeting Lobbyists Pays Off for GOP," *Washington Post*, June 26, 2003, p. A1.

12. Quoted in Julie Kosterlitz, "On the Ropes?" *National Journal*, September 6, 2003, p. 2683.

13. Morton Kondracke, "GOP Has Scored Major Gains in Swing States," *Roll Call*, November 10, 2003.

14. Quoted in Dana Millbank, "History's Tea Leaves Point to Bush's Reelection," *Washington Post*, November 18, 2003, p. A23.

15. Fred Barnes, "The (Finally) Emerging Republican Majority," *The Weekly Standard*, October 27, 2003, pp. 24–26.

16. David Brooks, "The Promised Land," *New York Times*, November 29, 2003, p. A33.

17. Michael Barone, "Life, Liberty, and Property," in *The Almanac of American Politics 2004*, ed. Michael Barone with Richard E. Cohen (Washington, D.C.: National Journal, 2003), p. 35.

18. Robert Kuttner, "America as a One-Party State," *American Prospect*, online, February 1, 2004.

19. John Micklethwait and Adrian Wooldridge, *The Right Nation: Conservative Power in America* (New York: Penguin Press, 2004).

20. Quoted in John F. Harris, "Was Nov. 2 Realignment—Or a Tilt?" *Washington Post*, November 28, 2004, p. A1.

21. Stanley B. Greenberg, *The Two Americas: Our Current Political Deadlock and How to Break It* (New York: Thomas Dunne Books, 2004).

22. John Sperling, Suzanne Helburn, Samuel George, John Morris, and Carl Hunt, *The Great Divide: Retro Versus Metro America* (Sausalito, CA: Polipoint Press, 2004).

23. See, for example, Dan Balz and Ronald Brownstein, *Storming the Gates: Protest Politics and the Republican Revival* (Boston: Little, Brown, 1996).

24. Stanley B. Greenberg and Theda Skocpol, eds., *The New Majority: Towards a Popular Progressive Politics* (New Haven, CT: Yale University Press, 1987).

25. Paul Starr, "An Emerging Democratic Majority," in *The New Majority: Towards a Popular Progressive Politics*, ed. Stanley B. Greenberg

and Theda Skocpol (New Haven, CT: Yale University Press, 1987), pp. 221–37.

26. Christopher Caldwell, "The Southern Captivity of the GOP," *The Atlantic Monthly*, June 1998, pp. 55, 82.

27. Judis and Teixeira, *The Emerging Democratic Majority*.

28. Ruy Teixeira, "Deciphering the Democrats' Debacle: Why the Republican Majority (Probably) Won't Last," *Washington Monthly*, June 2003; Ruy Teixeira, "Post-Industrial Hopes Deferred: Why the Democratic Majority Is Still Likely to Emerge," *Brookings Review*, Summer 2003, pp. 40–42. Also see Teixeira's website http://www.emergingdemocraticmajorityweblog.com/donkeyrising/.

29. Greenberg, *The Two Americas*.

30. Robert B. Reich, *Reason: Why Liberals Will Win the Battle for America* (New York: Alfred A. Knopf, 2004).

31. E. J. Dionne, *They Only Look Dead: Why Progressives Will Dominate the Next Political Era* (New York: Simon and Schuster, 1996). Walter Dean Burnham suggested in 2000 that a backlash against conservative economic policies might help a "progressive realignment," too. See Walter Dean Burnham, "Whole Lotta Shakin' Goin' On: A Political Realignment Is on the Way," *The Nation*, April 17, 2000, pp. 11–15.

32. Matthew Dowd and Bill McInturff in "The GOP Seeks A Broader Base," Thomas B. Edsall, *Washington Post National Weekly Edition*, January 6–12, 2003, pp. 12–13.

33. For more on the National Election Studies, see The National Election Studies, Center for Political Studies, University of Michigan, and *The NES Guide to Public Opinion and Electoral Behavior* at http://www.umich.edu/~nes/nesguide/nesguide.htm.

34. About once a month Gallup asks respondents to a survey, "Do you approve or disapprove of the way X Is handling his job as president?"

35. Jonathan Chait, "Mad About You," *New Republic*, September 29, 2003, pp. 20–23.

36. Quoted in Robin Toner, "Anger at Bush Smolders on Democratic Turf," *New York Times*, August 4, 2003, p. A8.

37. Robert Novak, "The Anti-Bush," from townhall.com Web site, August 7, 2003, http://www.townhall.com/columnists/robertnovak/rn20030807.shtml.

38. Robert C. Byrd, *Losing America: Confronting a Reckless and Arrogant Presidency* (New York: Norton, 2004); Richard A. Clarke, *Against All Enemies: Inside America's War on Terror* (New York: Free Press, 2004); John W. Dean, *Worse than Watergate: The Secret Presidency of George W. Bush* (New York: Little, Brown, 2004); Kevin Phillips, *American Dynasty: Aristocracy, Fortune, and the Politics of Deceit in the House of Bush* (New York: Viking, 2004); Ron Suskind, *The Price of Loyalty: George W. Bush, the White House, and the Education of Paul O'Neill* (New York: Simon &

Schuster, 2004); Craig Unger, *House of Bush, House of Saud: The Secret Relationship between the World's Two Most Powerful Dynasties* (New York: Scribner's, 2004); Joseph Wilson, *The Politics of Truth: Inside the Lies That Led to War and Betrayed My Wife's Identity* (New York: Carroll and Graf, 2004). Michael Scheuer's book was published under the pseudonym "Anonymous" as *Imperial Hubris: Why the West Is Losing the War on Terror* (New York: Brassey's, 2004).

39. Quoted in Adam Clymer, "Buoyed by Resurgence, GOP Strives for an Era of Dominance," *New York Times*, May 25, 2003, p. 1.

40. Quoted in Adam Nagourney and Richard W. Stevenson, "Some See Risks as Republicans Revel in Power," *New York Times*, January 24, 2005, p. A14.

41. There is a large literature on more gradual changes in voter coalitions than those envisioned by the traditional theory of realignment. See, for example, Edward G. Carmines and James A. Stimson, "The Dynamics of Issue Evolution: The United States," in *Electoral Change in Advanced Industrial Democracies: Realignment or Dealignment?* ed. Russell J. Dalton, Scott C. Flanagan, and Paul Allen Beck (Princeton: Princeton University Press, 1984) and V. O. Key Jr., "Secular Realignment and the Party System," *Journal of Politics* 21, no. 2 (1959), pp. 198–210. For examples of those who see gradual political changes in the last thirty or so years helping Republicans, see James E. Campbell, "The Presidential Pulse and the 1994 Midterm Congressional Election," *Journal of Politics* 59 (August 1997): 830–57; Everett C. Ladd, "The 1994 Congressional Elections: The Postindustrial Realignment Continues," *Political Science Quarterly* 110 (Spring 1995): 1–23; Richard Wirthlin, "Partisan Change in the 1980s: A Rolling Realignment," *Public Perspective* 1 (November/December 1989): 13–15.

42. Kenneth T. Walsh, "Keeping the Plan That Got Him Here," *U.S. News and World Report*, October 2, 2000, p. 23.

43. Daniel Casse, "An Emerging Republican Majority?" *Commentary*, January 2003, pp. 17–22.

44. Rove quoted in Dan Balz and Mike Allen, "Four More Years Attributed to Rove's Strategy," *Washington Post*, November 7, 2004, p. A1. See also, Michael Barone, "American Politics in the Networking Era," *National Journal*, February 26, 2005, pp. 590–96.

45. Jeffrey Bell and Frank Cannon, "The Bush Realignment," *The Weekly Standard*, November 15, 2004, pp. 9–11.

46. Quoted in Chuck McCutcheon, "Republicans in Congress Call Election a Mandate," *New Orleans Times-Picayune*, November 4, 2004, p. 9.

47. Quoted in Adam Nagourney, "Kerry Advisers Point Fingers at Iraq and Social Issues," *New York Times*, November 9, 2004, p. A16.

48. Ronald Brownstein, "After Four Years Bush Is No Closer to Building a GOP Majority," *Los Angeles Times*, November 1, 2004, p. 14.

CHAPTER 2

1. James Madison, *Federalist 39*, in Alexander Hamilton, James Madison, and John Jay, eds., *The Federalist Papers*, (New York: Mentor Books, 1961), p. 243.

2. Ibid.

3. Daniel Lazare, *The Frozen Republic: How the Constitution Is Paralyzing Democracy* (New York: Harcourt Brace, 1996).

4. Michael Lind, "Seventy-Five Stars: How to Restore Democracy in the U.S. Senate (And End the Tyranny of Wyoming)," *Mother Jones*, January–February 1998, pp. 44–49.

5. Francis E. Lee and Bruce I. Oppenheimer, *Sizing Up the Senate: The Unequal Consequences of Equal Representation* (Chicago: University of Chicago Press, 1999), pp. 158–85.

6. Citizens Against Government Waste, *The 2004 Congressional Pig Book* (Washington, D.C.: Citizens Against Government Waste, 2004). The group uses a variety of criteria to define pork, including appropriations serves a local interest, expenditures not requested by the president, and unauthorized spending.

7. Tax Foundation. Annual comparison of taxes to spending, http://www.taxfoundation.org/taxingspending.html.

8. Steven Hill, *Fixing Elections: The Failure of America's Winner Take All Politics* (New York: Routledge, 2002).

9. Jack Rakove, "Europe's Floundering Fathers," *Foreign Policy*, September–October 2003, p. 34.

10. Tom Geoghegan, "The Infernal Senate," *The New Republic*, November 21, 1994, pp. 17–23.

11. John Griffin, "Senate Apportionment as a Source of Political Inequality." Paper presented to the 2004 meeting of the American Political Science Association, Chicago.

12. Thomas L. Brunell, "Partisan Bias in the U.S. Congressional Elections: Why the Senate Is Usually More Republican than the House of Representatives," *American Politics Quarterly* 27 (July 1999): 316–37; Lee and Oppenheimer, *Sizing Up the Senate*, pp. 116–121.

13. There are 535 full voting members of Congress but 538 electors. Since 1961, the District of Columbia has had three votes in the Electoral College.

14. Alexander Hamilton, *Federalist 68*, in Hamilton, Madison, and Jay eds., *The Federalist Papers*, p. 412.

15. In some of these states the ballot is worded, "Presidential electors for [the name of the presidential candidate]." In others, even that information is omitted, and voters may have no idea that they are actually voting for a slate of electors and not, directly at least, a presidential candidate.

16. Quoted in Bill Kauffman, "The Elector Defector," *The American Enterprise*, March 2001, p. 49.

17. Lawrence D. Longley and Neal R. Peirce, *The Electoral College Primer 2000* (New Haven: Yale University Press, 1999), p. 113. I have seen it reported that she just wanted to bring attention to the fact that electors had the ability to vote for whomever they wanted.

18. For more, see Bernard Grofman, Thomas Brunell, and Janet Campagna, "Distinguishing between the Effects of Swing Ratio and Bias on Outcomes in the U.S. Electoral College, 1900–92," *Electoral Studies* 16 (December 1997): 471–87.

19. Longley and Peirce, *The Electoral College Primer 2000*, pp. 149–53.

20. George C. Edwards II, *Why The Electoral College Is Bad for America* (New Haven, CT: Yale University Press, 2004), p. 39.

21. Andrew Gelman and Jonathan N. Katz, "How Much Does a Vote Count? Voting Power, Coalitions, and the Electoral College," California Institute of Technology, Social Science Working Paper 1121, May 2001.

22. There have been modern occasions when the district plan would have made a difference, however. Nixon would have beaten Kennedy in 1960, and Carter and Ford would have been tied in 1976. See *The Rhodes Cook Letter*, March 2001.

23. Larry Rohter, "Florida Is Rethinking The Way Presidents are Elected," *New York Times*, June 7, 1992, p. I25.

24. Charles Krauthammer, "Avoiding the Electoral Train Wreck," *Washington Post*, May 29, 1992, p. A23; Martin Tolchin, "And If Perot Produces a Deadlock? The House Will Decide," *New York Times*, May 10, 1992, p. 1:18; George F. Will, "The Framers and Ross Perot," *Washington Post*, April 19, 1992, p. C7.

25. Susan Page, "Remember the Mess in 2000? How about a Tie?" *USA Today*, September 3–6, 2004, p. 2A.

26. Dana Milbank, "Electoral College Calculus," *Washington Post*, October 27, 2004, p. A1.

27. James C. Garand and T. Wayne Parent, "Representation, Swing, and Bias in U.S. Presidential Elections, 1872–1988," *American Journal of Political Science* 35 (November 1991): 1011–31.

28. John Maggs, "Divided We Stand," *National Journal*, March 20, 1999, pp. 748–52.

29. The two books are Earl Black and Merle Black, *The Rise of Southern Republicans* (Cambridge, MA: The Belknap Press of Harvard University Press, 2002); and David Lublin, *The Republican South: Democratization and Partisan Change* (Princeton, NJ: Princeton University Press, 2004).

30. "Bush's America: One Nation, Fairly Divisible, Under God," *The Economist*, January 20, 2001, pp. 19–22.

31. Quoted in Adam Nagourney, "Edwards Makes Rural Voters a Focus of His '04 Campaign," *New York Times*, May 22, 2003, p. A23.

32. Michael Barone, "The 49% Nation," in *The Almanac of American Politics, 2002*, ed. Michael Barone with Richard E. Cohen and Grant Ujifusa (Washington, D.C.: National Journal), pp. 21–45.

33. See Ronald Brownstein, "Midwest May Be Key to GOP Senate Hopes," *Los Angeles Times*, August 27, 2002, p. 1.

34. Quoted in Liz Clarke, "In Sunbelt Politicians Vie for NASCAR Dads," *Washington Post*, August 2, 2003, p. A1.

35. Quoted in Jeff MacGregor, "The New Electoral Sex Symbol: NASCAR Dad," *New York Times*, January 18, 2004, p. 4:1.

36. See Fox Butterfield, "For Democrats a Continental Divide on Guns," *New York Times*, February 27, 2002, p. 16.

37. "Cultural Issues in Rural America Gave Republicans a Wide Margin of Success in Recent Elections," Kellogg Foundation, November 2002.

38. Gregory L. Giroux, "Breaking the Tie: Parties Seek Formula for Majority Status," *Congressional Quarterly Weekly Report*, February 17, 2001, pp. 362–72.

39. On the issues currently facing Republicans in suburbia, see, for example, William Schneider, "In His Image: Now That President Bush Has Put His Face on the Republican Party, Can It Reclaim the Suburban Swing Voters the Democrats Wooed Away?" *Los Angeles Times*, January 5, 2003, p. 1.

40. Janet F. Gainsborough, *Fenced Off: The Suburbanization of American Politics* (Washington, D.C.: Georgetown University Press, 2001), pp. 116–33.

41. On the referendum, see Sue Fox and Patrick McGreevey, "Secessionists Weigh Options," *Los Angeles Times*, November 7, 2002, p. 2:1; Patrick McGreevey, "Stumbles Hurt Breakup Efforts," *Los Angeles Times*, November 8, 2002, p. 2:1.

42. Judis and Teixeira, *The Emerging Democratic Majority*, p. 73.

43. Joel Kotkin, *The New Geography: How the Digital Revolution Is Reshaping the American Landscape* (New York: Random House), pp. 38–44.

44. Kotkin, *The New Geography*, p. 39.

45. Joel Garreau, *Edge City: Life on the New Frontier* (New York: Doubleday, 1991).

46. Richard Florida, *The Rise of the Creative Class and How It's Transforming Work, Leisure, Community, and Everyday Life* (New York: Basic Books, 2002); David Brooks, *Bobos in Paradise: The New Upper Class and How They Got There* (New York: Simon & Schuster, 2000).

47. Greenberg, *The Two Americas*, p. 132.

48. For more on the effects of Sunbelt suburban construction on life, see Kenneth Jackson, *Crabgrass Frontier: The Suburbanization of the United States* (New York: Oxford University Press, 1985).

49. J. Eric Oliver, *Democracy in Suburbia* (Princeton, NJ: Princeton University Press, 2001), p. 161.

50. Evan McKenzie, *Privatopia: Homeowner Associations and the Rise of Residential Private Government* (New Haven: Yale University Press, 1994).

51. Robert E. Lang and Karen A. Danielsen, "Gated Communities in America: Walling Out the World?" *Housing Policy Debate* 8 (1999): 867–99.

52. Quoted in Haya El Nasser, "Gated Communities More Popular, and Not Just for the Rich," *USA Today*, December 16, 2002, p. 1A.

53. Oliver, *Democracy in Suburbia*, Chapter 2.

54. Although over the past decade the evidence is anecdotal, this certainly seems to be the case in growing suburban counties like Mecklenburg and Wake in North Carolina. In Wake County, for instance, a large and influential group of parents has formed Assignment By Choice, Inc. to shape school reassignment policy.

55. For more on the recent diversification of the suburbs, see William H. Frey, "The Melting Pot Suburbs: A Census 2000 Study of Suburban Diversity," *The Brookings Institution: Census 2000 Series*, June 2001.

56. This literature in political science, psychology, and sociology is huge. For a good overview and discussion on its application to race, see T.F. Pettigrew, "Intergroup Contact Theory," *Annual Review of Psychology* 49 (1998): 65–85. A recent argument in favor of the "power-threat" theory is, Marylee Taylor, "Local Racial/Ethnic Proportions and White Attitudes: Numbers Count," *American Sociological Review*, 63 (August 1998): 512–35.

57. Allport's "contact theory" can be found in his book, *The Nature of Prejudice* (Cambridge, MA: Addison-Wesley, 1954).

58. David Brooks, *On Paradise Drive: How We Live Now (And Always Have) in the Future Tense* (New York: Simon & Schuster, 2004), p. 45.

59. Ibid., pp. 53–63.

60. Barone, "The 49% Nation," p. 21.

61. David Brooks, "Democrats, Time to Meet the Exurban Voter," *New York Times*, November 10, 2002, p. 4:3.

62. Quoted in Ronald Brownstein and Richard Rainey, "GOP Plants Flag on New Voting Frontier," *Los Angeles Times*, November 22, 2004, p. A1.

63. Samuel Lubell, *The Future of American Politics* (New York: Harper, 1952).

CHAPTER 3

1. Jim Campbell has made an argument that verges on the contrary. He says the Democratic advantage is the direct consequence of a single-member plurality electoral system in which Democrats win a disproportionate number of low-turnout seats—often in uncompetitive districts in urban centers with large minority populations. See James E. Campbell, *Cheap Seats: The Democratic Party's Advantage in U.S. House Elections* (Columbus: Ohio State University Press, 1996).

2. Gary W. Cox and Jonathan N. Katz, *Elbridge Gerry's Salamander: The Electoral Consequences of the Reapportionment Revolution* (New York: Cambridge University Press, 2002).

3. J. Morgan Kousser, "Estimating the Partisan Consequences of Redistricting Plans—Simply," *Legislative Studies Quarterly* 21 (November 1996): 521–41.

4. On Indiana, see Gary C. Jacobson, *The Electoral Origins of Divided Government: Competition in U.S. House Elections, 1946–1988* (Boulder, CO: Westview Press), pp. 95–96.

5. Janet Campagna and Bernard Grofman, "Party Control and Partisan Bias in 1980s Congressional Redistricting," *Journal of Politics* 52 (November 1990): 1242–57.

6. Richard G. Niemi and Alan I. Abramowitz, "Partisan Redistricting and the 1992 Congressional Elections," *Journal of Politics* 56 (August 1994): 811–17.

7. The compactness dimension to Brennan's decision did not bind those who drew districts after the 1990s census. As a result, we saw districts like the North Carolina 12th District—often called the I-85 district because, as it snaked from Durham to Gaston County, west of Charlotte, it was sometimes as wide as the interstate—and Louisiana's 4th District—which, like the mark of Zorro, tore a Z-shape through the state connecting, at its tips, parts of Shreveport and Lafayette.

8. Although clearly not completely attributable to the establishment of "majority-minority" districts, African American representation in the House grew from twenty-six to thirty-eight and Hispanic representation from eleven to seventeen after the 1992 elections. For the argument that these districts help Republicans, see David Lublin, *The Paradox of Representation: Racial Gerrymandering and Minority Interests in Congress* (Princeton, NJ: Princeton University Press, 1997).

9. The cases were *Shaw v. Reno* (1993) and *Miller v. Johnson* (1995). The decisions stated that race could not be factored into the drawing of district lines. In *Georgia v. Ashcroft* (2003), the Court eroded the principle further. It found that reducing the size of black populations in certain "majority-minority" districts was not necessarily detrimental to the aggregate interests of African Americans in a state.

10. For more on the Iowa process, see Adam Clymer, "Democracy in Middle America: Why Iowa Has So Many Hot Seats," *New York Times*, October 27, 2002, p. 4:5; Phil Duncan, "New Iowa Map: No Gerrymandering Allowed," *Congressional Quarterly Weekly Report*, September 19, 1992, pp. 1798–1801; Joanne Dann, "Safe but Sorry: The Way We Redistrict Destroys the Middle Ground," *Washington Post*, December 2, 2001, p. B1.

11. See http://www.boozman.house.gov/ConstituentServices/.

12. Morris P. Fiorina, *Congress—Keystone of the Washington Establishment* (New Haven, CT: Yale University Press, 1977).

13. For more on how casework increases the vote of incumbents, see George Serra and Albert D. Cover, "The Electoral Consequence of Perquisite Use: The Case of Casework," *Legislative Studies Quarterly* 17 (May 1992): 233–46; George Serra, "What's In It for Me? The Impact of Congressional Casework on Incumbent Evaluation," *American Politics Quarterly* 22 (October 1994): 403–20.

14. Warren E. Miller, Donald R. Kinder, Steven J. Rosenstone, and the National Election Studies, *American National Election Study 1990: Post-Election Survey*, 2nd ed. (Ann Arbor: Inter-University Consortium for Political and Social Research, January 1992), pp. 166–70.

15. Norman J. Ornstein, Thomas E. Mann, and Michael J. Malbin, *Vital Statistics on Congress, 2001–2002* (Washington, D.C.: AEI Press, 2002), p. 129.

16. Kathleen Q. Seelye, "Congress Online: Much Sizzle, Little Steak," *New York Times*, June 24, 2003, p. A16.

17. There's a wealth of material that views congressional-election outcomes as largely the product of forces outside the direct influence of the candidates. See, for example, James E. Campbell, *The Presidential Pulse of Congressional Elections*, 2d ed. (Lexington: University Press of Kentucky, 1997); Douglas Hibbs, *The American Political Economy: Macroeconomics and Electoral Politics in the United States* (Cambridge, MA: Harvard University Press, 1987); D. Roderick Kiewiet, *Macroeconomics and Micropolitics* (Chicago: University of Chicago Press, 1983).

18. For more on the type of voters who are more predisposed to cast a personal vote, see Scott W. Desposato and John R. Petrocik, "The Variable Incumbency Advantage: New Voters, Redistricting, and the Personal Vote," *American Journal of Political Science* 47 (January 2003): 18–32.

19. Bruce Cain, John Ferejohn, and Morris Fiorina, *The Personal Vote: Constituency Service and Electoral Independence* (Cambridge, MA: Harvard University Press, 1987), p. 9.

20. Stephen Ansolabehere, James M. Snyder Jr., and Charles Stewart III, "Old Voters, New Voters, and the Personal Vote: Using Redistricting to Measure the Incumbency Advantage," *American Journal of Political Science* 44 (January 2000): 17–34; Steven D. Levitt and Catherine D. Wolfram, "Decomposing the Sources of Incumbency Advantage in the U.S. House," *Legislative Studies Quarterly* 22 (February 1997): 45–60.

21. Jeffrey H. Birnbaum, "Bringing Home the Bacon," *Wall Street Journal*, May 13, 1988, p. 17R.

22. R. Michael Alvarez and Jason Saving have shown that in the 1980s pork was especially helpful to Democratic incumbents, the marginal effect of an additional dollar in pork having five times the effects on the vote for a Democrat than a Republican. R. Michael Alvarez and Jason L. Saving, "Deficits, Democrats, and Distributive Benefits: Congressional Elections and the Pork Barrel in the 1980s," *Political Research Quarterly* 50 (December 1997): 809–31.

23. Steven D. Levitt and James M. Snyder, "The Impact of Federal Spending on House Election Outcomes," *Journal of Political Economy* 105 (February 1997): 30–53.

24. David R. Mayhew, *Congress—The Electoral Connection* (New Haven, CT: Yale University Press, 1974).

25. Armey quoted in Karen Foerstel, "A Bitter Day for the GOP," *Congressional Quarterly Weekly Report*, July 14, 2001, pp. 1676–77; Doolittle quoted in Karen Foerstel, "Mixed Signals, Hard Feelings," *Congressional Quarterly Weekly Report*, February 16, 2002, p. 443.

26. For more on Shays and Meehan's experience, see Diana Dwyre and Victoria A. Farrar-Myers, *Legislative Labyrinth: Congress and Campaign Finance Reform* (Washington, D.C.: Congressional Quarterly, 2001).

27. Ornstein, Mann, and Malbin, *Vital Statistics on Congress, 2001–2002*, p. 87.

28. Paul S. Herrnson, *Congressional Elections: Campaigning at Home and in Washington*, 3d. ed. (Washington, D.C.: Congressional Quarterly, 2000), pp. 151–63; Gary C. Jacobson, *Money in Congressional Elections* (New Haven, CT: Yale University Press, 1980).

29. Money seems to be the way to get a member to return a phone call, not necessarily to get him or her to vote in a particular way. See, for example, Gregory Wawro, "A Panel Probit Analysis of Campaign Contributions and Roll-Call Votes," *American Journal of Political Science* 45 (July 2001): 563–79.

30. Levitt and Wolfram in "Decomposing the Sources of Incumbency Advantage in the U.S. House" show the link between the quality of challengers and incumbency advantage.

31. For more on this argument, see Alan Ehrenhalt, *The United States of Ambition: Politicians, Power, and the Pursuit of Office* (New York: Times Books, 1991), p. 221.

32. Data supplied by Gary Jacobson.

33. See, for example, Diane Granat, "The House's TV War: The Gloves Come Off," *Congressional Quarterly Weekly Report*, May 19, 1984, pp. 1166–67. This was the first time a Speaker's words had been "taken down" since 1797.

34. For more on the COS, see Nicholas Lemann, "Conservative Opportunity Society," *Atlantic Monthly*, May 1985, pp. 22–36; and Mel Steely, *The Gentleman from Georgia: The Biography of Newt Gingrich* (Macon, GA: Mercer University Press, 2000), pp. 139–45.

35. Jill Lawrence and Jessica Lee, "Gingrich's Triumph and Debacle: GOPAC," *USA Today*, January 16, 1997, p. 8A; and Stephen Engelberg and Katherine Q. Seelye, "Gingrich: Man in Spotlight and Organization in Shadow," *New York Times*, December 18, 1994, p. A19.

36. The importance of encouraging candidates to run has been shown empirically. See L. Sandy Maisel, Walter J. Stone, and Cherie Maestas, "Quality Challengers to Congressional Incumbents: Can Better Candidates

be Found?" in *Playing Hardball: Campaigning for the U.S. Congress,* ed. Paul S. Herrnson (Upper Saddle River, NJ: Prentice Hall, 2001).

37. For more on the Wright resignation, see Janet Hook, "Passion, Defiance, Tears: Jim Wright Bows Out," *Congressional Quarterly Weekly Report,* June 3, 1989, pp. 1289–94.

38. Ornstein, Mann, and Malbin, *Vital Statistics on Congress, 2001–2002,* pp. 40–41.

39. Congressional term limits—both three for the House and two for the Senate and six for the House and two for the Senate (the so-called 6–12 and 12–12 plans, respectively)—were part of the House Republicans' 1994 "Contract with America." In 1995, however, the proposal suffered two severe blows. The Supreme Court ruled in *U.S. Term Limits v. Thornton* that states could not limit the terms of their members of Congress, and the House failed to get the two-thirds vote necessary to pass term limits as an amendment to the Constitution. The House failed to do this by an even bigger margin in 1997. The issue still has some support, but it is waning. Four state supreme courts have overturned limits at the state level, and two state legislatures—Idaho in 2002 and Utah in 2003—have repealed requirements.

40. The Safire quote is in Phil Kuntz, "Uproar over Bank Scandal Goads House to Cut Perks," *Congressional Quarterly Weekly Report,* October 5, 1991, p. 2843.

41. For more on 1992, see Jack W. Germond and Jules Witcover, *Mad as Hell: Revolt at the Ballot Box, 1992* (New York: Warner Books, 1993).

42. Gary C. Jacobson, "Congress: Unusual Year, Unusual Election," in *The Elections of 1992,* ed. Michael Nelson (Washington, D.C.: Congressional Quarterly Press, 1993), p. 167.

43. The nadir in public confidence in Congress produced a great amount of work on the issue. The figures are drawn from two books that were part of this literature: Joseph Cooper, ed. *Congress and the Decline of Public Trust* (Boulder, CO: Westview Press, 1999); John R. Hibbing and Elizabeth Theiss-Morse, *Congress as Public Enemy: Public Attitudes Toward American Public Institutions* (New York: Cambridge University Press, 1995).

44. Quoted in George Hager, "Defiant House Rebukes Leaders; New Round of Fights Begins," *Congressional Quarterly Weekly Review,* October 6, 1990, pp. 3183–88.

45. For more on the origin of the *Contract with America,* see James G. Gimpel, *Fulfilling the Contract: The First 100 Days* (Needham Heights, MA: Allyn and Bacon, 1996), pp. 16–21; Balz et al., *Storming the Gates,* pp. 37–43.

46. See David Barker, *Rushed to Judgment: Talk Radio, Persuasion, and American Political Behavior* (New York: Columbia University Press, 2002).

47. For an insightful treatment of the 1994 election, see Gary C. Jacobson, "The 1994 House Elections in Perspective," *Political Science Quarterly* 111 (Summer 1996): 203–23.

48. Robert D. Reischauer, "Light at the End of the Tunnel or Another Illusion? The 1997 Budget Deal," *National Tax Journal*, March 1998, pp. 143–65.

49. Ralph Z. Hallow, "Conservative Groups Break with Republican Leadership," *Washington Times*, January 16, 2004.

50. Demian Brady, "The First Eighteen Months of the 108th Congress: Ghosts of the Revolution," National Taxpayers Union Foundation Policy Paper 154, October 7, 2004.

51. Daniel J. Parks, "Earmarks, Back with a Vengeance," *Congressional Quarterly Weekly Report*, December 1, 2001, pp. 2828–33.

52. Frances E. Lee, "Geographic Politics in the U.S. House of Representatives: Coalition Building and Distribution of Benefits," *American Journal of Political Science* 47 (October 2003): 714–28.

53. Citizens against Government Waste, *The 2004 Congressional Pig Book*.

54. Brian M. Riedl, "Another Omnibus Spending Bill Loaded with Pork," Heritage Foundation, Web Memo 377, December 2, 2003, http://www.heritage.org/research/budget/wm377.cfm.

55. Quoted in John Cochran and Andrew Taylor, "Earmarks, the Booming Way to Bring Home the Bacon," *Congressional Quarterly Weekly Report*, February 7, 2004, p. 327.

56. Alan K. Ota, "Highway Law Benefits Those Who Held the Purse Strings," *Congressional Quarterly Weekly Report*, June 13, 1998, pp. 1595–96.

57. Quoted in Carl Hulse, "Veto Threatened on Highway Bill," *New York Times*, April 1, 2004, p. A19.

58. Quoted in Dan Morgan, "The GOP Congress, High on the Hog," *Washington Post*, January 18, 2004, p. B1.

59. Steven J. Balla, Eric D. Lawrence, Forrest Maltzman, and Lee Sigelman, "Partisanship, Blame Avoidance, and the Distribution of Legislative Pork," *American Journal of Political Science* 46 (July 2002): 515–25.

60. Kenneth N. Bickers and Robert M. Stein, "The Congressional Pork Barrel in a Republican Era," *Journal of Politics* 62 (November 2000): 1070–86.

61. Stephen Moore, "Tax Cut and Spend: The Profligate Ways of Congressional Republicans," *National Review*, October 1, 2001, pp. 30–34.

62. Quoted in David E. Rosenbaum, "Spending Discipline Proves Unfashionable This Year," *New York Times*, November 25, 2003, p. A18.

63. See Richard W. Stevenson and Edmund L. Andrews, "No Escaping the Red Ink as Bush Pens '04 Agenda," *New York Times*, November 29, 2003, p. A10.

64. Quoted in Alan K. Ota, "House Sets up Battle with Senate in Passing $218 Billion Roads Bill," *Congressional Quarterly Weekly Report*, April 4, 1998, p. 882.

65. For more on the tanker deal, see Renae Merle, "Documents Detail Maneuvers for Boeing Lease," *Washington Post*, August 31, 2003, p. A10; R. Jeffrey Smith, "Air Force Pitch for Boeing Detailed," *Washington Post*, November 20, 2004, p. A1; James Surowiecki, "Aim High," *The New Yorker*, September 22, 2003, p. 90; Edward Wong, "With Time Short, Boeing and Air Force Push Tanker Deal," *New York Times*, October 2, 2003, p. C1:6.

66. Quoted in Leslie Wayne, "The Flawed Plane Congress Loves," *New York Times*, March 24, 2005, p. C2.

67. Office of Rep. Curt Weldon, press release, July 25, 2003, http://www.house.gov/curtweldon/.

68. Juliet Eilperin, "Rep. Watts of Oklahoma Set to Retire; Decision Deprives GOP of Key Minority Leader, Gives Democrats an Opening," *Washington Post*, July 2, 2002, p. A2.

69. Alison Mitchell, "Congress's Sole Black Republican Is Retiring," *New York Times*, July 2, 2002, p. A17.

70. Benjamin Ginsberg and Martin Shefter, *Politics by Other Means: Politicians, Prosecutors, and the Press from Watergate to Whitewater* (New York: W.W. Norton, 2002), pp. 117–21.

71. The figures are from the Political Money Line Web site, http://www.tray.com/fecinfo/.

72. Gary W. Cox and Eric Magar, "How Much Is Majority Status in the U.S. Congress Worth?" *American Political Science Review* 93 (June 1999): 299–309.

73. The figures are from the Center for Responsive Politics, www.opensecrets.org.

74. See Thomas B. Edsall, "A Clinton Administration Foe's Equal Opportunity Watchdogging," *Washington Post*, March 10, 2002, p. A6.

75. See Jonathan Weisman, "House GOP Fundraisers Put a Price on Honors," *Washington Post*, February 22, 2003, p. A1.

76. Quoted in Juliet Eilperin, "Fundraising Focus Earns DeLay Wealth of Influence," *Washington Post*, July 22, 2003, p. A1.

77. R. Jeffrey Smith, "DeLay's Corporate Fundraising Investigated," *Washington Post*, July 12, 2004, p. A1.

78. See, for example, William F. Connelly Jr. and John J. Pitney Jr., *Congress' Permanent Minority? Republicans in the U.S. House* (Lanham, MD: Rowman and Littlefield, 1994); Douglas L. Koopman, *Hostile Takeover: The House Republican Party, 1980–1995* (Lanham, MD: Rowman and Littlefield, 1996). I discuss these divisions in more detail in Chapters 7 and 10.

79. See, for example, Eric Pianin, "GOP Whip's Skill Counted for Survival; In House Leadership Brawl, Nobody Challenged 'The Hammer'

DeLay," *Washington Post*, November 10, 1998, p. A1; Peter Perl, "Absolute Truth; Tom DeLay Is Certain That Christian Family Values Will Solve America's Problems. But He's Uncertain How to Face His Own Family," *Washington Post*, May 13, 2001, p. W12.

80. Quoted in Richard E. Cohen, "The Evolution of Tom DeLay," *National Journal*, November 15, 2003, p. 3479.

81. Quoted in Anne E. Kornblut, "Tom DeLay's Empire of Favors," *New York Times*, May 8, 2005, p. wk 3.

82. Gebe Martinez, "DeLay's Conservatism Solidifies GOP Base for Bush," *Congressional Quarterly Weekly Report*, July 12, 2003, pp. 1726–33.

83. See Richard E. Cohen, "The Crack-Up of Committees," *National Journal*, July 31, 1999, pp. 2210–17.

84. Quoted in E. J. Dionne, "The Democrats Take a Dive," *Washington Post*, November 25, 2003, p. A29.

85. Quoted in Alison Mitchell, "Redistricting 2002 Produces No Great Shake Ups," *New York Times*, March 13, 2002, p. A20.

86. For more on the fascinating technology of redistricting, see Mark Monmonier, *Bushmanders and Bullwinkles* (Chicago: University of Chicago Press, 2001), pp. 104–35.

87. Quoted in Juliet Eilperin, "GOP's New Push on Redistricting; House Gains Are at Stake in Colo., Tex." *Washington Post*, May 9, 2003, p. A4.

88. Quoted in R. Jeffrey Smith, "DeLay, FAA Roles in Tex. Redistricting Flap Detailed," *Washington Post*, July 12, 2003, p. A3.

89. *Vieth v. Jubelirer* (2004).

90. Gary C. Jacobson, "Terror, Terrain, and Turnout," *Political Science Quarterly* 118 (Spring 2003): 1–22.

91. Quoted in Richard L. Berke, "The 1998 Elections: Congress—The Reasons; Without a New Tune to Whistle, G.O.P. Kept Humming 'Scandal'," *New York Times*, November 5, 1998, p. A1.

CHAPTER 4

1. Quoted in Edward Walsh, "Ideological Appeals Rejected in Governors' Races," *Washington Post*, November 5, 1998, p. A40.

2. David Winston, "The GOP's Two Brands: Congress vs. The Governors," *Policy Review* 99 (February/March 2000): 41–53.

3. David Plotz, "The Peril of Faith: Should We Believe in the Republican Governors?" *Slate*, April 3, 1999, http://slate.msn.com/id/22949/.

4. Winston, "The GOP's Two Brands," p. 50.

5. See, for example, Carol Weissert, ed., *Learning from Leaders: Welfare Reform Politics and Policy in Five Midwestern States* (Albany, NY: Rockefeller Institute Press, 2000).

6. John J. Miller, "The GOP's Pataki Problem," *National Review*, Febraury 28, 2005, p. 32.

7. William Schneider, "The Secret Formula," *National Journal*, April 20, 2002, p. 1182.

8. For academic research explaining the Republican ascendancy in southern state politics, see Aubrey W. Jewett, "Partisan Change in Southern Legislatures, 1946–95," *Legislative Studies Quarterly* 26 (August 2001): 457–86; M. V. Hood III, Quentin Kidd, and Irwin L. Morris, "The Reintroduction of the *Elephas Maximus* to the Southern United States: The Rise of Republican State Parties, 1960 to 2000," *American Politics Research* 32 (January 2004): 68–101.

9. Paul Brace, Melinda Gann Hall, and Laura Langer, "Measuring the Preferences of State Supreme Court Justices," *Journal of Politics* 62 (May 2000): 387–413.

10. Quoted in Adam Liptak, "Judicial Races in Several States Become Partisan Battlegrounds," *New York Times*, October 24, 2004, p. 20.

11. Melinda Gann Hall, "State Supreme Courts in American Democracy: Probing the Myths of Judicial Reform," *American Political Science Review* 95 (June 2001): 315–30.

12. For more on Reagan's judicial selections, see Sheldon Goldman, *Picking Federal Judges: Lower Court Selection from Roosevelt to Reagan* (New Haven, CT: Yale University Press, 1997), pp. 284–345.

13. For more on both a Republican and Democratic view of the Bush judicial selection process, see Sheldon Goldman, Elliot Slotnik, Gerard Gryski, Gary Zuk, and Sara Schiavoni, "W. Bush Remaking the Judiciary: Like Father, Like Son?" *Judicature* 86 (May–June 2003): 282–309.

14. Clay Risen, "Understudies," *New Republic*, May 26, 2003, p. 10.

15. Quoted in Jeffrey Toobin, "Advice and Dissent: The Fight over the President's Judicial Nominations," *New Yorker*, May 26, 2003, p. 44.

16. Thomas M. Keck, *The Most Activist Supreme Court in History: The Road to Modern Judicial Conservatism* (Chicago: University of Chicago Press, 2004). Mark Tushnet disagrees and believes the Rehnquist court has not been revolutionary. See, Mark Tushnet, *The Rehnquist Court and the Future of Constitutional Law* (New York: W.W. Norton, 2005).

17. Andrew D. Martin and Kevin M. Quinn, "Dynamic Ideal Point Estimation via Markov Chain Monte Carlo for the U.S. Supreme Court, 1953–1999," *Political Analysis* 10 (Spring 2002): 134–53.

18. Bernard Grofman and Timothy J. Brazill, "Identifying the Median Justice on the United States Supreme Court through Multidimensional Scaling: Analysis of 'Natural Courts,' 1953–1991," *Public Choice* 112 (July 2002): 55–79.

19. The most important case dealing with statutory revocation of regulatory deals is *U.S. v. Winstar* (1996); that on bankruptcy protection is *FCC v. NextWave* (2003); those on employment arbitration are

Gilmer v. Interstate Securities (1991) and *Circuit City v. Adams* (2001); and on punitive damages the most important case is *State Farm v. Campbell* (2003). The ADA cases are *Toyota v. Williams* (2002), *Chevron v. Echazabal* (2002), *U.S. Airways v. Barnett* (2002), *Sutton v. United Air Lines* (1999), and *Murphy v. UPS* (1999).

20. *P.G.A. Tour v. Martin* (2001).

21. These cases are *44 Liquormart v. Rhode Island* (1996) and *Lorillard Tobacco v. Reilly* (2001).

22. *FDA v. Brown and Williamson* (2000).

23. *United States v. AT&T* (1982), *United States v. Microsoft* (2001).

24. *AT&T v. Iowa Utilities Board* (1999).

25. The cases were *Tahoe-Sierra Preservation Council v. Tahoe Regional Planning Agency* (2002) and *Brown v. Legal Foundation of Washington* (2003).

26. *Dolan v. City of Tigard* (1994) and *Palazzolo v. Rhode Island* (2001).

27. Tinsley E. Yarborough, *The Rehnquist Court and the Constitution* (New York: Oxford University Press, 2000), p. 268.

28. Robert S. Boynton, "The Tyranny of Copyright," *New York Times Magazine*, January 25, 2004, pp. 40–45.

29. *Eldred v. Ashcroft* (2003).

30. Linda Greenhouse, "Focus on Federal Power," *New York Times*, May 24, 1995, p. A1. This is not an uncontroversial argument. For opposing arguments see Timothy J. Conlan and Francois Vergniolle de Chantal, "The Rehnquist Court and Contemporary American Federalism," *Political Science Quarterly* 116 (Summer 2001): 253–75; Pietro S. Nivola, "Does Federalism Have a Future?" *Public Interest* (Winter 2001): 44–60.

31. *United States v. Printz* (1997).

32. *Kimel v. Florida Board of Regents* (2000). The family- and medical-leave case is *Nevada Department of Human Services v. Hibbs* (2003).

33. *Seminole Tribe v. Florida* (1996).

34. *Alden v. Maine* (1999) and *Federal Maritime Commission v. South Carolina Ports Authority* (2002).

35. *United States v. Morrison* (2000).

36. *Webster v. Reproductive Health Services* (1989).

37. *Atkins v. Virginia* (2002).

38. *Ring v. Arizona* (2002).

39. *Miller-El v. Cockrell* and *Wiggins v. Smith*.

40. *Missouri v. Seibert* (2004).

41. *United States v. Booker*.

42. *Ewing v. California* (2003) and *Lockyer v. Andrade* (2003).

43. *Smith v. Doe* (2003) and *Connecticut v. Doe* (2003).

44. Eric Lichtblau, "Ashcroft Limiting Prosecutors' Use of Plea Bargains," *New York Times*, September 23, 2003, p. A1.

45. Guido Calabresi, "The Exclusionary Rule," *Harvard Journal of Law and Public Policy* 26 (Winter 2003): 111–18.

46. *Indianapolis v. Edmond* (2000) and *Kyllo v. United States* (2001).

47. The 2000 case was *Dickerson v. United States*. In *Fellers v. United States* (2004), the Court iterated that accused persons must be informed of their rights before being interrogated.

48. *Arizona v. Evans* (1995) and *Illinois v. Wardlow* (2000).

49. *Lee v. Weisman* (1992).

50. *Good News Club v. Milford Central School*.

51. *Mitchell v. Helms* (2000).

52. *Hopwood v. Texas* (1996).

53. *Gratz v. Bollinger*.

54. *Ashcroft v. ACLU* (2004).

55. *Scheidler v. National Organization of Women* and *Boy Scouts v. Dale*.

56. *McConnell v. Federal Election Commission* (2003).

57. Herbert M. Kritzer, "The Impact of *Bush v. Gore* on Public Perceptions and Knowledge of the Supreme Court," *Judicature* 85 (July–August 2001): 37.

58. David Beiler, "Southern Trilogy: How Republicans Captured Governorships in Georgia, South Carolina, and Alabama," *Campaigns and Elections*, June 2003, p. 16.

59. *Texas v. Johnson*.

60. Quoted in Charles Lane, "U.S. Court Votes to Bar Pledge of Allegiance," *Washington Post*, June 27, 2002, p. A1.

61. Quoted in David Von Drehle, "Judge Blocks Pledge Decision during Appeals," *Washington Post*, June 28, 2002, p. A6.

62. Quoted in Carl Hulse, "House Passes Court Limits on Pledge," *New York Times*, September 24, 2004, p. A18.

63. *Grutter v. Bollinger*.

64. Robin Toner, "For GOP It's a Moment," *New York Times*, November 6, 2003, p. A1.

65. Quoted in Robin Toner, "Abortion's Opponents Claim the Middle Ground," *New York Times*, April 25, 2004, p. 4:3.

66. Quoted in Julie Kosterlitz, "Pious and Partisan," *National Journal*, October 23, 2004, p. 3220.

67. William Saletan, *Bearing Right: How Conservatives Won the Abortion War* (Berkeley: University of California Press, 2003), p. 234.

68. John J. Miller, "What Now, Lifers? Ditch Partial Birth," *National Review*, February 19, 2001, pp. 22–24.

69. *Stenberg v. Carhart*.

70. Quoted in Carl Hulse and David D. Kirkpatrick, "Even Death Does Not Quiet Harsh Political Fight," *New York Times*, April 1, 2005, p. A1.

71. Quoted in "The Doctor's New Right Wing," *The Economist*, April 30, 2005, p. 32.

72. Quoted in Helen Dewar, "Senate Passes Bill on Harm to Fetuses," *Washington Post*, March 26, 2004, p. A1.

73. *Locke v. Davey*.

74. *Santa Fe School District v. Doe* (2000).

75. Stacey Bielick and Kathryn Chandler, "Homeschooling in the United States: 1999," National Center for Education Statistics, July 2001.

76. Quoted in David D. Kirkpatrick, "College for Home-Schooled Is Shaping Leaders for the Right," *New York Times*, March 8, 2004, p. A14.

77. *Lawrence v. Texas* (2003).

78. Neil A. Lewis, "Conservatives Furious over Court's Direction," *The New York Times*, June 27, 2003, p. A19.

79. Lewis, "Conservatives Furious over Court's Direction," p. A19.

80. Quoted in Adam Nagourney, "Decision on Gay Marriage Creates a Thorny Issue for 2004 Race," *New York Times*, November 19, 2003, p. A1.

81. Quoted in David D. Kirkpatrick, "Conservatives Use Gay Union as Rallying Cry," *New York Times*, February 8, 2004, p. A20.

82. Alan Cooperman, "Gay Marriage as the 'New Abortion'," *Washington Post*, July 26, p. A3.

83. Quoted in David Von Drehle and Alan Cooperman, "Same-Sex Marriage Vaulted into Spotlight," *Washington Post*, March 8, 2004, p. A1.

84. Quoted in Joel Achenbach, "A Victory for 'Values,' But Whose?" *Washington Post*, November 4, 2004, p. C1.

85. Thomas Frank, "Failure Is Not an Option, It's Mandatory," *New York Times*, July 16, 2004, p. A27.

86. See, for example, Nicholas Confessore, "The Judicial Vigilantes," *The American Prospect*, May 1999.

87. See Keith Penne, "'Heightened Tensions' Fray Judicial-Legislative Relations," *Congressional Quarterly Weekly Report*, September 18, 2004, pp. 2148–53.

88. Michael Janofsky, "Review of TV Decency Law Looks beyond Bared Breast," *New York Times*, February 12, 2004, p. A1.

89. Jacques Steinberg, "Self-Censorship in Broadcasting Seen as Rising," *New York Times*, May 10, 2004, p. A1.

90. Political scientists believe that public opinion is thermostatic or, in other words, that it responds directly to changes in policy. In turn, continued policy success generally undermines the political support of governing parties because the public is ideologically moderate and wants sustained conservative or liberal policy-making to stop so that outputs can drift back to the middle. For more on this, see, James A. Stimson, *Tides of Consent: How Opinion Movements Shape American Politics* (New York: Cambridge University Press, 2004).

91. For more on Focus on the Family, see Micklethwait and Wooldridge, *The Right Nation*, pp. 186–88. See also Peter H. Stone and Bara Vaida, "Christian Soldiers," *National Journal*, December 4, 2004, pp. 3596–603.

92. Clyde Wilcox and Lee Sigelman, "Political Mobilization in the Pews: Religious Contacting and Electoral Turnout," *Social Science Quarterly* 82 (September 2001): 524–35.

93. See, for example, Mark Francis Cohen, "Hard Right," *Washingtonian*, April 2004.

94. See, for example, David D. Kirkpatrick, "Conservatives Using Issue of Gay Unions as a Rallying Tool," *New York Times*, February 8, 2004, p. 1:1.

95. Quoted in Alan Cooperman and Thomas B. Edsall, "Evangelicals Say They Led Charge for the GOP," *Washington Post*, November 8, 2004, p. A1.

96. Micklethwait and Wooldridge, *The Right Nation*, p. 189.

97. Greenberg and Greenberg, "Contesting Values."

98. See Frank Bruni, "The Changing Church," *New York Times*, October 13, 2003, p. A1.

99. William Haltom and Michael McCann, *Distorting the Law: Politics, Media, and the Litigation Crisis* (Chicago: University of Chicago Press, 2004).

100. See, for example, Robert Pear, "In a Shift Bush Moves to Block Medical Suits," *New York Times*, July 25, 2004, p. A1.

101. Quoted in Thomas B. Edsall, "Battle over Court Awards Takes More Partisan Turn," *Washington Post*, August 10, 2003, p. A1.

102. Quoted in Thomas B. Edsall and John F. Harris, "Bush Aims to Forge a GOP Legacy," *Washington Post*, January 30, 2005, p. A1.

103. Sarah Kershaw, "In Insurance Cost, Woes for Doctors and Women," *New York Times*, May 29, 2003, p. A16.

104. "Who Pays for Tort Liability Claims? An Economic Analysis of the U.S. Tort Liability System," Council of Economic Advisers, April 2002.

105. Joshua Green, "John Edwards, Esq." *Washington Monthly*, October 2001.

CHAPTER 5

1. Condoleezza Rice, "Promoting the National Interest," *Foreign Affairs* 79 (January–February 2000): 45–62; Robert Zoellick, "A Republican Foreign Policy," *Foreign Affairs* 79 (January–February 2000): 63–78.

2. Frederick W. Kagan, "War and Aftermath," *Policy Review*, September–October 2003, http://www.policyreview.org/aug03/kagan.html.

3. "U.S. National Security Strategy: A New Era," U.S. Department of State, December 2002.

4. Sebastian Mallaby, "The Irrelevant Election," *Foreign Policy* 120 (September–October 2000): 64–70.

5. Rice, "Promoting the National Interest," p. 53.

6. Quoted in Ivo H. Daalder and James Lindsay, *America Unbound: The Bush Revolution in Foreign Policy* (Washington, D.C.: Brookings Institution, 2003), p. 112.

7. Quoted in Kagan, "War and Aftermath."

8. Nicholas Lemann, "Real Reasons," *The New Yorker*, September 22, 2003, pp. 81–82.

9. Daalder and Lindsay, *America Unbound*, p. 13.

10. Zoellick, "A Republican Foreign Policy," p. 69.

11. Donald H. Rumsfeld, "Transforming the Military," *Foreign Affairs* 81 (May–June 2002): 31.

12. Joseph Nye, "U.S. Power and Strategy after Iraq," *Foreign Affairs* 82 (July–August 2003): 60–73.

13. Ole R. Holsti, *Public Opinion and American Foreign Policy* (Ann Arbor: University of Michigan Press, 1996), pp. 129–90.

14. See Stanley Hoffman, "The High and the Mighty; Bush's National-Security Strategy and the New American Hubris," *The American Prospect*, January 13, 2003, p. 38.

15. The quote is from the bill, H.R. 7 in the 104th Congress.

16. Stephen M. Walt, "Two Cheers for Clinton's Foreign Policy," *Foreign Affairs* 79 (March–April): 65. There is evidence, however, that many GOP members of Congress are extremely interested in foreign affairs. Newt Gingrich's academic background provides a good example. See, also, Eric Schmitt and Elizabeth Becker, "Insular Congress Appears to Be a Myth," *New York Times*, November 4, 2000, p. A9.

17. For more on the neoconservatives and their thinking and influence, see Stefan Halper and Jonathan Clarke, *America Alone: The Neo-Conservatives and the Global Order* (New York: Cambridge University Press, 2004); James Mann, *Rise of the Vulcans: The History of Bush's War Cabinet* (New York: Viking, 2004).

18. John Lewis Gaddis, "Grand Strategy in the Second Term," *Foreign Affairs*, January–February 2005, pp. 2–16.

19. Samantha Power, "Force Full," *The New Republic*, March 3, 2003, pp. 28–31.

20. See, for example, "Clinton's Foreign Policy," *Foreign Policy* (November–December 2000): 18–28; Stephen M. Walt, "Two Cheers for Clinton's Foreign Policy."

21. Terry L. Deibel, "Bush's Foreign Policy: Mastery and Inaction," *Foreign Policy*, Fall 1991, pp. 3–23.

22. Charles Krauthammer, "A War That Never Should Have Happened," *Washington Post*, December 21, 1989, p. A29.

23. On the fact that Bush had no real cohesive policy see, for example, David Gergen, "America's Missed Opportunities," *Foreign Affairs* 71

(December 1991–January 1992): 1–19; Jonathan Clarke, "The Conceptual Poverty of American Foreign Policy," *Atlantic Monthly*, September 1993, pp. 54–66.

24. Steven Kull, "Public Attitudes towards Multilateralism," in *Multilateralism and U.S. Foreign Policy: Ambivalent Engagement*, ed. Stewart Patrick and Shephard Forman (Boulder, CO: Lynne Reiner Publishers, 2002).

25. Holsti, *Public Opinion and American Foreign Policy*, p. 42.

26. Ibid., pp. 88–90.

27. James M. Lindsay, "The New Apathy," *Foreign Affairs* 79 (September–October 2000): 2–8.

28. Daalder and Lindsay, *America Unbound*, p. 79.

29. Melvyn P. Leffler, "Bush's Foreign Policy," *Foreign Policy* (September–October 2004): 26.

30. John H. Aldrich, John L. Sullivan, and Eugene Borgida, "Foreign Affairs and Issue Voting: Do Presidential Candidates 'Waltz before a Blind Audience'?" *American Political Science Review* 83 (March 1989): 123–41; Benjamin I. Page and Robert Y. Shapiro, *The Rational Public* (Chicago: University of Chicago Press, 1992).

31. The public's view on foreign aid is from "Vox Americani," *Foreign Policy* (September–October 2001): 29–38. Americans have been shown to have less knowledge of the world than citizens in other advanced industrialized countries. See Michael A. Dimock and Samuel L. Popkin, "Political Knowledge in Comparative Perspective," in *Do the Media Govern? Politicians, Voters, and Reporters in America*, ed. Shanto Iyengar and Richard Reeves (Thousand Oaks, CA: Sage Publications).

32. James Meernik and Michael Ault, "Public Opinion and Support for U.S. Presidents' Foreign Policies," *American Politics Research* 29 (July 2001): 352–73.

33. Richard N. Haas, "The Squandered Presidency: Demanding More from the Commander-in-Chief," *Foreign Affairs* 79 (May–June 2000): 136–40.

34. Chuck Todd, "Air Force Won," in *Midterm Madness: The Elections of 2002*, ed. Larry J. Sabato (Lanham, MD: Rowman and Littlefield, 2003).

35. Jacobson, "Terror, Terrain, and Turnout," pp. 1–22.

36. Adam Nagourney, "So What Happened in That Election, Anyhow?" *New York Times*, January 2, 2005, p. wk 3.

37. Quoted in Louis Menand, "Permanent Fatal Errors," *New Yorker*, December 6, 2004, p. 60.

38. Quoted in Adam Nagourney, "Democratic Party Leader Analyzes Bush's Victory," *New York Times*, December 11, 2004, p. A14.

39. Maureen Dowd, "Tizzy over Lezzies," *New York Times*, January 8, 2004, p. A33.

40. John Mueller, *War, Presidents and Public Opinion* (New York: Wiley, 1973). The quote is from Marc J. Hetherington and Michael

Nelson, "Anatomy of a Rally Effect: George W. Bush and the War on Terrorism," *PS: Political Science and Politics* 36 (January 2003): 37–42.

41. Quoted in Mike Allen, "Bush Cites 9/11 on All Manner of Questions," *Washington Post*, September 11, 2003, p. A12.

42. James Traub, "The Things They Carry," *New York Times Magazine*, January 4, 2004, p. 32.

43. Joshua Muravchik, "The European Disease," *The American Enterprise*, December 2002.

44. See, for example, Richard Bernstein, "Foreign Views of U.S. Darken after Sept. 11," *New York Times*, September 11, 2003, p. A1.

45. Quoted in Keith B. Richburg, "Kerry Is Widely Favored Abroad," *Washington Post*, September 29, 2004, p. A14.

46. Pew Research Center for the People and the Press, "Views of a Changing World 2003," June 2003.

47. Pew Research Center for the People and the Press, "America's Image Further Erodes, Europeans Want Weaker Ties," March 2003.

48. Quoted in Susan Sachs, "Poll Finds Hostility Hardening toward U.S. Policies," *New York Times*, March 17, 2004, p. A3.

49. Ziauddin Sardar and Merryl Wyn Davies, *Why Do People Hate America?* (New York: The Disinformation Company, 2003).

50. Emmanuel Todd, *After the Empire: The Breakdown of the American Order* (New York: Columbia University Press, 2003).

51. Quoted in Elaine Sciolino, "World Opinion Is Fragmented on Tighter Security for Visitors," *New York Times*, January 7, 2004, p. A1.

52. Robert Kagan, "America's Crisis of Legitimacy," *Foreign Affairs* 83 (March–April 2004): 67.

53. Daalder and Lindsay, *America Unbound*.

54. George Packer, "A Democratic World," *New Yorker*, February 16–23, 2004, p. 108.

55. Quoted in E. J. Dionne Jr., "Inevitably the Politics of Terror, Fear Have Become Part of Washington's Power Struggle," *Washington Post*, May 25, 2003, p. B1.

56. See, for example, James Atlas, "What It Takes to Be a Neo-Neoconservative," *New York Times*, October 19, 2003, p. W12.

57. Quoted in David E. Sanger, "The China Trade Vote: Rounding Out a Clear Clinton Legacy," *New York Times*, May 25, 2000, p. A1; Joseph Kahn, "On the Road again in Midwest, Clinton Promotes China Trade," *New York Times*, May 13, 2000, p. A6.

58. Mathis quoted in PBS Online News Hour report, May 2000, at http://www.pbs.org/newshour/bb/asia/china/pntr/qa_labor.html; Pope's argument is from a Sierra Club letter to Representatives, April 10, 2000.

59. Michael J. Hiscox, "Commerce, Coalitions, and Factor Mobility: Evidence from Congressional Votes on Trade Legislation," *American Political Science Review* 96 (September 2002): 593–608.

60. Edmund L. Andrews, "Democratic Candidates Differ on Economy, but Often Subtly," *New York Times*, December 31, 2003, p. A1.

61. Kerry and Gephardt are quoted from the September 25, 2003, Democratic presidential candidates debate at Pace University, New York.

62. Quoted in Jim Morrill, "Democrats Attack Bush over Lost Jobs," *Charlotte Observer*, February 13, 2004.

CHAPTER 6

1. Irving Kristol, "The Neoconservative Persuasion," *Weekly Standard*, August 25, 2003, pp. 23–25.

2. See, for example, David Brooks, "A Return to National Greatness: A Manifesto for a Lost Creed," *Weekly Standard*, March 3, 1997, p. 16.

3. David Brooks, "How to Reinvent the GOP," *New York Times Magazine*, August 29, 2004, pp. 30–56.

4. David S. Broder, "So Now Bigger Is Better?" *Washington Post*, January 12, 2003, p. B1.

5. George F. Will, "A Year to Clear the Decks," *Washington Post*, January 1, 2004, p. A25.

6. Bob Woodward, *The Agenda: Inside the Clinton White House* (New York: Pocket Books, 1995), pp. 80–87.

7. For more on this argument about Clinton, see John W. Burns and Andrew J. Taylor, "A New Democrat? The Economic Performance of the Clinton Presidency," *The Independent Review* 5 (Winter 2001): 387–408.

8. For more on the Clinton proposal, see Theda Skocpol, *Boomerang: Health Care Reform and the Turn against Government* (New York: Norton 1997).

9. Robert G. Kaiser, "There's a Reason Why There Hasn't Been Much of a Fight," *Washington Post*, February 16, 2003, p. B1.

10. Quoted in Nicholas Confessore, "Breaking the Code," *New York Times Magazine*, January 15, 2005, p. 38.

11. See Jonathan Weisman, "Anti-Tax Crusaders Work for Big Shift; White House Wary of Broad Changes," *Washington Post*, June 14, 2003, p. A1.

12. Paul Krugman, "Bad Heir Day," *New York Times*, May 30, 2001, p. A23.

13. Quoted in Greg Hill, John D. McKinnon, and Shailagh Murray, "Caution: Tax Cuts Are Bigger Than They Appear in Budget," *Wall Street Journal*, May 19, 2003, p. A6.

14. Joel Friedman, Robert Greenstein, and Richard Kogan, "The Administration's Proposal to Make the Tax Cut Permanent," Center on Budget and Policy Priorities, April 16, 2002.

15. Veronique de Rugy and Tad DeHaven, "On Spending, Bush Is No Reagan," Cato Institute, Tax and Budget Bulletin, August 2003.

16. David Hogberg, "Supply-Spend Economics," *The American Spectator*, November 26, 2003, http://www.spectator.org/dsp_article.asp?art_id=5831.

17. Ramesh Ponnuru, "Swallowed by Leviathan: Conservatism Versus and Oxymoron, 'Big Government Conservatism'," *National Review*, September 29, 2003, pp. 30–33.

18. Quoted in Mike Allen, "$3 Trillion Price Tag Left Out as Bush Details His Agenda," *Washington Post*, September 14, 2003, p. A1.

19. Quoted in Sheryl Gay Stolberg, "Shrink Government, the Right Tells the Right," *New York Times*, January 4, 2004, p. 4:1.

20. The lower estimate is from William G. Gale and Peter R. Orszag, "Fiscal Follies: The Real Budget Problem and How to Fix It," *Brookings Review* 21 (Fall 2003): 7–11. The higher estimate is from Howell E. Jackson, "It's Even Worse Than You Think," *New York Times*, October 9, 2003, p. A37.

21. Concord Coalition, "The Truth about Entitlements and the Budget," *Fax Alert*, October 1, 2003.

22. Cited in Edmund L. Andrews, "Medicare and Social Security Challenge," *New York Times*, March 2, 2004, p. C13.

23. Suskind, *The Price of Loyalty*, p. 291.

24. Jonathan Weisman, "2006 Cuts in Domestic Spending on Table," *Washington Post*, May 27, 2004, p. A1.

25. David S. Broder, "Stealthy Budget Cuts," *Washington Post*, February 27, 2005, p. B7.

26. Barry Goldwater, *The Conscience of a Conservative* (New York: Hillman Books, 1960), p. 23.

27. As told to Mara Liasson, National Public Radio, May 25, 2001.

28. Nicholas Lemann, "The Controller," *The New Yorker*, May 12, 2003, p. 82.

29. Quoted in Daniel Patrick Moynihan, *Came the Revolution* (San Diego: Harcourt Brace Jovanovich, 1988), p. 279.

30. Tom A. Coburn with John Hart, *Breach of Trust: How Washington Turns Outsiders into Insiders* (Nashville: WND Books, 2003).

31. Quoted in Joseph L. Schatz, "Lawmakers Call for Cuts, but Not in Their Programs," *Congressional Quarterly Weekly Report*, January 17, 2004, p. 152.

32. Quoted in Edmund L. Andrews, "Mutiny by Four Republicans over Bush's Tax Cutting Forces Delay on the Budget Vote," *New York Times*, May 21, 2004, p. A19.

33. Milton Friedman, "What Every American Wants," *Wall Street Journal*, January 15, 2003, p. A10.

34. Quoted in David E. Rosenbaum, "Laying Out 'Big Ideas,' Not Balancing the Ledger," *New York Times*, February 4, 2003, p. A21.

35. Quoted in David Firestone, "Conservatives Now See Deficits as a Tool to Fight Spending," *New York Times*, February 11, 2003, p. A22.

36. Quoted in Hans Nichols, "Leadership Lines Up with Deficit Doves," *The Hill*, February 5, 2003.

37. Paul Light, *The True Size of Government* (Washington, D.C.: Brookings Institution, 1999).

38. Ibid., pp. 13–45.

39. See Martin Kady II, "Congress Builds a Barrier to Bush Privatization Plan," *Congressional Quarterly Weekly Report*, October 11, 2003, pp. 2486–91.

40. Quoted in Stephen Barr, "Election Results Point to Imminent Battles over Bush's Agenda for Employees," *Washington Post*, November 4, 2004, p. B2.

41. P. W. Singer, *Corporate Warriors: The Rise of the Privatized Military Industry* (Ithaca, NY: Cornell University Press, 2003), p. 8.

42. Ann R. Markusen, "The Case against Privatizing National Security," *Governance* 16 (October 2003): 471–501.

43. David Issenberg, "The New Mercenaries," *Christian Science Monitor*, October 13, 1998, p. 19.

44. P. W. Singer, "Thinking Big, War Inc.: A Privatized Military Industry Is Taking over the Work of War," *Boston Globe*, October 19, 2003, p. L12.

45. David Barstow, "Security Companies: Shadow Soldiers in Iraq," *New York Times*, April 19, 2004, p. A1.

46. See David McGlinchey and Shawn Zeller, "Homeland Security Unveils Performance Pay Plan," GovExec.com, February 13, 2004; Christopher Lee, "Civil Service System on Way Out at DHS," *Washington Post*, January 27, 2005, p. A1.

47. Paul C. Light, "The Empty Government Talent Pool," *Brookings Review*, Winter 2000, p. 20.

48. Elizabeth C. Corey and James C. Garand, "Are Government Employees More Likely to Vote? An Analysis of Turnout in the 1996 U.S. National Election," *Public Choice* 111 (April 2002): 259–83.

49. Ginsberg et al., *Politics by Other Means*, p. 83.

50. Light, *The True Size of Government*, pp. 84–92.

51. The figures are from a February 2003 survey by the Federation of Tax Administrators, http://www.taxadmin.org/fta/rate/stg_pts.pdf.

52. Quoted in John Cochran, "Election System Revamp Stymied by Tight Federal Purse Strings," *Congressional Quarterly Weekly Report*, October 11, 2003, p. 2493.

53. Cited in James Vaznis, "U.S. Education Law Drawing Debate on Costs, Local Control Fear Is Funds May Be 'Left Behind'," *Boston Globe*, June 12, 2003, p. 1.

54. Eric Kelderman, "State Republicans Assail Bush Education Law," stateline.org, January 29, 2004.

55. General Accounting Office, "Characteristics of Tests Will Influence Expenses; Information Sharing May Help States Realize Efficiencies," May 2003, 03–389.

56. See, for example, Sam Dillon, "President's Education Law Is Finding Few Fans in Utah," *New York Times*, March 6, 2005, p. 21.

57. Quoted in Brian Friel, "The Bush Record," *National Journal*, March 20, 2004, p. 869.

58. See Eric Kelderman, "Feds Quell States' Revolt on No Child Left Behind," stateline.org, July 6, 2004.

59. The figures are from an April 2003 report undertaken by the National Conference of State Legislatures, http://www.ncsl.org/ standcomm/scbudg/budgmandates03.htm.

60. See John Holahan and Brian Bruen, "Medicaid Spending: What Factors Contributed to the Growth between 2000 and 2002?" Kaiser Family Foundation, September 2003.

61. National Association of State Budget Officers, "State Expenditure Report, 2003."

62. See, for example, David Gratzer, "Medicaid Needs Surgery," *Weekly Standard*, February 14–21, 2005, pp. 14–15.

63. Vernon Smith, Rekha Ramesh, Kathleen Gifford, Eileen Ellis, Victoria Wachino, and Molly O'Malley, "States Respond to Fiscal Pressure: A 50-State Update of State Medicaid Spending Growth and Cost Containment Actions," report of the Kaiser Commission on Medicaid and the Uninsured, January 2004.

64. National Governor's Association, National Association of State Budget Officers, *The Fiscal Survey of the States*, 2003, p. 6.

65. Rick Lyman, "Florida Takes Lead as States Struggle with Medicaid Cost," *New York Times*, January 23, 2005, p. 1.

66. Robert Pear, "U.S. Nears Clash with Governors on Medicaid Costs," *New York Times*, February 16, 2004, p. A1.

67. Robert Pear, "U.S. Says Medicaid Money Was Obtained Improperly," *New York Times*, April 12, 2005, p. A12.

68. Sandra Murillo and Holly Wolcott, "Community Colleges Hit Hard by Budget Woes," *Los Angeles Times*, December 14, 2003, p. B1.

69. Eric Kelderman, "States and Public Colleges Consider New Relationship," stateline.org, March 4, 2004.

70. See National Education Association, Press Release, June 2003, http://www.nea.org/esea/images/storiesfromfieldJUNE.pdf.

71. Elissa Gootman, "Lunch at 9.21, and Students Are the Sardines," *New York Times*, October 14, 2003, p. A1.

72. Fox Butterfield, "States Putting Inmates on Diets to Trim Budgets," *New York Times*, September 30, 2003, p. A18.

73. Fox Butterfield, "With Cash Tight, States Reassess Long Jail Terms," *New York Times*, November 10, 2003, p. A1.

74. Timothy Egan, "States, Facing Budget Shortfalls, Cut the Major and Mundane," *New York Times*, April 21, 2003, p. A1.

75. John M. Broder, "Despite Rebound, States' Budgets Are Still Reeling," *New York Times*, January 5, 2004, p. A1.

76. Leighton Ku and Sashi Nimalendran, "Losing Out: States Are Cutting 1.2 to 1.6 Million Low-Income People from Medicaid, SCHIP and Other State Health Insurance Programs," Report of the Center for Budget and Policy Priorities, December 22, 2003.

77. General Accounting Office, "Child Care: Recent State Policy Changes Affecting the Availability of Assistance for Low-Income Families," Report GAO-03-588, May 2003.

78. David S. Broder, "Budget Gloom, State By State," *Washington Post*, November 16, 2003, p. B7.

79. The figures are from, Elizabeth McNichol and Makeda Harris, "Many States Cut Budgets as Fiscal Squeeze Continues," Center on Budget and Policy Priorities, April 26, 2004; and the National Association of State Budget Officers, "The Fiscal Survey of the States," April 2004.

80. Pamela Prah, "Let the Meager Times Roll; Half of States Face Shortfalls," stateline.org, February 19, 2004.

81. Robert D. Behn and Elizabeth K. Keating, "Facing the Fiscal Crises in State Governments: National Problem; National Responsibilities," Taubman Center for State and Local Government, Harvard University, 2004, pp. 5–7.

82. See Jason White, "Experts Debate the Merits of Bush's Block Grants Plan," stateline.org, October 20, 2003.

83. Jonathan Walters, "Block That Grant," *Governing Magazine*, September 2003, p. 12.

84. On conservatives, welfare, and marriage, see Shawn Zeller, "Morality Play," *Government Executive Magazine*, March 1, 2002.

85. Walters, "Block That Grant."

86. *Congressional Record*, H12268, November 21, 2003.

87. The private plan figure is from Robert Pear, "Medicare Actuary Gives Wanted Data to Congress," *New York Times*, March 20, 2004, p. A8.

88. Quoted in Robin Toner, "An Imperfect Compromise," *New York Times*, November 25, 2003, p. A19.

89. Quoted in David Von Drehle, "For Democrats, a Wake-Up Call," *Washington Post*, November 26, 2003, p. A1.

90. Quoted in Elisabeth Bumiller, "For White House, Two Bills Offer Route to Political High Ground," *New York Times*, November 23, 2003, p. 1.

91. Robert Pear and Robin Toner, "Partisanship and the Fine Print Seen as Hindering the Medicare Law," *New York Times*, October 11, 2004, p. A1.

92. "Strengthening Social Security and Creating Personal Wealth for All Americans," Report of the President's Commission to Strengthen Social Security, December 2001.

93. See Mike Allen, "Bid to Change Social Security Is Back, Bush Aides Resurrect Plans for Personal Retirement Accounts," *Washington Post*, November 21, 2003, p. A14.

94. Quoted in John Tierney, "Can Anyone Unseat FDR?" *New York Times*, January 23, 2005, p. 4:1.

95. See John E. Chubb and Terry M. Moe, *Politics, Markets, and America's Schools* (Washington, D.C.: Brookings Institution, 1990).

96. *Zelman v. Simmons-Harris* (2002).

97. *Locke v. Davey*.

98. See, for example, Michael A. Fletcher, "Milwaukee Will Vouch for Vouchers: Parochial, Private Schools Draw Pupils—and Questions about Success," *Washington Post*, March 20, 2001, p. A1.

99. Quoted in Corine Hegland, "Making Faith-Based Funds Flow," *National Journal*, February 7, 2004, p. 390.

100. Alan Cooperman and Jim VandeHei, "Ex-Aide Questions Bush Vow to Back Faith-Based Efforts," *Washington Post*, February 15, 2005, p. A1.

101. Amy E. Black, Douglas L. Koopman, and David K. Ryden, *Of Little Faith: The Politics of George W. Bush's Faith-Based Initiatives* (Washington, D.C.: Georgetown University Press, 2004), pp. 103–105, 281–82.

102. Jonathan Rauch, "The Accidental Radical," *National Journal*, July 26, 2003, pp. 2404–10.

103. Ibid., p. 2408.

104. Quoted in Matt Bai, "The New Boss," *New York Times Magazine*, January 30, 2005, p. 68.

CHAPTER 7

1. The term is Leon Epstein's. See Leon D. Epstein, *Political Parties in the American Mold* (Madison: University of Wisconsin Press, 1986).

2. For more on Brock's contribution, see John F. Bibby, "Party Renewal in the National Republican Party," in *Party Renewal in America: Theory and Practice*, ed. Gerald M. Pomper (New York: Praeger, 1981); M. Margaret Conway, "Republican Party Nationalization, Campaign Activities, and Their Implications for the Political System," *Publius* 13 (Winter 1983): 1–17.

3. Quoted in Ken Auletta, "Fortress Bush: How the White House Keeps the Press under Control," *New Yorker*, January 19, 2004, p. 54.

4. Dana Milbank, "Florida Recount Prompts an Outpouring of GOP Activism," *Washington Post*, November 27, 2000, p. A9.

5. See Andrew Ferguson, "The Words That Move Americans: Frank Luntz Does It for the Children," *Weekly Standard*, September 22, 1997,

pp. 21–24; Deborah Tannen, "Let Them Eat Words: Linguistic Lessons from a Republican Master Strategist," *American Prospect*, online, August 31, 2003.

6. "Right Young Things," *The Economist*, July 26, 2003, p. 48.

7. For more, see John Colapinto, "The Young Hipublicans," *New York Times Magazine*, May 25, 2003, p. 30.

8. Dan Balz and Mike Allen, "2004 Is Now for Bush's Campaign," *Washington Post*, November 30, 2003, p. A1.

9. Matt Bai, "The Multilevel Marketing of the President," *New York Times Magazine*, April 25, 2004, pp. 44–47.

10. John F. Harris, "In Ohio, Building a Political Echo," *Washington Post*, May 12, 2004, p. A1.

11. Paul Farhi, "Parties Square Off in a Database Duel," *Washington Post*, July 20, 2004, p. A1.

12. Jon Gertner, "The Very, Very Personal Is the Political," *New York Times Magazine*, February 15, 2004, pp. 42–47.

13. Katherine Q. Seelye, "How to Sell a Candidate to a Porsche-Driving, Leno-Loving, Nascar Fan," *New York Times*, December 6, 2004, p. A16.

14. Quoted in Joyce Purnick, "Data Crunchers Try to Pinpoint Voters' Politics," *New York Times*, April 7, 2004, p. 1.

15. Howard Rheingold, *The Virtual Community: Homesteading on the Virtual Frontier* (New York: HarperCollins, 1993), p. 14.

16. Joe Trippi, *The Revolution Will Not Be Televised: Democracy, The Internet, and the Overthrow of Everything* (New York: Regan Books, 2004), pp. 228–29.

17. Anthony Corrado, "Elections in Cyberspace: Prospects and Problems," in *Elections in Cyberspace: Toward a New Era in American Politics*, ed. Anthony Corrado and Charles M. Firestone (Washington, D.C.: The Aspen Institute, 1996), p. 29.

18. Bruce Bimber and Richard Davis, *Campaigning Online: The Internet in U.S. Elections* (New York: Oxford University Press, 2003), p. 143.

19. Glen Justice, "Kerry Kept Money Coming with Internet as His ATM," *New York Times*, November 6, 2004, p. A10.

20. Nick Anderson, "Political Attack Ads Already Popping Up on the Web," *Los Angeles Times*, March 30, 2004, p. A13.

21. Michael Cornfield, *Politics Moves Online: Campaigning and the Internet* (New York: The Century Foundation Report, 2004), p. 107; Howard Rheingold, *Smart Mobs: The Next Social Revolution* (New York: Perseus, 2003).

22. For more on the Dean campaign and the Internet, see, Matthew Robert Kerbel, "The Media: The Challenge and Promise of Internet Politics," in *The Elections of 2004*, ed. Michael Nelson (Washington, D.C.: Congressional Quarterly Press, 2005), pp. 88–107.

23. Quoted in Todd S. Purdum, "So What Was *That* All About?" *New York Times*, February 22, 2004, p. 4:3.

24. John F. Harris and Paul Farhi, "Taking the Campaign to the People, One Doorstep at a Time," *Washington Post*, April 18, 2004, p. A1.

25. Balz and Allen, "2004 Is Now for Bush's Campaign."

26. Alan Cooperman, "Churchgoers Get Direction from Bush Campaign," *Washington Post*, July 1, 2004, p. A6; David D. Kirkpatrick, "Churches See an Election Role and Spread the Word on Bush," *New York Times*, August 9, 2004, p. A1.

27. Rhodes Cook, "Moving On," *Washington Post*, June 27, 2004, p. B1.

28. Dan Balz and Mike Allen, "Four More Years Attributed to Rove's Strategy," *Washington Post*, November 7, 2004, p. A1.

29. For more on the "72-Hour Project," see Dan Balz and David S. Broder, "Close Election Turns on Voter Turnout," *Washington Post*, November 1, 2002, p. A1; David E. Rosenbaum, "Last-Minute Efforts Shift from Talking to Walking," *New York Times*, October 31, 2002, p. A23; Jim VandeHei and Dan Balz, "In GOP Win, a Lesson in Money, Muscle, Planning," *Washington Post*, November 10, 2002, p. A1.

30. Abby Goodnough and Don Van Natta, "Bush Secured Victory in Florida by Veering from Beaten Path," *New York Times*, November 7, 2004, p. 1.

31. Donald P. Green and Alan S. Gerber, *Get Out the Vote! How to Increase Voter Turnout* (Washington, D.C.: The Brookings Institution, 2004).

32. See, for example, Ford Fessenden, "Both Parties See a Big Increase in New Voters," *New York Times*, September 26, 2004, p. 1.

33. Jeanne Cummings and Jackie Calmes, "In Final Showdown, Getting Voters to Go to the Polls Is Key," *Wall Street Journal*, November 1, 2004, p. A1.

34. David M. Halbfinger, "Going to Bush Rally, Finding Strings Attached," *New York Times*, September 28, 2004, p. A1; Dana Milbank, "Diverse Tactics on the Stump," *Washington Post*, October 12, 2004, p. A1.

35. See, for example, A. James Reichley, *The Life of the Parties: A History of American Political Parties* (Lanham, MD: Rowman and Littlefield Publishers, 1992), pp. 326–27; John Kenneth White and Daniel M. Shea, *New Party Politics: From Jefferson and Hamilton to the Information Age* (New York: Bedford/St. Martin's, 2000), pp. 197–98.

36. Quoted in Kosterlitz, "On the Ropes?" p. 2687.

37. Kimberly H. Conger and John C. Green, "Spreading Out and Digging In: Christian Conservatives and State Republican Parties," *Campaigns and Elections*, February 2002, p. 58.

38. Ronald G. Shaiko and Marc A. Wallace, "From Wall Street to Main Street: The National Federation of Independent Business and the

New Republican Majority," in *After the Revolution: PACs, Lobbies, and the Republican Congress*, ed. Robert Biersack, Paul S. Herrnson, and Clyde Wilcox (Boston: Allyn and Bacon, 1999), pp. 18–35.

39. Quoted in Juliet Eilperin, "Small Business Group Sticks to One Side of Political Fence," *Washington Post*, May 16, 2002, p. A23.

40. See James Dao, "N.R.A. Opens All-Out Drive for Bush and His Views," *New York Times*, April 16, 2004, p. A1; James Dao, "Gun Group's Radio Show Tests Limits on Advocacy," *New York Times*, June 16, 2004, p. A13.

41. See Nicholas Confessore, "Welcome to the Machine: How the GOP Disciplined K Street and Made Bush Supreme," *Washington Monthly*, July–August 2003, pp. 30–37.

42. See, for example, Sharon Waxman, "Valenti's Successor, but Not His Clone," *New York Times*, November 11, 2004, p. E1.

43. Kathleen Day and Jim VandeHei, "Congressman Urges Republican Lobbyist," *Washington Post*, February 15, 2003, p. A3.

44. Thomas B. Edsall, "Big Business' Funding Shift Boosts GOP," *Washington Post*, November 27, 2002, p. A1.

45. Quoted in Gail Russell Chaddock, "Republicans Take Over K Street," *Christian Science Monitor*, August 29, 2003, p. 1.

46. Gretchen Morgenson and Glen Justice, "Taking Care of Business, His Way," *New York Times*, February 20, 2005, p. 3:7.

47. Jeffrey H. Birnbaum, "Advocacy Groups Blur Media Lines," *Washington Post*, December 6, 2004, p. A1.

48. Jeffrey H. Birnbaum, "Businesses Point Workers toward Ballot Boxes," *Washington Post*, March 21, 2004, p. A1.

49. Michael Moss and Ford Fessenden, "Interest Groups Mounting Costly Push to Get Out Vote," *New York Times*, October 20, 2004, p. A1.

50. Micklethwait and Wooldridge, *The Right Nation*, p. 111.

51. Quoted in Dan Balz, "Ralph Reed Wants to Take Movement to New Political Level," *Washington Post*, April 25, 1997, p. A11.

52. Peter H. Stone, "Go-To Guy," *National Journal*, July 17, 2004, pp. 2234–38.

53. Quoted in Laura Blumenfeld, "Sowing the Seeds of GOP Domination," *Washington Post*, January 12, 2004, p. A1.

54. Quoted in Jill Zuckman, "Pipeline Leads to White House," *Chicago Tribune*, June 9, 2003, p. 1.

55. Quoted in John Maggs, "Grover at the Gate," *National Journal*, October 11, 2003, p. 3102.

56. Franklin Foer, "Fevered Pitch," *New Republic*, November 12, 2001, pp. 22–24.

57. Quoted in Nicholas Confessore, "The Myth of the Democratic Establishment," *Washington Monthly*, January–February 2004, pp. 22–29.

58. James Q. Wilson, *The Amateur Democrat: Club Politics in Three Cities* (Chicago: University of Chicago Press, 1962).

59. Quoted in Theodore H. White, *The Making of the President 1968* (New York: Atheneum, 1969), p. 90.

60. See, for example, Steve Fraser and Gary Gerstle, eds., *The Rise and Fall of the New Deal Order, 1930–1980* (Princeton, NJ: Princeton University Press, 1989).

61. Herbert B. Asher, Eric S. Heberlig, Randall B. Ripley, and Karen Snyder, *American Labor Unions in the Electoral Arena* (Lanham, MD; Rowman Littlefield, 2001), pp. 133–53.

62. Harold Meyerson, "Organize or Die," *American Prospect*, online, August 31, 2003.

63. For more on Stern, see Bai, "The New Boss," pp. 38–45, 62, 68–71; Aaron Bernstein, "Can This Man Save Labor?" *Business Week*, September 13, 2004, pp. 80–86; Steven Greenhouse, "Between Union Leader and Protégé, Polite but Firm Disagreement on Labor's Future," *New York Times*, December 5, 2004, p. 20.

64. Mike Allen, "Bush Courts Unions to Split off Votes," *Washington Post*, March 31, 2002, p. A5.

65. See, for example, Dan Balz, "Howard Dean's Unlikely Road to a Major Boost from Labor," *Washington Post*, November 12, 2003, p. A8.

66. Taylor Dark, *The Unions and the Democrats: An Enduring Alliance* (Ithaca, NY: Cornell University Press, 1999).

67. See, for example, R. W. Apple Jr., "An Insurgent Gains Status," *New York Times*, December 10, 2003, p. A1; David S. Broder, "Dean: A Milestone Not a Millstone," *Washington Post*, February 22, 2004, p. B7.

68. Kenneth S. Baer, *Reinventing Democrats: The Politics of Liberalism from Reagan to Clinton* (Lawrence: University Press of Kansas, 2000), p. 62.

69. Koopman, *Hostile Takeover.*

70. Michael Sokolove, "Can This Marriage Be Saved?" *New York Times Magazine*, April 11, 2004, p. 26.

71. Quoted in Philip Gourevitch, "Fight on the Right," *New Yorker*, April 12, 2004, p. 34.

72. Quoted in David Nather, "GOP Infighting: Not Fatal," *Congressional Quarterly Weekly Report*, May 31, 2003, p. 1309.

73. Martin P. Wattenberg, *The Rise of Candidate-Centered Politics: Presidential Elections of the 1980s* (Cambridge, MA: Harvard University Press, 1991).

74. William G. Mayer, *The Divided Democrats: Ideological Unity, Party Reform, and Presidential Elections* (Boulder, CO: Westview Press, 1996).

75. See, for example, James I. Lengle, Diana Owen, and Molly W. Sonner, "Divisive Nominating Mechanisms and Democratic Party Electoral Prospect," *Journal of Politics* 57 (May 1995): 370–83.

76. Anthony Corrado, "The Legislative Odyssey of BCRA," in *Life after Reform: When the Bipartisan Campaign Reform Act ... Meets*

Politics, ed. Michael J. Malbin (Lanham, MD: Rowman Littlefield, 2003), pp. 21–39.

77. Seth Gitell, "The Democratic Party Suicide Bill," *Atlantic Monthly*, July–August 2003, pp. 106–13.

78. Steve Weissman and Ruth Hassan, "BCRA and the 527 Groups," in *The Election after Reform: Money, Politics, and the Bipartisan Campaign Reform Act*, ed. Michael J. Malbin (Lanham, MD: Rowman, Littlefield, 2005).

79. For more on the Democratic 527s, see James V. Grimaldi and Thomas B. Edsall, "Super Rich Step into Political Vacuum," *Washington Post*, October 17, 2004, p. A1.

80. Quoted in James A. Barnes, "Where Democrats Might Have an Edge," *National Journal*, May 8, 2004, p. 1442.

81. Jim Rutenberg, "Ads for (And at No Cost to) Kerry Keep Flowing," *New York Times*, August 5, 2004, p. A1.

82. Quoted in Matt Bai, "Wiring the Vast Left-Wing Conspiracy," *New York Times Magazine*, July 25, 2004, p. 36.

83. Quoted in Eliza Newlin Carney, Peter H. Stone, and James A. Barnes, "New Rules of the Game," *National Journal*, December 20, 2003, p. 3808.

84. Quoted in Jeanne Cummings, "In New Law's Wake, Companies Slash Their Political Donations," *Wall Street Journal*, September 3, 2004, p. A4.

85. Citizens United and Progress for America are actually 501 (c) (4) groups that can run ads that address issues but cannot engage in explicit advocacy of a candidate. Such groups do not have to disclose their contributors.

86. Thomas B. Edsall, "After Late Start, Republican Groups Jump into the Lead," *Washington Post*, October 17, 2004, p. A15.

87. Quoted in Glen Justice and Jim Rutenberg, "Advocacy Groups Step Up Costly Battle of Political Ads," *New York Times*, September 25, 2004, p. A10.

88. Quoted in Glen Justice, "In New Landscape of Campaign Finance, Big Donations Flow to Groups, Not Parties," *New York Times*, December 11, 2003, p. A25.

89. Clyde Wilcox, Alexandra Cooper, Peter Francia, John C. Green, Paul S. Herrnson, Lynda Powell, Jason Reifler, Mark J. Rozell, and Benjamin A. Webster, "With Limits Raised, Who Will Give More? The Impact of BCRA on Individual Donors," in *Life after Reform*, ed. Michael Malbin, pp. 61–79.

90. On the relationship between the big donors and the Bush campaign, see Peter H. Stone, "Power Rangers," *National Journal*, October 30, 2004, pp. 3288–92.

91. Peter H. Stone, "The Texan's Rangers," *National Journal*, October 25, 2003, pp. 3260–63.

92. Thomas B. Edsall, Sarah Cohen, and James V. Grimaldi, "Pioneers Fill War Chest, Then Capitalize," *Washington Post*, May 16, 2004, p. A1.

93. Katherine Q. Seelye, "Both Sides' Commercials Create Brew of Negativity, at a Boil," *New York Times*, September 23, 2004, p. A22.

94. Anthony Corrado and Thomas E. Mann, "Despite Predictions, BCRA Has Not Been a 'Democratic Suicide Bill'," *Roll Call*, July 26, 2004.

95. Paul Farhi, "Small Donors Grow into Big Political Force," *Washington Post*, May 3, 2004, p. A1.

96. Michael J. Malbin, "Political Parties under the Post-*McConnell* Bipartisan Campaign Reform Act," *Election Law Journal* 3 (2) (2004): 177–91.

97. Daniel M. Shea, "The Passing of Realignment and the Advent of the 'Base-less' Party System," *American Politics Quarterly* 27 (January 1999): 33–57.

98. On the last point, see, for example, William C. Berman, *America's Right Turn: From Nixon to Bush* (Baltimore: Johns Hopkins University Press, 1994); Thomas Ferguson and Joel Rogers, *Right Turn: The Decline of the Democrats and the Future of American Politics* (New York: Hill and Wang, 1986).

99. Benjamin Radcliff, "Organized Labor and Electoral Participation in American National Elections," *Journal of Labor Research* 22 (Spring 2001): 405–14.

100. Dewayne Wickham, *Bill Clinton and Black America* (New York: Ballantine, 2002).

101. Maurice Mangum, "Psychological Involvement and Black Voter Turnout," *Political Research Quarterly* 56 (March 2003): 41–48; Priscilla L. Southwell and Kevin D. Pirch, "Political Cynicism and the Mobilization of Black Voters," *Social Science Quarterly* 84 (December 2003): 906–17.

102. Quoted in Maura Reynolds and Doyle McManus, "GOP Focus Is Already Fixed on Endgame," *Los Angeles Times*, February 1, 2004, p. A1.

103. Robert D. Putnam, *Bowling Alone: The Collapse and Revival of American Community* (New York: Simon and Schuster, 2000), p. 40.

104. Quoted in Jim Drinkard, "Parties Are Losing People Power," *USA Today*, August 31, 2000, p. 13A.

105. Priscilla L. Southwell finds no discernible partisan advantage in Oregon's system in her article, "Five Years Later: A Re-Assessment of Oregon's Vote by Mail Electoral Process," *PS: Political Science and Politics* 37 (January 2004): 89–93.

106. Quoted in Jo Becker, "Voters May Have Their Say before Election Day," *Washington Post*, August 26, 2004, p. A1.

107. Michael Moss, "Both Parties See New Promise When the Ballot Is in the Mail," *New York Times*, August 22, 2004, p. A1.

108. J. Eric Oliver, "The Effects of Eligibility Restrictions and Party Activity on Absentee Voting and Overall Turnout," *American Journal of Political Science* 40 (April 1996): 498–513.

109. Jeffrey A. Karp and Susan A. Banducci, "Absentee Voting, Mobilization, and Participation," *American Politics Research* 29 (March 2001): 183–95.

110. R. Michael Alvarez and Thad E. Hall, *Point, Click, and Vote: The Future of Internet Voting* (Washington, D.C.: Brookings Institution Press, 2004), pp. 31–53.

CHAPTER 8

1. Bernard Goldberg, *Bias: A CBS Insider Exposes How the Media Distort the News* (Washington, D.C.: Regnery Publishing, 2002), p. 24.

2. Alterman's quote is from Eric Alterman, *What Liberal Media? The Truth about Bias and the News* (New York: Basic Books, 2003), p. 42; Coulter's is from Ann Coulter, *Slander: Liberal Lies about the American Right* (New York: Crown, 2002), p. 96 and p. 114.

3. Robert K. Goidel and Ronald E. Langley, "Uncovering Evidence of Indirect Media Effects: News Coverage of the Economy and the 1992 Presidential Election," *Political Research Quarterly* 48 (June 1995): 313–28.

4. Paul Allen Beck, Russel J. Dalton, Steven Greene, and Robert Huckfeldt, "The Social Calculus of Voting: Interpersonal, Media, and Organizational Influences on Presidential Choices," *American Political Science Review* 96 (March 2002): 57–73.

5. Tim Groseclose and Jeff Milyo, "A Measure of Media Bias," typescript, September 2003. See also Robert J. Barro, "Bias beyond a Reasonable Doubt," *Weekly Standard*, December 13, 2004, pp. 14–15.

6. J. Wilson Mixon Jr., Amit Sen, and E. Frank Stephenson, "Are the Networks Biased? Calling States in the 2000 Presidential Election," *Public Choice* 118 (January 2004): 53–59.

7. Kenneth Dautrich and Thomas Hartley, *How the News Media Fail American Voters: Causes, Consequences, and Remedies* (New York: Columbia University Press, 1999).

8. Paul J. Maurer, "Media Feeding Frenzies: Press Behavior during Two Clinton Scandals," *Presidential Studies Quarterly* 29 (March): 65–79.

9. David Niven, "Partisan Bias in the Media? A New Test," *Social Science Quarterly* 80 (December 1999): 847–57.

10. David Niven, *Tilt? The Search for Media Bias* (Westport, CT: Praeger, 2002), pp. 73–95.

11. David Domke, David P. Fan, Michael Fibison, Dhavan V. Shah, Steve S. Smith, and Mark D. Watts, "News Media, Candidates and Issues, and Public Opinion in the 1996 Presidential Campaign," *Journalism and Mass Communication Quarterly* 74 (Winter 1997): 718–37.

12. David D'Alessio and Michael Allen, "Media Bias in Presidential Elections: A Meta-Analysis," *Journal of Communication* 50 (Fall 2000): 133–56.

13. Kathleen Hall Jamieson, *Everything You Think You Know about Politics ... And Why You're Wrong* (New York: Basic Books, 2000), p. 187.

14. William G. Mayer, "Why Talk Radio Is Conservative," *Public Interest*, Summer 2004, pp. 86–103.

15. Paul D. Colford, *The Rush Limbaugh Story: Talent on Loan from God* (New York: St. Martin's Press, 1993), pp. 66–67.

16. Rush H. Limbaugh, "Voice of America: Why Liberals Fear Me," *Policy Review*, Fall 1994, pp. 4–10.

17. David C. Barker, *Rushed to Judgment: Talk Radio, Persuasion, and American Political Behavior* (New York: Columbia University Press, 2002).

18. David C. Barker, "Rushed Decisions: Political Talk Radio and Vote Choice, 1994–1996," *Journal of Politics* 61 (May 1999): 527–39.

19. Quoted in Jim Rutenberg, "On the Air: Bush's Campaign Finds Platform on Local Radio," *New York Times*, December 29, 2003, p. 1.

20. Daniel Okrent, "Is the New York Times a Liberal Newspaper?" *New York Times*, July 25, 2004, p. 4:2.

21. David Brock, *The Republican Noise Machine: Right-Wing Media and How It Corrupts Democracy* (New York: Crown Publishers, 2004), p. 135.

22. Quoted in Francis X. Dealy Jr., *The Power and the Money: Inside the Wall Street Journal* (New York: Birch Lane, 1993), p. 212.

23. Michael Tomasky, "Whispers and Screams: The Partisan Nature of Editorial Pages," The Joan Shorenstein Center on the Press, Politics, and Public Policy, Research Paper R-25, July 2003.

24. David Carr, "White House Listens When Weekly Speaks," *New York Times*, March 11, 2003, p. E1.

25. The figures are from Lorraine Adams, "The Magazine of Restoration Washington," *Columbia Journalism Review*, September–October 2002, pp. 28–31.

26. For more on the development of conservative publishing, see Brock, *The Republican Noise Machine*, pp. 347–64.

27. David E. Rosenbaum, "His Conservative Connections Help to Put Novelist on Best-Seller List," *New York Times*, November 15, 2003, p. A8.

28. See, for example, Matthew Klam, "Fear and Laptops on the Campaign Trail," *New York Times Magazine*, September 26, 2004, pp. 43–49.

29. For more on the conservative blogs, see Jonathan V. Last, "What the Blogs Have Wrought," *Weekly Standard*, September 27, 2004, pp. 27–31.

30. Quoted in Jonathan D. Glater, "Liberal Bloggers Reaching Out to Major Media," *New York Times*, March 14, 2005, p. C6.

31. Don M. Flournoy and Robert K. Stewart, *CNN: Making News in the Global Market* (Luton, UK: University of Luton Press, 1997), p. 1.

32. Scott Collins, *Crazy Like a Fox: The Inside Story of How Fox News Beat CNN* (New York: Portfolio, 2004), pp. 77–79.

33. Quoted in Brian Anderson, "We're Not Losing the Culture Wars Anymore," *City Journal* 13 (Autumn 2003): 14.

34. Quoted in Alex S. Jones, "Fox News Moves from the Margins to the Mainstream," *New York Times*, December 1, 2002, p. 4:4.

35. Quoted in Ken Auletta, "Vox Fox," *The New Yorker*, May 26, 2003, p. 65.

36. Collins, *Crazy Like a Fox*, pp. 140–43.

37. Jim Rutenberg, "Cable's War Coverage Suggests a New 'Fox Effect' on Television Journalism," *New York Times*, April 16, 2003, p. B9.

38. Walter Isaacson, "Fighting Words: The White House Memoir Grows Claws," *New Yorker*, July 14, 2003, p. 98.

39. Quoted in Adam Clymer, "Democrats Seek a Stronger Focus and Money," *New York Times*, May 26, 2003, p. A12.

40. Quoted in Jim Rutenberg, "Outflanked Democrats Wonder How to Catch Up in Media Wars," *New York Times*, January 1, 2003, p. A12.

41. Hendrick Hertzberg, "Radio Daze," *New Yorker*, August 11, 2003, p. 24.

42. Mayer, "Why Talk Radio Is Conservative."

43. See, for example, James Bandler, "New York Times Criticizes Its Own Iraqi-Weapons Coverage," *New York Times*, May 27, 2004, p. A10; Howard Kurtz, "The Post on WMDs: An Inside Story," *Washington Post*, August 12, 2004, p. A1.

44. For more on the concentration of ownership, see Ben H. Bagdikian, *The New Media Monopoly* (Boston: Beacon Press, 2004).

45. Quoted in Howard Kurtz, "Troubled Times for Network Evening News," *Washington Post*, March 10, 2002, p. A1.

46. Martin Gilens and Craig Hertzman, "Corporate Ownership and News Bias: Newspaper Coverage of the 1996 Telecommunications Act," *Journal of Politics* 62 (May 2000): 369–86.

47. Alterman, *What Liberal Media?* p. 24.

48. See, for example, Thomas E. Patterson, "Doing Well and Doing Good: How Soft News and Critical Journalism Are Shrinking the News Audience and Weakening Democracy—And What News Outlets Can Do about It," The Joan Shorenstein Center on the Press, Politics, and Public Policy, 2000.

49. Marion Just and Rosalind Levine with Kathleen Regan, "News for Sale," *Columbia Journalism Review*, November–December 2001, pp. 2–3.

50. Richard A. Viguerie and David Franke, *America's Right Turn: How Conservatives Used New and Alternative Media to Take Power* (Chicago: Bonus Books, 2004).

51. For more on this see Paul Farhi, "Voters Are Harder to Reach as Media Outlets Multiply," *Washington Post*, June 16, 2004, p. A1.

52. Quoted in Brock, *The Republican Noise Machine*, p. 302.

53. Edith Efron, *The News Twisters* (Los Angeles: Nash, 1971).

54. David A. Jones, "Why Americans Don't Trust the Media: A Preliminary Analysis," *Harvard International Journal of Press/Politics* 9 (2) (2004): 60–75.

55. Pew Research Center for the People and the Press, "News Media's Improved Image Proves Short-Lived," August 4, 2002.

56. David M. Ricci, *The Transformation of American Politics: The New Washington and the Rise of Think Tanks* (New Haven, CT: Yale University Press, 1993).

57. R. Kent Weaver, "The Changing World of Think Tanks," *PS: Political Science and Politics* 22 (September 1989): 563–78.

58. James Allen Smith, *The Idea Brokers: Think Tanks and the Rise of the New Policy Elite* (New York: The Free Press, 1991), pp. 122–66.

59. Donald E. Abelson, *Do Think Tanks Matter? Assessing the Impact of Public Policy Institutes* (Montreal: McGill-Queen's University Press, 2002), p. 179.

60. Sidney Blumenthal, The *Rise of the Counter-Establishment: From Conservative Ideology to Political Power* (New York: Times Books, 1986), pp. 45–54.

61. For more on Heritage's strategies, see Edwin Feulner, "The Heritage Foundation," in *Think Tanks and Civil Societies: Catalysts for Ideas and Action*, ed. James G. McGann and R. Kent Weaver (New Brunswick, NJ: Transaction Publishers, 2000), pp. 67–86.

62. Peter H. Stone, "Conservative Brain Trust," *New York Times Magazine*, May 10, 1981.

63. Discovery's activities are described in some detail in Micklethwait and Wooldridge, *The Right Nation*, pp. 158–60; Chris Mooney, "Survival of the Slickest," *American Prospect*, online, December 2, 2002; Peter Slevin, "Battle on Teaching Evolution Sharpens," *Washington Post*, March 14, 2005, p. A1.

64. Russ Bellant, *The Coors Connection: How Coors Family Philanthropy Undermines Democratic Pluralism* (Boston, MA: South End Press, 1991), p. xv.

65. Robert Kaiser and Ira Chinoy, "How Scaife's Money Powered a Movement," *Washington Post*, May 2, 1999, p. A1.

66. Phil Kuntz, "Citizen Scaife," *Wall Street Journal*, October 12, 1995, p. A1.

67. Quoted in W. John Moore, "Wichita Pipeline," *National Journal*, May 16, 1992, p. 1171.

68. Quoted in Matt Bai, "Notion Building," *New York Times Magazine*, October 12, 2003, pp. 82–87.

69. Ibid.

70. Robert Kuttner, "Beyond Left and Right: A Guide for the Unwary," *The American Prospect*, online, April 1, 2003.

71. Richard Morin and Claudia Deane, "Big Thinker," *Washington Post*, December 10, 2001, p. C1.

72. Abelson, *Do Think Tanks Matter?*

73. Andrew Rich, "The Politics of Expertise in Congress and the News Media," *Social Science Quarterly* 82 (September 2001): 583–601.

74. Andrew Rich and R. Kent Weaver, "Think Tanks in the U.S. Media," *Harvard International Journal of Press/Politics* 5 (Fall 2000): 81–103.

75. Edwin Meese III, *With Reagan: The Inside Story* (Washington, D.C.: Regnery, 1992), p. 60.

76. Quoted in Bai, "Wiring the Vast Left-Wing Conspiracy," p. 37.

77. Eliza Newlin Carney, "Extreme Makeover," *National Journal*, February 26, 2005, pp. 598–603.

78. James K. Glassman, "The Trends Are All towards Republicans," Scripps Howard News Service, August 2, 2004.

CHAPTER 9

1. Daniel Bell, *The Coming of Postindustrial Society* (New York: Basic Books, 1973), p. 44.

2. See, for example, William A. Niskanen, *Reaganomics: An Insider's Account of the Policies and the People* (New York: Oxford University Press, 1988), pp. 51–52.

3. Quoted in David Leonhardt, "Egalitarian Recession Keeps Anger at Bay," *New York Times*, June 15, 2003, p. 4:1.

4. For such an interpretation, see Irwin M. Stelzer, "Larry Lindsey Was Right," *The Weekly Standard*, December 23, 2002, pp. 14–16.

5. Jacob S. Hacker, "Middle Class Tightrope: It's More Dire Than the Numbers Show," *Washington Post*, August 10, 2004, p. A19.

6. Quoted in David Leonhardt, "Defining the Rich in the World's Wealthiest Nation," *New York Times*, January 12, 2003, p. 4:16.

7. W. Michael Cox and Richard Alm, *Myths of Rich and Poor* (New York: Basic Books, 2000).

8. Robert H. Frank, *Luxury Fever: Why Money Fails to Satisfy in an Era of Excess* (New York: The Free Press, 1999).

9. Gregg Easterbrook, *The Progress Paradox: How Life Gets Better While People Feel Worse* (New York: Random House, 2003). The data on income are from page 9.

10. See, for example, Easterbrook, *The Progress Paradox*, pp. 121–62; Brian Goff and Arthur A. Fleisher III, *Spoiled Rotten: Affluence, Anxiety, and Social Decay in America* (Boulder, CO: Westview Press, 1999), pp. 109–94.

11. Frank, *Luxury Fever*, pp. 122–45.

12. Everett Carll Ladd Jr., *American Political Parties: Social Change and Political Response* (New York: W.W. Norton, 1970), pp. 243–311.

13. Ronald Inglehart, *The Silent Revolution: Changing Values and Political Styles among Western Publics* (Princeton, NJ: Princeton University Press, 1977).

14. Quoted in John Cassidy, "Tax Code," *New Yorker*, September 6, 2004, p. 75.

15. Cited in Barone, "Life, Liberty, and Property," p. 32.

16. John Hood, *Investor Politics: The New Force That Will Transform American Business, Government, and Politics in the Twenty-First Century* (Philadelphia: Templeton Foundation Press, 2001).

17. Ramesh Ponnuru, "Investor Class, Investor Nation," *National Review*, February 9, 2004, pp. 28–33.

18. Richard Nadler, "Portfolio Politics: Nudging the Investor Class Forward," *National Review*, December 4, 2000, pp. 38–40.

19. Quoted in Edsall et al., "Bush Aims to Forge A GOP Legacy," p. A1.

20. For more on this, see Margaret Levi, "Organizing Power: The Prospects for an American Labor Movement," *Perspectives on Politics* 1 (March 2003): 45–68.

21. See Steven Greenhouse, "Labor Federation Looks beyond Unions," *New York Times*, July 11, 2004, p. 18.

22. Max Green, *Epitaph for American Labor: How Union Leaders Lost Touch with America* (Washington, D.C.: The AEI Press, 1996), pp. 153–54.

23. Asher et al., *American Labor Unions in the Electoral Arena*, pp. 26–46.

24. Paul Burstein and Susan Wierzbicki, "Public Opinion and Congressional Action on Work, Family, and Gender, 1945–1990," in *Work and Family: Research Informing Policy*, ed. Toby B. Parcel and David B. Cornfield (Thousand Oaks, CA: Sage Publications, 2000).

25. Andrew Kohut, John C. Green, Scott Keeter, and Robert C. Toth, *The Diminishing Divide: Religion's Changing Role in American Politics* (Washington, D.C.: Brookings Institution Press, 2000), p. 25.

26. Michael Hout and Claude S. Fischer, "Why More Americans Have No Religious Preference: Politics and Generations," *American Sociological Review* 67 (April 2002): 165–90.

27. Kohut, Green, Keeter, and Toth, *The Diminishing Divide*.

28. Ibid., pp. 59–63.

29. See, for example, David D. Kirkpatrick, "Bush Appeal to Churches Seeking Help Raises Doubts," *New York Times*, July 2, 2004, p. A1; Kirkpatrick, "Churches See an Election Role and Spread the Word on Bush," p. A5.

30. Wilcox et al., "Political Mobilization in the Pews," pp. 524–35.

31. Quoted in Robin Toner, "Kerry Criticizes Bush's Definition of Values," *New York Times*, July 5, 2004, p. 13.

32. David M. Halbfinger and David E. Sanger, "Kerry's Latest Attacks on Bush Borrow a Page from Scripture," *New York Times*, October 25, 2004, p. A17.

33. Jim VandeHei, "Faith Increasingly Part of Kerry's Campaign," *Washington Post*, October 18, 2004, p. A1.

34. Sheryl Gay Stolberg, "Democrats Getting Lessons in Speaking Their Values," *New York Times*, February 11, 2005, p. A16.

35. Morris P. Fiorina, with Samuel J. Abrams and Jeremy C. Pope, *Culture War? The Myth of a Polarized America* (New York: Pearson Longman, 2005), pp. 95–106.

36. Jeffrey Bell and Frank Cannon, "The Rise of the Values Voter," *Weekly Standard*, October 11, 2004, pp. 11–12.

37. Matt Barreto and Nathan D. Woods, "Latino Voting Behavior in an Anti-Latino Political Context," in *Diversity in Democracy: Minority Representation in the United States*, ed. Gary Segura and Shaun Bowler (Charlottesville, VA: University of Virginia Press, 2003).

38. Greenberg, *The Two Americas*, p. 122.

39. Micklethwait and Wooldridge, *The Right Nation*, pp. 240–41.

40. Quoted in Kirk Johnson, "Hispanic Voters Declare Their Independence," *New York Times*, November 9, 2004, p. A16.

41. Gregory L. Giroux, "Pursuing the Political Prize of America's Hispanic Vote," *Congressional Quarterly Weekly Report*, June 29, 2002, pp. 1710–15.

42. Carol A. Cassel, "Hispanic Turnout: Estimates from Validated Voting Data," *Political Research Quarterly* 55 (June 2002): 391–408.

43. Quoted in "The Manana Vote," *National Journal*, June 5, 2004, p. 1762.

44. Louis DeSipio, "Building America One Person at a Time: Naturalization and Political Behavior of the Naturalized in Contemporary American Politics," in *E Pluribus Unum? Contemporary and Historical Perspectives on Immigrant Political Incorporation*, ed. Gary Gerstle and John H. Mollenkopf (New York: Russell Sage Foundation, 2001), pp. 67–106.

45. Nicolás C. Vaca, *The Presumed Alliance: The Unspoken Conflict between Latinos and Blacks and What It Means for America* (New York: Rayo, 2004), pp. 185–202.

46. Jorge Ramos, *The Latino Wave: How Hispanics Will Choose the Next President* (New York: HarperCollins, 2004). Roberto Suro is quoted in Martin Kasindorf, "Parties Target Hispanics in Four Battleground States," *USA Today*, July 20, 2004, p. 1A.

47. Paul Frymer, *Uneasy Alliances: Race and Party Competition in America* (Princeton, NJ: Princeton University Press, 1999).

48. Peter W. Wielhouwer, "Releasing the Fetters: Parties and the Mobilization of the African-American Electorate," *Journal of Politics* 62 (February 2000): 206–22.

49. Mangum, "Psychological Involvement and Black Voter Turnout," pp. 41–48.

50. Theda Skocpol, *Diminished Democracy: From Membership to Management in American Civic Life* (Norman: University of Oklahoma Press, 2003), p. 220.

51. Ibid., p. 220.

52. Rodney E. Hero, "Social Capital and Racial Inequality in America," *Perspectives on Politics* 1 (March 2003): 113–22. The full citation for Putnam's book is Robert D. Putnam, *Bowling Alone: The Collapse and Revival of American Community* (New York: Simon & Schuster, 2000).

53. Hero, "Social Capital," pp. 115–16.

54. See, for example, Matt Labash, "Getting Out the Phat Vote," *Weekly Standard*, August 9, 2004, pp. 23–26.

55. Priscilla L. Southwell and Kevin D. Pirch, "Political Cynicism and the Mobilization of Black Voters," *Social Science Quarterly* 84 (December 2003): 906–17.

56. This is Thomas Byrne Edsall's argument about Nixon and Reagan's race policies. See Thomas Byrne Edsall with Mary D. Edsall, *Chain Reaction: The Impact of Race, Rights, and Taxes on American Politics* (New York: Norton, 1991), pp. 74–98 and pp. 172–97. The importance of Nixon's and Reagan's racial conservatism is explained by Edward G. Carmines and James A. Stimson, *Issue Evolution: Race and the Transformation of American Politics* (Princeton: Princeton University Press, 1989), pp. 52–58.

57. Quoted in Henry Louis Gates Jr., "Swallowing the Elephant," *New York Times*, September 19, 2004, p. 4:11.

58. Thomas B. Edsall, "Group Runs Anti-Kerry Ads on Black Radio Stations," *Washington Post*, August 12, 2004, p. A1.

59. Quoted in Ramesh Ponnuru, "Tell It! A Republican Outreach Program to Black Voters," *National Review*, February 10, 2003, pp. 17–19.

60. Isaac Shapiro and Joel Friedman, "A Comprehensive Assessment of the Bush Administration's Record on Cutting Taxes," Center on Budget and Policy Priorities, April 23, 2004.

61. Larry Bartels, "Unenlightened Self-Interest: The Strange Appeal of Estate-Tax Repeal," *The American Prospect*, online, May 17, 2004.

62. Micklethwait and Wooldridge, *The Right Nation*, pp. 307–8.

63. These are all reasons cited by Garry Orren in his essay, "Fall from Grace: The Public's Loss of Faith in Government," in *Why People Don't Trust Government*, ed. Joseph S. Nye, Jr., Philp D. Zelikow, and David C. King (Cambridge, MA: Harvard University Press, 1997), pp. 77–107.

64. John R. Hibbing and Elizabeth Theiss-Morse, *Stealth Democracy: Americans' Beliefs about How Government Should Work* (New York: Cambridge University Press, 2002), p. 46.

65. William G. Mayer, *The Changing American Mind: How and Why American Public Opinion Changed between 1960 and 1988* (Ann Arbor: University of Michigan Press, 1992); James A. Stimson, *Public Opinion in America: Moods, Cycles, and Swings*, 2d ed. (Boulder, CO: Westview Press, 1999).

66. Donald Green, Bradley Palmquist, and Eric Schickler, *Partisan Hearts and Minds: Political Parties and the Social Identities of Voters* (New Haven, CT: Yale University Press, 2002).

67. Barry C. Burden and Casey A. Klofstad, "Affect and Cognition in Party Identification," manuscript, Harvard University.

CHAPTER 10

1. David R. Mayhew, *Divided We Govern: Party Control, Lawmaking, and Investigations, 1946–1990* (New Haven, CT: Yale University Press, 1991).

2. For more on money in Gilded Age presidential politics, see Mark Wahlgren Summers, "Party Games: The Art of Stealing Elections in the Late-Nineteenth-Century United States," *The Journal of American History*, September 2001, http://www.historycooperative.org/journals/jah/88.2/summers.html.

3. Sarah A. Binder and Steven S. Smith, *Politics or Principle? Filibustering in the United States Senate* (Washington, D.C.: Brookings Institution, 1997); Gregory Wawro and Eric Schickler, "Redoubtable Weapon: Obstruction and Lawmaking in the U.S. Senate," paper presented to the annual meeting of the American Political Science Association, 2004.

4. Eric Schickler, *Disjointed Pluralism: Institutional Innovation and the Development of the U.S. Congress* (Princeton, NJ: Princeton University Press, 2001), pp. 32–43.

5. O. O. Stealey, *Twenty Years in the Press Gallery* (New York: Publishers Printing, 1906), p. 113.

6. Herbert Croly, *Progressive Democracy* (New York: Macmillan, 1915), p. 87.

7. See, for example, Dana Milbank, "Bush Seeks to Rule the Bureaucracy," *Washington Post*, November 22, 2004, p. A4; Jim VandeHei and Mike Allen, "A Domestic Policy in Sharp Focus," *Washington Post*, December 10, 2004, p. A1.

8. See, for example, Paul Singer, "By the Horns," *National Journal*, March 26, 2005, pp. 898–904.

9. See, for example, "Don't Worry. It's Only Little Brother," *The Economist*, March 19, 2005, p. 37.

10. Charles E. Walcott and Karen M. Hult, "The Bush Staff and Cabinet System," in *Considering the Bush Presidency*, ed. Gary L. Gregg II and Mark J. Rozell (New York: Oxford University Press, 2004), p. 64.

11. Alexis Simendinger, "Power of One," *National Journal*, January 26, 2002, p. 230.

12. John G. Geer, *From Tea Leaves to Opinion Polls: A Theory of Democratic Leadership* (New York: Columbia University Press, 1996).

13. E. E. Schattschneider, *Party Government* (New York: Holt, Rinehart and Winston, 1942), p. 37.

14. David A. Dulio, *For Better or Worse? How Political Consultants Are Changing Elections in the United States* (Albany: State University of New York Press, 2004), pp. 135–65; Stephen K. Medvic, *Political Consultants in U.S. Congressional Elections* (Columbus: Ohio University Press, 2001).

15. Dulio, *For Better or Worse?* pp. 41–64.

16. Susan B. Glasser, "Hired Guns Fuel Fundraising Race," *Washington Post*, April 30, 2000, p. A1.

17. George Stephanopoulos, *All Too Human: A Political Education* (New York: Little, Brown, 1999), pp. 328–41.

18. Wickham, *Bill Clinton and Black America*.

19. See Jonathan Rauch, "In 2004, the Country Didn't Turn Right— But the GOP Did," *National Journal*, November 13, 2004, pp. 3450–51.

20. For more on the government shutdown and the public's views on it, see James A. Stimson, *Tides of Consent: How Public Opinion Shapes American Politics* (New York: Cambridge University Press, 2004), pp. xi–xvi.

21. For a comprehensive synopsis of polling data on Clinton and impeachment, see Michael R. Kagay, "Presidential Address: Public Opinion and Polling during Presidential Scandal and Impeachment," *Public Opinion Quarterly* 63 (Fall 1999): 449–63.

22. Thomas Frank, *What's The Matter with Kansas? How Conservatives Won the Heart of America* (New York: Metropolitan Books, 2004), pp. 225–36.

23. For a short discussion of the many divisions, see Dan Balz and John F. Harris, "Some Republicans Predict Upheaval within the Party," *Washington Post*, September 4, 2004, p. A8.

24. William Safire, "Inside a Republican Brain," *New York Times*, July 21, 2004, p. A23.

25. Adam Nagourney, "Squabbles under the Big Tent," *New York Times*, April 3, 2005, p. 4:1.

26. John Judis, "Freed Radicals," *New Republic*, September 6, 2004, pp. 18–22.

27. See Sheryl Gay Stolberg, "A Senate Race in Oklahoma Lifts the Right," *New York Times*, September 19, 2004, p. 1.

28. See, for example, David Brooks, "The Era of Big Government Is Over," *New York Times Magazine*, August 29, 2004, pp. 32–56.

29. Frank Rich, "The O'Reilly Factor for Lesbians," *New York Times*, October 24, 2004, p. 2:1.

30. See, for example, Peter Beinart, "Great Divide," *New Republic*, September 13–20, 2004, p. 6.

31. Pat Buchanan, *Where the Right Went Wrong: How Neoconservatives Subverted the Reagan Revolution and Hijacked the Bush Presidency* (New York: Thomas Dunne Books, 2004).

Select Bibliography

Bell, Daniel. *The Coming of Postindustrial Society: A Venture in Social Fore-casting*. New York: Basic Books, 1973.

Black, Earl, and Merle Black. *The Rise of Southern Republicans*. Cambridge, MA: Harvard University Press, 2002.

Brock, David. *The Republican Noise Machine: Right-Wing Media and How It Corrupts Democracy*. New York: Crown, 2004.

Brooks, David. *On Paradise Drive: How We Live Now (And Always Have) in the Future Tense*. New York: Simon & Schuster, 2004.

Burnham, Walter Dean. *Critical Elections and the Mainsprings of American Politics*. New York: Norton, 1970.

Cain, Bruce E., John A. Ferejohn, and Morris P. Fiorina. *The Personal Vote: Constituency Service and Electoral Independence*. Cambridge, MA: Harvard University Press, 1987.

Campbell, Colin, and Bert A. Rockman, eds. *The George W. Bush Presidency: Appraisals and Prospects*. Washington, D.C.: Congressional Quarterly Press, 2004.

Collins, Scott. *Crazy Like a Fox: The Inside Story of How Fox News Beat CNN*. New York: Portfolio, 2004.

Connelly, William F., and John J. Pitney Jr. *Congress' Permanent Minority? Republicans in the U.S. House*. Lanham, MD: Rowman and Littlefield, 1994.

Cornfield, Michael. *Politics Moves Online: Campaigning and the Internet*. New York: Century Foundation Press, 2004.

Daalder, Ivo H., and James M. Lindsay. *America Unbound: The Bush Revolution in Foreign Policy.* Washington, D.C.: Brookings Institution, 2003.

Easterbrook, Gregg. *The Progress Paradox: How Life Gets Better While People Feel Worse.* New York: Random House, 2003.

Edwards, George C. III. *Why the Electoral College Is Bad for America.* New Haven, CT: Yale University Press, 2004.

Fiorina, Morris P. *Congress: Keystone of the Washington Establishment.* New Haven, CT: Yale University Press, 1977.

Florida, Richard L. *The Rise of the Creative Class: And How It's Transforming Work, Leisure, Community and Everyday Life.* New York: Basic Books, 2002.

Frank, Thomas. *What's the Matter with Kansas? How Conservatives Won the Heart of America.* New York: Metropolitan Books, 2004.

Frymer, Paul. *Uneasy Alliances: Race and Party Competition in America.* Princeton, NJ: Princeton University Press, 1999.

Garreau, Joel. *Edge City: Life on the New Frontier.* New York: Doubleday, 1991.

Green, Donald P., Bradley Palmquist, and Eric Schickler. *Partisan Hearts and Minds: Political Parties and the Social Identities of Voters.* New Haven, CT: Yale University Press, 2003.

Greenberg, Stanley B. *The Two Americas: Our Current Political Deadlock and How to Break It.* New York: Thomas Dunne Books, 2004.

Greenstein, Fred I., ed. *The George W. Bush Presidency: An Early Assessment.* Baltimore: Johns Hopkins University Press, 2003.

Gregg, Gary L., III, and Mark J. Rozzell, eds. *Considering the Bush Presidency.* New York: Oxford University Press, 2004.

Halper, Stefan, and Jonathan Clarke. *America Alone: The Neo-Conservatives and the Global Order.* New York: Cambridge University Press, 2004.

Inglehart, Ronald. *The Silent Revolution: Changing Values and Political Styles among Western Publics.* Princeton, NJ: Princeton University Press, 1977.

Judis, John B., and Ruy Teixeira. *The Emerging Democratic Majority.* New York: Scribner, 2002.

Kohut, Andrew, John C. Green, Scott Keeter, and Robert C. Toth. *The Diminishing Divide: Religion's Changing Role in Politics.* Washington, D.C.: Brookings Institution, 2000.

Koopman, Douglas L. *Hostile Takeover: The House Republican Party, 1980–1995.* Lanham, MD: Rowman and Littlefield, 1996.

Kotkin, Joel. *The New Geography: How the Digital Revolution Is Reshaping the American Landscape.* New York: Random House, 2000.

Lee, Frances E., and Bruce I. Oppenheimer. *Sizing up the Senate: The Unequal Consequences of Equal Representation.* Chicago: University of Chicago Press, 1999.

Lublin, David. *The Republican South: Democratization and Partisan Change.* Princeton, NJ: Princeton University Press, 2004.

Mann, Jim. *Rise of the Vulcans: The History of Bush's War Cabinet.* New York: Viking, 2004.

Mayhew, David R. *Congress: The Electoral Connection.* New Haven, CT: Yale University Press, 1974.

———. *Electoral Realignments: A Critique of an American Genre.* New Haven, CT: Yale University Press, 2002.

Micklethwait, John, and Adrian Wooldridge. *The Right Nation: Conservative Power in America.* New York: Penguin Press, 2004.

Oliver, J. Eric. *Democracy in Suburbia.* Princeton, NJ: Princeton University Press, 2001.

Phillips, Kevin P. *The Emerging Republican Majority.* Garden City, NY: Anchor Books, 1970.

Putnam, Robert D. *Bowling Alone: The Collapse and Revival of American Community.* New York: Simon & Schuster, 2000.

Saletan, William. *Bearing Right: How Conservatives Won the Abortion War.* Berkeley: University of California Press, 2003.

Shafer, Byron E., ed. *The End of Realignment? Interpreting American Electoral Eras.* Madison: University of Wisconsin Press, 1991.

Skocpol, Theda. *Diminished Democracy: From Membership to Management in Amercian Civic Life.* Norman: University of Oklahoma Press, 2003.

Steely, Mel. *The Gentleman from Georgia: The Biography of Newt Gingrich.* Macon, GA: Mercer University Press, 2000.

Viguerie, Richard A., and David Franke. *America's Right Turn: How Conservatives Used New and Alternative Media to Take Power.* Chicago: Bonus Books, 2004.

Index

About the Author

ANDREW J. TAYLOR is Associate Professor at North Carolina State University. He has contributed frequently to scholarly journals, has made over 200 appearances on television, been interviewed over 100 times for radio, and has been quoted regularly in national and local newspapers.